Cooperatives in New Orleans

Cooperatives in

NEW ORLEANS

COLLECTIVE ACTION AND URBAN DEVELOPMENT

Anne Gessler

University Press of Mississippi / Jackson

The University Press of Mississippi is the scholarly publishing agency of
the Mississippi Institutions of Higher Learning: Alcorn State University,
Delta State University, Jackson State University, Mississippi State University,
Mississippi University for Women, Mississippi Valley State University,
University of Mississippi, and University of Southern Mississippi.

www.upress.state.ms.us

The University Press of Mississippi is a member
of the Association of University Presses.

A version of chapter two first appeared as Anne Gessler, "Warriors
for Lower Prices: The New Orleans Housewives' League and the
Consumer Cooperative Movement, 1913–1921," *Journal of Southern
History* LXXXIII, no. 3 (August 2017), pp. 573–616.

A version of chapter three was first published as Anne Gessler, "'A Formula
for Freedom': The Utopian Promise of the 1940s New Orleans Cooperative
Movement," *Utopian Studies* 26, no. 1 (May 2015). Copyright © 2015. This
article is used by permission of the Pennsylvania State University Press.

First printing 2020
∞

Library of Congress Cataloging-in-Publication Data

Names: Gessler, Anne, author.
Title: Cooperatives in New Orleans: collective action and urban
development / Anne Gessler.
Description: Jackson: University Press of Mississippi, 2020. |
Includes bibliographical references and index.
Identifiers: LCCN 2019053409 (print) | LCCN 2019053410 (ebook)
| ISBN 9781496827616 (hardback) | ISBN 9781496827579 (trade
paperback) | ISBN 9781496827586 (epub) | ISBN 9781496827593
(epub) | ISBN 9781496827609 (pdf) | ISBN 9781496827562 (pdf)
Subjects: LCSH: Cooperative societies—Louisiana—New
Orleans—History. | New Orleans (La.)—History.
Classification: LCC HD3446 .G47 2020 (print) | LCC HD3446
(ebook) | DDC 334.09763/35—dc23
LC record available at https://lccn.loc.gov/2019053409
LC ebook record available at https://lccn.loc.gov/2019053410

British Library Cataloging-in-Publication Data available

CONTENTS

vii   Acknowledgments

3   Introduction: Unearthing a Genealogy of Grassroots Economic Development

SECTION ONE: Utopian Socialist Cooperatives

23   Chapter One: The Brotherhood of Co-operative Commonwealth: Modernizing Infrastructure and Public Welfare at the Dawn of the Twentieth Century

SECTION TWO: Rochdale Cooperatives

51   Chapter Two: The New Orleans Housewives' League: White Women's Political Equality and Consumer Reform

83   Chapter Three: The Consumers' Co-operative Union: Embedding Integrated Popular Front and War on Poverty Social Programs in the South

SECTION THREE: Hybrid Racial Justice Cooperatives

115   Chapter Four: Albert Dent and the Free Southern Theater: Intergenerational Civil Rights Cooperatives and the Fight Against Racialized Economic Inequality

150   Chapter Five: The Louisiana Association of Cooperatives and Gathering Tree Growers' Collective: Rebuilding a Cooperative Food Economy in Katrina's Aftermath

179   Conclusion: Hope for a Cooperative Life: Forecasting Cooperative Trends

189   Notes

239   Reference List

277   Index

ACKNOWLEDGMENTS

This book would not have been possible without the enduring support of my family, friends, and colleagues. The University of Texas at Austin's Louann Atkins Temple Endowed Presidential Fellowship and Graduate School Continuing Fellowship, as well as the Louisiana State University Libraries Special Collections Research Fellowship, provided financial support and time to research and write. The University of Houston-Clear Lake Faculty Development Support Funds funded academic conference travel so I could further hone the project's argument. Thank you to colleagues past and present for being models of intellectual rigor: Andrew Busch, Sean Cashbaugh, Carly Kocurek, and Joshua Specht. Susannah Anderson welcomed me to New Orleans and introduced me to invaluable cooperative contacts. John Clark, Macon Fry, Sally Golub, Liz Lichtman, Harvey Reed, Matt Robinson, Sally Stephens, Jocine Velasco, and many others graciously allowed me to pester them about the city's cooperative movement.

Thank you to Shirley Thompson, Elizabeth Engelhardt, Sarah Dooling, and Paul Adams, and particularly Janet Davis, who read innumerable drafts of this manuscript. My writing group members Jeannette Vaught, Andrew Friedenthal, Andrew Hamsher, and Irene Garza gave me a sense of direction when I was mired in minutiae. Stalwart writing buddies Kirsten Ronald, Lily Laux, Diana Bowen, and Kim Case extended moral support over endless cups of tea, while my champion Robin Riehl offered incisive feedback on multiple iterations of multiple chapters. Others generously commented on the manuscript: the UHCL Faculty Writing Group, as well as Andrea Baldwin, Declan Gould, Joanna Eleftheriou, Amy Lucas, Max Rayneard, Jim and Jenny Gessler, Nori Thorne, and Jamie Eakin. Fellow conference panelists and attendees Etta Madden, Michelle Tiedje, and Aaron Windel challenged me to delve deeper into my research's implications. Finally, my parents Nori Thorne and Jim Gessler supplied endless patience and love during the entire process. This book is dedicated to them.

Cooperatives in New Orleans

Unearthing a Genealogy
of Grassroots Economic Development

In late August 2005, Melissa Hoover, executive director of the United Federation of Worker Cooperatives (USFWC), watched from her San Francisco headquarters as Hurricane Katrina's devastating winds and flooding brutally exposed New Orleans's entrenched racial and class inequalities.[1] In the aftermath, neighborhood rebuilding collided with city and federal efforts to privatize medical, housing, and educational systems, which indelibly altered the city's physical and cultural fabric. Developers and city planners offloaded onto the private sector responsibility for the design of ethical, broad-based urban redevelopment plans that addressed intertwined neighborhood environmental, economic, and social issues. Between 2005 and 2008, the city demolished four intact public housing complexes and erected privately managed, mixed-use residential apartments with thousands fewer affordable units. While some developers touted on-site, nonprofit social service and job training providers, the lack of subsidized apartments discouraged low-income African American flood victims from returning to New Orleans.[2]

Community economic development activists accused state level officials of resorting to "generic and recycled policies and plans" that awarded disaster aid contracts to favor major commercial and recreational interests, to the disadvantage of small, minority-owned businesses.[3]

Treading the same path generations of outside activists had beaten, Hoover was convinced that beleaguered New Orleanians could tap the energy of the national worker cooperative movement to repair their neighborhoods. She decided to hold the USFWC's 2008 annual meeting in New Orleans. For Hoover, the event represented "the first time the USFWC had reached out as a movement," and the conference's ideological stakes were high.[4] A volunteer workweek would pair visiting and local cooperatives to jumpstart a "solidarity economy," in which member-controlled and employee-owned businesses would return profits to marginalized communities and swiftly and justly reconstitute New Orleans. Hoover strove to publicly demonstrate that ordinary citizens could "rebuild a city using the co-op model" grounded in democratic, neighborhood-based economic development.[5]

Adhering to a particular conception of cooperation, however, the USFWC overlooked long-established working-class black self-help networks already mobilized to aid neighborhood recovery. Two months before the meeting, conference organizer Erin Rice declared that after spending ten to fifteen hours a week "sending out tons of emails" and "tracking down leads," she could not find enough grassroots economic development projects for USFWC attendees to assist.[6] She concluded, "there was not much cooperative presence in New Orleans." Instead, the USFWC shifted focus toward educating New Orleanians about the basics of cooperative development. By June, 200 cooperative representatives convened to "spread the fertile soil of cooperation and sow some skillful seeds." After the conference, some New Orleanians complained that the city's political torpor and intractable inhospitality to cooperation had sabotaged an opportunity "to use the energy from the conference to get more people to start [worker cooperatives]."[7] These attitudes echoed generations of non-Louisianan reformers committed to "embedding" the national cooperative movement's principles "in the thinking of [southern] people."[8] To many outside activists confounded by the "rural provincialism of the South" and "poverty unknown in the industrial and agricultural North," New Orleans was the last frontier of cooperative organizing.

Yet the city's rich history of cooperative-driven neighborhood development lay hidden in plain sight. For over 200 years, Louisianans of color had honed a locally rooted, African diasporic-inspired cooperative model buffering residents from manmade and natural disasters they now harnessed to guide recovery efforts. New Orleans native Harvey Reed, a conference panelist and director of the Louisiana Association of Cooperatives (LAC), admonished disaster response officials and outside cooperative activists, "maybe in your mind [Louisianan cooperatives] don't exist, but they do."[9] Convening in the relative safety of neighborhood social spaces, for generations economically precarious residents negotiated community and international identities to form a complex, cosmopolitan sense of self and duty to the world. They fused international alternative economic theories, grassroots social movements, and local communal traditions to create a neighborhood-based cooperative model they believed would stoke American progress and promote economic well-being. Additionally, sustained socializing across difference integrated dispersed neighborhoods into ideologically and geographically expansive cooperative resource networks that instantiated working-class producers and consumers' influence over city economic and political life.

Most significantly, Reed argued that preexisting cooperatives' track record of spurring historical local and regional growth offered a more ethical framework to guide the state's economic expansion than did private developers. He pointed to the "resilient, active, strong" black-run cooperative stores, agricultural businesses, and credit unions that spread throughout Louisiana from the 1960s to the 1980s. Affiliating with the Federation of Southern Cooperatives and inspired by Catholic cooperative examples from Antigonish, Nova Scotia, they battled rural poverty and political powerlessness among people of color.[10] In 2007, the LAC revived and extended the federation's dormant state cooperative network. It scattered cooperative enterprises across forty-one of sixty-four parishes, while supporting land security and economic justice initiatives in both Louisiana and developing countries.[11]

Simultaneously, New Orleans neighborhood activists and public housing residents deployed a robust mutual aid network to protest developer McCormack Baron Salizar's plan to demolish 4,600 units. They paraded from City Hall to Mid-City's St. Bernard Public Housing Project, forming a "Party with a Purpose" second line that danced to the Hot 8 Brass Band, a New Orleans mainstay. Soon-to-be arrested demonstrators sang, "I need my home / We need our homes / Don't take my home away."[12] Former public housing residents also joined leftist nonprofits the Common Ground Relief Collective and the People's Hurricane Relief Fund to jointly purchase property as housing cooperatives and community land trusts.[13] As gentrification shrinks affordable housing stock, land trusts stabilize poor neighborhoods by maintaining and expanding affordable housing and promoting community asset building.[14] Fundamentally, the LAC and its contemporaries speak to an unbroken lineage of internationally inspired, community-driven cooperative formation molding Louisiana's economic growth.

Taking a long historical view of cooperative development clarifies how ordinary New Orleanians have mandated equitable, community-responsive urban growth in ways at odds with linear progress narratives that dismiss alternative economic models to naturalize corporate capitalism.[15] Using the methodologies of women's and gender studies, social history, cultural geography, and oral history, *Cooperatives in New Orleans* mines fragmented, scattered cooperative archives and oral histories to unearth a parallel history of

New Orleans's modernization. Occupying the "margins of struggle" within New Orleans's conservative cultural milieu, intergenerational cooperatives run by women, immigrants, and people of color devised multifaceted solutions to class and race inequality still visible today.[16] They helped upgrade New Orleans's inadequate flood control plan; implemented citywide welfare programs and consumer protections; constructed non-exploitative farmers' markets and grocery stores facilitating regional economic growth; integrated formerly excluded citizens into financial markets; and provided local job opportunities for the unemployed. Finally, New Orleanian cooperative models address today's economic and political realities by illustrating how marginalized communities can collaboratively decide what cities should look like, how they should function, and whose economic interests they should serve.

Clarifying Murky Cooperative Categories

Yet, due to the fact that New Orleanian cooperatives are an outgrowth of unpredictable interactions between culturally specific communities and global cooperative trends, they are ensnarled in a knot of overlapping alternative economic practices with muddied definitional categories, objectives, and constituents. Cooperatives' historical reluctance to formally align with a single political and economic worldview has led to their enthusiastic adoption by a constellation of economic and political interests. At times, tension among competing cooperative models have complicated their vision for urban development and enabled policymakers to efface their ongoing contributions to democratic urban growth. Politicians have paid lip service to cooperative principles and ideology to justify deregulating markets and dismantling public welfare programs like government-supervised affordable housing.[17] A patchwork of local, state, and national legislative policies and zoning codes that poorly understand cooperatives' purpose can impede "people-controlled system[s] of goods and distribution" from stabilizing marginalized communities that the free market and governmental programs have neglected.[18]

In spite of what Pierre Bourdieu describes as the late capitalist "programme of . . . methodological destruction" of collectives threatening "the logic of the pure market," New Orleanian institutions and infrastructure still reflect a confluence of cooperative ideals.[19] To resurrect cooperatives' role in modernizing the city, it is worthwhile, then, to briefly chart how sustained social mixing within and across communities nourished the globally influenced communal culture that reshaped New Orleans.

Creole of Color Mutual Aid Associations

From its earliest days, New Orleanians established patterns of cross-ethnic and transnational social, economic, and intellectual exchange that would drive their cooperative culture. Because the built environment guides how we move through our city and how we interact with one another, it also organizes our social order and institutions and, by extension, expands or constricts our capacity to envision other possible, better societies.[20] Following Henri Lefebvre's theory of dialectical social relations, the physical form of New Orleans is shaped by the dynamic interaction between the "perceived space" of cooperative activists' everyday social practices and neighborhood boundaries, the "conceived space" of city planners' development goals, and a more transcendent "lived space" in which citizens can collectively implement alternatives to exploitative land use policies and social hierarchies.[21]

At the same time, as social movement historian Robin Kelley argues, the spaces in which activists live, work, and mobilize constitute multiple "worlds" informed by constituents' particular cultural beliefs, ideologies, unique lived experiences, as well as their degree of marginality.[22] Depending on one's dominant or peripheral socioeconomic and political status, living and meeting in segregated social spaces can strengthen in-group identity, while potentially limiting cooperative benefits to that group at the expense of a more expansive view of community belongingness. Restricting sociality therefore narrows the kinds and scope of economic redress people seek. In contrast, communicating across difference can reconcile clashing ideological visions favoring, for example, affluent white women's enfranchisement and economic independence, black assertions of personhood, or workers' confrontation with capitalism, in order to realize all citizens' full economic inclusion.

Until post-Hurricane Katrina redevelopment, New Orleans enjoyed somewhat fluid racial relations. Historically, white residents have settled in a demographic area geographer Richard Campanella terms "the white teapot."[23] Wealthy whites collected along the strip of high land bordering the Mississippi River, between the Carrollton and Bywater neighborhoods, and including the French Quarter. Recent white immigrants and descendants of French and Spanish colonists crowded the teapot's chamber near the Central Business District (CBD) and French Quarter commercial centers. Poor African Americans resided on marginal, low-lying swampland, while ethnically diverse laborers populated the Mississippi waterfront. Creoles of color—free French-speaking Louisianans of African, Indian, and mixed ancestry—inhabited Sixth and Seventh Ward neighborhoods north and east of the French Quarter. Residential trends reflected and reinforced a tripartite social structure dividing whites from Creoles of color and English-speaking, often enslaved African Americans, whose intergroup animosities stemmed from religious, occupational, educational, neighborhood, political, and associational differences.[24]

While residents' class, racial, and religious identities closely mapped onto their street and block, New Orleans was far from a quaint, backwater city of atomistic neighborhoods. Pockets of English-speaking black slaves and laborers lived behind wealthy Uptown white employers or were interspersed among immigrant enclaves and newer suburbs, while many Creoles of color lived among Caribbean immigrants and white Creoles.[25] As historian Shirley Thompson notes, residential proximity supported "a long tradition of locally sanctioned interracial intimacy" and even a measure of social equality among white Creoles, Haitian refugees, recent immigrants, free people of color, and enslaved Africans all debating citizens' ideal relationship to the state.[26] In fact, until the end of the nineteenth century, interracial participation was evident in cultural institutions such as Catholic churches, saloons, and sports teams.[27] Consequently, a porous social geography whose diasporic communities remained intellectually linked to their homeland cultivated a utopian model for democratic city and regional economic growth.

An inspection of New Orleans's rich social fabric reveals how working-class residents routinized informal economic and cultural exchanges into a complex web of mutual aid organizations helping neighborhoods weather manmade and natural disasters and systemic inequality. In his study of southern colonial "mortuary politics," historian Vincent Brown argues that enslaved Africans' collective funeral processions and burial ceremonies allowed participants to share experiences of death and dislocation; as such, they became powerful conduits through which impoverished black southerners could democratically exchange material goods and construct communities.[28] The Haitian Revolution and Louisiana's transfer from French to American ownership in 1803 politicized these nascent community distributive systems, as waves of colonial, enslaved, and free people of color sought asylum in New Orleans. While free black Haitians tested Creole of color charitable institutions, they also revived an elastic Caribbean understanding of race and class and an enduring commitment to French republicanism and racial pride underpinning political mobilizing among Creoles of color. In the face of discriminatory antebellum policies designed to restrict their mobility and ability to acquire property and status, Creoles of color pitched legal battles and held neighborhood parades celebrating black soldiers of the Haitian Revolution and the War of 1812. Collective practices reinforced a performative Creole of color identity centered on community economic and political resistance.[29] Rather than operating between two poles of ideological purity that falsely pitted native cultural authenticity against outsiders' cosmopolitan broadmindedness, Creoles of color blended external economic survival tactics with street-level communalism to combat racialized poverty and state oppression.[30]

Community economic exchanges were often clandestine because black residents recognized that to publicly criticize New Orleans's dominant social relations or to fraternize across race and class risked grievous bodily harm or even death. The murder of Creole of color labor organizer Rudolph Charles underlines the precarity of black working-class resistance. The roof slater had frequently clashed with Tremé police over the course of the 1880s and 1890s. He was repeatedly arrested for gambling and brawling outside disreputable saloons. Unafraid to protest state repression, he was jailed for impeding white officers apprehending black residents.[31] By the 1893 to 1897 national depression, Charles had joined an integrated, Tremé-based labor association whose rallies and editorials spurred the City to provide unemployment relief for all laborers, regardless of race.[32]

Charles's civil rights advocacy came to an abrupt, violent end one evening in 1905, as he played cards in an Italian-owned neighborhood bar patronized by black dockworkers. The *Daily Picayune* reported that off-duty police officer Matthew Fredricks drunkenly stumbled into the saloon and confronted Charles. Slurring that he "gave a 'nigger' a 41 [pistol] last week," the white patrolman fired a bullet straight into the victim's chest. Charles slumped to the floor, dead. Ironically, the officer had "known [Charles] for a long time and . . . considered [him] a good man." In light of Creole of color and immigrant eyewitness testimony, Fredricks was fired for engaging in "unnecessary conversation," while a grand jury indicted him for murder.[33] Sidestepping Fredricks's deep-seated racial prejudice, investigators suggested that interracial conversation provoked the tragedy; citizens' safety was ensured through restricting mobility and sociality to racial enclaves rather than expanding political and social equality.

To subvert official attention that so often threatened their autonomy, marginalized neighborhoods' fugitive, communal networks became etched into what French historian of memory and identity Pierre Nora calls "true memory," embodied "in gestures and habits, in skills passed down by unspoken traditions" within the city's communities of color.[34] For example, generations of rural black migrants lent their horticulture skills to building vibrant backyard and community gardens that operated as collective spaces of cultural transmission, sociability, and economic stability.[35] One neighborhood activist observed that the black working-class Gert Town's community garden had long been run by "a bunch of really old families."[36] Neighbors used the site as "a place where they can get food if they need it," such as one man who "has picked kumquats off [the garden's] tree for as long as it's been around here." As a result, many neighborhoods of color implicitly "functioned like cooperatives." Residents would "come together and take . . . goods and services and trade and market to those who are going to use it."[37]

By the early 1800s, communal gatherings and under-the-radar distributive systems converged into discrete mutual aid associations. From *ad hoc* organizations to chartered entities, voluntary organizations united members around shared geography, ethnicity, religion, profession, or other commonalities. Unlike corporations, they existed not to enrich stockholders but to provide a mechanism by which members could financially support each other and improve their community. Pooled resources subsidized grocery and medical bills, rent, and funerals for the elderly, infirm, or impoverished.[38]

While New Orleanians of all backgrounds formed mutual aid associations, those organized by Sixth and Seventh Ward Creoles of color continued to serve as a private refuge from state and employer surveillance. French critic of mass culture Michel de Certeau suggests that covert social spaces permit individuals to safely appropriate or invert traditions, symbols, art, and consumer goods to cultivate alternative economic and political ideologies.[39] To that end, successive generations of benevolent associations, fraternal orders, churches, second lines, social aid and pleasure clubs, brass bands, and Mardi Gras Indians remained largely invisible to dominant power structures to protect community members from public scrutiny, reflect on daily and institutionalized racism, and create a working-class identity necessary for political movement formation.[40] Further, black-run mutual aid associations residing on black-owned properties helped Creoles of color amass wealth and spur urban development in their community and throughout the city.[41] For these grassroots organizations, preparing local leadership for social movement mobilization was inextricable from maintaining the neighborhood's safety and economic self-sufficiency.

Among the city's integrated labor unions, mutual aid was a vital means of transforming the South into a laboratory for racial equality and radical economic reform. After the Civil War, for example, influential Creole of color political activists such as Paul Trevigne worked with unions and other mutual aid organizations to advocate political reform, practice self-governance and collective action, and organize community-based cooperative enterprises. Similarly, from 1869 until the late nineteenth century, the Knights of Labor, the first major national labor organization in the United States, organized men and women into sporadically integrated local affiliates across industries rather than individual crafts. They sought to establish a "cooperative commonwealth," in which the laboring classes democratically controlled the national government and cooperative modes of production.[42] For example, in 1887, female unionists opened a three-story, steam-powered cooperative clothing manufacturing company along Canal Street based on Parisian industrial models. The *Daily Picayune* crowed that workers no longer received "insufficient pay for honestly performed labor" and now shared in the profits of the business. The Knights of Labor's cooperative commonwealth vision deeply influenced subsequent New Orleanian unions. As it struck for improved working conditions, opened cooperative stores, and lobbied for workers' legal protections, organized labor systematically reordered employer-employee relations governing the city's economic growth.[43]

New Orleans's fraternal lodges also reconfigured the city's ethical landscape. Although many ethnic groups established secret societies, Creole of color fraternal orders were uniquely situated to bolster black political and economic life. In 1797, Prince Hall founded the first black fraternal order, the African Lodge of Freemasons in Philadelphia, whose focus on rituals, secrecy, and belongingness contributed to the consolidation of disparate ethnic identities into a dynamic African American culture. While French-speaking Creoles of color did not establish their own Prince Hall Masonic lodge until 1842, the order institutionalized efforts to counter legalized white supremacy by celebrating and politicizing a common African historical and religious past. After the Civil War, fraternal orders like Eureka Grand Lodge, Scottish Rite Order, and Prince Hall Masonic Lodge dispensed aid to the needy, while aligning with the state's white northern Republican government and black Catholic and secular social justice organizations to promote French egalitarianism and republicanism. Reconstruction-era Masons joined activists fighting to safeguard and extend the provisions of the 1868 Louisiana Constitution, such as universal male suffrage, legalized interracial marriage, desegregated schools and transportation systems, fair labor standards, and black political office-holding.[44]

Male- and female-run French-speaking and Caribbean-heritage benevolent associations also emerged as indispensable nodes in a politically charged Creole of color survival economy built to resist Jim Crow *de jure* and *de facto* segregation and disenfranchisement. When President Andrew Johnson ended federal occupation of the South in 1877, Louisiana succumbed to what was effectively a one-party system. While affluent, reformist business and civic leaders vied against a powerful Regular Democratic Organization representing immigrants and labor, both Democratic Party factions reinforced white supremacy in city and state politics. For instance, Louisiana's 1880 Poor Law criminalized vagrancy and indigence, which allowed parish police juries to disproportionally imprison poor blacks and reinstituted slavery in all but name. In the absence of state-run welfare programs, benevolent associations joined a Sixth and Seventh-Ward-based network of unions, fraternal orders, and Catholic churches and charities to offer medical insurance, health care, and funeral services to impoverished French-speaking Creoles of color and English-speaking freedpeople.[45]

In addition to providing an economic safety net for vulnerable residents, working-class Creole of color benevolent associations honed street-level, oppositional aesthetic rituals whose principles of mutualism bound disin-vested neighborhoods together and primed members to participate in the city's equal rights and cooperative movements.[46] In addition to defraying medical expenses, neighborhood-specific social aid and pleasure club dues funded annual parades and picnics, as well as members' jazz funeral marches. As the central community event of working-class African Americans by the late nineteenth century, up to a thousand people congregated on Sundays to follow the societies wending their way through city wards. The Seventh Ward's oak-shaded Claiborne Avenue was one magnet for these communal gather-ings; camped out on the grassy neutral ground, residents threw parties, pic-nicked, and watched Zulu Social Aid and Pleasure Club's Mardi Gras parades and second lines roll down the street. Hired brass bands played elegiac and celebratory music, while club members danced behind them in matching, fes-tive suits. Lastly was the second line, neighbors who danced together while expressing their own creativity. Social aid and pleasure clubs thus cultivated a sense of individual autonomy while solidifying community belongingness among Creoles of color. Most significantly, the parades challenged racial repression by declaring black people's right to freely move about their city.[47]

Despite considerable friction between African Americans and Creoles of color, Six and Seventh Ward mutual aid associations tacked between enshrining a unique Creole of color community identity rooted in French democratic rhetoric and sustaining broader black American and diasporic political equality movements.[48] After prominent Creole of color freemasons and notary publics Louis Martinet and Rene Metoyer incorporated French-speaking black fraternal lodges, benevolent associations, and cooperatives, their officers formed recruiting and fundraising channels for city and national campaigns seeking civil rights for all people of color. For example, mutual aid members belonged to Martinet's Citizens' Committee to Test the Constitu-tionality of Louisiana's Separate Car Act and fought racial segregation before the Supreme Court in the 1896 case *Plessy v. Ferguson*.[49]

Creole of color mutual aid activists' commitment to racial justice thus was inextricable from community economic development. Many benevolent associations only contracted with doctors and funeral directors who were explicitly "RACE [men] in every detail" to ensure black businesses flourished.[50] Ultimately, their fierce desire to overturn a capitalist system corrupted by racial discrimination would lead Creole of color mutual aid organizers to experiment with globally informed, culturally resonant cooperatives demanding black mobility as a precondition for urban growth.[51]

Cooperative Development: A Fluid Distinction

Confronting the conundrum of operating egalitarian economic and political enterprises within an unequal, capitalist framework eventually propelled mutual aid organizers toward cooperative economics.[52] The dividing line between New Orleanian cooperatives and other democratically organized ventures remained fluid: the cooperatives profiled in this story emerged out of older mutual aid traditions, were managed by larger mutual aid organizations, or later reframed themselves as other kinds of mutual aid. Nonetheless, cooperatives formalized the process for redistributing wealth and promoting civic participation among marginalized residents that mutual aid associations had pioneered. Broadly speaking, cooperatives are a type of mutual aid organization in which members collectively own and democratically run their organization in order to benefit their community and customer base. Each member-owner enjoys one vote, shares in their association's profits, can be elected to its board of directors, and decides daily operations and organizational goals.[53]

Cooperatives run the gamut in terms of who organizes them and for what purpose. For example, worker and producer cooperatives, such as farms or factories, are designed to improve working conditions and wages for their employee-owners, while producer cooperatives when affiliated with larger cooperative associations, collectively market and distribute members' cooperatively produced goods to better compete with powerful corporations. Consumer cooperatives, in contrast, are businesses that lower the cost of goods and services for the consumer. While member-patrons own the cooperative, such as a utility company or grocery store, they often hire outsiders to manage and staff the business. Additionally, credit unions are cooperative banks that enable members united by common residency, occupation, or organizational affiliation to save money and access consumer and home loans with reasonable interest rates. They have been fundamental to increasing property ownership and entrepreneurship among underserved communities.[54]

The social practices that frame cooperative development reveal an accretion of ongoing social protest and grassroots mobilization driving local economic activity. Replicating the process by which they formed mutual aid organizations, neighborhood activists harnessed the intellectual production emanating from the vibrant tapestry of the migrant and immigrant communities of New Orleans to open cooperative businesses. The permeable racial and class borders limning the city's neighborhoods enabled concerned residents to meet in peripheral ethnic and integrated union halls, clubs, galas, restaurants, bars, conferences, and libraries. There, they honed the oppositional cultural beliefs, ideologies, and daily practices crucial to forming cooperatives that undermined the conflicting logics of citizenship otherwise flowing from hierarchical social relations. Progressive venues hosted diverse discussions of European socialist philosophy, Japanese consumer cooperatives, Israeli kibbutzim, and Third World Left collectives—progressive economic models that would animate successive waves of homegrown cooperative traditions. As a result, the city's highly adaptable system of cooperative development amplified mutual aid efforts to end racial and gender inequality, labor oppression, and environmental exploitation inscribed in citywide urban planning.

Chapter Map

Cooperatives in New Orleans examines how three strands of cooperative development—utopian socialist, Rochdale, and hybrid racial justice cooperatives—variously modernized the economic and political structures of the city. Historically and theoretically anchoring our story are seven cooperatives, from 1897 to the present, whose social bonds with local and international labor, political, and consumer activist networks cemented concrete strategies for fashioning a new, egalitarian economy. The neighborhood-specific case studies provide what historian Glenda Gilmore calls "deep local context for broader historical changes" by tracing how members' complex negotiation of social, economic, and political policies perpetuating systemic gender, class, and racial inequality knits together seemingly discrete cooperative projects and eras.[55] Each chapter illustrates how a particular cooperative built on or diverged from previous cooperatives to further contribute to city growth.

Section One: Utopian Socialist Cooperatives

The first section of *Cooperatives in New Orleans* examines the extent to which utopian socialist cooperatives pushed the state apparatus to grant ostracized New Orleanians full inclusion in civic life and protection from economic exploitation. Some of the earliest propagators of formal cooperation, Creole of color utopian socialists engaged in cross-racial socializing to incorporate European intellectual trends into their own brand of radical urban coopera-tives. In 1808, the French philosopher Charles Fourier theorized that poverty could be eliminated if society were reorganized as a collection of socialis-tic, worker-owned rural communes. His "Fourier phalanxes" would organize units of 1,600 people of all classes into cooperative joint-stock companies that equally distributed profits among members. American utopian socialists reproduced his agrarian model with varying degrees of success, particularly between 1837 and 1844, the years of national economic depression. In Loui-siana, white abolitionists advocated transforming white-owned plantations into democratic, worker-controlled agrarian colonies so that freed people could accumulate wealth and escape the exploitative planter system. By 1865, however, a committee of elite, French-speaking Creoles of color and English-speaking freedmen applied Fourierism to an urban, antiracist context. In spite of considerable cultural friction between white New Orleanians, Creoles of color, and African Americans, they published their vision in black progressive newspapers such as *The Tribune*. The group planned to open an integrated cooperative called the People's Bakery as a means of democratizing industrial relations between blacks and whites.[56]

While the bakery never opened, other ethnic cooperatives would replicate its call for a socialized economic order grounded in a network of loosely affili-ated and worker-owned voluntary associations.[57] During the bloody Russian pogroms of 1881 to 1884, Jewish refugees collaborated with the New York-based Hebrew Emigrants' Aid Association and New Orleanian Christian politicians and German Jewish benevolent societies to purchase land in Catahoula Par-ish's Sicily Island. They settled twenty families in a short-lived, disease-ridden agrarian colony in 1881.[58] The mutual aid organizers' brand of utopian social-ism promoted cooperative land cultivation to counter Christians' perception of Jewish peoples as commercial swindlers and prevent the passage of oppres-sive, anti-Semitic policies that had persecuted them in Europe. Further, Sicily Island advocates and their offspring continued to urge cooperative develop-ment as key members of New Orleans's Progressive movement.

Our story begins a generation after these early utopian socialist experi-ments, in 1897, when a four-year national depression, interracial violence, unpredictable flooding and epidemics, and legalized segregation and disen-franchisement spelled intense social disruption for New Orleanians of color and impoverished whites. Tremé-based Creole of color contemporaries of People's Bakery organizers joined a renewed effort to bring utopian social-ism to bear on state-sanctioned economic and political oppression. Meeting in integrated labor halls and saloons, multiracial socialists and labor activists translated American, Caribbean, and European utopian socialist theory into a cooperative blueprint for equitably integrating unemployed workers into the city's economic structure. While the People's Bakery and Sicily Island fizzled before their economic theories could be tested, the interracial utopian socialists of 1897 built coalitions with labor, women's rights, and political reform allies to temporarily reknit the city's fractured labor movement, improve the city's crumbling infrastructure, and implement an egalitarian public welfare system to benefit all New Orleanians.

Section Two: Rochdale Cooperatives

However, one charge consistently lobbied against utopian socialism was that its diffuse program for social change was often disconnected from pressing political and economic realities. Instead, reformers seeking a more practical cooperative approach turned to the Rochdale cooperative model. Among the most widely recognized and adopted cooperative archetype, it represented a confluence of working-class European organizing traditions and Christian socialism. In 1844, displaced tradesmen in Rochdale, England, responded to the Industrial Revolution and the proletarianization of skilled labor by opening a wholesale store to sell essential goods to subscribers. Their "Rochdale Plan" mandated that cooperative member-owners retain democratic control over their business, bar speculative stock trading, and receive regular dividends and patronage rebates, by which businesses returned profits to members as a percentage of their store purchases. Additionally, influenced by the contemporary Christian socialist movement, Rochdale cooperatives instituted market rates for all goods sold and encouraged cash-only transactions. Finally, to build an independent network of democratic, worker-controlled states, members educated the public about cooperative principles and goals; expanded into other industries to achieve regional economic stability; and federated with neighboring cooperatives to ultimately build a global cooperative society.[59]

By the 1870s, marginalized New Orleanians seeking strategies to immediately and efficiently economically empower their communities were clamoring for information about Rochdale businesses, the success of which they deemed "undoubted."[60] Low-income African Americans, dockworkers, farmers, wholesalers, and women established a range of credit unions, consumer and marketing cooperatives, and other enterprises throughout the late nineteenth-century to establish a flexible "producer-consumer market organizing [system] that cuts out capitalist middlemen."[61] Nonetheless, New Orleans's adoption of the Rochdale model was neither widespread or systematized until after the creation of the socialistic Consumer Cooperative League of America (CLUSA) in 1916, which created a national resource and advocacy network for member cooperatives. Rochdale's popularity also rose in tandem with the emergence of New Orleans as the face of the New South; relocating to profit off the city's proximity to national and international markets, white Midwestern and northern technocrats already familiar with Rochdale formed close political and economic partnerships with native Progressive reformers yearning to modernize New Orleans and position it as a leader in global democracy.[62]

To that end, section two explores how early-to-mid-twentieth century New Orleans socialists grappled with two central questions: could an embattled Rochdale consumer cooperative model thrive within a capitalist system, or should it presage a fundamental social, political, and economic transformation? Chapter two traces cooperatives' overlooked contributions to Progressive female economic institution-building and white women's enfranchisement during the 1910s and '20s. White Uptown New Orleanian women studied contemporary American and British socialists who equitably wove women, laborers, and agricultural producers into a national economic plan encompassing cooperative housing, production, health insurance, medical care, and education. Specifically, educated, affluent, and ethnically heterogenous cooperative activists replicated CLUSA's chain store cooperative networks, which they folded into a broad-based consumer rights platform modernizing and expanding the city's grocery retail industry and public market system.[63]

Yet, by the 1930s, CLUSA's Rochdale cooperatives eschewed overt political agendas in favor of a gradualist approach to economic reform. After protracted, bitter infighting between communists, liberals, conservatives, and socialist members, politically neutral Rochdale cooperatives exploded in popularity, so that 300,000 middle- and lower-income rural, urban, and suburban Americans had joined cooperatives in thirty-seven states, while over 50 percent of England's population had joined housing, insurance, consumer, producer, marketing, and financial cooperatives by the end of the decade.[64] Chapter three analyzes radical Depression- and World War II-era consumer cooperatives in the working-class Freret neighborhood as their explicitly antiracist, socialist calls for a complete overhaul of the capitalist system careened into their constituents' desire for economic expediency. Opening an integrated grocery store and host of affiliated cooperatives, organizers muted their Popular Front sympathies to lower the cost of living for racially mixed Freret residents and implement New Deal economic reforms in the South. Although critics charged that apolitical Rochdale cooperatives lacked a "broad vision of social change," and while radicals' principles were co-opted to serve a capitalist agenda, chapter three illuminates how the city's mid-twentieth-century credit union movement embedded Popular Front ideals into Great Society social policies.[65] Credit unions operated as a political channel for marginalized communities, situating New Orleans urban growth within the context of the long civil rights movement.

Section Three: Hybrid Racial Justice Cooperatives

While New Orleanians of all races, genders, and classes opened Rochdale cooperatives, oppressed citizens did not have the luxury of studied political neutrality. Chapter four follows the generational shift from African American activists' celebration of Rochdale cooperatives as vehicles for political equality and economic self-sufficiency, to their eventual rejection of the form as hopelessly complicit in American imperialism and white supremacy. Accelerating in the 1930s, segregationist practices such as deed restrictions and slum clearance increasingly concentrated impoverished African Americans in geographically isolated public housing and in low-lying drained marshland vulnerable to flooding.[66] Georgia-born hospital administrator Albert Dent believed informal, poorly funded Creole of color mutual aid associations could not effectively address blacks' lack of access to equitable housing, much less tackle mounting disparities in health care and education. Between the 1930s and '40s, Dent fused black southern civil rights activism and global cooperative philosophy to create a modern cooperative insurance plan and public health system serving poor blacks. Collaborating with white southern liberals implementing New Deal policies ensured the future Dillard University president could instantiate his broad vision of black economic justice and self-advocacy at the city and state level.

Writer and playwright Tom Dent took up his father's cooperative mantle, incorporating Albert Dent's down-to-earth cooperative vision, coalition-building strategies, and regional cooperative institution building into the leftist Free Southern Theater Collective, active from the 1960s to the '80s and based in black neighborhoods like the Ninth Ward and Central City. However, steeped in the rhetoric of the Black Arts Movement, civil rights movement, and the southern cooperative movement, Dent and his radicalized New Orleans peers argued the Rochdale cooperative form had discarded its ideological commitment to achieving social and economic transformation in favor of narrow economic reform.

Instead, the cooperative theater company combined militant communist organizational rhetoric, a non-hierarchical collective structure, and African diasporic ideology that blurred collective social protest with spiritual and aesthetic practices. Rather than depend on a manager and board of directors, collectively organized cooperatives mandated that all members participate in the entities' decision-making process, either through group consensus or by committee.[67] Further, Dent's arts organizations strategically blended African and Creole of color mutual aid traditions to advance the project of local and global worldwide liberation: New Orleanian writers and artists created a political, aesthetic, and "cultural 'kitchen,'" inspired by the "international scope" of "Black New Orleans."[68] Additionally, working with antipoverty officials and nonprofit organizations, the FST contributed to a sprawling southern network of producer and consumer cooperatives seeking to "[gain] volume savings and collective market power" for poor African Americans without replicating capitalist "structural features that lead to bigness and centralization."[69]

Chapter five documents the legacy of hybrid racial justice cooperatives on post-Hurricane Katrina recovery projects. New racial justice cooperatives reenacted the historical circulation of goods, people, and ideas across neighborhood, national, and international channels to thread seemingly isolated ethnic enclaves into a robust regional network promoting egalitarian food policy into city and state economic development, labor policies, and land-use plans. In keeping with the International Cooperative Alliance's aims, minority cooperative activists like Harvey Reed have opened autonomous food cooperatives that spread workplace democracy regionally, nationally, and internationally.[70]

New Orleanian cooperatives make manifest utopia's forward drive. Literary scholar Fredric Jameson writes that despite their "unreliable form," the "idea and the program of Utopia" serve a "very real political function" to theorize and enact social change.[71] Even failed cooperatives extend tendrils of social change entwining subsequent social movements to elucidate a genealogy of street-level activism with citywide economic impacts. Asked how he determined whether a given performance was good or bad, experimental, improvisational music composer George Lewis replied that he avoids thinking in terms of success or failure. Real life is unexpected; we make mistakes we must live with, but at the same time, we might reevaluate them later. We live in a state of "temporal flux" in which individuals and societies constantly reassess and recontextualize historical moments.[72] What matters instead is that the performance structure functions as a social contract in which musicians can express themselves creatively while creating a cohesive composition. The invitation to another artist to "play with me," a fellow performer added, is a joyful, intimate experience.

Similarly, cooperatives extend to us a joyful, intimate invitation to collectively renegotiate our social structure. Regardless of cooperative collapses and ideological shortcomings, members reflect on their failures, resist oppressive economic and political systems, and expand the vision of the possible for the next spate of activists. Cooperatives' everyday "infrared" oppositional tactics, or as anthropologist James C. Scott terms them, "infrapolitics," empower citizens to collectively envision new ways of relating to power structures and pressure government leaders to incorporate constituents' concerns into city planning.[73] After mining New Llano, an early twentieth-century Louisianan socialist colony, for organizing strategies, current New Orleans cooperative activist John Clark was amazed by "how much people can do—relatively poor people—when they pool efforts and skills and imaginations. . . . They failed. . . . But the history is there. True communities developed, and communities will emerge, hopefully on larger scale."[74] The regularity with which New Orleanian communal institutions have emerged reflects citizens' ongoing desire for egalitarian discourse within the context of formal political organization.[75] Offering an elastic model of rupture and continuity, cooperatives persist as a reliable means of political mobilizing across geographical, racial, class, gender, and religious divides to promote ethical economic growth.

UTOPIAN SOCIALIST COOPERATIVES

The Brotherhood of Co-operative Commonwealth: Modernizing Infrastructure and Public Welfare at the Dawn of the Twentieth Century

Throughout July 1897, unemployed laborers in New Orleans circulated mysterious "flaming red hand bills" amongst themselves, inviting all to march a mile from Congo Square's Globe Hall to City Hall in Lafayette Square. The fliers' socialist writers demanded government-funded economic relief to counter the lingering 1893 to 1897 national depression. On July 16, the appointed day, a "motley crowd from seventy-five to a hundred men, who needed no credentials as to their being out of employment" converged on the sweltering Congo Square, a hub for integrated, working-class social activity. Globe Hall was locked tight, and black and white workers milled about with "no center, head, nor tail to them." Hours later, there was still no sign of an organizer.[1]

Fearing the restless gathering would ignite into a race riot, police dispersed the crowd. Finally, two figures emerged from the chaos to claim responsibility for the abortive march: twenty-eight-year-old Eugene Bacarisse and thirty-year-old August Graf, leaders of the New Orleans branch of the Brotherhood of Co-operative Commonwealth, a multiracial utopian socialist cooperative and unemployed workers' union. The would-be agitators could neither afford the two-dollar rent for Globe Hall nor the event permit fee, and the morning culminated in their arrest by the sweating and "corpulent form of Sergeant Gabriel Porteous."[2]

Back at the police station, Police Chief Dexter Gaster sternly lectured Bacarisse and Graf on the futility of their cause: as "foreigners over here out of employment," they should not presume to "teach the American people anything."[3] Rather than stir up trouble in New Orleans, why didn't the Cuban-born Bacarisse help his fellow revolutionaries "lick" the Spanish colonizers

in skirmishes wracking his home country? As for Graf, the Bavarian émigré was surely a "Dutchman, and an anarchist: that's a dead easy guess." He
conceded, "there is a great deal of distress because of men not being able to
secure employment, but they are never going to obtain any relief from such
fellows as you." Both organizers rejected violent political revolution, endors-
ing instead peaceful resolutions to worker-employer conflict. Temporarily
appeased, Gaster reluctantly dismissed the two men.

Lampooned in the local color section of the *Daily Picayune*, this small
scene belies the concrete ways racially diverse utopian socialists helped
modernize the city's infrastructure and public welfare policies in turn-of-
the-century New Orleans. Understanding that laborers were the backs upon
which city planners would build their cosmopolitan metropolis, the brotherhood responded to the city and nation's imperialist ambitions in three successive economic development campaigns. First, between February and July
1897, founder Eugene Bacarisse drew on his family's Cuban revolutionary
ties to espouse French republicanism and universal brotherhood and oppose
global industrial capitalism's mistreatment of poor whites and people of
color. Then, between July and October 1897, veteran Creole of color activists
launched the brotherhood's operational arm, the Laboringmen's Protective
Association (LMPA), regularly staging highly visible meetings and protests in
the racially heterogeneous Tremé neighborhood's array of integrated venues.
Rejecting both segregation and immigration policies that threatened Creole of color dockworkers' economic mobility and political influence, LMPA
president Albert Holmes suggested that New Orleans's centrality within an
international marketplace hinged on protecting all "home" labor. Finally, from
October 1897 to October 1898, August Graf presided over a splinter group, the
White Laboringmen's Protective Association (WLMPA). It reflected a theatrical craft unionism that, in the months leading up to the Spanish American War,
legitimized members' direct actions and ethnic pride by asserting a homogeneous American identity rooted in patriotism and white supremacy. Aided by
white Progressive city planners and women's rights advocates, the organization restricted the city's nascent public welfare plan to white citizens.

The sorely overlooked story of the brotherhood decenters a common historical narrative that points to the late 1890s as the nadir for labor and political rights activism in New Orleans. The post-Reconstruction era of the 1870s
and 1880s steadily eroded black civil rights, exemplified by the 1890 Separate
Car Act, which mandated different railroad cars for white and black passen-
gers. It presaged a slew of state segregationist laws restricting black access
to streetcars, transit terminals, hotels, restaurants, and entertainment venues.
Nonetheless, cooperation among working-class blacks and whites had been

common and culminated in a general union strike in 1892. Yet a four-year-long national depression ignited months of racial violence in 1894 and 1895 as hundreds of white longshoremen viciously attacked black dockworkers competing for work, eviscerating once powerful, integrated labor unions. White dockworker unrest echoed the rash of lynchings and race riots sweeping Louisiana and the South.[4]

Amplifying racial antagonism, by upholding "separate but equal" public accommodations in 1896, the US Supreme Court case *Plessy v. Ferguson* drew a firm line between citizens' social and political equality. It emboldened Louisiana to endorse the "grandfather clause" restricting freedmen's enfranchisement, requiring voters to reregister after January 1897, and barring electoral officials from assisting illiterate voters. Finally, in February 1898, Democrats at the Louisiana Constitutional Convention voted to permanently disenfranchise blacks and poor whites. In New Orleans, this prevented 50 percent of whites and 90 percent of African Americans from voting.[5] Stalwart Creole of color equal rights activist Rodolphe Desdunes bemoaned that *Plessy v. Ferguson* plunged black New Orleanians into "forlorn hope and noble despair."[6] United action to remedy residents' common oppression seemed impossible as economic and political conditions reordered New Orleans's blurred racial geography.

Yet integrated Brotherhood members did not share Desdunes's gloomy assessment. In contrast, the utopian socialist cooperative broadens the scope of institutionalized Creole of color efforts to overturn Jim Crow laws: members exploited the city's murky racial categories and porous racial geographies to lodge daily, sustained challenges to restrictions on multiethnic socialization, mobilization, and civic participation. Creole of color and English-speaking black political equality advocates, Cuban revolutionaries, and ethnic white unionists labored together, belonged to the same clubs and benevolent societies, and conversed in Tremé's integrated union and dance halls. Prolonged, powerful social mixing remapped the terms of neighborhood identity and citizenship around a shared understanding of voluntary aid, refining a pattern of internationally inspired, community-based cooperative organizing operating in New Orleans.

Additionally, the brotherhood bridges the devastating 1894 longshoremen's riots and a return to widespread interracial union organizing in 1901. Historians have largely neglected the productive interconnections among Louisiana's late nineteenth-century utopian socialist, labor, and cooperative activists that helped mend the city's fractured labor movement. As labor historian Eric Arnesen observes, the scant scholarship on urban Louisiana labor history reflects the labor movement's refusal to "conform to established paradigms."[7] Pairing Christian socialist economic theory with indigenous

mutual aid traditions, the brotherhood demanded universal enfranchisement, financed floundering union chapters, and brokered city construction
contracts for the unemployed when cross-racial union collaboration was supposedly non-existent.

Finally, the brotherhood fundamentally reconceptualized the state's
responsibility to its citizenry. As a first step toward realizing a national cooperative commonwealth in which a socialist government would supervise a
nationalized industrial economy, the brotherhood persuaded the city to hire
unemployed multiracial laborers to improve an extensive infrastructure system of levees, floodwalls, and pumps that would protect all residents.[8] Consequently, thousands of laborers constructed a revamped municipal public
works system still largely in operation today.[9] The brotherhood's mutualistic welfare plan mirrored Jacob Coxey's theory that "Workingmen Want
Work, Not Charity," sentiments that President Franklin Delano Roosevelt's
Depression-era Works Progress Administration would echo as it sought the
"preservation of the skill of the worker, and hence the preservation of his
self-respect."[10] On a broader scale, the organization's blend of evolutionary
socialism and local organizing traditions also influenced subsequent New
Orleans cooperatives for the next sixty years. Beginning our story with the
brotherhood establishes a framework for understanding how the intensely
local, lived experience of cooperative action informs social movements' economic programs and stimulates urban growth.

The Interracial Roots of the Brotherhood of Co-operative Commonwealth

Representing the apex of Creole of color and immigrants' thirty-year-long
experimentation with urban utopian socialism, the brotherhood was forged
out of persistent socializing among Creoles of color and Cuban émigrés
whose French Quarter and Tremé-based mutual aid institutions propelled
radical economic activity. At the same time, the brotherhood's socialistic
worldview and economic policies drew on members' social networks extending far beyond the borders of the Fifth, Sixth, and Seventh Wards. Steeped in
the French republicanism common to Tremé's overlapping Cuban independence and Creole of color political rights movements, its Cuban American
founder, Eugene Bacarisse, sought to peacefully transform the nation into a
cooperative commonwealth that was inclusive of all.

Born in Havana in 1867 on the eve of the Ten Years' War, Cuba's bloody
struggle for independence from Spain, Bacarisse was baptized in the fires of
revolutionary ardor and emancipatory zeal. As a young clerk of twenty-two,

in 1839 his paternal grandfather, Louise Jerome Charles Bacarisse, emigrated from Bordeaux, France, to New Orleans, fleeing the wealthy bourgeoisie's politically repressive July Monarchy regime. He married Cuban-born, New Orleans-raised Lise Augustine Cohen, a young woman of French and Dutch extraction, and his descendants would also marry Cuban-, Spanish-, and French-born spouses. The Bacarisses comfortably inhabited three identities—French, Cuban, and American—as Gulf Coast mercantile traders regularly traversing the narrow strip of water between Cuba and New Orleans.[11]

However, the Bacarisses' livelihoods were ensnared in Cuba's unstable political climate, as well as America's evolving expansionist policies and diplomacy with Spain. Eugene's father, Jean Baptiste "Charles" Bacarisse, was a multilingual shipping clerk and ardent supporter of Cuban independence.[12] After weathering the country's economic crisis in 1867 and a sugar planters' political revolt that sparked the Ten Years' War, Cubans like the Bacarisses fled to the United States, where the burgeoning tobacco trade provided steady employment in cigar factories in New Orleans, New York, and Key West.[13] Moving to New Orleans permanently in 1869, the family joined growing numbers of educated, politicized Cubans settling in the French- and Spanish-speaking Fifth, Sixth, and Seventh Wards. They collaborated with New Orleans's political and commercial interests who sought to expand American markets by funding Cuban revolutionaries' filibusters and liberation campaigns. Similarly, the New Orleans shipping industry, on which the Bacarisses' fortunes depended, advocated an American-negotiated end to hostilities in order to maintain a profitable line of Cuban sugar imports.[14]

The Bacarisses were intimately familiar with Tremé's community of Ten Years' War veterans and professionals helping organize and fund the Cuban separatist movement leading up to the 1898 War of Independence. Cuban political and social clubs held banquets, street parades, and balls close to the Bacarisses' French Quarter home.[15] For his part, as a poet and coeditor of *La Libertad*, a French- and Spanish-language Cuban nationalist weekly paper, Charles Bacarisse contributed to an outpouring of incendiary propaganda circulating between Cuba and America. Bacarisse and his coeditor and neighbor, Dr. Juan G. Hava, demanded a Cuban-directed military victory over Spain without American annexation.[16] In a missive that informed Eugene's own complicated antiracism, they contended Cuba's economic health could only be secured through gradual emancipation of slaves, financial compensation to slaveholders, and labor reform.

Significantly, the Bacarisses' slippery racial and ethnic identity made them sensitive to the ways in which race and class privilege reproduced inequality. While the family considered itself white "Creole" for its European ancestry, whiteness alone could not grant Cubans social and political equality in the face of America's mounting imperialist ambitions. The United States undermined Cuban fitness for self-determination, fearing autonomy would jeopardize its Anglo-Saxon right to Latin American and Caribbean markets to export millions of dollars in goods, stimulate the US economy, and relieve labor-capital tensions.[17] Consequently, to be Cuban was to be racially suspect.

That the United States Census branded the Bacarisses "mulatto" into the 1900s reflected the family's political and community allegiances as much as its racial entanglements. The Bacarisses shared a French Quarter home with propertied, mixed-race descendants of Haitian Revolution refugees driving the neighborhood's development and lived alongside cigar makers, tailors, brick masons, coopers, and plasterers constituting the backbone of Cuban and Creole of color political equity and self-help movements.[18] Cubans and Creoles socialized in the same neighborhood spaces, staging meetings at Congo Square's Globe Hall and picnics and concerts at Loeper's Park.[19]

Regular socializing translated into political action: Charles Bacarisse was arrested during the Civil War for stealing Confederate mail and eventually befriended Creole of color abolitionist and education reformer Thomy Lafon. Ultimately, the family would remain a fixture in the French Quarter and Tremé's multiethnic neighborhoods even as white Creoles moved north to newly drained, segregated suburban plots along Lake Pontchartrain by the end of the nineteenth century.[20] Sharing a similar ideological perspective with Creole of color antiracist activists, Cubans like the Bacarisses integrated into Tremé's culture of interracial, cooperative sociability.

Collectively, Creole of color and Cuban mutual aid organizations constituted a politicized neighborhood landscape that actively resisted the violent repression of marginalized citizens' civil rights, physical well-being, and economic stability. Lacking access to reliable and affordable healthcare, Creoles of color depended on benevolent associations to subsidize doctors' visits, prescriptions, and, inevitably, funeral expenses when the cost of racialized poverty, from bullet wounds, venereal disease, diphtheria, and tetanus, to chronic illness, exacted its deadly toll.[21] When president J. B. Prados contracted a fatal throat disease, for example, his insurance cooperative defrayed his medical expenses because he had "not made a dollar in three months [and] not being able to work, [it] would be somewhat hard to face this alone."[22] Similarly, Cuban cigar workers, galvanized by factory lectors reading political treatises, tended to support anarchist and collectivist ideologies. As with their Cuban compatriots in New York and Key West, New Orleanian cigar packers joined integrated city strikes with industrial and craft unions and union-operated cooperatives.[23] Most significantly, however, mutual aid organizations of color folded local economic self-determination into broader advocacy for global political equity.

Demonstrating a fierce sense of class solidarity and progressive racial relations, both Creoles of color and Cuban revolutionaries saw Cuba's liberation as part of a coordinated Caribbean and American battle for political justice. For example, Creole of color political activists Cuban-Haitian Rodolphe Lucien Desdunes and Walter L. Cohen, as well as Cuban separatist Andrés Alpízar, all worked in the cigar industry. Accordingly, when Desdunes and notary Louis Martinet formed the radical Citizens' Committee to Test the Constitutionality of the Separate Car Law in 1891 to challenge state segregation laws, their newspaper, *The Crusader*, chronicled local Creole of color as well as Cuban political events.[24] Additionally, they invited Cuban revolutionary and local Cigar Makers Union president Ramón Pagés to speak at committee meetings.[25] While Martinet conceded Pagés was a "stranger by his language," he was aligned "heart and soul" with the committee's objectives: "The sun did not divide off a portion of its rays for one class and a portion for the other, a part of the whites and a part for the blacks; but shone equally for everybody."[26]

Further entwining European, Cuban, and Creole of color mutual associations' political outlooks was a pointed embrace of French democratic ideals as an antidote to avaricious American imperialism. For example, as members of L'Athénée Louisianais Society, the Bacarisses labored to preserve and promote the French language, literature, and scholarly research in Louisiana.[27] In the French Democracy Club, Eugene honored the French Republic of 1792 by advocating "Liberté, Egalité, Fraternité, [and] Solidarité." His "Universal Social Progress" speech at a club event also reflected the French Second Republic's institutionalized Fourierist ideology that embraced associationalism and a gradual, state-led evolution toward socialism.[28] Similarly, Creole of color social aid and pleasure clubs, secret societies, labor associations, and cooperatives joined intellectuals campaigning to protect the 1868 state constitution's fusion of American and French Revolutionary democratic ideals from white supremacist incursions.[29] Joining Tremé's tight-knit social clubs gave Eugene a public platform to hone the French intellectual and political principles he would advocate in the brotherhood.

At the same time, theosophy's millennial philosophy imbued Bacarisse's French republicanism and Cuban revolutionary sympathies with cosmic urgency. Founded by Colonel Henry Steel Olcott and Helena Blavatsky in 1875, the nonsectarian Theosophist Society fostered a class-, race-, and gender-inclusive "Universal Brotherhood of Humanity." They studied ancient and contemporary religion, science, philosophy, and art to understand the "laws of nature" and the "divine powers in man."[30] Theosophists believed that the world was emerging from a 5,000-year period of chaos, and that a new age of universal brotherhood would dawn between 1897 and 1898. To prepare, in 1896 the society mounted a national educational "crusade," championing social reform and cooperation over individualistic self-improvement. For Cuban and white Creole leaders of the New Orleans chapter, an independent Cuba was the ideal proving ground for theosophy's utopian world order. Throughout February 1897, Eugene helped lecture French-, German-, and English-speaking clubs in the immigrant-heavy CBD on Cuban self-determination, racial harmony, and communitarianism.[31] During these classes, Bacarisse befriended the idealistic socialists constituting the brotherhood's beating heart.

The Brotherhood of Co-operative Commonwealth Forms

Ultimately, the Panic of 1893 transformed Bacarisse from an abstract "thinker, philosopher, poet, sociologist and humanitarian" into a committed cooperative organizer.[32] What once had been an academic argument for socialized government and cooperative economics became deeply personal as Bacarisse's shifting fortunes testified to the stark failings of an industrial capitalist society. Despite being a "competent stenographer and correspondent, having a fair knowledge of the English, French and Spanish languages," he searched in vain for a "living salary."[33] The Bacarisses sold their elegant five-bedroom French Quarter townhouse to squeeze into cramped quarters above a dingy Mississippi Riverfront shop, before eventually settling into a modest Tremé shotgun home less than a mile from Congo Square, surrounded by lower-middle-class and working-class black and white Creoles.[34]

Seeking economic relief, Bacarisse joined the Populist Party. On the eve of the depression, his brother and father had worked as stenographers and clerks for the populist Farmers' Union Commercial Association of Louisiana, an integrated self-help organization.[35] Active between 1890 and 1893, it decried monopolistic corporations that forced small, independent farmers into debt by dropping crop prices. To compete with powerful agrarian operations and avoid unscrupulous middlemen, the Farmers' Union organized a profitable statewide wholesale and retail cooperative network in which small farmers sold produce directly to a dozen affiliated grocery stores. Eventually a national cooperative economic system would harmonize relations between farmers, urban labor, and capital. The Farmers' Union worked in concert with the national, integrated People's Party (or Populist Party), formed in 1892 by the Knights of Labor, sharecroppers, reformist Democrats, and Republicans to eliminate political corruption and improve working conditions and educational opportunities for the poor. In Louisiana, the Populists campaigned in 1896 to defeat *laissez-faire* Regular Democratic governor Murphy Foster and a state legislature hostile to silver currency, accessible land ownership, and income tax reform. Although they failed, Bacarisse harnessed the People's Party's integrated coalitional and cooperative network model to serve the city's racially heterogeneous populace.[36]

In particular, Bacarisse closely followed the development of the National Union of the Brotherhood of Co-operative Commonwealth, a product of the Socialist Party, Populism, and socialist writer Edward Bellamy's utopian communalism. Bellamy's 1887 wildly popular treatise *Looking Backward* described a future society featuring community cooperation and state-owned industry as the basis of its government and economic structure. *Looking Backward* and its 1897 sequel, *Equality*, inspired nationwide "Bellamy Clubs" that publicized Bellamy's vision of a socialist society and even formed cooperative colonies throughout the 1890s and 1900s.[37]

Likewise, after experimenting with small utopian colonies in Maine, Populist Norman Wallace Lermond created the National Union in early 1897, a Christian socialist organization tasked with educating Americans about socialism, uniting socialists into one cooperative society, and financially and materially supporting pioneer settlements across the country. Establishing a cluster of cooperatives in Skagit County, Washington, its white middle-class professionals, cooperative sympathizers, and laborers aimed to peacefully convert the state to socialism before tackling the federal government. Advertising the National Union's progress in national Populist and socialist publications, Lermond implored readers like Bacarisse to form their own locals and affiliate with the National Union. Radicals across the country donated thousands of dollars to the cooperative project that would initiate "Mutualism or the Kingdom of Heaven Here and Now."[38]

Inspired to make manifest a cooperative commonwealth in depression-struck New Orleans, Bacarisse spent the early months of 1897 debating cooperating economics with his Theosophical Society and Populist colleagues in Tremé and the CBD's many immigrant-run, integrated saloons and beer halls, cementing his disparate social connections into a grassroots cooperative organization. The CBD's border, Canal Street, was as a point of cultural exchange between uptown Anglos and downtown Francophones.[39] As labor historian Daniel Rosenberg observes, such in-between social spaces sheltered "startling examples of continued integration and so-called social equality," fostering a common working-class identity Bacarisse and his multiracial compatriots deployed to fully integrate marginalized residents into the civic body.[40]

In February 1897, Bacarisse quit his low-paying stenographic job to head the first chapter of the Socialist National Union of the Brotherhood of Co-operative Commonwealth. While scholars have characterized the National Union as a single, ill-fated Equality Colony in Washington State, the New Orleans Brotherhood claimed affiliation six months before the Pacific Coast colony was operational in November 1897.[41] Brotherhood cofounder August Graf, a Bavarian bartender and staunch Republican, joined after he lost his streetcar conducting job and spent months fruitlessly searching for work to support his young family.[42] Similarly, the brotherhood's forty charter members were a mix of labor organizers and political operatives representing under-employed German, Irish, and white and black Creole bartenders, machinists, dockworkers, and day laborers dispersed along the Mississippi waterfront and in the Creole Fifth, Sixth, and Seventh Wards.[43]

Reflecting its immigrant membership and ideological worldview, that month the cooperative convened in the CBD's segregated Spiritualists' Hall, where white Creole bartender Paul Banch's violin stylings serenaded attend-ees and the blustery Bacarisse expounded on "The Solution of the Human Problem and the Advantages of Socialism and Communism." Structurally, it practiced cooperative governance. All members, black or white, voted demo-cratically on directors during regular elections and collectively decided on brotherhood actions during long, contentious monthly meetings. Program-matically, the brotherhood established urban worker cooperatives, hosted prominent political figures, staged unemployment marches, wrote editorials in local papers, and met with city leaders.[44]

In practice, the urban New Orleans chapter barely resembled the National Union in outlook or organization. Equality Colony rejected the industrial sys-tem, professing an abiding faith in communal agricultural labor. Residents lived together, collectively farmed and processed food, ate in common din-ing halls, and educated their children in the colony's schoolhouse. Nor did American Railway Union president Eugene V. Debs's brief attempt to merge National Union's utopian socialism with industrial unionism encapsulate the goals of the New Orleans chapter. Before he resigned as its national represen-tative, Debs promoted Equality as a refuge for aging, ailing railway unionists, rather than as a project to systematically remodel society.[45]

In contrast, Bacarisse used a synthetic approach when applying the National Union's political program to an urban, southern context. He laid out his com-prehensive cooperative philosophy, "The Problems of Industrial Life," in the *Daily Picayune*, a major New Orleans newspaper, in June 1897. While theoso-phists distinguished their "common brotherhood" from socialism, Bacarisse felt Christian socialism, sociology, and theosophy were analogous in their

pursuit of "truth." Central to this "truth" was the clear renunciation of racist, classist religious and anthropological theories that justified an avaricious
capitalist system. First, theosophists rejected the racist antebellum "science" of
polygenesis in favor of monogenesis: humans had a common origin and were
bound by the principle of universal harmony. Second, Bacarisse argued that
capitalists'"survival of the fittest" mentality underwrote working-class exploitation. Specious religious education fostered individualistic competition, hindering society from realizing its cooperative utopia. He condemned churches
for instructing the poor that they had duty to obey society's dictates without
enjoying basic rights.[46] According to New Orleans theosophist Charles Lopez,
society's laws and commerce had embraced "the habits of cheating, lying, etc.,
[which] have become part of our lower nature."[47] Yet surely, Bacarisse rea-
soned, society had advanced to a point at which no one needed to be "humili-
ated [or] brutalized" by eking out a "mere physical existence."[48]

Rather than using the animal kingdom as a model for social organization,
Bacarisse urged economists and reformers to turn to "cooperative sociology."[49]
He echoed British Positivist sociologists like Frederic Harrison who believed
a robust trade union movement arbitrated by intellectuals would improve
laborers' workplace and domestic sphere to insulate them from capitalistic
exploitation. Citizen sociologists surveying regional housing, urbanism, and
geography would guide the gradual creation of republican city-states and
elevate the moral fabric of the industrial economy and civic life.[50] Similarly,
Bacarisse saw the brotherhood as a scientific blueprint for societal advancement that transcended petty political jockeying, the "province of statesmen
and lawmakers of the country."[51] Societal "evolution was the law, not revolution." When combined with theosophy, a socialist society could best harness
the "Christian principle of cooperation [to] improve industrial relations."

To spur peaceful social transformation, Bacarisse replicated contemporary
socialist-labor coalitions like the Socialist Trade and Labor Alliance (STLA)
and Socialist Labor Party, which strove to radicalize flagging Knights of Labor
chapters and conservative American Federation of Labor (AFL) craft unions
and yoke them to a national network of cooperative factories undergirding a
socialist government and economy.[52] For example, when Louisianan lumber
mill owners forced employees to work ten hours a day without compensation during their off-season, disgruntled operators organized the Mill Hands
Union and, along with a carpenters' union, struck in March and April 1897. The
brotherhood advised strikers to open a cooperative lumber mill in the lower
Ninth Ward to compete with nonunionized rural and New Orleans mills. The
cooperative pledged to operate fewer than nine hours a day and pay laborers high wages. While the mill never opened, the *Daily Picayune* reported in

March and April 1897 that "every class of labor" in the building trades supported the cooperative. Its broad appeal validated Bacarisse's hope that a coalition of socialists, labor unions, and Populists could engineer a national political and economic system that cooperatively distributed resources and, consequently, eliminated "unnatural human miseries and social anxieties."[53]

Yet some Brotherhood members rejected Bacarisse's gradualist, often nebulous socialist proselytizing in favor of expeditious, concrete political programs that would swiftly materialize New Orleans's cooperative commonwealth. Specifically, they proposed that city funds supplement private charities and mutual aid societies to provide relief for down-on-their-luck residents. To that end, August Graf invited Ohio businessmen and gubernatorial candidate Jacob Coxey to promote his Non-Interest-Bearing Bonds Bill, a public welfare plan, at the brotherhood's first public event on February 27, 1897.[54]

Bacarisse kicked off the Spiritualist's Hall event by breathlessly extolling the virtues of Christian socialism and Coxey's Non-Interest-Bearing Bonds Bill. Public works projects would enable the "masses" to "earn an honest living" and deliver society from poverty-created "tramps and criminals." After two hours, a restless moderator "tugged violently and frequently at the enthused speaker's coat tails" until Bacarisse finally yielded Coxey the floor. The guest of honor thrilled the audience with Coxey's Army exploits. In 1894, he had assembled 500 unemployed men and women into the United States Industrial Army to march on Washington, DC, and promote his bill. To improve the nation's public infrastructure and reduce an 18 percent unemployment rate, the federal government should establish a $500 million investment plan.[55] The US Treasury Department would loan non-interest-bearing bonds in paper currency to municipal and state governments to establish public works projects employing thousands of out-of-work laborers, regardless of race. Coxey stressed that his plan was the "sole and only remedy for the diseased condition of the American people."[56] The brotherhood applied Coxey's non-interest-bearing bonds program to a local context. By borrowing money from the state or federal government, city-funded public works projects would aid the unemployed while modernizing New Orleans infrastructure.

The brotherhood's call for a city public works plan took shape in the midst of raging environmental management debates and a reformist political landscape. For decades, New Orleans's crushing Reconstruction debt had stalled dock renovations and the construction of new drainage, sewage, and water treatment systems.[57] A crumbling infrastructure exacted a heavy toll on the city's low-income citizens. Excess water from Lake Pontchartrain often flooded Bayou St. John, Old Basin, New Basin, and other levees. One Tremé denizen recalled, "the cry would go out that the Old Basin was overflowing," and residents would rush with "casks of mud and sand to bolster up the banks and try and stop the water coming over."[58] Poor drainage also flooded neighborhoods, forcing locals to travel by canoe or skiff for up to a week until waters subsided. Floodwaters spread disease, damaged house foundations, and ruined merchandise "unprotected against the ravages of the scummy and dirty waters." As New Orleans chronicler John Kendall observed, "at no time in its history was the city in such grave peril of inundation."[59]

While the city repaid its Reconstruction debt in 1895, reformist entrepreneurs and laborers blamed cronyism within the Bourbon Democrat political machine for the city's economic stagnation and public infrastructure mismanagement. In 1896, they formed the nonpartisan Citizens' League and launched a mayoral campaign promoting local commercial investment, a balanced budget, and improved schools. When reform Democrat Walter Flower was elected mayor, he used the league's economic and political clout to create a Levee Board, updating the city's infrastructure and emergency response measures. Nonetheless, in March 1897, a deluge opened thirty-eight crevasses in Louisianan levees, while strong winds swept water over New Orleans's Canal and Bienville Street embankments, swamping stores. Lacking sufficient public emergency funds, the city depended on private loans to pay 2,500 men to frantically erect 20 miles of levees and riverfront embankments.[60] Even so, floodwaters took three months to recede. The Army Corps of Engineers and the Mississippi River Commission concluded that only a comprehensive levee system featuring levees built two feet higher than the recent floodwaters would eliminate the risk of flooding.[61] Brotherhood activists believed they could persuade city leaders to combine the Army Corps' infrastructure redevelopment proposal with their racially egalitarian city welfare program on the basis of sound economics and public safety, if not moral rectitude.

However, the cooperative's status as an integrated socialist organization committed to democratic decision-making and economic equality deeply perturbed conservative political, media, and business interests. One editorial in the *Daily Picayune* on June 3, 1897, contended that immigrant agitators like Graf had been "ruled over [by] emperors or other autocrats" with no understanding of American politics. Only the federal government, not the state, could distribute money to needy cities, employ "at a moment's warning an army of men" for public works projects, or pass substantial economic reforms. In any case, a government-supervised social safety net was an economically ruinous "fantasy." Under the brotherhood's direction, "the government [would own] everything and the people nothing . . . A rich man is an impossibility."

In Summer 1897, August Graf planned two Tremé-based mass marches to boldly counter such objections. The brotherhood's first march distills how the cooperative traversed the thorny entanglements of racial antagonism and oppositional grassroots performance to create a multiracial socialist cooperative movement. Evoking Coxey's Army, Graf called on unemployed men to assemble at Globe Hall in Congo Square on June 4, 1897.[62] He invited allies like the Carpenters' Union and other trade organizations to march a mile "in a peaceful column" to City Hall in Lafayette Square.[63] There, the brotherhood would petition Mayor Flower and Governor Murphy Foster, a staunch segregationist and Bourbon Democrat, to borrow from the state or federal treasury to create an emergency work relief fund.[64] The protest publicly communicated the brotherhood's commitment to political and economic equality for all workers.

By holding the march at Congo Square, the brotherhood clearly renounced Jim Crow strictures dictating socializing patterns. Since the 1700s, the park had harbored Afro-Creole cultural practice, religious ritual, and political organizing. Until the 1880s, Sunday evening visitors might observe or participate in diasporic musical and dance performances using African and the West Indies percussion instruments. In turn, weekly performances influenced turn-of-the century jazz originators like cornetists Buddy Bolden and Manuel Perez, who played to black Globe Hall audiences. Organizers of all ethnicities also rented the venue for political events, union meetings, and campaign rallies.[65]

At the same time, Graf traded on Congo Square's notoriety for high political drama. He strategically juxtaposed integrated labor protest for economic survival against the violent, extralegal gatherings held under the square's dusty, whitewashed trees. In 1891, after nineteen Sicilian Americans were acquitted of the murder of Police Chief David Hennessy, a vigilante mob of 10,000 people, including city leaders, dragged eleven Italians from the Orleans Parish Prison near Congo Square. The crowd shot and clubbed nine men to death, before lynching one man under a lamppost and another under a Congo Square tree.[66] Graf complained police unfairly hampered brotherhood peaceful protests yet no one had stopped the permit-less, murderous lynch mob. Nonetheless, the potential for interracial rioting "aroused some uneasiness" among city officials and the press "in the face of disturbances in other cities when meetings of a . . . similar kind had been . . . held."[67] Mayor Flower and City Council member Abraham Brittin refused the brotherhood a parade permit because the "incendiary" event was "unnecessary and calculated to cause harm."[68] Instead, the brotherhood should form a committee to formally meet with city officials rather than disturbing "the peace and quiet of New Orleans."[69] Consequently, the brotherhood was forced to cancel the march.

Furious, Graf stormed into Flower and Brittin's offices to demand redress. When Brittin rebuffed him, Graf "made himself so objectionable that he was finally ordered out of the office."[70] As Graf was hustled away, Brittin warned him that city police would closely monitor future brotherhood meetings. The city was true to its word; at subsequent events, officers threatened to arrest attendees discussing inflammatory topics such as political revolution, whether gradualist or not. In July, police shut down a planned mass march from Congo Square to City Hall because the brotherhood had not arranged parade permits, rented Globe Hall, or decided who would address the befuddled protestors.[71] Bacarisse complained that he had become wary of trumpeting too enthusiastically the "socialistic metamorphosis throughout . . . the world" for fear of being "combated and antagonized."

Worried that the impetuous August Graf had jeopardized a working relationship with the Flower administration, and by extension, the possibility of realizing universal brotherhood, Bacarisse labored to institutionalize and professionalize the brotherhood. In a series of summertime letters to the *Daily Picayune*, he criticized Graf for flaunting proper organizational channels.[72] Graf should have submitted his direct action proposal to a local Brotherhood committee, which would have contacted the National Union's "entire order throughout the country" to organize a national worker protest.[73] Instead, Graf had seized authoritative control, rejecting socialists' "dissipation of all autocratic powers—whether vested in individuals or in the body politic." While Bacarisse contained Graf's messy, performative working-class direct tactics within a rigid respectability politics, he also hinted he could invoke the power of a vast, coordinated socialist movement. Accordingly, in July, the brotherhood unveiled its operational arm, the Laboringmen's Protective Association (LMPA), an integrated lobbyist organization and cooperative labor union whose alliances with local and national social movements would enable it to more systematically advocate for "the whole laboring element."[74]

Creole of Color Organizing within the Laboringmen's Protective Association

On July 17, 1897, after yet another botched march on City Hall, several hundred men convened at Globe Hall for the LMPA's first meeting. In his opening remarks, Bacarisse cheekily addressed the police's bar on inflammatory speech by skirting the "very danger line of incendiarism" before "declaring he was not advocating violence and bloodshed. The time for [class] warfare had passed." Fifty members were black dockworkers, craftsmen, and office workers, making the thicket of lurking police officers again leery of a race riot.[75] They had been active within the failed 1896 Populist, Republican, and Democrat "fusion" campaign to defeat Governor Foster and saw the LMPA as a renewed opportunity to secure "the poor man's rights" in the midst of accelerating disenfranchisement.[76] While it endorsed a socialistic society, the LMPA first worked with veteran political operatives and Creole of color labor activists to secure city drainage contracts for depression-struck workers, regardless of race and occupation.[77]

Uniting multiracial, unemployed workers across industries, the LMPA sheltered the cross-class and -racial socializing necessary to repair an integrated, citywide labor movement. In contrast, while AFL's collective bargaining tactics won higher wages and a shorter workday for black and white workers during the Panic of 1893, the rapidly expanding labor organization limited membership to master craftspeople in skill-specific, segregated state and regional assemblies. Likewise, white New Orleanian socialists claimed that "each race [should] have charge of its own affairs."[78] When the Socialist Party of Louisiana formed in 1903, it initially refused to admit black members before forming segregated local chapters. Even antiracist socialists avoided the question of black social equality for fear of splintering fragile interracial labor coalitions.[79] Instead, the LMPA harkened back to the AFL's 1886 founding principles, when president Samuel Gompers organized unions "irrespective of creed, color, sex, nationality or politics."[80] Bacarisse averred that "the pre-eminent aim of a truly conscientious civilization" was open and equal discourse among "happy human creatures . . . without distinction of color, race, creed or previous condition."[81]

Most significantly, the LMPA's nine Creole of color and English-speaking African American directors forced white leadership to translate their vague declarations of racial equality into practice. Meeting in integrated Tremé venues like Globe Hall and the nearby Hopes Hall, a dance hall that served as the Citizens' Committee's headquarters while it drafted the *Plessy v. Ferguson* lawsuit, black members shaped the LMPA in ways impossible when the brotherhood convened in segregated CBD spaces.[82] They "insisted upon having the floor" at meetings, served on committees, gave speeches, and met with city officials and business leaders.[83] Tremé thus remained a vital staging ground where diverse LMPA members, following historian Richard White, cultivated an "in between culture" characterized by "new systems of meaning and of exchange" that rejected Jim Crow's stultifying segregationist customs and practices.[84]

Creole of color activist Louis Henry Mathieu vividly illustrates how clandestine Tremé meetings supported the generative intellectual exchanges producing the LMPA's synthetic structure and economic reform proposals. Mathieu himself was the product of Tremé's liminal Creole of color and

Cuban community life: a Cuban-Creole of color plasterer, Mathieu lived in Tremé's Cuban enclave within blocks of Bacarisse and other prominent émigrés and liberationists.[85] At the same time, his family dedicated their lives to expanding Creole of color political influence and economic security. Mathieu's father was a Republican political appointee who had supervised presidential elections and supported the Citizens' Committee.[86] His uncle helped found a benevolent association and was secretary of a Masonic Fusion Lodge, a Scottish Rite temple bristling with Creole of color political leaders.[87] Like Bacarisse, Mathieu's faith in French republicanism, American democracy, and mutualism was reinforced by political dialogue and sociability between radical Cubans and Creoles of color.

Mathieu believed cooperative principles would form a bulwark against the Separate Car Act and *Plessy v. Ferguson*. As secretary of the Senior Co-operators' Benevolent and Fraternal Association and president of its offshoot, the Juvenile Co-operators Fraternals Benevolent Mutual Aid Association serving Catholic Creole of color boys under the age of twenty-one, he expanded vulnerable New Orleanians' access to health insurance, medical care, funeral services, and pensions. Signaling his politicized mission, in 1897 Mathieu enlisted Citizens' Committee lawyer Louis Martinet to formally incorporate Juvenile Co-operators as a state-recognized organization. The cooperative was democratically run: members voted on directors, a committee supervising patient care, and service providers.[88]

Yet confining its services to Seventh Ward Catholic Creoles of color meant that the cooperative operated within a world bounded by race, religion, culture, and place. Ethnic-, craft-, and neighborhood-specific benevolent associations reinforced cultural distinctions and biases among demographic groups. Downtown-based Creoles of color and Uptown-concentrated English-speaking African Americans often clashed. Evincing a distinct political worldview rooted in French democratic republicanism and colorism, Creoles of color disdained black Americans.[89] In contrast, the LMPA's rank-and-file English-speaking black, German, Irish, and white Creole dockworkers living along the Mississippi riverfront eagerly collaborated with Creole of color craftsmen and clerks residing in the French Quarter, Tremé, and Seventh Ward. The cooperative urged black and white industrial workers to recognize they were both "in a worse condition of bondage" than slaves.[90] Because "no color line [was] drawn in this aggregation," the LMPA's citywide membership offered Mathieu an expanded resource network to press for civil rights, while his ties to Seventh Ward benevolent associations and political organizations lent the LMPA credibility within the radical Creole of color community.[91]

The nomination of black Creole US Customs House employee Albert J. Holmes for vice president further tied the LMPA's economic recovery plan to broader calls for black civil rights. During a directors' election on July 26 at Globe Hall, Bacarisse declared that both white and black workers, enslaved to monopolistic corporations, must unite to overthrow their capitalist oppressors. Yet white members bitterly protested when Holmes was nominated for vice president. Graf professed in "fractured English" that according to socialist principles, Holmes should be permitted to run for office, while a northerner observed that the city labor movement suffered from "dissension with the negro and refusing to organize with him." Swept up in class solidarity, the LMPA elected Holmes as first vice president and later as president. As a director, Holmes channeled his managerial skills into corralling the LMPA's philosophical meanderings into action. He was adept at "hold[ing] the unruly down" and enforcing parliamentary law during meetings.[92] Most importantly, unlike reviled immigrant outsiders Bacarisse and Graf, Holmes's federal position and familiarity with institutional procedures granted him a modicum of respectability necessary for negotiating favorable labor contracts for the unemployed.

Holmes saw his LMPA directorship as a chance to reassert black political and economic rights in wake of dockworker rioting, *Plessy v. Ferguson* social segregation, and threats to African American enfranchisement. As a Custom House sugar weigher, he was a federal political appointee at a time when black New Orleanians had vanishingly few opportunities for political participation.[93] When Henry Clay Warmoth, a former Reconstruction-era governor of Louisiana, was appointed Commissioner of Customs for the Port of New Orleans in 1890, he gave many loyal black Republicans plum Custom House positions, turning the federal building into a hotbed of black leadership. For instance, Holmes's co-workers included cooperative insurance organizer Walter Cohen, as well as Citizens' Committee founders Martinet, Desdunes, and Paul Trévigne, also an organizer of the People's Bakery.

Assistant weigher, politician, and union man Robert Boyer Gould also had captured the public's attention during the 1894 dockworker riots. On a foggy March morning, two white longshoremen fired shotgun rounds into a group of black screwmen loading cotton onto the steamship *Engineer* docked at Harrison Wharf. Gould hid between two bales of cotton as a mob of 200 to 300 white longshoremen stormed the surrounding wharves. While Gould escaped with only a flesh wound to his calf, his co-worker, John Payne, was fatally shot.[94] He would later address the LMPA's first meeting, understanding, as did its black members, that the cooperative could be an extension of Creole of color battles against *de jure* and *de facto* segregation.

The LMPA's Utopian Vision Constricts: Home Labor, Sicilians, and Yellow Fever

While the brotherhood had been a ramshackle affair, the LMPA's success hinged on recruiting established unionists and city government employees who, like Holmes, were well-versed in negotiating with politicians and commercial interests. They valued political expediency and rejected radical sloganeering because "the rich" could accuse the LMPA of "stir[ring] up the masses to discontent, strife, and strikes." They vetted new members for respectability, and those spouting "inflammatory or revolutionary remarks or speeches" were fined a dollar (a day's wage), required to apologize to the LMPA body, and expelled for a second offense. Although Bacarisse still professed that socialism benefitted "the legitimate, honest rich man all the way gradually down to the lowest class or wage earners," the LMPA adopted conservative trade unions' "bread and butter" agenda for higher wages and worker benefits.[95] Accordingly, in July 1897, the LMPA's first action was to join Populists, reformers, and the AFL petitioning the New Orleans Drainage Commission to award levee and drainage contracts with a fixed minimum wage to union members.[96]

Yet the LMPA's moderate consensus-building tactics began to narrow the cooperative's expansive worldview that multiracial laborers "organize to liberate themselves" to overturn competitive capitalism.[97] While immigrants clamored to join, the cooperative's constitution now required members be native-born or naturalized citizens.[98] Competing with Sicilian immigrants for dockyard jobs, both LMPA and AFL members upheld "home labor" as the only recipient of the coalition's municipal public welfare plan. Although global intellectual exchanges had informed the LMPA's cosmopolitan, democratic worldview, disruptive international trade tested its broad conception of citizenship and belongingness.

The LMPA's anti-Sicilian stance was rooted in dockworkers' economic dependence on a stable sugar trade. Beginning in the 1880s, cheap Cuban imports flooded the American market, jeopardizing Democrat sugar cane planters' stranglehold over Louisianan politics and economy. In response, wealthy growers drained and cultivated large swaths of Louisiana's swamps to ramp up domestic sugar production. They also strategically collaborated with black and white Republicans, Knights of Labor, and Populist agricultural and urban laborers to win federal protective sugar tariffs between 1894 and 1897. The LMPA denounced the uneasy alliance as expeditious. Even though tariffs had allowed the sugar industry to recover, it exploited black field hands as well as an influx of Chinese and Italian laborers.[99] State labor bureaus, company labor agents, and established family and friends' promise of quick cash had funneled 30,000 Sicilians and Italians into Louisiana's sugar parishes and urban dockyards by the late 1890s.[100]

Echoing Populist and Knights of Labor organizers struggling to unionize Louisiana's black and poor white sugar growers, the LMPA predicted a cascade of calamities. Sicilians undercut domestic field hands' wages, driving rural blacks to New Orleans "in direct competition with our city labor."[101] Worse yet, the stagnating waterfront economy had already ignited dockyard race riots, and a surfeit of urban Sicilian sugar workers further fanned racial tensions by snatching precious sugar refinery and warehouse jobs from black and white unionists.[102] After slashing wages, unscrupulous city contractors capitalized on "pauper labor . . . gradually crowding [New Orleanian] negroes out of the sugar districts." The net effect was "starvation" wages for all, as well as rampant "crimes and depravations" across the city as indigents overburdened charitable institutions. Hiring more police to monitor vagrants and "keep in order this foreign element" would only further tax depleted municipal funds.[103]

The LMPA's experienced political operatives understood that harnessing the Citizens' League's business acumen while working through established institutional channels was key to capturing the city's reformist administration's attention. The coalition shrewdly contended that unemployment relief would benefit home labor, business leaders, and the public alike. Building an efficient and cost-effective drainage system would protect New Orleanian assets while ameliorating Sicilian and migrant job competition and "a vast army of unemployed."[104] On July 23, Acting Mayor Brittin met with the joint labor committee to discuss the terms of their municipal drainage contract proposal. Committee representatives praised him for aiding "home labor" but requested that the city and its contractors pay unemployed levee workers a fixed, fair wage of $1.50 a day, twenty-five cents above the state average.[105] Impressed, Brittin presented their proposal to the Drainage Commission the same day, while contractors promised "drainage work [would] be given to home labor."[106]

Brotherhood president Albert Holmes's plan to improve city infrastructure and safeguard citizens' physical and economic health gained further credence in August 1897, when a deadly yellow fever outbreak paralyzed the city.[107] The epidemic infected 4,000 people and killed 500 across nine southern states. New Orleans's large population of non-immune residents suffered inordinately, with 300 deaths. City trade and worker wages stagnated for months due to strict port quarantines and conflicting regional public health and security measures. Across the South, laborers urged federal officials to standardize coastal quarantine laws regulating interstate trade and keep dockyards running during public health crises.[108] Holmes joined a committee representing the brotherhood, AFL, and the Central Trade and Labor Assembly, an integrated labor body of over thirty city unions, to protest Louisiana's "numerous and cowardly" commercial shipping quarantines. The committee explained to Mayor Flower that a city-administered public health fund to employ home labor in public works and sanitation would both ease unemployment and halt the spread of disease.[109]

Mayor Flower conceded that recent flooding and epidemics highlighted the city's desperate need for a comprehensive drainage, sewerage, and water supply system. He assured Holmes and his colleagues that the state Board of Health would listen to their recommendations.[110] The Commissioner of Public Works began hiring unemployed workers, while private sanitary squads employed laborers to patrol neighborhoods for health violations. Finally, by late August, drainage system draftsman and LMPA officer Henry Zander used his professional connections within the Drainage Commission to win city contracts for his fellow cooperative members.[111] The levee project Holmes helped launch literally remapped the city and challenged the logic of Jim Crow segregation with each new contract.

Restricting Home Labor to White Labor

Yet the seeds of the multiracial organization's destruction were sown in its expeditious pursuit of unemployment relief for American citizens rather than all laborers. LMPA members' access to contracts turned on the definition of "home labor," which was increasingly conflated with "white labor." Mayor Flower and commercial contractors' promise to award drainage and levee contracts to "home labor without regard to color" was largely a rhetorical flourish; they were reluctant to meaningfully expand black employment.[112] For example, in July, the National Contracting Company of New Orleans extended its drainage contracts to home labor. However, Holmes reported that only applicants holding poll tax certificates, indicating voter eligibility, were hired. In practice, this meant precious few black workers met the company's requirements. The policy mirrored Louisiana's 1877 poll tax laws, which disenfranchised many blacks and poor whites because few could afford the poll tax fee.[113]

Further, white Populists and AFL members within the LMPA evinced deep discomfort with its black leadership, viewing it as a bellwether for societal "negro supremacy." By the end of the 1893–97 depression, the AFL dispensed with racial inclusionary language entirely and closed membership to African Americans.[114] Similarly, at an October 1897 meeting of New Orleanian

Populist ward clubs, Bacarisse joined white LMPA and AFL representatives in drafting platform recommendations for the state party. Embittered by their 1896 state electoral defeat, the clubs now accused Republicans and their "sable allies" of stuffing ballot boxes and buying "ignorant and corrupt" black and immigrant votes. They advised the 1898 Louisiana Constitution Committee to eliminate universal manhood suffrage to prevent Republican corporate and political interests from elevating "the illiterate negro element of the state" above poor whites.[115] Repeating Populist sentiments, on October 25, 1897, Bacarisse, Graf, and other white unionists shattered the LMPA to form a new, segregated unemployed workers' union, the White Laboring Men's Protective Association (WLMPA).[116]

The LMPA might have fractured along radical versus conservative racial politics, but its Creole of color members' subsequent careers constituted vibrating strings of cooperative life that resonated with future social movements. After Democrats voted to disenfranchise African Americans at the 1898 Louisiana Constitution Convention, Creoles of color enlisted in the Spanish American War to demonstrate their patriotism and civic fitness. When President William McKinley created black "immune regiments" based on the racist belief that they were immune to yellow fever and could withstand Cuba's tropical climate, former LMPA head and Civil War veteran Albert Holmes saw the war as "the opportunity of their lives" for African Americans to serve as officers.[117] Other black LMPA activists recruited for and served in Louisiana's Ninth US Volunteer Infantry. Returning soldiers did not receive the franchise and were often denied pensions, so black members' unions, spiritual associations, and mutual aid societies provided veterans economic and medical aid, while allying with national civil rights advocates pressing for full citizenship rights. Operating in dialogue with African diasporic and global equality movements, they maintained a neighborhood-based economic safety net that Depression-era and countercultural black liberationist collectives continued to evolve.[118]

In contrast, WLMPA members repudiated racial justice and comprehensive social transformation for moderate economic reform. The national discourse around the Spanish American War and US imperialism enabled the WLMPA's ethnic whites to leverage a broadening definition of whiteness dependent on colonizing people of color.[119] Just months prior, city officials and the press had pilloried Bacarisse and Graf's "foreignness" and, by extension, the soundness of their political critique.[120] Now, as journalists filed Spanish American War reports contrasting "lazy, inefficient, hungry Cuban bodies with the spectacle of American manhood," WLMPA members more persuasively asserted a common white American identity.[121]

August Graf's dominance within the WLMPA reflects this new identity formation. As state organizer, he exploited his German heritage, union affiliations, and associational memberships as WLMPA recruitment channels. Immigrating to the United States as a teenager, Graf rotated through New Orleans's white ethnic enclaves like the Irish Channel and the Lower Ninth Ward, which imposed an assimilating influence on him.[122] Speaking before the German American Republican Club in 1896, he argued that since German leaders cared for the "Fatherland" and not émigrés, new citizens must prize "the interests of this country, and no longer . . . those of Germany."[123]

For Graf, German barroom sociability solidified the WLMPA as a refuge for ethnic whites. The cooperative's new meeting space at Teutonia Hall starkly rejected Tremé's multiracial cosmopolitanism. Located at the corner of Exchange Place and Customhouse Street, Teutonia Hall was a significant node in the CBD's German bar culture and immigrant union organizing. It hosted German social and political functions, including Graf's political club meetings.[124] Graf himself was a bartender and eventually owned a CBD saloon. Neighborhood bars fostered working-class loyalty to the Regular Democratic Party chiseling away at black enfranchisement and mobility. As precinct captains, bar owners dispensed jobs, financial aid, and other charity to faithful voters.[125] Likewise, a majority of WLMPA members were German or worked in the beer industry. Many belonged to the AFL-affiliated Hotel and Restaurant Employees and Bartender's Union, which disavowed radical politics to win wage increases for skilled white workers.[126] Unlike former LPMA president Eugene Bacarisse, who unequivocally pointed to industrial capitalism as the fundamental cause of unemployed workers' misery, the WLMPA blamed the lingering depression and yellow fever outbreak on "the all-wise creator of the universe."[127] Casting the depression as an "act of God," Graf legitimized unemployment relief as an "emergency" measure, not the harbinger of widespread political change.

Ironically, WLPMA members used the social and professional networks, ideological models, and organization-building techniques the integrated Brotherhood and LMPA had perfected to restrict New Orleans's nascent government-funded public works program to white workers. Allying with the same labor and civic groups, the WLMPA argued that if the city were to pay white employees a $1.50 daily salary and mandate a shorter workweek, it could hire even more laborers.[128] Consequently, aspects of the WLMPA's plan were incorporated into the unemployment relief program Mayor Flower unveiled in late October. A private-public partnership, the Mayor-Mullen-McGary Relief Plan created an emergency fund to employ white laborers in public works projects. New Orleans Public Works Commissioner W. L. McGary and National Contracting Company Frank P. Mullen agreed to pay WLMPA members a dollar a day to gravel roads in the city. Additionally, new WLMPA president Michael Nestor, a city Board of Health clerk, used his insider status to pressure the agency to hire cooperative members as private watchmen monitoring yellow fever hotspots.[129] Further, new city-run levee and pump systems and public health measures solidified the segregationist edict of *Plessy v. Ferguson* by cleaving neighborhoods and isolating black communities from basic resources.[130] Finally, after reading reports that city levee contractors were hiring African Americans and transient whites, a Terrebonne Parish sawmill 40 miles outside New Orleans employed 75 WLMPA members as skilled mechanics and laborers.[131] The WLMPA thus enlarged the geographic scope of racially contingent relief efforts far beyond city boundaries.

Although the WLMPA disbanded in late 1898 when the yellow fever epidemic subsided and the national economy recovered, the WLMPA's impact on city infrastructure extends beyond its mayfly's lifespan. As Louisianan legislators restricted black voting rights, they permitted women property holders to vote on tax laws, opening new opportunities for some women to influence New Orleans urban development. In January 1898, the Local Council of Women, a Progressive civic group, formed to document and publicize the city's myriad public sanitation problems. Prominent suffragists and white supremacists Kate and Jean Gordon mobilized white women to approve a bond for the city to purchase privately managed water, sewerage, and drainage systems. Throughout 1898, the Local Council joined the WLMPA, the AFL, the Board of Health, and reformist businesses petitioning to modernize city infrastructure.

Their coalition was unusual: New Orleans's white, affluent suffragists had consistently overlooked working-class organizations as potential political allies, while male labor officials often dismissed the unskilled positions many women filled as unworthy of unionizing. Yet Bacarisse, a member of the Local Council-affiliated and women-dominated Stenographers' Association, linked female suffrage to city improvement.[132] During the Spring 1897 floods, he published a poem contending that if women were enfranchised, they could have voted for "herculean levees" to protect the city and avoid future catastrophes.[133] Further, the WLMPA and the Local Council shared a mistrust of black voters and capitalist machinations. They decried poor white neighborhoods' inability to afford current water or sewerage rates, their resulting unsanitary conditions, and skyrocketing sewerage rates for all without city regulation.[134]

The coalition's campaign to hold city leaders accountable to constituents was successful, plotting a new urban geography in the process. In 1899, voters approved the necessary city utilities bond. City Council member Abraham Brittin also created a single city agency to oversee public works projects hiring impoverished laborers. By 1915, New Orleans had spent $27.5 million overhauling water, sewer, and drainage systems, dramatically reinvesting in the previously bankrupt city.[135]

One member of the union-Local Council utilities battles, Ida Weis Friend, extended the Brotherhood of Co-operative Commonwealth's internationally inspired socialist vision for responsive local government and equitable economic policies well into the twentieth century. A key architect of a women-led Southern cooperative movement, she helped direct the Housewives' League Co-operative Store, an Uptown-based Rochdale grocery store lowering the cost of living for female consumers and their families during the 1910s and '20s.[136] Its comprehensive cooperative plan strove to reorder southern homes, neighborhoods, and cities, with white women's needs solidly at the center.

ROCHDALE COOPERATIVES

CHAPTER TWO

The New Orleans Housewives' League:
White Women's Political Equality and Consumer Reform

During the 1914–15 depression, a harrowing food crisis gripped New Orleans and the nation. The Housewives' League, a white middle- and upper-class female consumer advocacy group composed of former Local Council members like Ida Weis Friend and Kate Gordon, believed that President Woodrow Wilson's "call for the South to feed itself" could break the city's dependence on northern and western agriculture. However, retailers and wholesalers monopolized regional produce distribution and artificially inflated food costs to the detriment of the family pocketbook. The league avowed that an alliance between small farmers and women consumers would ameliorate the high cost of living. Beginning in December 1915, the Housewives' League opened several cooperative curb markets across the affluent Uptown New Orleans neighborhood so that Louisiana truck farmers could sell directly to female customers. Caught up in the nascent women's club and consumer rights movements sweeping the industrializing South, it emulated contemporary consumer activist groups opening cooperatives as emergency food distributors for economically precarious families.[1]

Operating four days a week, New Orleans cooperative markets were sites of frenetic activity. Dozens of produce carts jammed together on small plots of city land. Desperate for fresh and inexpensive produce, black, Chinese, and white customers arriving by car, by streetcar, and on foot rushed the laden wagons "with upstretched arms eager for their bargains."[2] Patrons carted away their finds "in wheelbarrows pushed by the small boys of the families, or in baby perambulators," and gloated over "[l]ettuce as big and solid as cabbage," "[e]xcellent sweet potatoes," "[t]he finest and tenderest spinach," "turnips and mustard greens, and endive and shallots."[3] League members "arose before daylight, in rain or shine, in cold or heat, and went to the various market places and sold . . . fresh country eggs," homemade breads and jellies, and crafts.[4] Farmers praised the arrangement, citing profits far exceeding those at public markets.[5] Market member-owners contracted directly with producers and distributors to circumvent the corrupt wholesalers and retailers whom the public blamed for perennial food supply crises.[6]

The history of the league's cooperative projects deepens our understanding of how white Southern progressive women's organizations operated in the 1910s and '20s and their impact on New Orleans's economic development. Viewing the Housewives' League through the lens of the national cooperative movement positions New Orleans as a cosmopolitan site of intellectual foment, a swiftly modernizing city enriched by the circulation of international goods, bodies, and political thought. The league yoked white women's cooperative enterprise to the same evolutionary socialism and social democratic thought Eugene Bacarisse had promoted. Even as post-World War I Red Scare propaganda threatened to dismantle radical labor, feminist, and socialist advances, participating in cooperatives hardened league members' belief that unchecked capitalism disadvantaged ordinary women. Debating over downtown hotel luncheons and Association of Commerce library gatherings, the league proposed that New Orleanians should emulate socialists and Progressives erecting egalitarian global economic and political structures rather than kowtowing to the insular planter aristocrats who controlled the city's social life and politics. As league president Inez Meyers declared, "I think we are all socialistic, or will get there soon, the longer we find that we can't do the things we want to do."[7]

While historians have posited that pre-Depression consumer activism was hyper-localized and shambolic, the Housewives' League thrived on highly organized regional coordination among diverse New Orleans civic groups and between urban and rural clubwomen to form a women-driven, cooperative economy.[8] To that end, between 1913 and 1921, the league rolled out several women-run consumer cooperatives—curbside produce stalls, World War I cooperative kitchens, and a grocery store—each of which connected rural producers to urban consumers. Their Rochdale cooperatives dispensed money- and labor-saving strategies so white middle-class women could devote themselves more fully to integrating New Orleans into the global marketplace, as well as achieving broader Progressive reforms and enfranchisement. As religious and cultural outsiders in New Orleans, Housewives' League president Inez Meyers, cooperative committee chair Edna Egleston, and consumer advocate Ida Friend gathered disparate Louisianan consumer activists, labor unionists, Progressive entrepreneurs, small farmers, woman suffragists, and rural clubwomen under the mantle of a new moral economy rooted in community cooperation and gender parity.

Yet the Housewives' League is fundamentally a study in contrasts. Historians Landon Storrs and Pamela Tyler suggest that large white southern women's organizations blocked institutional change and enforced conservative ideologies antithetical to radical reforms.[9] Because middle- and upper-class league women's campaign to curb capitalism's excesses required eroding the very foundation upon which their social class rested, Meyers, Egleston, and Friend's cooperative plans clashed with white women's dogged adherence to New Orleans class hierarchies. Although the league claimed that a socialized cooperative system would democratize local and national political and economic institutions, members hoped to reform capitalism from the inside. After encountering European consumer cooperatives in their studies and travels abroad, members hailed the pragmatic Rochdale model, not Bacarisse's utopian socialism, as a revolution in modern, egalitarian food distribution. The Housewives' League professionalized and institutionalized its economic activities by blending modern business practices with Rochdale principles in order to secure financing from Progressive politicians and businessmen.

Additionally, like the WLMPA's German membership, the Housewives' League's inner circle of Jewish, northern, and immigrant outsiders used African Americans as a foil to solidify their own tenuous hold on citizenship and civic voice. For instance, while the league allied with white labor unions, it sabotaged a black domestic workers' union made up of league members' own employees. Finally, its cosmopolitan understanding of cooperative economics as a conduit for egalitarian global trade was rooted in imperialism and did not extend to colonized people of color. Nonetheless, the Housewives' League's evolving eight-year cooperative vision improved public markets, raised wages for farmers, and reduced the cost of living for average families by adapting international socialist ideas to the neighborhood level.

The Origins of the Housewives' League

To Housewives' League movers and shakers Meyers, Egleston, and Friend, 1910s-era New Orleans teetered maddeningly on the cusp of economic revival, while national market instability, corrupt political regimes, yawning class and gender divides, and antiquated infrastructure threatened the city's progress at every turn. The distinct social geography of New Orleans profoundly shaped its reformers' understanding of the possible. Racial and ethnic segregation tightened as affluent Anglo American civic leaders concentrated in western

"streetcar suburbs" in the Garden District, Uptown, Audubon Park, Carrollton, and northern neighborhoods like Metairie. English-speaking black and
white domestic workers lived behind their employers' spacious estates in
cheaper residential blocks, forming a grid of spatial inequality.[10]

The city's racial and class topography also influenced economic revitalization efforts throughout the 1910s. Fearing that the Citizens' League's body of
Progressive commercial elites would loosen the conservative Regular Democratic Organization's stranglehold on city politics, Mayor Martin Behrman
appointed reformist entrepreneurs to administrative positions. Civic-minded
white entrepreneurs touted municipally driven economic development as
an effective tool to limit Downtown working-class and immigrant patronage while improving government efficiency and responsiveness.[11] However,
between 1910 and 1915, a series of national recessions, food shortages, and
consumer goods price increases tested Regular Democrat and Progressive
business leaders' resolve to collaboratively safeguard laborers and consumers'
living standards while attracting commercial investors.[12]

Commercial development in the city was racialized and unequally distributed. Policy makers fretted that the decaying French Quarter's "shiftlessness"
and its Creole character discouraged vital outside financial backing and tourism. Instead, city leaders concentrated on bolstering the city's flagging Warehouse and Cotton Districts, which contained the factories, banks, agents, and
factors dependent on Louisiana's languishing cotton industry, as well as the
commodity exchange houses and businesses supporting agricultural trade.
The Association of Commerce and other civic groups also hosted business
conventions showcasing "made-in-New-Orleans" products and pushed funding extensive waterfront, canal, and railroad modernization projects that
expanded domestic and Latin American trade. Seeking greater profits and
smoother workflows, the shipping industry and cotton trades largely abandoned an autocratic managerial model that had provoked decades of labor
strikes and boycotts in favor of maintaining cooperative relations with black
and white waterfront unions to stimulate the urban economy.[13]

Into this potent mix of economic growth and Progressive reform stepped
Housewives' League directors Meyers, Egleston, and Friend, wealthy women
of vision eager to make their mark on the city's economic and political landscape. Their political sympathies, religious beliefs, and class backgrounds
shaped the contours of the Housewives' League cooperative campaign.
League president Inez Beryl MacMartin Meyers was born in 1868 in Iowa
to a Wisconsin-born homemaker and a Scottish-Canadian carpenter. As a
young woman, Inez and her family moved to Jennings, a rural town then in
Calcasieu Parish, Louisiana. After marrying railway mail agent Henry Buford

Meyers in December 1887, the couple settled in Uptown New Orleans, where Henry became assistant superintendent of the United States Postal Service's railway department. Inez acted as treasurer of the family business, the Meyers Printing and Advertising Company.[14] She was an assistant magazine editor in the 1910s before editing one of the city's first women's columns for the *New Orleans Item*. Until her death in 1923, Meyers was "one of the best known and most wide awake newspaper women of the far south," working with national media to publicize women's efforts to improve film regulation, prison and women's working conditions, public health, and family nutrition.[15]

As a printer and a journalist, Meyers joined a circle of affluent Uptown women civic leaders and urban professionals deeply invested in New Orleans's commercial future. Doctors, teachers, clerical workers, social workers, and journalists who formed the core of the Housewives' League membership were also married or related to Progressive businessmen directing the city's technological modernization and import-export industries. Husbands managed engineering offices, post offices, dry docks, steamship companies, and telephone and telegraph offices. For example, Edna Egleston's husband was a prominent railroad and bridge engineer who had helped construct the Panama Canal as well as railroad lines in Mexico, Florida, and Louisiana. Exploring Cuban, Puerto Rican, and Central and Latin American markets, Housewives' League spouses and relatives exported and imported cotton, sugar, chicory, rice, oil, and lumber to make the port of New Orleans the second largest in the nation.[16] Keen to forge diplomatic and commercial partnerships with "these tropic lands to which we have so long been aliens," New Orleans manufacturing industries enriched themselves on Latin America's "vast resources."[17]

However, women's religious beliefs, weak cultural and familial attachments to the South, and active civic engagement crystallized into a comprehensive critique of industrial capitalism, often in opposition to husbands who sought low-cost labor at the expense of working women and consumers' well-being.[18] Of eighty-three active Housewives' League members, 82 percent were either themselves not from Louisiana or had parents who were not native to the state. A quarter were married to northern-born or naturalized men. And 12 percent were German American Reform Jews prominent within the city's commercial and philanthropic circles. Even Louisianan members were frequently educated or had spent significant periods outside the Jim Crow South. Frequent voyages to Europe and Latin America enabled this band of outsiders to witness firsthand how different economic and political systems were organized, as well as how women might take advantage of New Orleans's flourishing international trade. The British-born publisher Winifred Dabney traveled to Panama, Costa Rica, and Guatemala with her investigative reporter husband, while Midwestern suffragist Margaret Elliot was a classical violinist who toured the United States, Canada, and Mexico.[19] Imbued with a cosmopolitan curiosity about the world, women's clubs studied how to adapt Russian women's rights advances and cooperative kitchens, Finnish cooperative grocery stores, Austrian cooperative housing, and British fishing cooperatives to a New Orleans context.[20]

New Orleans activist Ida Weis Friend exemplifies how outside affiliations and religious-based sociality pushed women's civic groups politically leftward. Friend was born in 1868 in Natchez, Mississippi, to a wealthy German Jewish cotton broker. Educated in New Orleans, France, and Germany, she married a Milwaukee native and moved to Chicago. When she returned to New Orleans for good, Friend faced considerable religious discrimination. Sequestered within St. Charles Avenue's Reform Jewish neighborhood and excluded from Protestant- and Catholic-affiliated social clubs, Friend and her Uptown Jewish peers began to challenge the racial, religious, and class-based presumptions that elevated such institutions.[21] They poured their energies into secular suffrage, consumer rights, civil equality, and antipoverty organizations. Investigating a host of urban ills, well-heeled Progressives discovered industrial labor's detriment to working-class women and children.[22]

For all their ambition, Progressive white women were politically hamstrung by the anti-woman suffrage Regular Democrats, which blocked their enfranchisement and passed measures counter to consumers' interests. Worried that women's enfranchisement would lead to sweeping political reform, Mayor Behrman instructed every city ward leader to turn out the vote against state woman suffrage in 1912 and 1918. Similarly, when female reformers accused the mayor of hiking consumer fuel rates to lavishly fund the city's Industrial Canal improvements, Regular Democratic-supporting husbands barred wives from attending consumer activist meetings.[23]

To combat Regular Democrats' persistent obstructionism and expand women's political and economic protections, wealthy white Progressive women rallied behind the New Orleans suffrage movement. Inez Meyers was secretary of the Era Club, which white social elites Kate and Jean Gordon had formed in 1895 to advocate for and implement women's rights reforms, including stumping for a state suffrage amendment, monitoring public sanitation, building playgrounds, enforcing child and women's labor laws, and establishing juvenile courts. Yet when Meyers and her Jewish, northern, and immigrant peers championed the federal amendment campaign sponsored by the National American Woman Suffrage Association (NAWSA), the virulently racist Gordons feared that the federal measure would allow black women to vote. They ousted Meyers and federal amendment supporters in 1913.[24]

Meyers cofounded the NAWSA-affiliated Woman's Suffrage Party (WSP) to counter the Gordons' autocratic leadership and recruit white working women to the federal amendment cause. WSP representatives spoke before schoolteachers, labor unionists, shop girls, and factory workers and even contemplated visiting "the cotton field in order to talk suffrage to the workers." Democratically run, the WSP held officer elections and eschewed party business "conducted too much along drawing-room lines."[25] Its nonhierarchical organization dovetailed with individual members' interest in a gender-equitable socialized state. Meyers chaired a 1913 suffrage convention in leafy City Park in which German Jewish lawyer and cooperative supporter Solomon Weiss argued that as society accepted "that distinction[s] of class and creed, of wealth and station are largely the creations of chance," it would also develop "a more Socialistic regard for the relation between man and woman—a more fraternal, a more equitable, relation."[26] State organizer Mrs. E. J. Graham explained the symbolic power of the park's weekly suffragist meetings to transform society: "Formerly men of Louisiana . . . met in the gray of morning dawn to settle matters of . . . life or death with bullets. Now men and women meet under the beautiful oaks to discuss and settle matter of life by means of the ballots." To recruit WSP members to join the Housewives' League, the league integrated the party's egalitarian structure and political program into its own version of socialistic female cooperation.

At the same time, the burgeoning women's club movement provided a robust institutional framework to help Louisiana suffragists like Meyers collaboratively address local, regional, and national issues concerning American women. Although the club movement had organized women around self-improvement and education since the mid-1800s, it was not until the South began to industrialize and urbanize that large, national organizations like the General Federation of Women's Clubs extended to Louisiana.[27] Later a national General Federation press committee member, Meyers chartered the New Orleans chapter in 1912 and was elected its "able" and "beloved" president.[28] As GFWC directors and affiliated club leaders, suffragists like Meyers mustered New Orleanians to fight for a kaleidoscopic array of Progressive reforms. One Louisiana clubwoman characterized the "key woman" as "she who strives for the solution for the questions of wage-earning women, of the underage working children, of the Consumers League, of the Sanitation Clubs, of the political equality movement."[29] Recognizing that "[t]here is force in numbers, and twenty or fifty clubs co-operating heartily can naturally accomplish more than one working by itself," New Orleans clubwomen like Meyers incorporated these community-building skills into future Housewives' League cooperative projects.[30]

Most important, by regularly convening at the Association of Commerce's CBD offices to discuss urban ills that disproportionately affected women, Meyers and her peers developed a holistic understanding of the institutionalized classism and sexism dividing their city. New Orleans spent the least money on social welfare in Louisiana, with little relief for its most vulnerable residents. Private, often religious, charities and social agencies were forced to fill the gaps. Interacting with the General Federation's Christian socialist, social gospel, and evolutionary socialist social workers inspired by the Chicago settlement house movement particularly impacted the Housewives' League's cooperative philosophy. Hull House settlement founder Jane Addams and acolyte Florence Kelley's evolutionary socialism held that social transformation would slowly be achieved via legislation and cultural shifts, not political revolution.[31] Similarly, in 1913 Meyers discerned a sea change among urban socialites seeking to professionalize social work and public relief: "many a frivolous, pleasure-loving woman, lured into the [General Federation] club by the refreshments and the social side, becomes gradually interested in the more serious work of the organization, and at length develops into an efficient, hard-working member."[32]

Like Eugene Bacarisse before them, Christian socialist groups also exposed Meyers and her peers to formal cooperative organization. Meyers learned "the value of co-operation and united effort" by campaigning for temperance with St. Mark's Hall Methodist settlement workers.[33] As social gospel adherents, they strove to physically manifest an egalitarian Kingdom of God in the disinvested French Quarter, experimenting with cooperative housing and educational programs to aid white female immigrants.[34]

Housewives' League members also attended the venerated Trinity Episcopal Church. Its Christian socialist minister, Reverend Beverly Warner, believed that unchecked capitalism drove class inequality and that cooperatives would replace sinful economic competition. In 1899, he opened the nonsectarian Kingsley House settlement to serve the Irish Channel's poor white residents. Head resident and Housewives' League member Eleanor McMain organized a housing cooperative and neighborhood buying club to improve tenement housing, stabilize rent, and enforce sanitation laws. The league later opened extensions at both St. Mark's Hall and Kingsley House to showcase home economic techniques to impoverished women. Interacting with radical social workers spurred future league members to develop on-the ground solutions to urban poverty rather than merely donating to philanthropies.[35]

Simultaneously, Meyers's colleagues belonged to a coterie of socialistic "material feminists" who argued that white women's political and economic equality hinged on their liberation from devalued domestic work. Pre-World War I female Progressives and socialists often debated platforms, joined each other's groups, and echoed each other's rhetoric. Reformer and novelist Charlotte Perkins Gilman's 1898 socialist treatise *Women and Economics* outlines the material feminist cooperative program.[36] Women must organize professionally run collective kitchens, cleaning services, nurseries, and kindergartens so that capitalism and its attendant gender exploitation could yield to a socialist, industrialized society whose democratic household structures freed women to pursue careers. Likewise, to prevent the "[e]normous social waste from educated women becoming mere domestic drudges after marriage," New Orleans clubwomen believed that "household life . . . becoming socialized" would enable experts to use new communication and transportation technology to democratize the domestic sphere.[37]

Accordingly, Meyers and the Era Club sponsored Gilman's 1911 talk on "cooperative housekeeping," while in 1920 the Housewives' League cooperative committee head Edna Egleston spoke alongside Florence Kelley and Jane Addams on shared housekeeping's ability to reduce settlement workers' living expenses to better aid their target demographics.[38] Holding Kelley and Addams's talk in the First Presbyterian Church of New Orleans, the oldest Presbyterian congregation in Louisiana, and Gilman's lecture at the Athenaeum, a Jewish-affiliated institution better known for hosting Mardi Gras balls "[reigning] in a riot of color, a profusion of masks and a depth of balloons" than socialist lectures, lent their political messages credibility for respectable women leery of controversy.[39]

However, white supremacy tainted even the staunchest New Orleans material feminists, who replicated Louisiana socialists' particular brand of Jim Crow racism. For instance, the Socialist Party of Louisiana advocated collective ownership of all means of production, women's suffrage, and direct democracy alongside nationwide racial segregation.[40] Even radical socialists supported black economic rather than social or political parity. Local Socialist Party member and suffragist Martha Porter averred, "socialism was really a protection for the home" and devoted herself to "the brotherhood of man . . . by aiding impoverished families." She barred black and white socialists from mingling at her boardinghouse and advocated slum clearance "for hygienic as well as social reasons."[41] Similarly, by locating league cooperatives in wealthy white Uptown neighborhoods, material feminists like Meyers implicitly promoted a racially bounded communal society whose cooperative economy elevated white women's financial and political standing.

With a cooperative philosophy forged in the fires of material feminism, members of the Housewives' League found that their ability to bind white women's suffrage, Progressive reform, and consumer advocacy to cooperative economics was tempered by a series of severe economic recessions and food shortages between 1910 and 1915. State legislators, US Senate committees, and private institutions furiously debated the constricting market's causes and effects, but unwilling to enforce strict market controls, they left consumers to navigate high prices alone.[42] Condemning policy makers' complacency, Meyers declared that the "remedy" for price fluctuations "lies in the hands of the housewives."[43] She echoed British Fabian socialists who believed that civic-minded consumers were rational, ethical agents acting above self-interested capitalists and laborers. First, Meyers advised female consumers to join municipal and state consumer and labor committees to ensure government consumer agencies protected constituents. Then in 1913, influenced by the national consumer movement, Meyers and Friend chartered the New Orleans chapters of the National Consumers' League (NCL) and the National Housewives' League (NHL) to force city and federal officials to strictly regulate corporations' affairs.[44]

The "Housewife" and the Female Consumer: The Housewives' League Forms

The Housewives' League "took a deep breath and girded its armor" to "advance the mutual interests of producer and consumer" by supervising daily consumption practices and ensuring women's equitable treatment in the marketplace.[45] After the Panic of 1910, Jennie Dewey Heath formed the NHL to offset rapid inflation by training the American housewife "to recognize her economic position" as an efficient, responsible consumer.[46] The NHL's journal, *Housewives League Magazine*, outlined agricultural policy, reported on branches' public health campaigns, and deployed new nutrition and home economics theories to help women source high-quality, cheap food. Proclaiming "food is our most vital necessity," the local Housewives' League allied with the NCL, the General Federation, and the NAWSA to install city health inspectors in public markets and pressure retailers and wholesalers to standardize weights and measures affecting food costs. The league also distributed a "white list" of honest factories and retailers and instructed women to boycott price-gouging stores.[47]

While the New Orleans chapters of the NCL and the NHL overlapped in membership and platforms, the Consumers' League consciously pursued cross-class alliances that diluted white southern women's paternalism. Since

1899, NCL head Florence Kelley had focused on extending political and economic equality to the urban working classes, countering the market's "invisible hand" with labor legislation. The local Consumers' League researched
women's and children's salaries, domestic life, and industrial working conditions and requested that the city implement minimum wages. It allied with
labor unions like the Retail Clerks' Protective Association to protest female
employees' unequal pay, their long, unpredictable work hours, and retail
stores' inadequate heating systems and fire escapes.[48]

In contrast, the Housewives' League had a complicated relationship to
capitalism. While the league positioned itself as a social justice organization
protecting consumers from globalized industrial capitalism's economic disparities, it also welcomed women's integration into new, international consumer markets as a theoretical social good. Reflecting members' commercial
ties, it advised women to organize along corporate business models and, as
cooperative entities, to ally with government and economic leaders to force
retailers to sell fairly priced, quality goods.[49] In 1913, the New Orleans chapter
unveiled an eight-year-long cooperative initiative that, by improving mainstream businesses, helped struggling families stretch their incomes to have
"a better chance to live, to own a home, and to climb up to higher things."[50]

Building a Regional Cooperative Economy through Public Markets

A severe national depression in 1915 kicked off the Housewives' League's
cooperative plan in earnest. Cotton Belt populists, farmers, and unionists
had long established a web of cooperative associations to combat middleman
retailers and wholesalers who inflated prices for substandard foods, and Meyers enlisted key representatives to help women do the same in New Orleans.
Reviving the regional exchanges between urban laborers and rural producers that Louisianan populists had constructed a generation prior, in May the
league collaborated with the Louisiana State Farmers' Educational and Cooperative Union of America (LSF) to open a cooperative produce market along
Prytania and Carrollton Streets accessible to public transit.[51]

A rural populist organization, the LSF was a branch of the militant National
Farmers' Union, active in the Deep South since 1902. The National Farmers'
Union recruited farm laborers and allied with trade unions to organize credit
unions and supply-purchasing, marketing, grain elevator, and grocery cooperatives. It also lobbied the federal government to ban commodity market
speculation and regulate agricultural prices to aid small farmers.[52] LSF state
agent J. H. Craig asserted that cooperation between "the farmers or the farm

wives and [women's] clubs" was "a recognized condition imperative for the common weal."[53] Meyers also hoped social mixing at the curb market would "[bring] producer and consumer together, that the higher prices of foodstuffs might be cut in some measure."[54] The cooperatives operated until the scorching summer heat drove league volunteers from the markets.

Despite public acclaim, challenges to the Housewives' League's farm-to-table movement tormented the women. Retailers and wholesalers feared that cooperative markets would destroy their businesses and "industriously circulated" a rumor that the farmers were actually hucksters reselling French Market produce at a markup.[55] Federal agricultural agents sniffed, "You cannot eliminate the middleman."[56] Farmers doubted female consumers' constancy and the league's organizational abilities; as league president Inez Meyers complained in January 1916, "We know for a surety that many [farmers], if not all, have been importuned [by wholesalers] to disappoint us, to take their produce elsewhere to market."[57]

Further, as rapidly mechanizing industries threatened to displace workers and undercut unions' wage advances, close ties to the Association of Commerce muddied the league's working relationship with white unions. Often married to association members, Housewives' League members saw no contradictions among pursuing economic imperialism abroad, promoting New Orleans's businesses, and denouncing industrial capitalism. Because their livelihoods depended on the city's commercial vibrancy, city boosters like league member and journalist Julia Truitt Bishop demanded female inclusion in New Orleans's conversion into "one of the best and busiest and most economical ports in the entire country."[58] While immigrant members might have spurred other organizations to be more reflective about US foreign relations, the league's affluent newcomers belonged to the merchant class and hailed from countries with strong colonial histories: Britain, Germany, Spain, and France by way of the West Indies and Mexico. Relying on Progressive entrepreneurs to endorse and fund their cooperative projects, leaguers worked in the Association of Commerce's CBD offices and partnered in citywide commercial promotions, such as "Made-in-New-Orleans" and "Buyers Week" campaigns. League headquarters were even nestled in the association's library.[59]

Notwithstanding grocers' opposition to cooperative curb markets and the league's own ambivalence toward capitalism, Meyers brought the local Housewives' League's 800 members to bear on high living costs. She declared, "We are going to give the farmers a chance, and, at the same time, enable thousands of families in the city to receive quantities of fresh green vegetables."[60] Consequently, from 1915 to 1917, the LSF and Housewives' League partnership tangibly benefitted both farmers and consumers. First, it appreciably reduced urban food costs while profiting producers. The market offered bulk vegetables, poultry, and fruit at discounted prices. Additionally, when crop failures, railroad delivery disruptions, and wartime food demands sparked a nationwide food crisis in 1916, market women sold fresh eggs from their own backyard hens to desperate customers. Finally, local grocers and peddlers agreed to match the league's reasonable prices, while rural clubwomen started their own markets.[61]

Second, the Housewives' League pressured the city to open additional public markets so farmers and consumers could avoid unethical middlemen monopolizing produce distribution. League members monitored the markets for consistent pricing, and city health inspectors ensured stalls maintained proper sanitation. Finally, league women learned how to manage cooperative ventures by contracting with farmers, budgeting, and coordinating rail transportation for produce shipments.[62] They also collaborated with other women's organizations, government officials, and farmers to, in the words of member Julia Truitt Bishop, erect an effective "barrier between the people of New Orleans and the ever-climbing wave of hard and harder times."[63]

Women's Wartime Cooperation

World War I provided another concrete, publicly acceptable outlet for the Housewives' League's evolving woman-centered cooperative philosophy. In a time of nationalistic fervor and restricted civil liberties, mainstream suffragists decided that instead of controversial protesting, they would coordinate industrial labor, military enlistment, volunteer work, and civilian defense training to exemplify women's readiness for full citizenship.[64] Speaking before New Orleanian suffragists to promote civil defense work in 1918, NAWSA and Woman's Committee of the Council of National Defense (WCCND) representative Anna Howard Shaw predicted that "when this war is ended the entire world will come to a stronger realization of democracy and the work which the women have done will receive its full measure of recognition. I believe the war will prove the greatest step in the development of equal suffrage."[65] The Housewives' League also forged government alliances to legitimate calls for enfranchisement while building a welfare state framed by patriotic food relief activities.

Accordingly, league women strategically served on wartime consumer committees organized by Progressive officials crucial to the passage of state and federal suffrage amendments. In 1918, at the behest of Louisiana's Food Administration head and Progressive politician John M. Parker, league members monitored the state's wartime food supply to prevent shortages, hoarding, price inflation, and food riots.[66] Governor Ruffin G. Pleasant also appointed Housewives' League representatives to the New Orleans chapter of the WCCND, which coordinated civilian women's defense work at the state and national levels. Consumers' League president Ida Friend chaired the WCCND's Women in Industry Committee, which demanded "just and health-ful conditions in industry" for low-income female industrial and government employees. Meeting in the City Hall Council Chamber, the Women's Commit-tee rubbed elbows with future corporate and government League allies.[67]

Wartime patriotism sparked greater public interest in women's coopera-tive projects targeting consumers and marginalized citizens. In 1917, journalist and Progressive reformer Ida M. Tarbell observed that WCCND cooperative canning centers, food exchanges, buying clubs, and storage facilities aided "all classes of the community" and were "dangerous opponents of food specu-lators and food hoardings." Similarly, Housewives' League members and prominent philanthropists Eleanor McMain, Eva Dibert, and Catherine Van Meter helped finance the Hope Haven Industrial Farm, which redressed poverty through cooperative means. Linking the charity to military goals, Kingsley House social worker McMain vowed that assisting the vulnerable would "win the war and save the state." Hope Haven, located ten miles south of New Orleans on Bayou Barataria, featured a dairy and industrial complex that employed, housed, and educated people with disabilities, widows with dependent children, and orphaned boys, while supplying the city with milk and produce. The nonsectarian, self-supporting farm aimed to "patriotically do its share by raising its own food and distributing the surplus to the poor." Galvanized by the power of women-led cooperative enterprises to improve vulnerable populations' economic plight, the league echoed Tarbell's predic-tion that a women-run postwar cooperative democracy would direct "great economic and social readjustments, reforms and undertakings." By the end of the war, the league's cooperative committee chair Edna Egleston decreed that cooperation was "an instrument of universal public interest."[68]

The Racial Borders of Female Cooperation

While Housewives' League members celebrated the advent of a postwar cooperative commonwealth, their maternalist model of interracial cooper-ation overlooked racial equality as a precondition for true democracy and humane capitalism. Working with black women in segregated WCCND sec-tions to coordinate Louisiana women's war work inspired a few league members, like Ida Friend, to join integrated partnerships to enfranchise all women and end workplace gender and racial discrimination, while others devoted themselves to alleviating poverty and illness within black communities. More common was black journalist and political activist Alice Dunbar-Nelson's observation that interracial WCCND interactions were merely a facade of "lovely co-operation, and general foggy feeling of goodwill and sisterly love." Most league members resolutely regarded African Americans as beneficiaries of their aid and expertise rather than as allies. For instance, black suffragist and Progressive educator Sylvanie Williams had for years demanded equitable and free vocational education for one of the few New Orleans schools for black students, the Thomy Lafon School, only to have the parish school board repeatedly deny her requests. As part of a fundraising effort by white business leaders and black parents in 1918, Housewives' League member and Anti-Tuberculosis League president Melanie Wilkinson donated $150 to furnish the campus with home economics equipment. Nonetheless, the black community continued to shoulder the vast majority of the time and resources required to maintain the school and its facilities.[69]

Other interracial partnerships were largely self-serving: in 1917, the Housewives' League offered black cooks instruction in canning and food conservation, ostensibly to reduce white employers' costs rather than to economically empower their staff.[70] Similarly, when black social reformer and prisoner rights activist Frances Gaudet complained that the city was intentionally keeping the cost of living at its "zenith" by inconsistently enforcing food sale laws, league members supported her proposal to deliver low-cost produce to New Orleans housewives.[71] Deploying racial tropes, white women bought cabbage and lettuce from Gaudet Normal and Industrial School's black students who "work[ed] willingly and cheerfully in the fields," while boycotting the "huckster wagons" driven by "loudly yelling negroes and Italians [who] ply their trade through the streets of the city ignoring any law to the contrary."[72] While collaborating with African Americans on narrow issues, the Housewives' League never considered integrating its organization, rallying against Jim Crow legislation, or securing enfranchisement for all women.

Against this backdrop, in the summer of 1918 domestic labor shortages and black unionizing efforts threw the league's latent racial, class, and ethnic prejudices into sharp relief. Its resulting, revised cooperative vision reasserted divisions between white capital and black laborers. In 1917 and 1918, a boom in the cotton, sugar, timber, and petroleum industries, as well as a federally funded enlargement of New Orleans's maritime facilities, expanded black women's occupational opportunities. Domestic workers, drawn to higher industrial wages, quit their jobs in increasing numbers. White homemakers sneered that "the prospect of a few dollars a month" from government employers prompted black women to collectively "avoid work." Yet African Americans who joined wartime nonprofit organizations and government agencies quickly discovered they remained confined to janitorial positions, while domestic workers in private homes chafed at employers' continued mistreatment.[73]

In response, in May 1918, a Creole of color domestic worker, Elenora Alcorn Peete, formed the Colored Domestic Union, one of only ten domestic workers' unions in the nation affiliated with the AFL. She demanded that employers pay cooks twenty-five dollars a month, limit their duties to food preparation, and reduce their daily work shift to eleven hours.[74] The labor organizing of Peete reflected her family and community's activist inclinations. Her father, Seymour Alcorn, had enlisted in the First Louisiana Native Guard, the first official black Union regiment to see combat during the Civil War. Her husband, Sylvester Peete, was president of the black freight handlers' union and active in dockworker strikes.[75] Residing near the racially and ethnically diverse Irish Channel and militant dockyards a few miles from wealthy white employers' Uptown homes, Peete and her family attended St. Peter African Methodist Episcopal Church alongside other black labor leaders. Drawn to Peete's platform, the National Association for the Advancement of Colored People (NAACP) embraced the Colored Domestic Union, and black "ministers . . . preached from the pulpits that [women] should all join a union and strike for higher wages." Consequently, by July, the union's ranks swelled to nearly a thousand laundresses, cooks, maids, and nurses. Its members convened at the CBD's Pythian Temple, a well-known center for black fraternal, business, and political organizations.[76]

Positioning the Colored Domestic Union within the larger black labor movement mobilizing new industrial sectors and organizing strikes along the city's docks, white clubwomen feared the union would incite a potentially violent "servant problem." Some claimed the union's slogan was "join or take a beating." While evolutionary socialists like Inez Meyers and Ida Friend endorsed women's labor laws and cooperative curb markets, they lacked a coherent, intersectional economic analysis to accept black servants' collective action. Instead, white progressive clubwomen strove to dismantle the union through improved staff management on an individual level: "sympathy and kindness," clear communication, higher pay, and shorter hours were "the best way[s] to keep a servant" from unionizing or seeking better employment. For their part, racial conservatives within the Housewives' League flatly rejected Meyers and her peers' mild suggestion to standardize staff workdays and howled that unionists were now "dictat[ing] to white women what remuneration [servants] shall receive."[77]

As a result, in July, an anti-labor faction split from the Housewives' League to form the Homemakers' Association, a single-issue group consumed by destroying the Colored Domestic Union. Both white housewives' organizations adopted middle-class housekeeping cooperatives and community kitchens to blacklist unionized servants, blocking black working-class women from achieving economic stability through collective action and alternative economics. While the memberships overlapped, the Homemakers' Association was composed of a preponderance of wealthy New Orleans-born philanthropists and suffragists whose activities were splashed across the society pages' chronicle of tea parties and exotic summer trips.[78] Often also belonging to the United Daughters of the Confederacy, they longed to return to the "simple life," while promoting an interventionist government that monitored and punished recalcitrant black labor, forcing "colored women . . . to go to work."[79]

Socialist-leaning reformers also backed the Homemakers' Association. British émigré Jessie Gessner presided over institutional homes for the female poor and infirm and joined Jane Addams's socialistic Women's International League for Peace and Freedom to reject American xenophobia and militarism. Yet Gessner also attended women's club parties where "place cards which consisted of original verses in negro dialect . . . were cleverly illustrated with character sketches." WCCND volunteers also weighed white and black infants to promote the racialized "Better Baby" eugenics movement. Association members felt no compunction about rejecting black political equality while reforming capitalist-employee relations.[80]

The Homemakers' Association first attempted to shame black servants into capitulating by exploiting a delicate New Orleans interracial alliance forged around domestic servant training and black middle-class uplift ideology. Association cofounder Carrie McWilliams and United Daughters of the Confederacy officer Mrs. D. A. S. Vaught crowed that the respected black home economics instructor Blanche Armwood Perkins had dismissed the domestics' union because only "education and more efficiency" would lead to "more wages for servants." Opening in 1917, Perkins's School of Domestic Science taught hundreds of black women scientific food preparation and conservation methods. The school's financial ties to wealthy white women, corporations, and religious reformers pressured Perkins to advertise gradualist civil rights advocate Booker T. Washington's self-help philosophy. Black women would "better home conditions" by collaborating with white home economists to cultivate "a kee[n]er appreciation of advantages already granted." When the NAACP criticized her anti-union stance (which she denied taking), Perkins avowed that her mission was "to increase the efficiency of the colored womanhood of this city" through home economics rather than labor reform.[81]

Deploying respectability politics to police black working-class behavior failed to deter the domestic workers streaming into Elenora Peete's union headquarters, however. The Homemakers' Association consequently ramped up its assault on black servants. In late July, the association barred black workers from taking home food, eating more than one meal at work, or arriving late, regardless of "toothaches, illness and society funerals." It also joined the city police and American Protective League, an anti-espionage organization, in accusing the union of spreading German propaganda. As the police superintendent alleged, "servants and cooks in private households are in a position to learn many secrets which other spies could not learn." Association women claimed the union was part of an evil "Hun" agenda to "[stir] up race hatred" and distract white women from vital war work. Lending credence to these denunciations, the WCCND, whose members also belonged to the Homemakers' Association, stated that the union, and the labor movement in general, smacked of Bolshevism. That the association's radical reformers endorsed such rhetorical tactics is particularly ironic given that their own organizations, like the Consumers' League and Women's International League for Peace and Freedom, also drew the ire of conservative politicians and military officials labeling criticism of current political and economic policy dangerously communistic.[82]

The Colored Domestic Union dismissed the Homemakers' Association's smear campaign as baldly disingenuous. Unionist Sarah P. Williams reminded white women, "We have given our sons and husbands [to the war] and without protest. My race has bowed in submission to all laws and is loyal." To Williams, the labor movement was "one of the greatest things that has happened in years amongst the negro women" because it provided a formal structure to redress grievances. Mirroring Housewives' League member Ida Friend and other labor reformers' efforts to improve white mothers' "lowest wages, longest hours, and poorest working conditions," Williams admonished the Homemakers' Association to "not stand in the way of the negro woman's effort to make a day's . . . honest pay." Through organized and persistent agitation, a Department of Labor representative observed, by 1920, unions like the Colored Domestic Union had compelled reasonable white employers to "more scientific [consider] . . . household problems" to promote "higher standards in home economics." The Colored Domestic Union continued to set workplace standards until the mid-1920s.[83]

While the Colored Domestic Union did compel some white women to renegotiate work relations with their staff, responding to such pressure fundamentally shifted the role of female-run cooperatives from aiding vulnerable consumers to shoring up racial and class divides. Between 1918 and 1920, white clubwomen used cooperatives to exclude black servants and to transform white immigrant and Creole women into docile domestics. For example, both the Homemakers' Association and the City Federation of Women's Clubs co-opted Progressive cooperative kitchens to bypass the Colored Domestic Union. Association members Jeanie Raymond and Cora Moran worked in home economics instructor Adele Stewart's WCCND municipal kitchen, teaching white women to can, preserve, and pickle. Stewart's kitchen was a model for an association-backed vocational school that trained nonunionized white women to cook for wealthy employers without complaint. Holding classes in institution or state-funded community kitchens, the school imparted the "proper practice of the obliteration of self" to prevent "sloppy help" from "demand[ing] impossible wages."[84]

Similarly, in 1920 the City Federation of Women's Clubs appropriated the Housewives' League French Quarter community kitchen as a demonstration center for white cooks. Jeannette Hayes Moser, director of the federation's Americanization committee and wife of an immigration inspector, originally founded the community kitchen in 1918 to lower living costs for immigrant families while "Americanizing" them.[85] Nationally, social workers and female philanthropists promoted public cooperative kitchens during economic crises to provide poor women nutritious, inexpensive food while offering cooking, food safety, and consumer education courses. Women from the French Quarter's Syrian, Greek, Italian, and French enclaves gathered at the Louisiana State Museum auditorium to watch home economics experts explain the Food Administration's wartime food substitutions and model new cooking techniques. Herself the daughter of an unnaturalized British ironworks machinist, Moser was praised for community kitchens that fostered "loyalty among alien residents of New Orleans and the surrounding parishes" and generated "greater unity as a nation."[86]

While many home economists promoted an American cultural identity by dismissing ethnic cuisines, the Housewives' League's German Jewish food demonstrator Rosa Michaelis taught students to inexpensively prepare regional dishes like hominy grits, Creole boiled bacon, and bacon and oysters. Yet by 1920, the City Federation suggested homemakers capitalize on the French Quarter kitchen by sidestepping its antipoverty mission. Members should fire unionized black staff from their homes and form a cooperative cooking service that employed the kitchen's "fine [white] Creole cooks" to "prepare dinner for many families at the same time."[87]

Simultaneously, the Homemakers' Association and the Housewives' League both asserted that the modern housewife could avoid the Colored Domestic

Union's demands by starting white middle-class cooking and housekeeping cooperatives. Convening in members' comfortable Uptown homes, the Housewives League agreed that "wise" women would "slowly but surely [be] emancipated from the old-time all-day drudgery of housekeeping" to pursue their own professional and personal ambitions. The league implemented socialist utopian writer Edward Bellamy's 1889 proposal that cooperative kitchens running on a contract basis would promote democratic values while ridding housewives of "a succession of casual employees." Female home economists also touted cooperative cooking and cleaning services as the solution to food waste, poor family nutrition, and ultimately, "aggressive and tyrannical" servants.[88]

To that end, Housewives' League president Inez Meyers argued that middle-class women's domestic efficiency would be improved by replacing incompetent, expensive staff with new electric appliances, purchased on a "community plan." In an April 1919 league workshop on "Housework Minus Servants," Meyers suggested to attendees crowded into her Arabella Street parlor that women's cooperative buying clubs could collectively purchase and share large laborsaving appliances like washing machines, dishwashers, and vacuum cleaners. Meyers asserted that "every woman has the right to be mistress of her own home," but she omitted how working-class women might afford expensive modern appliances to relieve themselves of household work.[89] The league's cooperative housekeeping schemes entrenched affluent white women's racial and class status in the face of black labor unrest. While material feminists such as Florence Kelley and Jane Addams urged housewives and their staff to socialize domestic labor for their mutual benefit, league members clung to the conveniences afforded them by self-serving domestic arrangements. After the war, the league continued to overlook the racialized inequalities structuring black women's lives to focus on how white consumers alone could transcend the unstable labor market.[90]

Combatting the High Cost of Living with Cooperative Grocery Stores

Having enjoyed a modicum of wartime political influence as high-ranking WCCND volunteers, in 1919 Housewives' League members were thrust into a volatile postwar economic and labor landscape reeling from market deregulation, inflation, and demobilization. That year, President Woodrow Wilson terminated local labor adjustment committees, and Congress returned state-owned railroads and other industries to private hands. While the labor movement had rapidly expanded during the war, New Orleans industrialists and

Association of Commerce entrepreneurs now argued they could modernize city infrastructure only by instituting open shop, mechanization, strikebreaking, wage cuts, and hours increases. Louisiana reform governor John Parker claimed that unions stymied port development and helped commercial elites dismantle them. At the same time, President Wilson repealed the federal wartime regulation of utilities, transportation, and food industries that had stabilized living costs. Severe postwar inflation exacerbated the disproportionate impact that Wilson's economic and labor policies had on working-class citizens in doubling rent, clothes, food, and other living expenses by 1920.[91]

As working-class livelihoods constricted, consumer and labor protest shook post-World War I-era New Orleans. In August 1919, the Association of Commerce warned, "Mob spirit is spreading. If we try now to tell people that present prices of food are right and must stand they will not listen. They may act." Rejecting slashed wages, workers regularly shut down New Orleans ports and railways in massive labor strikes between 1919 and 1921. Cooperatives surged in popularity nationwide, including in Louisiana, as "low cost of living" clubs drove down consumer prices by buying in bulk directly from farmers and wholesalers and avoiding grocers' markups. Frequently organized along gender, occupation, racial, or ethnic lines and run out of members' homes, buying clubs typically had between 20 and 300 members.[92]

In New Orleans, just as they had in the 1893–97 depression, union cooperatives ensured unemployed and striking workers' economic survival. After a May 1920 strike, the Sheet Metal Workers Union opened a cooperative sheet metal factory to compete against former employers. It hired union laborers at union wages and hours, secured contracts, and produced sheet metal only a month into its operations. Additionally, new chain stores and cooperatives like the New Orleans Council of Railway Workers' dry goods store kept food prices low by purchasing items in large lots, selling the same items across affiliate stores, receiving discounts from processors and suppliers, and operating its own processing and wholesale subsidiaries.[93]

Even as individual Housewives' League members continued to agitate against black domestic unionists, the league as a whole joined white unions and female consumer activists across the nation organizing boycotts, leading marches, and fomenting riots to lower consumer costs while democratizing capitalism. Between 1919 and 1921, the Housewives' League launched a multifaceted campaign to mandate ethical consumption at the individual, city, state, and federal levels. First, women reduced household food expenses by growing, canning, preserving, and cooking inexpensive foods. Second, they staged boycotts—when milk prices rose sharply in October 1919, Meyers announced that the league's 1,600 members were "under moral obligation" to cut consumption by 50 percent, compelling retailers to reduce dairy prices. Third, women served on league, city, and state consumer committees to assiduously investigate consumer abuse and draft policy recommendations. Fourth, the league urged the federal government to regulate commodity prices and reduce living expenses. Finally, Meyers established a cooperative research committee, with Indiana native and Midwestern consumer cooperative veteran Edna Egleston as chair.[94]

In April 1919, Egleston had joined the Housewives' League to monitor public markets and promote Rochdale cooperatives to the public. She concluded that the league curb markets and "the common practice of a few housekeepers buying jointly, various and sundry supplies" had not "result[ed] in either economy or satisfaction" because individual consumers could not procure the low wholesale rates that retailers enjoyed. Instead, a civic-minded Rochdale grocery cooperative would provide citizens "all the necessities of life at the lowest possible cost" by eliminating "to a very large extent the [middleman's] present handling charges."[95]

Consequently, the committee unveiled the league's final cooperative experiment: the female-run League Co-operative Store. Egleston's socialistic grocery store attracted white and integrated unions' endorsement, yet avoided Homemakers' Association vitriol by remaining silent on racial equality. The cooperative specifically invited white women to combine their purchasing power as joint owners, contract with wholesalers at a reduced price, and receive rebates and quarterly dividends. In November 1919, illness forced Meyers to cede the Housewives' League presidency, and Egleston became the new face of the league's cooperative campaign.[96]

Egleston initially intended the cooperative store to operate alongside government market regulations to provide consumers a comprehensive cost reduction program. In 1919 the federal High Cost of Living Division began selling surplus canned foods and dry goods below market value in national army retail stores to redistribute wartime food stores and alleviate widespread economic hardship. Between 2,500 and 3,000 New Orleans residents daily thronged these "quartermaster stores." Yet by early 1920, the US War Department had closed the enterprises because they were too burdensome to maintain. Convinced that army retailers were inherently "Unfair, Un-American, [and] Un-Democratic," New Orleans wholesalers and grocers applauded the decision. Since the federal government was returning railways, telegraphs, and other service corporations to private hands, it should also cease meddling with the nation's food supply.[97]

Women's clubs, veterans, and labor unions countered that a permanent government-consumer cooperative partnership would guarantee public control over food production and distribution. As regulatory bodies contracted during reconversion, federal officials lauded buying clubs as practical substitutes to government intervention in consumer markets. Army retailers suggested that the Housewives' League Co-operative Store could moderate economic inflation in their stead. Yet Egleston implicitly rebuked laissez-faire politicians who suggested that cooperatives replace government market supervision. In February 1920, she warned that individualistic solutions could not solve large-scale economic problems. Unaffiliated with larger consumer advocacy organizations, most cooperative buying clubs failed to sufficiently expand to reduce regional consumer costs. As Egleston observed, "Experience has shown that when a small [cooperative] store grows beyond the stage of the voluntary and unpaid selling staff, it goes to pieces on the rocks of overhead costs."[98]

In contrast to the informal and dispersed buying-club movement, the Housewives' League envisioned cooperatives propelling a comprehensive, democratic transformation of national production, distribution, and consumption systems. Accordingly, Egleston aligned the league with the Rochdale consumer cooperative movement, which by 1920 included 2,600 American cooperatives and buying clubs seeking a corrective to economic inequality. She announced that the Housewives' Co-operative Store would be "a pioneer in the movement to reduce the high cost of living in the South on the same plan as that which has been in successful operation for three-quarters of a century in European countries and in the North and West." As a southern American version of the British Fabian Society's "Socialist Commonwealth," neighborhood cooperatives would reorganize the state's domestic political and economic activities, while serving as international agents of US economic and political interests. They would exploit modern infrastructural and communication technology to connect New Orleanian consumers to a socialist, global economy.[99]

Condemning the pursuit of profit at the expense of the common good, Egleston affiliated with the socialist Cooperative League of America (commonly known as CLUSA), the most well-known American Rochdale cooperative organization. Since its founding in 1916, CLUSA and its avowedly anti-capitalist affiliates facilitated cooperative organizing, coordinated regional wholesale activities, and crafted educational programs, according to secretary Albert Sonnichsen, to spur "a radical social reconstruction based on an all-inclusive collectivism." Egleston planned to implement CLUSA's 1919 economic blueprint in which local cooperatives would socialize farms and control manufacturing and service industries. Cooperative farms and factories would then ship their products to CLUSA stores across the country.

Likewise, Egleston envisioned cooperative farms supplying the league's chain stores and interfacing with regional and national, professionally managed cooperative federations to propel a national cooperative economy. To that end, she distributed CLUSA literature "among the housewives of this city with a view of preparing them for further action in this matter."[100]

To Egleston, the lynchpin in expanding a socialist cooperative movement "in its infancy in the South" continued to be a housewife-labor alliance. Pointing to the pro-union and socialist Tri-State Cooperative Association and Pacific Cooperative League's network of meat markets, grocery stores, bakeries, and laundries aiding labor unions in their struggles along the Pacific coast, Egleston queried, "Why should not the New Orleans housewife have similar economic advantage?" The league unabashedly and publicly "waged active warfare on behalf of lower prices and municipal cleanliness" alongside socialists and the labor movement.[101]

Echoing the Local Council and WLPMA's successful 1898 coalition to expand city infrastructure, city trade unionists supported the league. The integrated Street Carmen's Union was still reeling from army retail closings and readily helped the Housewives' League locate storefront property along Uptown's Prytania Street. Reflecting their shared interests, in July 1920 the union went on strike against the streetcar and railroad industries, which the Housewives' League also accused of manipulating utilities rates. The following year, the league endorsed the AFL's national campaign to circumvent profiteering and inflation by promoting union-run Rochdale cooperatives. Female consumers also advocated for government-regulated pipelines bringing cheaper natural gas into New Orleans in order for unprincipled utilities companies to "die a natural death." Because both female consumers and laborers were victims of government deregulation, unions avidly aided the league's cooperative development.[102]

The league's alliance with socialists and unions to reform capitalism provoked immediate backlash from politicians and businesses, highlighting a creeping conservatism and repression in the nation's post-World War I political landscape. In the wake of the 1917 Russian Revolution, unions and cooperatives calling for nationalized industries or collectivized production and distribution systems were regarded as subversives orchestrating a communist coup on American soil. For example, the Brotherhood of Railroad Trainmen complained in 1920 that New Orleans unions "have [been] slam-banged right and left, called 'pro-German,' 'Bolshevik,' and everything else under the sun." Targeted for their progressive politics and labor sympathies, cooperative activists were among the thousands of suspected provocateurs arrested during the Department of Justice's 1919–20 Palmer raids.[103]

Egleston's socialistic Housewives' Co-operative Store risked being painted with the same red brush. Like other material feminists, Housewives' League members studied Soviet communal kitchens, cafeterias, laundries, and childcare to lower the cost of living. Critics condemned suffragists and reformers who celebrated Soviet women's enfranchisement and housekeeping cooperatives as secret Bolsheviks whose social equality propaganda would topple racial hierarchies and ignite race riots. Though just two years earlier the Homemakers' Association had branded black servants as Bolshevik spies, the Red Scare unleashed a torrent of government and corporate investigations into white women's political organizing, vilifying reformers like National Consumers' League head Florence Kelley as alien and subversive. The backlash spurred moderate NAWSA suffragists to disassociate from leftists, chilling Progressive activism. Nonetheless, as activist Bessie Beatty affirmed before the Senate Judiciary Committee on Bolshevik Propaganda in 1919, she had "a great passion in [her] heart to do away with poverty"; therefore, she, like the New Orleans Housewives' League, was "interested in any program which may help to bring that about," even socialism or communism.[104]

The league recognized that female consumers' "constant, continual, everlasting agitation" and determination to "voice their protests where the people's rights are involved" undermined southern conservatives profiting from their disenfranchisement. During a bitter two-year battle to ratify the Nineteenth Amendment, Mayor Behrman and the Regular Democratic Organization lent tepid support for women's voting rights, while erstwhile suffrage ally Governor Parker blocked the federal amendment's ratification in the Louisiana legislature in July 1920. Louisiana politicians stymied the Housewives' League's plan to use women's political and economic leverage to reform abusive production, distribution, and consumption systems.[105]

Additionally, wholesalers and retailers were convinced that cooperatives were illegal monopolies restraining trade. Abstruse legislation made prosecuting wholesalers difficult when they blacklisted cooperatives: local district attorneys admitted that wholesalers were only "probably . . . laying themselves liable if through any combination or agreement they declined to sell" to consumer cooperatives. Consequently, businessmen excluded Egleston from market meetings. When she served on the US Department of Justice's local fair price committee as the only woman and consumer advocate, its body of wholesalers, grocers, sugar brokers, and Association of Commerce representatives purposely fixed household commodities prices without her. Egleston grumbled, "I can't help feeling that the average consumer might quarrel with the percentage of profit allowed." Worse yet, some league members' husbands dissuaded their wives from subscribing to the Housewives' Co-operative

Store. Despite the league's years of cooperative experience, "many a mascu-line eyebrow was raised, and many a man of business made dubious conjugal comment" about whether a woman-run cooperative could succeed.[106]

Ongoing corporate and government resistance to the Housewives' Co-operative Store forced Egleston to reconsider the grocery store's core iden-tity. The league's condemnation of corporate and political practices inflating living costs, exploiting workers, and denying women the right to vote had encouraged "[p]eople from all walks of life and from every quarter of the city and from surrounding towns" to subscribe to the cooperative, paying ten dol-lars per share. However, the cooperative store needed $10,000 in stock sub-scriptions to secure a grocery storefront, an amount that required Egleston to moderate overtly socialistic messaging to soothe wary businessmen. Sim-ilar to the LMPA's pragmatism, she duly "appeal[ed] to our public-spirited wealthy men to help us." Egleston assured potential investors, "If a few men can be made to see how much good they can do their city by assisting the housewives, I know the store will be a 'going concern' without delay."[107]

Egleston averred that the Housewives' League cooperative was rooted in liberal economic principles, not revolution. The difference between conven-tional and cooperative stores was a matter of degree. As with a retail store, a successful cooperative must handle large volumes of sales and raise prices to cover overhead costs. To ensure that the venture would be "more businesslike and better" than transient buying clubs or underhanded chain stores selling discounted, substandard goods, the Co-operative Store sought mentorship from "professionals in the grocery business" and established an advisory board that included respected businessmen.[108] One of Egleston's fellow Trin-ity Episcopal Church congregants, Philadelphian banker John Shober, served as board treasurer. Similarly, British pharmacist Ernest Vacher bought ten shares, "scor[ing] a significant point in favor of the plan." In addition, noted Creole grocer Rene Vivien pledged to be "one of the factors contributing to [the Housewives' Co-operative Store's] success" by ordering supplies and orga-nizing its food distribution and collection, while "a prominent attorney" had been retained and an "advantageously located" storefront secured. Progressive Jewish entrepreneurs such as Meyer Eiseman, a Jewish real estate magnate, suffrage sympathizer, and cooperative supporter, also eagerly subscribed. By August 1920, affluent immigrant, Jewish, and northern reformist businessmen had contributed over $8,000, which represented enough to open the store.[109]

While dependent on wealthy benefactors to jumpstart the cooperative store, the Housewives' League refused to cede control over the enterprise's direction to male investors, maintaining that the grocery cooperative was "primarily a women's movement, for the housewife, by the housewife." First, adhering to Rochdale Plan principles, Egleston permitted "[e]ach stockholder, whether he owns one or a hundred shares of stock, . . . only one vote." Such a system "keeps the organization democratic." Second, all employees, "from the sales force to the truck driver," would be women. Egleston and an advisory council of grocery retailers hired and directly supervised five experienced white saleswomen and one African American maid to assist customers. Third, once the Nineteenth Amendment was ratified, the Housewives' League mobilized women's newfound political agency around consumer issues. In June 1921, Meyers announced plans for members to "use not only their influence, but their votes" to elect legislators who would advocate for "a pure food supply" and "the welfare of the home, women and children." Harkening back to Fabian socialism, the cooperative would instill grassroots civic engagement in its customers and members.[110]

Finally, rejecting male contempt for women's consumer advocacy and entrepreneurship, Egleston cultivated solidarity among female cooperative activists. As City Federation president Ida Friend contended, "I don't think there is more than one opinion among women on these matters": the Co-operative Store, when combined with government economic regulation, was certain to reduce women's living expenses. Similarly, Mary O'Hara, manager of the Catherine Club, a boardinghouse for white "working ladies of high moral character," had once belonged to a Brainerd, Minnesota, food cooperative. She championed the Co-operative Store as a surefire "method to reduce the cost of living." Rural Louisiana and Mississippi clubwomen patterned their own cooperatives after the Co-operative Store. In the spring of 1920, Mississippi clubwomen reported "a very decided note of friendly co-operation and mutual helpfulness," as women-owned cooperative grocery stores, repair shops, and dry goods stores sprang up across the state. Hundreds of women bought stock to "keep down the high cost of living by turning back profits into the pockets of purchasers."[111]

A Women-Led Cooperative Economy:
The Housewives' League Cooperative Store Opens

Regional cooperation was solidified in January 1921, when the Housewives' League rented and finally renovated a small wooden building at 4900 Prytania Street. Located next to the bustling Prytania Street Market, and near the league's former cooperative curb markets, the store's convenient setting enabled Uptown women to complete all their shopping at once. As the "neat little store" neared completion, "dozens of women" came by each day "anxious

to see how it [was] 'getting on.'" The Housewives' Co-operative Store threw
its grand opening celebration on February 26, 1921. Stockholders and New
Orleans clubwomen browsed the shop's "well-equipped line of groceries,"
canned fruits, and vegetables nestled on tall, white enamel shelves. Bouquets
from the Louisiana Federation of Women's Clubs overflowed on the counters,
and the telephone rang with congratulations.[112]

In operation for nine months, the grocery store became a productive social
space to debate the extent to which feminized cooperative economics could
transform women's daily lives. As a Rochdale cooperative, the Housewives'
Co-operative Store was open to the general public; one did not have to be a
stockholder to shop there. While members received dividends in proportion
to their purchases at the end of each quarter, all customers bought goods
at a fair market rate. For example, the grocery store sold the least expensive eggs in the city and discounted cheese, sugar, boiled ham, and canned
items like salmon, sardines, and tomatoes. Appealing to busy women, the
grocery cooperative permitted customers to telephone in their orders and
specify parcel pickup or home delivery via a woman-driven truck service.
Member-owners also prepared foods for sale, working in the modern kitchen
at the rear of the building. Cooking demonstrator Mary Boynton managed
the cooperative's delicatessen, selling homemade "dainty cakes," salad dress-
ings, and "other delicacies." She stocked ready-to-order pastries and baked
raisin, lemon, and coconut cream pies and custom-made cakes.[113] Within two
months, the Housewives' Co-operative Store had generated $5,900 in sales,
which although a below-average profit, represented evidence that women's
businesses could prosper.[114]

Reflecting its members' Progressive political agenda, the Housewives' Cooperative Store cast itself as a middle-class oasis of ethical consumption and
female autonomy. Primarily, it offered a female space for those seeking con-
viviality as well as guidance in modern, sanitary food preparation and retail.
Reporters praised the store's "New York apartment house efficiency," enu-
merating features like its electric ceiling fans, "commodious refrigerator," and
ovens that "may be raised or lowered like window shades." Staff led in-store
cooking demonstrations on easy, healthful, and economical dishes using the
latest home appliances. Shoppers eager to streamline their cooking stocked
up on convenience foods like mayonnaise and potato chips. Finally, in line
with the "light lunch" nutritional fad, working women supped on sandwiches,
sodas, and ice cream during their breaks in the store's lunchroom.[115]

The Housewives' Co-operative Store also emulated both the conventional
corner grocery and the modern chain store. League members claimed that
neighborhood grocery stores were complicit in maintaining the high cost

of living. Because corner stores did not post prices, items' values were not standardized. Consequently, every purchase required a fraught negotiation that hinged on the customer's and shop clerk's class, gender, ethnicity, and religious affiliations. In contrast, the cooperative incorporated chain stores' efficient, innovative business methods to standardize and lower consumer prices. Yet the grocery cooperative also retained the intimacy of the local corner store. Directors staunchly refused to sacrifice good customer service to chain store convenience, favoring "a competent manager and sales force" over self-service models.[116]

In essence, Egleston argued, the Housewives' Co-operative Store was part of a national cooperative impulse to remodel the country's economic relations and expand democratic institutions. She asserted, "The idea that the cooperative store is . . . an ordinary small grocery store . . . is very much belittled by such limit." Speaking at the 1920 National Conference on Social Work, Egleston articulated her fervent belief that cooperatives should educate citizens to transform the nation into a true democracy. While she conceded that "we are at this time appealing to the people of New Orleans from the angle of the pocket-book," Egleston argued that as a moral and political entity, the cooperative "in its truest sense and fullest scope can and should go much farther than the mere saving of money for its adherents." She praised Progressive cooperatives around the country for making significant contributions to social welfare. Similarly, fellow conference speakers and social workers contended that cooperatives would help America's "industrial and economic problems," assimilate and empower immigrant communities, and, finally, make "democracy more efficient."[117]

On a larger scale, Egleston and her cosmopolitan colleagues argued that the Co-operative Store would help establish world democracy while linking the city's postwar economy to new foreign markets. She concurred with sociologist, feminist, and CLUSA cofounder Agnes Warbasse that a cooperative movement would "improve the lot of the world." Egleston observed that cooperatives' annual dividends and rebates "helped unbelievably in solving the problem of the high cost of living in many communities" across the world. However, she uncritically embedded imperialism into cooperative economics.[118]

Citing Great Britain's profitable postwar cooperatives, Egleston yearned to build an international economy revolving around "immense wholesale cooperative organizations supplying the thousands of retail stores, and being supplied in turn by their own factories, tea and coffee plantations, wheat lands, fruit farms, coal fields, etc., the products of which are transported in their own ships." She believed that cooperative enterprise would redeem American capitalism and enlighten global citizens, but she ignored the exploitative working conditions under which colonized Sri Lankans and Indians toiled on cooperative plantations. Even Fabian socialists promoted a "trusteeship" model of gradual self-rule in which European governments strictly supervised "non-adult races" practicing cooperative economics while still extracting profit from supposedly democratic modes of production.[119]

The End of the Housewives' Co-operative Store

The Co-operative Store's "ultimate purpose of national and world co-operation" did little to stimulate infrequent, apathetic patronage. Because bureaucratic "red tape" delayed the league's acquiring its storefront, "public interest had waned" by the time the cooperative opened in February 1921. Despite strong sales and regular advertising, by May, only a third of the store's 338 stockholders were regular customers. Flagging visits stemmed from the activist directors' and wealthy investors' differing expectations on what constituted reform work. Egleston implored stockholders to move beyond financial support and share the grocery store's day-to-day operations. While Egleston freely donated "her time and her ability" to run the store and appreciated "the staunch backing of a few men and women," a prevailing attitude of "let George do it" undermined the project. Directors failed to delegate tasks and "did a greater share of the work than co-operation calls for." Most members, in contrast, "promised co-operation (on their stock certificate) [but] failed to co-operate."[120]

While league advocates sought to halt rising inflation and to lower food costs for ordinary New Orleanians, the cooperative store's geographical and spiritual bonds to members' affluent Uptown neighborhoods implicitly limited cooperative democracy's fruits to wealthy white women. Although the store offered daily deliveries across the city, its location "lessened its value as a purchasing depot to stockholders living below Canal Street," namely, white Catholic Creole women from Downtown neighborhoods like the French Quarter, Esplanade Ridge, and Mid-City. Anglo American suffragists had long bemoaned the reluctance of the "conservative Creole element" to join voting or reform efforts. Similarly, stockholders were "disloyal in buying stock in an enterprise they were not willing to support." More than fifty subscribers had abandoned the organization. When a stockholders' meeting to discuss the cooperative's future adjourned due to the lack of a quorum, Egleston called for its dissolution and declared bankruptcy. By January 1922, the store filed its state-of-the-art refrigerators, scales, slicing machines, electric fans, and remaining assets with the civil district court as part of a bankruptcy agreement.[121]

Although the Housewives' Co-operative Store's staffing and patronage problems shuttered the store after only nine months of operation, its demise was also indicative of the economic and political structures decimating cooperatives nationwide. In early 1920, a recession caused commodities prices to fall precipitously, and the period of economic uncertainty extended into Spring 1921. Consumer cooperatives like the Co-operative Store drew customers with low prices, but they could not compete with large retailers who could slash prices and still stay solvent. In June 1921, the league lobbied for federal legislation that, had it passed, would have enabled cooperatives to compete with chains by fixing prices among cooperative affiliates. The lack of adequate funding, declining membership, and infighting within cooperatives resulted in their widespread closing by the mid-1920s.[122]

Nonetheless, the store successfully reduced New Orleans food prices. League members used the agricultural connections they had cultivated while running curb markets to turn the grocery store into a distribution channel for small farmers and manufacturers. Despite the opposition of wholesalers, the league partnered with truck farmers to open new cooperative produce markets, a strategy that, farmers believed, was "the opening wedge in tumbling down the structure of . . . a combine" among wholesalers that depressed producers' profits and inflated consumer prices. The Housewives' League stimulated regional agricultural trade as individual farmers who desired fair prices for their produce contracted with the cooperative store rather than with conventional wholesalers or retailers. Finally, true to his promise to support the cooperative movement even after the league suspended operations, grocer Rene Vivien offered "former customers . . . the same prices, quality and service as formerly given them by Mrs. Eggleston [sic]."[123]

Housewives' League cooperative curb markets, community kitchens, and cooperative grocery stores demonstrate how northern, Jewish, and immigrant women used the national Rochdale cooperative movement's model of decentralized collective action to challenge New Orleans's provincialism and democratize corporate and government institutions. Its cooperative plan was formed amid Jim Crow segregation, male chauvinism, and religious and ethnic insularity, but Uptown and CBD social spaces nurtured surprising collaborations with rural women, urban trade unions, and national cooperative and consumer activists that spurred the Housewives' League to adapt broadscale socialistic solutions to local labor and consumer exploitation. However, competing agendas within this coalition compromised the league's cooperative vision; concessions to pernicious contemporary racial and class biases restricted the league to expanding only affluent white Uptown women's political and economic autonomy.

Nevertheless, in its vision of a more humane political and economic system, the league's cooperative legacy extends beyond the benefits immediately conferred on white subscribers. Although a majority of league women resolutely maintained white supremacy, by the 1930s some were pushing the city cooperative movement leftward by cementing ties with black activists, socialists, and radical labor organizers to develop a comprehensive critique of social mores. For example, Ida Friend pursued her lifelong interest in cooperation by supporting the Co-operative Store as a Consumers' and Housewives' League member; chairing the Woman's Exchange Fair, a retail cooperative encouraging women's home production and economic stability; joining parent-teacher cooperatives; and participating in the Louisiana Co-operative Educational Association, which promoted state history documentation and preservation.[124]

As the Housewives' League faded into memory, its members nonetheless bequeathed a utopian vision for a "co-operative society . . . made up of co-operators" to a new cohort of Popular Front cooperative activists blending socialism and interracial cooperation during the 1930s and '40s. In 1938, Friend joined the New Orleans Committee for the League for Industrial Democracy (LID), a socialist organization tied to Florence Kelley and based at Tulane University. The LID's popular speaking engagements educated the public about the international, interracial cooperative movement's economic advantages.[125]

Most notably, Friend's socialist colleagues opened the New Orleans Consumers' Co-operative Union in 1941, a cross-class and multiracial Rochdale grocery store whose CLUSA affiliation and commitment to a socialized state echoes the Housewives' Co-operative Store's philosophical underpinnings. As will be discussed in chapter three, Popular Front activists built on the alliances the league made with government, academic, business, and labor allies to integrate *all* citizens into a technologically advanced, egalitarian cooperative economy connecting civically engaged consumers and producers around the world.

The Consumers' Co-operative Union: Embedding Integrated Popular Front and War on Poverty Social Programs in the South

A fiery socialist barber, German-born Henry Hermes cut an eccentric figure in New Orleans's mid-twentieth-century cooperative movement. During the Great Depression, Freret Street passersby were as likely to spot Hermes proselytizing socialist doctrine from atop a curbside milk crate as they were to see him shaving local clients in his barbershop. Hermes's rabble-rousing would cost him dearly. On a hot summer's day in August 1937, he interrupted the French Quarter union meeting he was conducting to peer warily from the podium as several policemen filed into Socialist Hall.[1] They harassed the audience and confiscated literature linking corrupt gambling interests to recently assassinated senator Huey Long's Old Regular Democratic political machine, with acolyte and New Orleans mayor Robert Maestri as its head. In an uncanny repetition of the Brotherhood of Co-operative Commonwealth's legal troubles, the police gave Hermes a "great deal of rough handling" before dragging him to jail, where a Maestri crony, Police Chief John Grosch, roared that he would "beat him to a pulp" and "run him out of town." Under the State War Emergency Act of 1917, Hermes was charged with "attempting to incite riot by distributing slanderous literature attacking our City and State Governments."[2]

Kept in isolation for eighteen hours and further manhandled by police, Hermes suffered a nervous breakdown before the League of Industrial Democracy (LID), Ida Friend's socialist organization of college faculty and students, posted his bail. Soon thereafter, while walking down Cadiz Street to his Freret neighborhood barbershop, two thugs jumped Hermes and kicked him to the ground. In between vicious blows, the men snarled, "So you don't like our governor [Huey Long supporter James Noe], huh?" Hermes sus-

pected his attackers were muscle for the city's slot machine racket and was
unsurprised when police refused to investigate the incident. As his socialist lawyers observed, Hermes's case was one of "scores, maybe as many as
100 [lawsuits] involving similar [police] abuses" perpetrated that year. Like
Bacarisse forty years before him, Hermes's arrest and beatings for proposing
equitable economic structures made him brutally aware of the urgency with
which Louisiana's political machine must be dismantled and egalitarian governance erected in its place.[3]

To that end, Hermes professed that national cooperative economic and
political institutions would end America's persistent racial and class inequality.
He picked up the brotherhood and Housewives' League's mantle of cooperative infrastructural development: while replicating the multiracial brotherhood's coalition of union, benevolent association, and leftist political activists
advocating government welfare, Hermes also advanced the league's campaign
to protect and empower consumers. Cooperative economics became a lynchpin in socialists' larger political and economic project compelling elected
officials to repeal the city and state sales tax benefitting large corporations,
create postwar jobs and higher living standards for civilians and World War
II veterans, initiate "slum clearance," and lower utilities rates.[4]

Between 1941 and 1965, Hermes and immigrant, Latin American, black,
and female consumer activists ran the New Orleans Consumers' Co-operative Union (CCU), an integrated Rochdale grocery store and credit union in
the working-class Freret neighborhood. Inspired by the international cooperative movement promoting worldwide economic cooperation and peace,
the CCU buffered southerners from wartime austerity measures and postwar economic inflation by purveying inexpensive, culturally appropriate
foods, practicing egalitarian worker-employee relations, hosting educational
programming, extending consumer loans, and prompting economic and
infrastructural improvements. The CCU expanded the Housewives' League's
skeletal network of community-driven consumer, producer, and financial
cooperatives, suturing geographic, racial, gender, and class divides to incorporate *all* Freret residents and marginalized southerners into a reformed economic marketplace and federally administered social safety net.

Just as significant, when the CCU suspended grocery operations in the face
of 1950s white flight, anti-communist hysteria, and urban decline, Hermes
parlayed his cooperative experience into a lifelong career in credit union
organizing. His second profession further refined the Housewives' League's
efforts to institutionalize and scale up New Orleanian mutual aid traditions.
While the league's dreams of a socialist, cooperative society died with its grocery store, the CCU diversified its cooperative businesses to include a credit

union, pushing New Orleanian cooperative economics into new territories. As a director of the Louisiana Credit Union League, Hermes bridged New Deal and Great Society ideas about cooperative democracy to grant tens of thousands of low-income Louisianans access to financial institutions and services crucial to increasing wealth among oppressed communities.

Hermes' work with the CCU and local credit unions disrupts our notion of insular neighborhood cultures, illuminating the complicated and overlapping political geography of local and international cooperative activism sparking economic growth in New Orleans between the 1930s and '80s. At the same time, a central tension animated Hermes's cooperative career: how to divest oneself from exploitative political and economic institutions and translate Rochdale cooperative ideology into pragmatic, impactful action benefitting the broadest population possible. Just as Eugene Bacarisse and Edna Egleston before him had been bound to the economic health and sociocentric biases of their immediate communities, Hermes grappled with fully renouncing white supremacy and capitalism in favor of fostering a participatory and egalitarian cooperative economy for all.

The Social and Political Geography of the Freret Neighborhood

Born in 1899, in Cologne, Germany, Heinrich W. Hermes immigrated to New York to join his father when he was fourteen. While working as a barber in Brooklyn, Hermes married Amelia Mendez, a native of Guatemala and resident of New Orleans. Mendez was of mixed British, Spanish, Mexican, and Honduran descent, and her family was involved in the export industry as well as international diplomacy. By 1928, the couple moved back to New Orleans to be closer to Amelia's family. The Hermeses were part of a wave of new immigrants and migrants taking advantage of early twentieth-century drainage, railroad, streetcar, and port improvements transforming the low-lying, marshy area sandwiched between the elite Uptown and Claiborne districts into the racially heterogeneous, working-class Freret neighborhood. There, they joined the city's Spanish and Latin American community, while Henry opened a barbershop on Freret Street, the neighborhood's bustling commercial hub.[5]

Freret was a close-knit community, fostered in part by its mixed-use development and pedestrian-friendly layout. Small entrepreneurs and their families often lived above their stores or nearby, which nurtured collective responsibility essential to the CCU's success. However, Freret was racially segregated at the street level; while African Americans comprised 40 percent of the population, their homes and businesses were concentrated along Soniat

Street. In contrast, small Jewish, Italian, and Eastern European businesses such as Cardaro's Poultry and Seafoods, Herman Bagalman's Pharmacy, Olga Pollock Beauty Salon, and Morris's Kosher Delicatessen lined Freret Street. Erasing ethnic divisions while shoring up racial difference, white shop owners belonged to segregated civic organizations like Freret Carnival Club and Freret Business Men's Association (FBMA), which lobbied for infrastructural improvements to make Freret "the best shopping center this side of Canal Street." As in other ethnic enclaves, Freret's Mardi Gras parades and neighborhood events drew much-needed business while establishing a white ethnic identity. By the 1940s, Freret had become a popular and inexpensive shopping district, and the St. Charles streetcar line transported eager bargain-hunters of all races to the neighborhood.[6]

While bound to Jim Crow racial codes, the Great Depression spurred white Freret residents to consider economic and political alternatives to unchecked capitalism. Although many supported the "Share Our Wealth" campaign of state governor (and US senator) Huey Long to modernize Louisiana via highway, bridge, charity hospital, and school construction, residents eventually rejected his followers' racialized populism and corruption scandals. They embraced President Franklin Roosevelt's activist federal government and New Deal welfare programs that protected average citizens. Also, because Hermes advocated for the unemployed and allied with familiar political institutions such the Democratic Party, white Freret residents tolerated his integrationist, socialist politics. The community affectionately dubbed Hermes the "neighborhood socialist," and local Popular Front sympathizers who protested alongside him at anti-fascist, civil liberties, and workers' rights groups would later join the CCU. Fundamentally, residents believed the CCU and Freret mutual associations' commitment to community-oriented economic development would sustain the neighborhood.[7]

The Barbers' Union Consolidates Working-Class Political Identity

To that end, over the course of the Depression, Hermes joined unions, consumer activists, and socialists who asserted that neighborhood and national cooperatives would resolve marginalized citizens' financial instability and political disempowerment. Between 1930 and 1936, the worsening national economy and vicious rivalry between Regular Democratic Organization (RDO) supporter T. Semmes Walmsley and Huey Long pushed the city to the brink of bankruptcy. As governor, Long and the RDO had brokered an uneasy alliance to consolidate power over Louisiana politics and stimulate state infrastructural development. However, the RDO grew leery of Long's anti-New Deal populism and tremendous sway over state politics. For instance, he was able to reliably capture the labor vote despite never sponsoring pro-labor union legislation or hiring union workers for state construction projects. Consequently, it backed conservative, pro-business state politicians like Walmsley running on "law-and-order" platforms actively suppressing unions and their allies.[8]

When Walmsley was elected mayor in 1933, the local RDO repudiated its alliance with Long. Now a US senator, Long eliminated state funding for New Orleans and revoked much of its ability to regulate its own affairs or collect revenue. Tensions escalated, and on the eve of the 1934 senatorial election, Long declared martial law in New Orleans. He deployed 3,000 National Guard members, who, armed with tear gas, occupied the voter registrar's office and posted machine guns in the windows facing City Hall. In response, 400 city police officers surrounded City Hall. While the conflict was defused, state legislators sympathetic to Long continued to economically punish the city.[9]

Outraged by the city's precipitous financial decline, as well as Louisiana's staunchly anti-labor policies, voter disenfranchisement, and chronic unemployment, New Orleanians joined national leftist political and labor movements in droves. Protesting local and state RDO corruption, Hermes joined the Associated Master Barbers of America in 1931 and served as vice president soon thereafter. Barber events were neighborhood fixtures that facilitated cross-ethnic, citywide and international alliances through a shared commitment to a worldwide industrial workers' movement. Like the cooperatives profiled in previous chapters, the barbers' union was supported by ethnic and professional mutual aid organizations whose sustained social exchanges in community spaces and economic survival programs cultivated the multiethnic union's cohesive identity and oppositional worldview.[10] In addition to providing burial insurance and medical services, immigrant benevolent societies fostered cross-class exchanges at ethnic meeting halls and social functions celebrating common hometowns and traditions. Similarly, Hermes mingled with German, Italian, and white Creole peers at Master and Journeyman's Barbers Band and Booster Club fundraisers, picnics, film screenings, and concerts at the verdant Audubon Park. The club also hosted meetings and parties at fraternal organizations' rooftop gardens. Unionized barbers' interest in community self-help and economic reform propelled Hermes's cooperative research, and his compatriots would form his cooperatives' core.[11]

As union director, Hermes zealously safeguarded barbers' economic livelihood. In 1932, Hermes had a young boot polisher arrested "for practicing barbering without a license when [Hermes observed him] shampooing the head of the owner of the barber shop." Shortly thereafter, the union accused Long of stacking the state barber board with allies who refused to enforce sanitation regulations protecting the public. During Walmsley's 1934 reelection campaign, Hermes was forcibly ejected from a rally for "disturbing the peace." When a conservative craft union president asserted that the mayor had always supported labor unions, Hermes repeatedly shouted, "I challenge that statement!" Officers bundled the protestor into a waiting police car, drew the window shades, and allegedly pummeled his face so hard they left bruises. Suffering the bodily cost of worker advocacy pushed Hermes further leftward.[12]

The New Orleans Popular Front and the Search for Global Democracy

After being elected secretary of the New Orleans Socialist Party, Hermes, along with other southern party officials, became a broker for Communist Party alliances rejecting "dictator" Huey Long's so-called populism to support black and white urban laborers, sharecroppers, and tenant farmers. In 1935, after the Seventh Comintern Congress called for a Popular Front, the small but active New Orleans Communist Party proposed a "united front" of interracial Communists, Socialists, leftists, and industrial unions promoting anti-fascism, collective bargaining, and civil liberties. The Popular Front integrated vulnerable Louisianans into an emerging New Deal welfare state rooted in local economic development, voter enfranchisement, labor regulation, and market reform.[13]

Radical critiques of labor, consumer, and capitalist relations deeply unsettled the state political apparatus. City and state efforts to squelch the Popular Front from convening to discuss policy and coordinate direct action accelerated after 1936, when the RDO forced Mayor Walmsley to resign and installed real estate magnate and Long loyalist Robert Maestri without an election.[14] While Maestri helped the city regain financial footing, he was a master of political patronage, tolerated prostitution and gambling, and, like Walmsley, attacked industrial unions. The mayor instructed Chief of Police Grosch to crack down on the industrial union Congress of Industrial Organization's (CIO) citywide organizing drive. According to historian Adam Fairclough, Grosch "raided homes and offices, seized documents, arrested strikers, threatened union lawyers, turned a blind eye to the AFL's thugs, and beat up CIO organizers" in jail.[15]

Working with conservative New Orleanian businesses, the police and Maestri officials widened their net to repress all political critique, criminalizing speech as well as the spaces in which such acts were performed. A city ordinance prohibiting the "teaching, uttering, printing, or advocating of anarchistic, communistic, or radical doctrines" targeted leftist college professors, public speakers, anti-fascist protestors, and Communist and Socialist Party members.[16] Protestors like Socialist Party president Louise Jessen were jailed for refusing to pay $10 street meeting permit fees and faced sentences of up to ninety days in prison. Furthermore, civil liberties activists reported, "Benevolent institutions permitting anyone on the [blacklist] to speak in their buildings are threatened with reprisals, including exclusion from the Community Chest," a major community funding organization. Accounts of city police brutality spread across the nation; a 1936 *St. Louis Dispatch* headline blared, "Police Make Their Own Laws: Their Fists Their Warrants." Political discussion was pushed underground to avoid bodily or economic harm: "avowed Communists and certain labor leaders live in a state of terror. They dodge from place to place in flight from the police, communicating with one another by trusted messenger."[17]

Constant police harassment reveals both the precarity and tenacity of Popular Front spaces of political dissent. While at any time police officers or hired goons might violently intimidate leftists at marches, union halls, newspaper offices, courtrooms, and even jail cells, such sites remained conduits for socioeconomically diverse protesters to share hardships and cooperatively confront institutional oppression. Dissidents' common experiences of police repression fostered a well-organized criminal law reform movement in New Orleans and Louisiana to protect all citizens' "liberties essential to keeping a liberal democratic government." Accordingly, the Louisiana League for the Preservation of Constitutional Rights' (LLPCR) body of liberal, mostly Jewish, Uptown intellectuals and lawyers took up activists' cases on the grounds that their arrests violated their civil liberties.[18]

Battling Hermes's 1937 arrest for distributing subversive literature hinged on activating the city's politicized social geography. Local socialists convened at the French Quarter-based Workers Center to spearhead letter-writing campaigns to government officials and newspapers, provide Hermes legal and financial assistance, and host national speakers. The Workers' Defense League, a legal and financial aid organization aiding victims of civil liberties abuses, arranged for national Socialist Party head Norman Thomas to protest Hermes's mistreatment at the Leopold Weil Community Center, a Jewish-run French Quarter educational and spiritual institution. Thomas compared New Orleans's pervasive political corruption to the rise of European totalitarianism. He intoned, "I found that Louisiana could grow almost anything—but freedom. . . . Your land is rich, but you have the poverty of exploitation." Alluding to the threat of fascism, socialists argued that if Hermes could be arrested for exercising free speech, so could any American. Their efforts were successful, and his case was dropped.[19]

Hermes understood New Orleanian political repression as a sign of encroaching authoritarianism domestically and abroad. His familial connections to the city's small Latin American community exposed the barber to the ways in which white supremacy and capitalism implicated Louisiana in the rise of totalitarian regimes. Cofounding the Louisiana Division of the North American Committee to Aid Spanish Democracy with Spanish-speaking anti-fascists in March 1937 forced Hermes to confront the impact of southern racial politics on a multiracial populace. Facing vocal opposition among segregationists and fascist supporters, the committee struggled to motivate an apathetic public to support the elected Second Spanish Republic during the Spanish Civil War. The public's disinterest stemmed from the longtime racialization of Spanish and Latin American peoples shoring up an expanding Anglo American identity rooted in imperialism and white supremacy.[20] In contrast, common experiences with southern racial prejudice prompted black, Jewish, and immigrant leftists to join Spanish anti-fascists and Latin American refugees from colonialism united in their resistance to Spanish nationalism. Meeting in the French Quarter, committee officers hosted national black civil rights activist and anti-fascist Thyra Edwards, held fundraisers and telegram-writing campaigns, and organized Spanish-language meetings.[21]

Further, being attuned to the international rise of totalitarianism prompted Hermes and his Spanish and Latin American colleagues to join other radical labor and socialist organizations to prevent domestic fascism from poisoning American democratic institutions. Throwing her support behind the CIO-affiliated United Mine Workers strike, Spanish American cooperative activist Lillian Muniz declared that by undermining organized labor, companies jeopardized miners' safety and economic well-being. Worse yet, corporations' "limitless appetites for profit" aided "Axis powers."[22] Hermes and Latin American organizers also joined the China Aid Council of New Orleans to protest Japanese imperialism, arguing that "[f]ascism will eventually absorb all democracies if a policy of isolationism and non-intervention is followed." Meeting in the French Quarter's Jerusalem Temple, Chinese, Latin American, black, and white committee members boycotted Japanese goods, screened anti-fascist documentaries, and sent food and clothing to noncombatants in China and Spain.[23] Hermes's partnerships with Spanish, Argentine, and Mexican immigrants informed his lifelong commitment to uniting "[a]ll thinking people" around "the maintenance of democratic rights" at home and abroad, while securing a recruiting channel for the CCU.[24]

Indeed, Hermes's diverse socialist and Popular Front colleagues identified cooperatives as the agents that would invest ordinary Americans with
the self-confidence and self-sufficiency needed to lead an economic revolution. Recalling the brotherhood and Housewives' League's platforms, socialist
cooperatives called for a national socialist government working in tandem
with a strong labor and cooperative movement to organize laborers into
cooperative factories and collective farms controlling the means of production and distribution. As a step toward discarding corporate capitalism as
a threat to democratic ideals, Upton Sinclair's "End Poverty in California"
gubernatorial campaign inspired the formation of 2,000 cooperatives in 1932
alone. Additionally, Sinclair proposed that California assist its unemployed
by creating state-owned cooperative colonies, a comprehensive industrial
system comprised of worker-owned cooperative factories, and social welfare programs. On a grander scale, socialists like CLUSA cofounder James
Warbasse and national peace activist Emily Greene Balch argued that an
international cooperative movement would inoculate nations from totalitarianism and repressive capitalism by engendering world peace.[25]

Convinced that Americans desperately "need[ed] . . . a cooperative social
order," Hermes and local socialists met in Popular Front enclaves to discuss
how to adapt a socialistic cooperative movement to the particular economic
needs of New Orleans.[26] Having taught at Commonwealth College, a socialist
labor school and commune founded by Louisiana's New Llano Cooperative
residents in 1923, chapter Socialist Party president Louise Jessen was interested in pairing cooperative living while educating industrial unionists to
resist imperialism and fascism. New Llano representatives traveled from their
socialist intentional community in Leesville, Louisiana to speak at the party's
humble French Quarter meeting hall. Colonists expounded that a "new social
fabric" of national economic and political cooperation would soon "cover the
back of advancing humanity after the old and torn one of capitalism [was]
discarded." Additionally, the socialist LID regularly hosted lectures on radical
cooperative economics, even staging national Socialist Party presidential candidate Norman Thomas's 1936 campaign rally at the Young Women's Christian Association (YWCA). There, Thomas discussed his vision for a national
"cooperative commonwealth," a democratic system of economic collectivism,
which would end soaring unemployment rates and improve living conditions
for "the masses."[27] The utopian socialist language of the "cooperative commonwealth" that once inspired Bacarisse and Egleston now propelled Hermes
and his ilk toward cooperative organizing.

An outgrowth of these cooperative discussions, in 1934 Hermes and the
New Orleans Socialist Party unfurled their first cooperative manifesto: coop-

eratives, rather than corporations or corrupt state governments, could best provide the essential infrastructural services necessary for the city's development. Exacerbating the feud between Walmsley and Long's cronies, Louisiana legislators had denied municipal government the power to regulate public utilities, so that the city could no longer effectively manage basic city services. Echoing the Local Council and Housewives League's campaign for utilities reforms, the Socialist Party demanded New Orleans Public Service Incorporated, the city's gas and electricity provider, impose fair rates for individual and corporate customers or permit the public to manage its utilities. The party ran a write-in mayoral candidate, Walter Smith, who proposed citizens "take over, own, and operate the Public Service, and sell electricity, gas, and streetcar service to ourselves AT COST." Socialists hailed electric cooperatives as competitive alternatives to exploitative private utilities companies. In fact, they would drive Louisiana's rural electrification between 1937 and 1940.[28]

New Orleans Consumers' Co-operative Union and Neighborhood Development

Yet by 1939, Hermes had distanced himself from a crumbling Socialist Party, making his vision of a socialized government and cooperative economy more palatable to average New Orleanians. The Socialist Party severed ties with CPUSA in the wake of the Soviet Union's Great Purge of 1937, in which Joseph Stalin ordered the political repression, police surveillance, imprisonment, and execution of millions of suspected counterrevolutionaries within the Communist Party and government, as well as ethnic minorities, intellectuals, religious figures, and the upper-classes. The Socialist Party too was soon riven with factions. In response, Hermes joined the Democratic Party and unsuccessfully ran for state representative on a reformist, anti-Earl Long administration ticket protesting the governor's history of embezzlement and extortion scandals. Reflecting the legacy of Jacob Coxey's economic proposals that the brotherhood advocated in New Orleans, Hermes championed New Deal social security and old age pensions under Roosevelt's Social Security Act of 1935. His faith in a society governed by the egalitarian interaction between neighborhood-based cooperatives, civically engaged citizens, and a federal social safety net would be embedded in the statewide cooperative businesses and credit unions Hermes seeded during his long cooperative career.[29]

Symbolizing his more moderate political platform, Hermes aligned with new generation of consumer movement-inspired cooperatives countering exorbitant consumer prices. During the 1930s and '40s, organized protest over mass retailing and older forms of food marketing and distribution once again swept the country. The rank-and-file consumer cooperative member was, according to historian Tracey Deutsch, part of a "broader network of liberal (though not necessarily leftist) citizens who organized advocacy groups to oppose a range of consumer abuses." Most, like CLUSA, adhered to the Rochdale Plan's consumer-oriented set of economic and organizational principles and rejected overt political action. As cooperative advocate John Dietrich observed in 1933, by forming local "non-political, voluntary association[s] of people," consumers would gradually and organically form a new, egalitarian economy. No government apparatus was needed because "people can conduct their own business without profit and without the state." Abandoning their socialist vision for a national cooperative democracy, by the 1930s, CLUSA cooperatives increasingly applied modern business practices to compete within, rather than replace, a capitalist framework.[30]

Like CLUSA's more moderate advocates, Hermes now studied how cooperatives could immediately benefit Freret, before tackling broader economic transformation. As in neighborhoods across the country, supermarkets and chain stores consolidated their hold over Freret's retail markets. Drawn to its middle- and working-class urban demographics and proximity to streetcar lines, three grocery chains dominated the neighborhood by 1944. New Orleans's new supermarket, with its vast stock and competitive prices, siphoned off patrons from independent businesses. Grocery cooperatives created regional umbrella organizations to compete with large retailers and independent grocers. While they reduced overhead costs for struggling store owners by sharing warehouses and brokering directly with producers and suppliers, they did not organize consumers.[31]

In contrast, Hermes convinced Freret residents to fund a Rochdale consumer cooperative store that would pressure local government and corporations to respect small businesses' solvency. Taking advantage of a 1940 federal law that protected consumer cooperatives through nontaxable patronage refunds and general incorporation, in July 1941, Hermes opened the integrated New Orleans Consumers' Co-operative Union (CCU) near his Freret Street barbershop. The Rochdale grocery store's inaugural meeting was small, Hermes conceded, "largely because President Roosevelt was broadcasting an address at the same time." However, after several picnic fundraisers, fifty former Popular Front activists and Freret residents enthusiastically paid the CCU's one-dollar membership fee. Blending neighborhood mutual aid organizations' self-help ethos with consumer-driven New Deal economic policies and international socialist ideology, the CCU gave its members a "stake in the economic system," in which the "monopoly" business model lost out to "democratic business."[32]

The unassuming two-story stucco building functioned as a middle ground welcoming both newcomers and established residents working in New Orleans's wartime munitions factories, military bases, and shipyards looking to spend their higher wages on culturally familiar foods. Nationally, Popular Front organizations disintegrated during the 1940s under mounting cultural-, spatial-, and religious-based friction among Catholic and Jewish industrial workers and newly arrived rural Protestant southern migrants looking for wartime work. In contrast, the CCU grocery store was a salve against an emerging "archipelago of cities," or residents' spatial segregation based on socioeconomic status. Unlike the Housewives' League's segregated store, CCU customers participated in egalitarian dialogue that crafted a community of vision empowering individual expression while promoting understanding across difference.[33] By appealing to the consumer cooperative movement's tenet "*everybody* is a Consumer, from the day of birth until we die," the grocery store bound its ethnically heterogeneous clientele to democratic institutions across the South. In the process, it successfully applied federally mandated rationing, grade labeling, and price controls to protect New Orleanians against unhealthful food, inflation, the black market, and hoarding throughout World War II.[34]

CCU's Latin American and Black Activists Pursue an Antiracist Agenda

Hermes's familial and political ties to the Latin American and Spanish community ensured the CCU soon looked beyond the Freret neighborhood to weigh cooperative economics' impact on society as a whole. While half of the CCU's directors were female consumer activists, Latina leftists led the store's campaign to protect customers from widespread economic instability and hardening government policies on industrial relations.[35] CCU's president, Mexican-born textile machinist Angelina Lopez Prior, was a prototypical "citizen consumer" advancing racial justice when doing so risked one being branded as a communist propagandist. Some southern cooperators fretted that if they had to sit next to black members, white racists might flee meetings or discredit their organizations. Others barred blacks from holding officer positions and attending events alongside their white peers. As head of the local AFL-affiliated United Garment Workers Union, she believed the federal government should not only intervene in the market to enforce product quality standards, but that laborers and consumers had a moral imperative to construct an equitable cooperative economy open to all. Likewise, Spanish and

Latin American CCU directors challenged Freret's segregationist practices by fostering direct action, meeting at black institutions and integrated spaces, granting equal voting privileges to black members, and electing people of color to the store's board of directors.[36]

CCU director and social worker Lillian Muniz in particular provided integrated social spaces the cooperative occupied as it framed its guiding philosophy and educated New Orleanians about economic cooperation. She represented the Louisiana State University YWCA chapter at integrated southern cooperative league conferences pairing labor and consumer advocacy.[37] YWCA members promoted interracial cooperation and racial justice, advocated collective bargaining and federal labor legislation, and joined national consumer agencies and cooperatives to build a "Christian nation" and "world commonwealth" free of exploitative capitalism. Accordingly, Muniz regularly booked multiracial CCU events and meetings at an integrated YWCA auditorium bordering the French Quarter. She organized lectures at the CCU, such as an integrated, pro-labor Southern Conference for Human Welfare talk on implementing New Deal economic policies and advancing civil rights, electoral reform, and social justice in the South.[38] Black consumers thus believed that the YWCA would be a "medium through which the right kind of contacts can be made" between "fine outstanding Negroes" and "other groups within [the New Orleans] community" to promote "human welfare in their region."[39]

Consequently, the CCU's racially progressive worldview attracted black civil rights activists intimately familiar with mutual aid organizations' ability to stimulate neighborhood economies. Freret resident Fletcher Sherrod balanced his duties as CCU auditor with serving as Postal Relief and Benevolent Association of New Orleans recording secretary.[40] As a mutual aid society providing medical and burial benefits to black postal workers and their families, its cooperative ethos propelled members to seek institutional redress for racial discrimination in their field and in society. Black postal workers were at the forefront of equality work, becoming core NAACP members by the 1940s. Also, Sherrod's brother was a doctor at Dillard University's Flint-Goodridge Hospital, which offered a nationally recognized cooperative insurance plan for black New Orleanians. As we shall see in the next chapter, the hospital's black supervisor, Albert Dent, believed sustained economic development in the South would end racism and halt the spread of fascism among southern segregationists. African Americans' integral participation in New Orleans's cooperative movement counters historians' claims that integrated racial justice organizations did little to concretely challenge Jim Crow in wartime New Orleans.[41]

Community Culture in the CCU

As secretary and publicist, Hermes crafted an imagined community of cooperators in order to move customers patronizing the CCU primarily to reduce
their grocery bill toward mobilizing to dismantle capitalism. A common
member identity also helped the cooperative weather service disruptions and
complaints. Like the Housewives' League grocery store twenty years prior,
although CCU's sales trebled between 1941 and 1944, it operated on a shoe-
string budget stretched thinner to accommodate wartime headaches. As did
many small grocery stores during World War II, the CCU struggled to keep
basic items in stock. When the store's delivery truck broke down in 1944, it was
unable to procure fresh produce, which measurably decreased its sales. Also,
the CCU struggled to retain grocery clerks and delivery truck drivers because
war industries offered higher wages. Hermes conceded, "no-one desires to
work behind the counter at a minimum pay," despite the cooperative's ethical
mission. The CCU was frequently mobbed with anxious shoppers waiting in
long lines for frazzled, short-staffed cashiers to count wartime ration points
and purchase totals. While its prices were comparable to those of larger retail
operations, narrow profit margins meant that the store could not offer the
cut-rate prices Freret consumers craved. Hermes bemoaned bargain-hunters
who would rather "patronize their competitors" like nearby corner stores, or
worse, far-flung chain stores, than "protect their investment and interest, not
mentioning CO-OPERATION."[42]

In response, Hermes used the CCU's monthly newsletter, the *New Orleans
Cooperator*, to promote social events, educational programs, and member services that associated cooperation with wartime patriotism and civic duty. Its
monthly "Gossip" column highlighted CCU members' shared experience of
World War II to cement a nascent sense of community. Bordering the Gulf
of Mexico and featuring many war production facilities and training camps,
Louisiana was considered vulnerable to Axis attack; several torpedo explo-
sions on the mouth of the Mississippi and the Gulf fanned public suspicion of
any group appearing anti-American. By illustrating politically, ethnically, and
racially diverse cooperators' commitment to the war effort, activists headed
off claims of subversion. Columnists bade farewell to members deployed
for active duty and noted that Hermes's daughter Marion was employed as
a nurse, while his son had enlisted in the navy. Hermes announced he had
joined the National Defense Council of Louisiana as a Freret air-raid warden,
while CCU president Angelina Prior sewed uniforms for the war effort. Additionally, the CCU credit union sold war bonds, explaining to readers that they
"belong in every budget, as Democracy belongs in every heart."[43]

During World War II, Americans conflated domestic consumption with good citizenship, and the CCU was no different. Elevating the CCU above avaricious, unpatriotic corporate retailers, Hermes asserted, "We give the service that people are entitled to and paying for but not receiving in the 'chains.'" In contrast, unscrupulous New Orleans retailers inflated their prices, and mainstream grocers blacklisted any protestors. While other independent grocery stores threatened to use the black market to circumvent the Office of Price Administration's (OPA) "red tape and technicalities" mandating market and rent controls, the CCU faithfully adhered to wartime rationing mandates. Like the Housewives' League, it joined national consumer activists who parlayed their influence within federal food agencies to legitimize calls for national social welfare and public works programs curbing capitalism's excesses.[44]

Key to the cooperative's patriotic identity were female consumers. While both men and women belonged to the CCU, American women were responsible for daily food purchases, often squeezing in shopping trips between wartime work shifts. Female consumer choice was therefore a primary polemical tool the CCU used in its battle to purify corrupt economic and political systems. Appealing to working-class women juggling war jobs and domestic duties, it sold convenience foods like chocolate syrups and Jell-O and purchased produce and dry goods in bulk to maintain chain store prices. Hermes also bragged that CCU customers gladly adhered to federal meat substitute campaigns. Wartime Californian growers marketed avocados to women as a healthful and elegant salad topping as well as a viable meat substitute for rationing families: avocados were "veritable grenades of glamor." Similarly, the CCU crowed, "we were the first on Freret Street with Avocados [sic] which sold like hot-cakes."[45] Likewise, when food administrators encouraged Americans to reduce their dependence on scarce canned items by purchasing or growing their own produce, women flocked to purchase the CCU's fruits and vegetables, sourced from open-air city markets. The CCU cast its members as female "citizen consumers" who upheld OPA regulations and bankrolled the greater war effort.[46]

CCU women's patriotic character was further bolstered by their status as ethnic paragons of wartime consumption. In stark contrast to the assimilationist efforts of the public kitchens of World War I, government food administrators urged native-born Americans to frequent Italian markets and emulate "Deep South" cooks to procure inexpensive food substitutes and eliminate food waste. Broadening the definition of American identity, the CCU stocked foods that honored its members' ethnic and racial diversity. The grocery store supplied New Orleans staples such as fresh fish, lobster, and Carnival, Easter, and picnic hams, while catering to immigrant families with imported specialty goods like sardines packed in oil and Pompeian olive oil. The CCU's delicatessen also targeted ethnic and black customers seeking organ meats, neck bones, and hot sausage. While the general public long distained spicy, garlicky foods or mixed stews as redolent of inassimilable otherness, food reformers now hailed immigrant and black housewives for their efficient food-stretching methods born out of prewar economic necessity.[47] Effectively, the CCU's food selections reflected its belief that a racially and ethnically diverse cooperative could demonstrate civic values while promoting systemic political and economic transformation.

The SCEA and Regional Economic Development

Their sense of fellow-feeling fostered among CCU members a shared commitment to democratic economic growth beyond the Freret neighborhood. Hermes was intimately familiar with contemporaneous efforts to establish farmers' cooperatives across the state, particularly those countering ineffective New Deal policies that accelerated rural displacement among tenant farmers. Headquartered in New Orleans and active within Hermes's leftist social circle, the Louisiana Farmers' Union's (LFU) communist organizer Gordon McIntire mobilized Cajun, Italian, black, Slavic and German fruit and vegetable growers to improve marketing conditions at the French Market and access federal agricultural programs. He also called for city cooperative creameries to secure fair prices for both producers and consumers. McIntire soon sought the legal aid of the New Orleans civil liberties community after white supremacist planters, furious with his attempts to unionize black sharecroppers, ran him out of Louisiana.[48]

Although Hermes too believed cooperatives could break the cycle of consumer dependency across the South, he avoided McIntire's disgrace by joining the more moderate Southeastern Cooperative Educational Association (SCEA) in 1941.[49] Active between 1939 and 1948, the interracial network of regional and sub-regional cooperatives drew on the Catholic cooperative tradition of Antigonish, Nova Scotia, to provide educational resources to southern colleges, unions, financial institutions, churches, and nonprofit organizations establishing cooperatives. The SCEA argued that southern poverty was rooted in damaging federal agricultural policies, as well as rural communities' dependence on exploitative corporations, bankers, and wholesalers. Its comprehensive regional development plan comprised cooperative-friendly legislation and trainings and workshops to link rural wholesale cooperatives to urban Rochdale consumer cooperatives. A cooperative network would help ordinary southerners, regardless of race or class, regain control over economic and political institutions. According to SCEA director Ruth Morton, the Rochdale model was more than "simply . . . a business enterprise" but rather, was "one of the means by which the common man attains his democratic ideal."[50]

Affiliating with the SCEA gave Hermes strategies and institutional resources to strengthen Freret's local economy while connecting the CCU to a regional cooperative economy. Over the course of the 1940s, Hermes studied various cooperative organizational structures at SCEA conferences and eastern cooperative site tours, applying his research to Freret needs. For instance, SCEA-inspired financial readiness workshops and educational film series inculcated economic independence in CCU members. Further, by 1949, Hermes had established a small universe of cooperative enterprises nestled along Freret Street. In addition to the CCU's cooperative laundry service next door, Myrtle Crow managed the Consumers' Co-operative Ice Cream Parlor inside the grocery store, while independent meat dealer Rusty Rusbridge ran the cooperative's deli. At the same time, the CCU invited representatives from SCEA-affiliated labor unions, churches, and civic organizations to speak at public meetings and member picnics. Members learned to contextualize their activities within the larger regional cooperative movement's postwar economic progress.[51]

Most significantly, Hermes forcefully applied SCEA's democratic lessons to modernize Freret infrastructure. One CCU member received a $25 war bond in 1945 for winning a local essay competition on how best to improve the neighborhood. Hermes coordinated a letter writing campaign among local business owners requesting city investment in more frequent policing, daily garbage collection, cleaner streets, paved roads leading into Freret, and well-maintained streetcar tracks. By 1947, the FBMA, of which the CCU was a member, had "persuade[d] the New Orleans Public Service and our city fathers to give us modern transportation" in the form of repaved roads, new trolley cars, and a convenient trolley line that intersected cross-city bus routes. At the neighborhood's Trolley Car Celebration Day, the city promised to install more streetlights in Freret as soon as it could raise funds. Officials praised cooperative organizations for "promot[ing] the business and welfare of the community," and the FBMA assured attendees that "to this, we dedicate ourselves."[52]

The International Cooperative Movement and Postwar Utopian Thought

The CCU's street-level successes gave Hermes the confidence to tackle an even larger cooperative project: joining a postwar global cooperative movement that aimed to reestablish peace, expand democracy, and ensure economic justice worldwide. While public figures like historian David Potter argued that natural resources and democratic principles had fostered a utopian "politics of abundance" that elevated postwar Americans' living standards above all others, leftist cooperators countered that, in the absence of truly democratic governance, America was not an example for other nations. Hermes predicted that unscrupulous corporations will be "enriched by wartime profits" and "[r]ace and minority problems will be loaded with dynamite. Much of the World hate or fear us."[53]

Instead, to achieve a visionary "economy of abundance," Hermes argued that postwar Americans should elect a socialistic government and implement a national cooperative economic system.[54] The state would control industries, regulate employment, heavily tax corporations, maintain wartime price controls and rationing, and finally, regulate farm and city land speculation to stabilize property values. To ensure long-term economic growth, a postwar government would convert industries into large-scale worker-controlled cooperatives. A national cooperative network would not only stimulate the economy, but it would also improve workers' standards of living, eliminate racial tension, and revitalize democratic values.

Additionally, Hermes declared that only "international economic co-operation based on democracy and economic justice" would secure the "opportunity for the people to help themselves to permanent peace." Likewise, CLUSA executive director Jerry Voorhis argued that despite the polarizing events of the Cold War, the current geopolitical context still brimmed with utopian, transformative potential. Voorhis posited that an international cooperative movement rooted in mutual aid and community participation was fundamental to an equitable global society. After World War II, the International Cooperative Alliance (ICA) promoted global trade among cooperative federations and training for new cooperative managers. Voorhis urged American cooperatives to battle political repression by uniting with the ICA and sharing modern agricultural and democratic organizational strategies with impoverished nations. Unlike corporate giants, American cooperatives were true emissaries of "people's capitalism"; average citizens, regardless of race or creed, worked together to achieve self-determination and economic security. Accordingly, American cooperatives like CLUSA and Cooperatives for American Relief Everywhere (CARE) formed cooperatives to facilitate community-driven economic recovery in war-torn countries. Voorhis hoped global citizens could build "bridges of understanding and of peace and of a practical kind of brotherhood."[55]

Even as other liberal thinkers conflated utopian idealism with repressive Stalinism, American and international cooperators offered a positive socioeconomic and political alternative to both communism and imperialist capitalism. Hermes's and Voorhis's postwar programs echoed humanists who responded to World War II's mass genocide and violence by proposing a new cooperative and democratic international society. René Cassin, framer of the 1948 United Nations Universal Declarations of Human Rights, rejected Cold War militarism and political dogmatism. He contended that nations could safeguard global peace by recognizing the essential human rights of all people and judiciously using technology to ensure everyone's economic, social, and political well-being. Additionally, physicist Leo Szilard demanded that nations cease nuclear weapon production. Instead, they should apply defense funds toward raising world and domestic standards of living and implementing an international, voluntary system of enforceable peace.[56] As the CCU similarly declared, the global "democratic movement" would end poverty and political dependency by "supplying the inspiration and the 'know how' for folks to help themselves."[57] Ultimately, a world cooperative system "is a formula for FREEDOM, both for the individual and for society."

One Door Closes, Another Opens: The End of the CCU

Yet even as the CCU demonstrated that a comprehensive cooperative economy was not only possible but profitable, the political and economic conditions sustaining the grocery store were rapidly eroding. Throughout the late 1940s and '50s, it remained dangerous to be a cooperative activist fighting for economic and political equality in the South. Desperate to preserve "the southern way of life," conservative white southerners sought to quash civil rights and unionizing efforts by raising the dual specter of black rebellion and foreign agitation.[58] The House Un-American Activities Committee (HUAC) initiated a southern Red Scare, a twenty-year period in which "southern nationalists," politicians committed to stamping out Communist-led racial equality, consolidated their hold over the region's politics. Established in 1938, HUAC investigated Roosevelt's New Deal coalition of labor, Jewish, Popular Front, and black activists. By 1947, legislators attempted to outlaw the Communist Party, while President Harry S. Truman initiated a federal loyalty program that barred employees from affiliating with "subversive" organizations.

Like the Housewives' League before them, Louisianan cooperatives did not escape anti-communist scrutiny, although their critics seemed confused about the entities' purpose and ideology. During a 1949 and 1950 US Congressional Ways and Means Committee investigation into the tax status of cooperatives, local businessmen wrote to Louisiana's congressional representative

Hale Boggs protesting the "socialistic movement" of unions and cooperatives that threatened to "destroy the [capitalist] system which has been in effect almost ever since this nation was founded."[59] Further, cooperative insurance companies were conspiring to exploit tax loopholes to swindle the federal government out of billions of tax dollars. Similarly, a New Orleans manufacturing agent charged that wealthy plantation owners and entrepreneurs used cooperatives to enrich themselves at the expense of "the small business man and the small farmer . . . the backbone of the Country."[60] He darkly echoed Louisianan segregationists' prediction that "if Communism comes to this country, it will come from within."

Former Louisianan Popular Front members faced severe political repercussions for their cooperative activism. In 1953, anti-communist federal investigators targeted Gordon McIntire, now a United Nations official, for his Depression-era work with the LFU.[61] He was fired, and the Federal Bureau of Investigations (FBI) tapped his telephone and monitored his mail. Claiming McIntire was a security risk, the State Department restricted his passport, and many countries refused him entry. McIntire described federal officials' circular logic, which conflated leftist activism with subversive activity:

> All they have against me is that I went to Commonwealth College and sponsored the Southern Conference for Human Welfare and worked for the Farmers Union. This seems to build up to Communist conspiracy. . . . The La.F.U. is said to have been Communist because I was its Secretary and I am said to be a Communist because I worked for the La.F.U.[62]

Anti-cooperative sentiment was so virulent that in 1950 Jerry Voorhis testified before Congress, maintaining that CLUSA and other cooperatives were bulwarks against communism and totalitarianism, which he defined as the "concentration of economic power in the hands of private individuals, depriving the people of economic opportunity and causing them to lose the right to determine their own course of action."[63] He posited that corporate monopolies were more communistic than were cooperatives. To preserve democracy, a system of cooperatives would decentralize economic and political power and "both ownership and responsibility [would be] restored to the people once again." Rather than operating as agents of extremism, voluntary cooperatives were "a middle road between dependence upon government on the one hand and control by private concentrations of power on the other."

Despite Voorhis's impassioned defense of cooperatives, over the course of the 1950s, the revanchist Cold War political climate decimated non-agrarian cooperatives while farm cooperatives purged radical activists critical of

American domestic and foreign policies from their membership rolls. Fearing redbaiting, surviving cooperatives eschewed politics altogether. Similarly, at the CCU, overtly socialist members faded from view, and Hermes's fellow barbers and Freret business owners populated its board of directors. What little political activism they advocated was channeled into legislative reform, while they concentrated on keeping the CCU alive in the midst of accelerating white flight and economic stagnation.[64]

Postwar settlement patterns permanently altered Freret's consumer culture, as well as its ability to sustain a grocery cooperative. When the Freret streetcar line closed in the late 1940s, the CCU lost significant patronage from cross-town shoppers, while the popularity of the family car drew Freret consumers to the suburbs and away from the pedestrian-oriented neighborhood. Supermarkets populated new, car-centric suburbs that made Freret Street's community of family-owned businesses and racially diverse residents seem shabby and outmoded in comparison. Across the city, the rise of large grocery stores spelled the end of corner grocery stores, street vendors, and city markets operating without the protection of powerful commercial and cooperative associations. Nationally, most neighborhood cooperatives dissolved during a postwar economic boom and dropping food prices. Likewise, the CCU could not compete with supermarkets and chains. It shuttered its grocery store in 1951 and formally disbanded in 1965. In a cruel twist of fate, a deli chain opened in its place.[65]

Henry Hermes and the New Orleans Credit Union Movement

Yet while the CCU's grocery store failed within an evolving grocery industry, its credit union continued to offer marginalized, ethnic Freret residents economic stability and wealth accumulation. In fact, the credit union launched Hermes's twenty-year credit union career, enabling him to finance working-class Louisianans' economic development on a scale the neighborhood-based CCU could not have imagined. The most concrete manifestation of the CCU's economic justice agenda, the briefly integrated credit union opened after World War II to "help a member help himself." Like radicals and labor unionists around the country, Hermes believed credit unions would expand working-class access to consumer credit. First established in 1900 and extending to Louisiana by the 1920s, credit unions are cooperative financial institutions dedicated to redressing the gap in consumer lending for low-income individuals. The Federal Credit Union Act of 1934 facilitated a national system of federal credit unions. The New Deal-era act encouraged credit union formation by permitting the Office of Financial Institutions, the National Credit Union Administration, an independent federal agency, and similar state agencies to charter and regulate credit unions. Consequently, the Louisiana Credit Union League (LCUL) formed in 1934 to promote economic cooperation, liaise with regulatory agencies, and provide legal aid for credit union members. LCUL cofounder and Roosevelt administration staffer Harold Moses crafted New Deal federal credit union legislation, rapidly spreading credit unions across Louisiana and the nation. The SCEA hailed their success as proof of "the growth of the cooperative philosophy and what it might do to help the South."[66]

Part of credit unions' appeal among working-class Americans was that they were run by and for the members themselves, unlike for-profit financial institutions. Freret's LCUL-affiliated credit union clients pooled money from inexpensive stock shares to open savings accounts, obtain loans at moderate interest rates, and receive dividends in proportion to their stock investment. Further, CCU directors and committees were democratically elected, and each member had one vote, regardless of how much stock she held in the institution. Like most other new occupational, residential, or associational credit unions, members were dependent on one another to stay solvent; limiting membership to those who belonged to the grocery cooperative established common bonds and mutual trust necessary to maintaining the cooperative. Echoing the SCEA, manager Peter Biewer likened the CCU credit union to "a miniature democracy" because "through group activity we can do much to solve common problems."[67]

Even as Louisiana's postwar industrializing economy expanded middle-class purchasing power and access to consumer credit, working-class whites and people of color remained excluded from mainstream lending institutions. Interest rates at loan offices and financial companies could be three times higher than those at credit unions, and fixed administrative costs made consumer loans prohibitively expensive for less affluent Americans.[68] Restrictive loan policies devastated black neighborhoods. Shreveport Federal Credit Union head Helen Godfrey-Smith recalls, "there was no opportunity for African Americans to have legitimate access to financial services that were responsive to what they needed." While postwar housing stock boomed for affluent whites, racial covenants and inadequate public housing resulted in a housing crisis for the poor, who squeezed into dilapidated, overcrowded housing stock. By 1950, vacancy rates for African American housing dipped to only 0.3 percent.[69]

Further, while white veterans secured federal housing financing through the Servicemen's Readjustment Act of 1944, or the GI Bill, African Americans were forced to pay large monthly payments and high interest rates on exorbitantly priced homes. For example, in 1951, fifty-five low-income white veterans who were evicted from Navy-owned public housing pooled their resources to build two cooperative housing divisions. The suburban Gentilly properties served 101 mostly Catholic Creole families. GI loans funded Legion Oaks Housing construction, and the cooperative restricted homeownership to white American Legion members, the organization instrumental in passing the GI Bill. Discriminatory lending practices stymied black property development and improvements; labeling clients of color "high risk," banks often denied them low-interest loans and mortgages.[70]

In contrast, the integrated CCU credit union helped vulnerable individuals avoid predatory or discriminatory lending agencies to gain financial solvency and spur substantial neighborhood investment. While black credit unions already offered their communities a measure of financial stability, the CCU was part of a small coterie of white credit unions that acknowledged the racialized service gap and recruited African Americans to join their ranks.[71] However, Hermes's active participation in segregated credit unions complicated a socialist vision for a racially egalitarian, community-led economic state.

Only a year after opening, in 1945 the CCU credit union renounced its integrated model for neighborhood economic advancement when it joined the segregated FBMA, and later, the FBMA Credit Union. The CCU grocery store's crusade against chain stores and large retail operations resonated with small business owners also suffering from corporate competition and discriminatory lending practices. Financial institutions repeatedly denied white Freret storeowners' loans because they viewed the racially diverse community as a liability. As credit union member Frank Barreca protested, "businessmen on [Freret] street had to have something to help themselves. Unless the small businessman has real estate, he has trouble getting money."[72]

In response, in 1951, Hermes cofounded the whites-only FBMA Credit Union. Offering easy loan repayment and low interest rates, credit unions offered cash-poor businesses preferable rates compared to commercial banks, department stores, and small loan companies.[73] While Hermes had envisioned a multiethnic, multiracial, and gender-inclusive cooperative society that would revitalize the democratic process and reject capitalism's exploitative profit motive, the FBMA credit union enabled Freret's white storeowners to profit from an entrenched, racially exclusionary capitalistic system. By extension, as director of both the FBMA and the Freret Civic Association, Hermes became complicit in barring black residents from self-help institutions and social spaces fundamental to the neighborhood's economic growth.

The segregated FBMA Credit Union and the neighborhood business and civic organizations it supported were barricades against shifting racial demographics they believed corroded Freret. For example, in 1949, in the midst of a severe housing crisis, civic associations attempted to demolish several predominantly black residential blocks as part of a "slum clearance" program. Similarly, when the Orleans School Board decided to convert Edwin T. Merrick Elementary into a black school in 1952, white organizations like the FBMA filed a civil suit against the board. They accused it of transferring white students to other schools to justify the conversion. New schools should be constructed in black neighborhoods "where they were most badly needed." Unwilling to accept the conversion, nearly 1,000 whites fled the neighborhood, while a 1960 mandate to integrate Orleans Parish public schools accelerated the white exodus of working- and middle-class whites from the Ninth Ward, Mid-City, and the Irish Channel. New suburban tracts sprung up along Lake Pontchartrain and the outskirts of New Orleans to accommodate their segregationist lifestyles. Inner-city black neighborhoods now encircled pockets of wealthy, exclusively white neighborhoods such as the Garden District.[74]

Although a strong postwar economy brought to New Orleans a reformed government, booming international trade, and new construction projects such as railroads, bridges, and public housing, mass white flight devastated Freret. Yet rather than incorporating black businesses and residents and stimulating a spiraling local economy, the FBMA Credit Union remained segregated by policy and practice. Member Frank Barreca's steakhouse hosted city and state credit union meetings and conventions to pump money into the declining neighborhood economy. Frank's Steak House remained segregated into the 1960s, barring African Americans from important credit union functions.[75]

Similarly, state and regional credit union meetings were strictly segregated. Richard Turnley, a civil rights activist who founded the Baton Rouge-based Southern Teachers and Parents Federal Credit Union in 1959, recalled that black board of directors and managers were forced to wait outside LCUL meetings. Sympathetic white credit union members snuck out to share the league's debates and literature so that black colleagues might disseminate the information to their constituents. The credit union movement's inability to reconcile its ideological commitment to equality with the realities of operating within a segregated society had severe economic consequences. Paralyzed by racial animosities, the Freret commercial district lost a third of its businesses between 1952 and 1972. Vacant lots depreciated property values and encouraged street crime.[76]

Frustrated by the segregated FBMA credit union's inability to revive the neighborhood, Hermes channeled his energies into LCUL, a statewide cooperative organization serving low- and moderate-income consumers. In 1955, Hermes became a board member of LCUL and in 1966 was elected Louisiana director of the Credit Union National Association (CUNA), a national trade and lobbyist organization. Because LCUL supervised hundreds of credit unions across the state, it depended on a network of field service district representatives to work directly with credit unions. Hermes coordinated credit union activity in Lafourche, Plaquemines, St. Bernard, and Terrebonne parishes and supervised a third of New Orleans's 1,100 credit unions. He gave operating procedure advice, arranged inter-credit union loans, suggested personnel placement, helped liquidations, and acted as liaison between LCUL and credit union affiliates. Over the course of his career, Hermes organized over twenty new credit unions whose low-rate loans during periods of economic recession between 1957 and 1962 insulated members from rampant inflation and job insecurity. In fact, by 1962, credit unions had superseded small loan companies as the second-most important purveyors of consumer loans in the state, enrolling 200,000 Louisianans in cooperative banks.[77]

While Hermes tempered his socialist worldview with a more moderate vision of "self-help" reforms, credit unions were by no means apolitical. The Louisiana credit union community was a refuge for Popular Front and New Deal cooperative activists run underground by Cold War anti-communist hysteria. Former SCEA members studded LCUL rolls, revealing an intact Depression-era southern cooperative network. For instance, after being inducted into LCUL's Founders Club in 1951, Hermes hobnobbed with old cooperators like the Right Reverend William J. Castel, one of the SCEA's "key people in the Roman Catholic Church," and CCU-LCUL liaison E. K. Watkins, now an international credit union advocate.[78] Further, Freret credit union member Joseph Barreca would serve as LCUL's legal counsel and legislative representative in the 1960s and '70s.[79] In 1973, he worked closely with Lindy Boggs, Louisiana's congressional representative, to pass the Federal Credit Union Act, which protected federally chartered credit unions and expanded their insurance services for low-income Americans. Linking New Deal and War on Poverty antipoverty initiatives, cooperative veterans lobbied influential city, state, and federal political leaders to pass credit union legislation that increased average Americans' access to consumer credit and political influence.[80]

The Louisiana Credit Union League and the War on Poverty

As a LCUL field director and eventual national director, Hermes had two goals: to incorporate the working class into the consumer economy and integrate African Americans into credit unions as equal members. His efforts dovetailed with the LCUL's participation in federal Great Society anti-poverty initiatives. In 1965, managing director Edgar Fontaine explicitly linked LCUL's New Deal past and War on Poverty present; not only would LCUL continue to assist ordinary Americans, but "we have been pioneering Christian principles and practices in the market place long before the giants of finance became responsive to consumer needs." In fact, President Lyndon B. Johnson's Economic Opportunity Act of 1964 galvanized cooperative activists confronting the effects of poverty and institutionalized racism within their communities. The law's Title II had far-reaching implications for cooperatives. Seeking to "eliminate the paradox of poverty in the midst of plenty . . . by opening to everyone the opportunity to live in decency and dignity," it called for "maximum feasible participation" among low-income and marginalized populations in planning and administering local anti-poverty initiatives.[81]

Between 1964 and 1970, the Office of Economic Opportunity (OEO) mandated the creation of state and local "Community Action Agencies" to supervise anti-poverty initiatives. Cooperatives could apply to operate as grant agencies.[82] Accordingly, Community Action Programs in New Orleans established credit unions and cooperative health programs, housing, and buying clubs to stimulate consumption among black, elderly, and impoverished citizens.[83] In 1966, LCUL began working with Total Community Action (TCA), the city administrator of OEO funds, the Bureau of Federal Credit Unions, and the Social Welfare Planning Council to establish federally chartered, community-run credit unions in white public housing project St. Thomas and black complexes Desire, Melpomene, and Fischer.[84] LCUL regularly advised residents on starting credit unions and following prudent saving and credit programs.

Throughout the 1960s, New Orleans was an important test site for low-income federal and state credit unions looking to expand across Louisiana. For example, in 1967, the city hosted "Project Moneywise," an OEO and Bureau of Federal Credit Unions initiative to train leaders of marginalized communities in "wise money management" to achieve neighborhood "economic survival." Officials hoped that community leaders would in turn educate poor residents to be smarter consumers by carefully budgeting, patronizing cooperatives and buying clubs, and borrowing at community-owned financial institutions. During month-long training sessions held in the Old Federal Building, participants made "comparative shopping trips," studied materials, and watched educational films like *Moneywise Family*, in which "Mr. Mighty Wise" saves a family of mice from the depredations of "Mr. Tiger Shark," an unscrupulous loan shark.[85]

Henry Hermes was instrumental in organizing two state and national credit union conferences that wholeheartedly endorsed the War on Poverty.

In March 1966, the Eighth District of CUNA, representing the organization's southern branch, announced an anti-poverty initiative that entailed lobbying for federal credit union legislation and increased minority membership. Two months later, the inner-city credit unions of New Orleans reported to LCUL conference attendees that they were aligning with War on Poverty programs. Notably, President Johnson, as well as high-ranking Louisianan and federal officials who had once attacked cooperatives for harboring communists, now congratulated the credit union cause.[86]

Representing credit unions at the local, city, state, and national level, Hermes was for the first time able to execute lasting economic policy by collaborating with the Democratic Party. After Hermes convened a 1968 LCUL conference, Congressman Boggs discussed the role credit unions would play in increasing impoverished consumers' purchasing power. While Boggs had been wary of the "socialistic" tendencies of cooperatives, he now claimed that credit unions were "the most essential parts of our consumer economy" and should be established "wherever possible."[87] Echoing President Johnson, Boggs believed social welfare programs were springboards to greater personal responsibility and civic engagement. Low-income credit unions in "ghetto areas" were crucial to ameliorating economic inequality because credit unions, "rather than offering a handout, offer a helping hand." Outlining his plan to pass several credit union measures and form an independent federal credit union administration to supervise the nation's 12,000 federal credit unions, Boggs proclaimed that credit unions had "virtually eliminated" the loan shark and "sharp practice operators." Mirroring the language of consumer empowerment, Boggs incorporated credit unions into a reformed, ethical capitalism. Systemic poverty required incorporating black and other marginalized individuals into the consumer market.

However, rather than investing in broader welfare programs, white government and credit union officials exploited the cooperative movement's principle of self-help because it resonated with their calls for the black community to develop greater self-reliance. As War on Poverty Taskforce member John Baker concedes, "We were just absolutely in a system, because we were convinced that in a really tough social structure intertwined with economic structure, the only solution for poor folks was to get co-ops."[88] In 1967, Project Moneywise director William O'Brien argued that to break the cycle of poverty, communities required extensive job training and consumer education. It was credit unions' duty to train "economic illiterates" to "save for the first time in their lives," because the poor could not distinguish needs from desires. Similarly, LCUL director Edgar Fontaine replicated white politicians' atomized perspective when he contended that a successful black credit union movement would require "[developing] a savings habit in these people; [and changing] their entire concept of economics." Although LCUL was committed to eradicating institutionalized poverty in New Orleans and Louisiana, it conflated economic and racial justice with consumer protections. Ultimately it was the individual's responsibility to climb out of financial dependency by becoming a better citizen consumer.[89]

Indeed, civil rights activists keenly felt the limits of War on Poverty's credit union initiatives. Traditionally, Godfrey-Smith recalls, "in spite of the segregation of the external world, within . . . [individual community] credit unions, there was some integration."[90] Further, because all members had the same account policies and voting privileges, African Americans could be elected to otherwise majority white credit union boards. Yet even as African Americans assumed credit union leadership, they were isolated and misunderstood within a white male-dominated movement. In 1970, tensions flared between smaller black credit unions and the National Credit Union Administration (NCUA) when the national regulating body attempted to close nearly a quarter of registered credit unions. Many Community Action Program-, OEO-, and NAACP-funded black credit unions buckled under competition from other financial institutions and NCUA's strict regulatory environment. Often serving low-income and disadvantaged members, they lacked critical resources, and regulators advocated closure, ignoring the racial dimensions of their insolvency. For black credit union members, then, the War on Poverty offered only a tenuous entry into economic solvency and community self-governance.

Despite officials' often condescending and racialized characterization of the poor, Hermes still believed credit unions offered black Louisianan important avenues for economic and political power as directors of OEO-sponsored cooperative financial institutions.[91] For their part, civil rights organizers used credit unions as tools to engender community self-sufficiency, autonomy, and individual political empowerment. Many Community Action Programs across Louisiana, credit unions, and civic organizations prepared community leaders for formal political action. In 1971, Ninth Ward community organizer Mrs. George Ethel Warren ran for state representative, contending that her "background and participation in varied activities in the community" best qualified her to represent the Lower Ninth Ward. A board member of TCA and the TCA-administered Ninth Ward Federal Credit Union, Warren was also active in black civic, voting registration, and educational organizations serving the Ninth Ward, New Orleans, and Orleans Parish. Her community organizing experience made Warren "certain I know the problems and have some of the solutions" to pervasive economic and political disparity in the neighborhood.[92]Activists like Warren and Hermes envisioned black-run credit unions as part of a wider civil rights agenda to improve neighborhood infrastructure and municipal services.

A Multiracial Freret Redevelopment Initiative

By the 1970s, Freret's growing black population and attendant rise in black-owned businesses forced the neighborhood's segregated civic organizations to finally cater to and admit African Americans as members. Freret community organizations like the FBMA Credit Union became outlets for biracial cooperation for the first time since the CCU closed in 1951. In 1971, long-time black resident August Weber stemmed declining business by opening a successful garden store in an abandoned Church's Chicken restaurant along Freret Street. To attract middle-class customers to the neighborhood, Weber cultivated personal relationships with patrons: "Being nice to people, picking up the package for the little old lady. . . . Satisfy the customers . . . and they'll come back." His commitment to neighborhood revival led to his election as co-president of the FBMA's successor, the Freret Street Merchants Association (FSMA), in 1981.[93]

The neighborhood also profited from an influx of oil industry money in the 1970s and early '80s, which remapped the city's landscape. To counter racialized housing disparities and concentrated inequality, the federal Housing and Community Development Act of 1974's Section 8 Program provided low-income families vouchers to rent privately managed residences across the city and expanded affordable housing in the form of multifamily apartment complexes. Developers began "investing in buying vacant lots and buying run-down properties to renovate them," in order to expand tourism and commercial investment.[94] Young professionals streamed into the city's core, drawn to new finance, real estate, and insurance jobs and inexpensive housing. Historically black enclaves in the CBD, lower Garden District, and Old Algiers became sites of white preservation activism and, simultaneously, urban renewal. At the same time, community civic leaders partnered across blighted neighborhoods and between public and private sectors in order to coordinate local revitalization campaigns.[95]

Additionally, Freret's interracial cooperative organizations took advantage of a political sea change when Ernest "Dutch" Morial, a longtime civil rights advocate, became the city's first black mayor in 1978. Morial channeled a burgeoning oil economy and federal redevelopment grants into reviving the tourist industry, diversifying the city's economy, and revitalizing impoverished neighborhoods. Accordingly, the FSMA received funding through Morial's Neighborhood Commercial Revitalization Program to halt Freret's population loss among both blacks and whites.[96] Heartened, August Weber watched as "everybody [did] some facelifting." Three years later, civic organizations comprised of multiracial residents and storeowners received nearly $2 million in federal and city grants to further improve the neighborhood's appearance and infrastructure. Commercial facade improvement loans enabled the Barrecas to renovate Frank's Steak House, still a beloved community institution, as well as the aging FBMA Credit Union building. Other "rat-infested buildings" were fumigated and renovated. While Freret did not regain financial stability until after Hurricane Katrina, it provides a model for how multiracial credit unions and neighborhood associations can pursue a range of funding sources to prevent neighborhoods' physical decay and social dissolution.[97]

For over twenty years, Hermes and the New Orleans Consumers' Co-operative Union's body of immigrant and multiracial members sought homegrown and international cooperative inspiration to improve the Freret neighborhood while offering a blueprint for self-help among oppressed peoples across the globe. Further, Hermes's work as part of LCUL and alliances with Democratic state and federal officials not only provided thousands of working-class black and white Louisianans access to consumer credit but sped community reinvestment on a vast scale. However, Hermes's persistent struggle to transcend southern racial codes in building a broad cooperative movement illustrates the tenuousness of mid-twentieth century interracial activist projects. Profoundly aware of the precarious nature of building coalitions with white social justice organizations, the city's black cooperative advocates, erected separate but intersecting cooperative institutions inculcating racial solidarity and economic independence within black communities. The next chapter will delve into one such family's multigenerational cooperative career to understand how a unique blend of African Diasporic, European, and New Orleanian cooperative economics sustained the long civil rights movement while stimulating democratic economic development across the South.

HYBRID RACIAL
JUSTICE COOPERATIVES

Albert Dent and the Free Southern Theater: Intergenerational Civil Rights Cooperatives and the Fight Against Racialized Economic Inequality

On the eve of what they billed as the "first bi-racial 'Conference on Cooperative Education' ever to be held in Louisiana," white Southeastern Cooperative Educational Association (SCEA) directors Ed Yeomans and Lee Brooks fretted over "the matter of Negroes for dinner (not in the cannibalistic sense). It's all fine and dandy as far as our immediate group goes," but if "key people in labor, agriculture" come, "Mightn't some of them, upon finding themselves in a mixed dinner, suddenly go back to the old reaction and give us a terribly black eye as far as the rest of the meeting was concerned?"[1]

They needn't have worried. On April 14 and 15, 1941, 140 black and white southern students, social workers, "dirt farmers," and "workers for Uncle Sam" eagerly convened in Baton Rouge. Students from the historically black Southern University and a "terrible" Works Progress Administration soloist kicked off the conference with some light musical entertainment. Attendees listened to reports from a constellation of cooperatives before drafting action plans to assist labor, agricultural, and consumer cooperatives in their own states. As Brooks observed, "Co-operation come[s] by tasting, then biting into it, then reaching for more . . . , then digesting, and then by plowing and planting the neighborhood and community fields where study plus work will bring results." The integrated body showed "GREAT ENTHUSIASM" for "co-operative responsibility in terms of security for one's self and one's brother."[2]

Dillard University's African American president Albert W. Dent was one of these enthusiastic cooperative converts. Fresh from serving as administrator of black-serving Flint-Goodridge Hospital, Dent joined socialist firebrand Henry Hermes in championing Rochdale consumer cooperatives empowering ordinary Americans to seize control of political and economic institutions. After studying cooperatives in an integrated committee of CIO leaders, Highlander Folk School supporters, and leftist Catholic priests, Dent pledged to "actively promote purchasing cooperatives on [Dillard] campus and the teaching of cooperation, and [to] promote establishment of medical cooperatives in the New Orleans housing projects."[3] Dent's participation in the SCEA mirrored his activism within other integrated government, academic, and professional coalitions wielding middle-class respectability as a weapon to seize political and economic equality for blacks and poor whites.

All the same, the stakes of Rochdale cooperation were very different for black civil rights activists like Dent than for white southern liberals like Hermes. Bookended by the deprivation of the Great Depression and marginalized American and colonized people's mounting calls for community-led economic advancement after World War II, the Georgia-born Dent professionalized New Orleans cooperatives and integrated them within a regional and transnational social justice movement. Racial exclusion and everyday violence encouraged African Americans to continue to consider themselves as a collective, studying black history, celebrating black diasporic material culture, and debating racial destiny. A groundswell of black activists, from racial accommodationist Booker T. Washington to pan-Africanist and integrationist W. E. B. Du Bois and black nationalist Marcus Garvey, hailed cooperatives as an expedient means to construct a black "cooperative State" eliminating global capitalism grounded in racial exploitation. While cooperatives "promote[d] the commercial and financial development of the Negro," they were also mechanisms to win full inclusion within American civic society, and ultimately, "work out [their] own salvation" as a united people.[4]

To that end, in 1942, Dent was elected to the SCEA's board of directors, linking him to a web of black cooperative experts discarding older, informal Creole of color mutual aid traditions in favor of a professionalized, institutionalized cooperative network aiding vulnerable black southerners. His statewide Mother's Clubs, hospitalization insurance plan, and university consumer cooperatives indelibly altered black sociability patterns, the fabric of the city's racial geography, and an economic marketplace weighted against black citizens. Foreshadowing black liberationists' 1970s marriage of cooperative economics with political revolution, Dent and his Dillard colleagues believed Rochdale cooperatives "offer[ed] a more fruitful way of living in *this* world, until the requisite social changes materialize" to "renounc[e] capitalism."[5]

As director of the New Orleans-based Free Southern Theater Collective (FST), Tom Dent extended his father's regional cooperative movement while advancing his own vision for black political and economic empowerment. Between 1963 and 1985, the FST's cooperative ethos guided its "collective method of theater work," organizational structure, and philosophical framework.[6] It made significant contributions to the Black Arts Movement by modeling collective action through art, producing black-authored plays featuring local student-activists, and documenting the civil rights struggle for southern black audiences. The FST allied with southern cooperative leagues, theater collectives, War on Poverty agencies, and nonprofit funding sources to provide the state's poorest citizens low-cost, politicized community theater and poetry workshops that "stimulate[d] creative and reflective thought" and nurtured a black theatrical movement.[7]

At the same time, the collective translated its mission to combine "art and social awareness" that "address[ed] the problems within the Negro himself, and within the Negro community" into a pragmatic cooperative program rebuilding black economies in New Orleans's Lower Ninth Ward and Central City, as well as in southern rural communities.[8] Mirroring the coalition-building strategies Albert Dent had modeled a generation prior, the FST joined a network of moderate antipoverty and black liberationist cooperatives working at the block and regional level to stabilize and integrate vulnerable communities into Louisiana's civic society.

Yet the ways in which the integrated, anti-fascist New Deal cooperative movement profoundly shaped the FST's economic development strategies are largely unacknowledged by either scholars or civil rights activists. Such a disavowal partly stems from Albert Dent's later complicity in perpetuating a conservative 1940s and '50s university system whose gradualist integrationist worldview was fundamentally at odds with the FST's black liberationist politics, a retrenchment that obscures the radical potential both the black working class and intellectual elites saw in the city's Popular Front cooperatives. Additionally, the FST rejected Rochdale cooperatives complicit in repressive regimes' surveillance and containment of revolutionary movements both domestically and globally. Consequently, historians often discuss the FST within the narrow confines of the Black Arts Movement's cultural politics, rather than recognizing its cooperative predecessors or its twenty-year-long contribution to improving regional economies.[9] As part of the Third World Left, the FST embraced what historian Cynthia Young defines as a "distinct cultural and political formation . . . [that] melded the civil rights movement's focus on racial inequality, the Old Left's focus on class struggle and anti-colonialism, and the New Left's focus on grassroots, participatory democracy."[10] While retaining Albert Dent's vision of an international cooperative movement serving vulnerable black citizens, the FST created a new, hybridized racial justice cooperative model. Pan-African socialist rhetoric, African dia-

sporic community organizing practices, and Creole of color informal cooperative traditions, such as social aid and pleasure clubs and second lines, now
informed FST theatrical aesthetics, organizational structure, and economic
development plans.

The historical neglect of the Dent family's cooperative legacy obscures
how the intertwined trajectories of international cooperative and equal rights
movements created a synthetic form of black-led neighborhood and regional
economic development. Even scholars who recognize the role cooperatives
played in civil rights and economic justice initiatives have inadvertently
constructed southern cooperative history as fractured and rooted in rural
communities. Civil rights scholar Greta de Jong demonstrates that Popular
Front and War on Poverty cooperatives were crucial components of Louisianan racial equality projects, yet her studies focus on agricultural cooperatives largely unaware of their predecessors or urban contemporaries. Social
movement historian Adam Fairclough grapples with the stark political dis-
juncture between integrated civil rights and black liberationist mobilizing
in New Orleans. However, an extensive network of community cooperatives
simmered below institutionalized organizing that liaised between these two
ideological strands. Finally, while other social historians like Hasan Kwame
Jeffries reveal black mutual aid societies' role in transforming local, informal
protest into a "sustained, organized, public effort to secure freedom rights,"
they subsume cooperatives within larger civil rights movement history rather
than discuss cooperatives as separate entities with their own goals and philosophical grounding.[11]

Because on-the-ground cooperatives have continually provided black
residents essential medical care, work relief, food, and educational services,
they do not disappear after mass movements form or fall apart; they knit
together seemingly discordant social movements and provide a template for
coalescing grassroots movements driving ethical economic growth. Chart-
ing the evolution of black cooperative institutions from Albert Dent's New
Deal-inspired insurance cooperatives to Tom Dent's cultural liberationist
FST threads together interwar and postwar organizing and interweaves racial
justice movements in New Orleans, the South, and the world to provide a
genealogy for civil rights-inspired economic development more broadly.

Albert Dent: Assessing Black New Orleanian Needs in the Great Depression

Albert Walter Dent was born in 1904 in Atlanta to a day laborer and house-
cleaner. In an act that would shape his cooperative career, a prominent black

insurance businessman became Dent's mentor and, according to Tom Dent, instilled in the young man a "starkly realistic sense of political and economic power. [His] racial strategies were based on the realization that blacks had very little of either." Accordingly, after majoring in accounting at the historically black Morehouse College, Dent worked for his mentor's Atlanta Life Insurance Company in 1926.[12]

Historically, white life insurance companies refused to insure black clients because they were too "risky." A burgeoning black economy in the late nineteenth and early twentieth century spurred African American mutual aid organizations in Atlanta and across the country to reinvent themselves as formal financial institutions to better invest in black communities' stability and "racial posterity." Starting in 1905, W. E. B. Du Bois and the national Niagara Movement hailed the emerging "New Negro" as a community-focused identity whose adherents demanded equal suffrage, civil liberties, improved education, and economic advancement. Because they injected value into black bodies and disinvested neighborhoods, cooperative insurance companies steeped in Progressive idealism and commercial acumen expanded the black economy while advancing racial solidarity. By working within the cooperative insurance industry, Dent joined Du Bois and later, the NAACP, in campaigning to end widespread racial violence and discrimination.[13]

John Hope—Morehouse College's African American president, renowned civil rights activist, and later vice president of the SCEA—was deeply impressed with the impact Dent's insurance companies had on black Atlantans' fiscal well-being. After hiring him as university alumni secretary, Hope alerted Dent to an exciting job opportunity in New Orleans. In 1932, the Julius Rosenwald Fund, a Jewish, northern philanthropy with familial connections to New Orleans, and the General Education Board, a medical and educational charity, merged Flint-Goodridge Hospital, New Orleans University, and Straight University to create a new university and hospital complex for African Americans called Dillard University. Hope's colleague Reverend William W. Alexander, a white Commission on Interracial Cooperation member committed to exposing the travesties of racism, including lynching, mob justice, and the tenant system, was appointed as president.[14]

Throughout the Depression, Alexander would use his political connections as a federal Resettlement Administration staffer to integrate black professionals into a broad network of government antipoverty programs and cooperative institutions in the South. Hope saw Alexander as a useful node in a constellation of white liberal civil servants, religious figures, and commercial leaders whose influence within the New Deal administration African Americans could leverage as they lobbied for full citizenship rights and economic advancement. Hope introduced the twenty-seven-year-old Dent to Alexander, who promptly hired him to manage Dillard's finances and serve as superintendent of Flint-Goodridge Hospital, a teaching hospital for black doctors, while grooming him to eventually assume the university's presidency in 1941. Accepting the position, Dent moved his young family to New Orleans in 1932.[15]

The New Orleans that Dent encountered was riven by cultural, racial, and class animosities. As historian Kent Germany notes, Jim Crow laws and customs "helped to control labor, regulate behavior, and obscure poverty. . . . [Segregation] kept down costs of governing and of economic production."[16] Most starkly, segregation fundamentally remapped the city's settlement patterns. Late nineteenth century technological advancements in levee and water management systems drained swamp water out of low-lying areas, which encouraged development into previously uninhabitable land. Easy access to extended streetcar lines and racially exclusionary neighborhood deed covenants encouraged the white middle-class to skip over black neighborhoods to settle in the outer suburbs.[17]

Additionally, between the 1920s and the 1950s, federal housing authorities amplified urban development patterns imposing a new raced and classed logic onto the city's muddy racial landscape. Under the US Housing Act of 1937, for instance, the Housing Authority of New Orleans (HANO) began demolishing older, often racially heterogeneous neighborhoods, concentrating poor blacks and whites in segregated low-income housing complexes. Slum clearance in racially mixed neighborhoods displaced up to half of the black population now excluded from the areas' newly erected white housing complexes. Most white housing projects were located on high ground close to the affluent "front-of-town" along the Mississippi River, while black projects were situated in lower elevations in the impoverished "back-of-town." Because HANO did not compensate former inhabitants or equitably replenish housing stock, it considerably hindered African Americans' ability to locate affordable housing.[18]

Increasing racial isolation cloaked uncomfortable realities. For instance, African Americans accounted for half of the city's unemployed, while only comprising a third of the city's population. Racialized poverty also led to disproportionate rates of tuberculosis, syphilis, and maternal and infant mortality among black Louisianans. At the same time, medical facilities languished in the segregated South. Out of Flint-Goodridge's staff of thirty-five licensed black doctors, only ten had completed a medical internship. Consequently, southern African Americans patronized black doctors only for minor ailments, assuming white physicians possessed superior skills and resources.

White-run hospitals reinforced this belief by refusing to hire black doctors as part of their regular staff. In their absence, inexpensive midwives lacking knowledge of basic sanitation or sterilization performed 90 percent of black women's deliveries in rural Louisiana and 22 percent in New Orleans. Segregated New Deal welfare programs targeting these issues were inefficient and woefully inadequate.[19]

With fewer opportunities to socialize, efforts to build black and integrated civil rights institutions that dismantled racialized inequities lagged behind those in other states. Small, daily acts of individual resistance were common, such as "remov[ing] the barriers [white officials] would put up without anybody knowing about it," as one Seventh Ward resident remembers, or ripping up "signs on the bus saying 'colored to the rear of the bus.'"[20] Communists, socialists, and labor leaders also organized blacks and whites. Yet historians argue that formal racial justice organizations struggled to substantively change New Orleans's racial dynamics because blacks lacked political and economic clout, while white liberals' small numbers and social ostracism made them reluctant to aggressively oppose Jim Crow laws. Consequently, white liberals often left the South or adopted gradualist integration strategies for expediency.[21]

At the same time, cultural divisions within black communities delayed mass movement mobilization. Taking root in city centers with large, marginalized black populations, between 1919 and the late 1920s, Marcus Garvey's pan-Africanist Universal Negro Improvement Association (UNIA) had mobilized working-class New Orleanians to start collective enterprises, seize political influence, and practice self-love as they raised money to create a separate black nation in Africa. New Orleanians saw the Jamaican benevolent society's expedient, community-driven solutions to residents' most urgent needs as an extension of their own Caribbean-inflected mutual aid traditions, likening the UNIA to "our church, our clubhouse, our theatre, our fraternal order, and our school." Despite considerable police intimidation, the city chapter opened soup kitchens and homeless shelters, while also training young men in industrial education and women in domestic science and hygiene. *En masse*, ordinary New Orleanians uprooted socioeconomic discrimination at home and rejected Western imperialism and colonialism abroad. However, as the Depression shuttered UNIA-supported churches, banks, and insurance companies, the movement splintered, leaving an institutional void mainstream civil rights organizations struggled to fill.[22]

While blurring by the 1930s, a stratified black social structure still separated middle-class Catholic Creoles of color from working-class black Protestants. The city's poorly funded black Creole-led NAACP chapter, battling to coordinate legal challenges to *Plessy v. Ferguson* without a strong statewide associational network, discovered its elitist reputation blocked broader public support. Despite rising numbers of working-class officers, the NAACP chapter's clerical leaders perpetuated a class-based hierarchy that hindered black voter registration campaigns from becoming fully grassroots efforts.[23]

Assessing black Louisianans' precarious status in 1932, Dent decided that his goals for Flint-Goodridge Hospital were threefold: to serve as a postgraduate school of medicine for regional black doctors, provide black Louisianans low-cost preventative and diagnostic healthcare, and train impoverished New Orleanian youths for steady employment. Conceding that New Orleans hospitals refused to hire black doctors but employed low-paid black orderlies and nursemaids, he partnered with New Deal agencies to place disadvantaged black youths in these positions. At the same time, however, Dent raised southern black doctors' reputations by establishing residencies and organizing a free two-week summer training course that, by 1939, had graduated one-third of Louisiana's black doctors and one-fifth of those from six southern states. To treat poverty-related ailments such as syphilis, tuberculosis, infant and maternal mortality, diphtheria, and diabetes, he hired Dillard-trained midwives and nurses to staff seven mobile outpatient clinics administering to parishes without black doctors. Dent also slashed admittance costs and provided doctors, medicines, and hospitalization for a week to encourage rural mothers to deliver their babies at Flint-Goodridge. By 1939, Dent boasted, "More white women than Negro women in New Orleans now employ [untrained] midwives," and births increased by 400 percent at the hospital. Further, the American Medical Association approved Flint-Goodridge to provide medical internships, and the hospital was admitted to the Fully Approved List of the American College of Surgeons, the highest rating for American hospitals.[24]

Dent's politically expedient partnerships established pockets of interracial sociability and exchange that subverted Jim Crow's totalizing effects on the city's racial landscape. For instance, he temporarily installed white, often Jewish, Tulane and Louisiana State University faculty as department medical consultants. Operating as important brokers between white medical institutions and Flint-Goodridge, they served as *de facto* department heads until Dent could promote black doctors who had completed internships. In a city disinclined to participate in meaningful interracial cooperation, Dent became, according to Dillard trustee Fred Brownlee, a "past-master in the art of applying the methods of the sun. Some would storm the walls of segregation; Mr. Dent would melt them down."[25] Yet for all his accomplishments, Dent, like other southern hospital administrators, grappled with conforming to Jim Crow dictates while creatively and steadily eroding them.[26]

In response, by 1932, Dent began experimenting with black-run medical cooperatives to ensure Flint-Goodridge Hospital's services remained geographically and financially accessible to low-income Louisianans while also generating community development across the state. As a member of the rising "New Negro" middle-class, Dent believed that the "modern health educator" and other black professionals should attend to poor African Americans' moral and physical health while training them to "work out their own solutions to their health problems."[27] To that end, Dent and his wife, Ernestine Jessie Covington, started cooperative Mothers' Clubs throughout the state to improve Louisiana's abysmal prenatal care for black women. A Julius Rosenwald Fund-sponsored social worker taught women basic prenatal care and advised them to avoid midwives in favor of Flint-Goodridge hospital births.[28]

Institutionalized since the late 1890s, in large part due to civil rights activist Mary Church Terrell's efforts to uplift "the lowly, the illiterate, and even the vicious to whom we are bound by the ties of race and sex," southern Mothers' Clubs improved housekeeping and public hygiene while promoting active participation among "the masses of our women."[29] Ultimately, self-help cooperatives reflected activists' broader concern that poor physical health threatened black racial survival. Just as important as the NAACP's legal challenges to segregation, black women's healthy sexuality and reproductive powers would direct African Americans' collective destiny.[30]

Casting Off a New Orleans Model of Mutual Aid

Ironically, establishing northern-funded and expert-directed cooperative Mothers' Clubs challenged New Orleans's community of benevolent associations that had been committed to rooting out the brutalizing effects of racialized poverty since the nineteenth century. Without a coordinated, well-funded mainstream civil rights movement, Depression-era mutual aid associations helped black New Orleanians circumvent *de jure* segregation and their continued exclusion from white-dominated commercial institutions. They subsidized members' education, groceries, rent, medical bills, and funeral services despite maintaining a neighborhood-based and largely Catholic Creole of color resource network disconnected from the regional web of white liberal New Dealers and black middle-class professionals Dent cultivated.[31]

In Tremé, for instance, cooperatives and other mutualistic organizations lined North Claiborne Avenue, a hub for the "vast amount of black businesses that catered to us and that we patronized" to avoid Canal Street's discriminatory stores.[32] Just as Louis Mathieu had done in 1897, Juvenile Co-operators

funeral director and embalmer Emile Labat orchestrated respectful, affordable funerals for Tremé residents because white providers refused to do so.
For $50, clients received "one white or black coffin, neatly trimmed, one auto-
mobile hearse, 2 limousines, crepe, candles, veil for face, [and] recording of
death certificate with the Board of Health." Embalmers and undertakers also
associated as a buffer against workplace abuse and to exchange medical information to remain current on the "developments and technique[s] . . . for the
proper embalming of cadavers." Believing that "education was the religion of
racial advancement after Emancipation," they opened the only embalming
school for black practitioners.[33] Similarly, city cooperatives funded Catholic
institutions educating black neighborhood children otherwise without access
to public schools.[34] These cultural, religious, and political mutual associations
successfully constructed self-contained, democratic economic ecosystems.

On a broader scale, representing 300 organizations with 20,000 rank-and-
file members, mutual aid associations connected ordinary citizens to the city's
civil rights movement. Even as the mainstream Catholic Church denounced
priests and laypeople's focus on black survival politics and cooperative activity as a distraction from their religious duties, for black Louisianans, spiritual
and social planes were inextricable.[35] Black Catholic cooperative members
patronized affiliated enterprises in a show of racial solidarity and uplift. In
1933, Dr. Ernest Cherrie, a general practitioner, was only able to retain his
contract with the Seventh Ward-based Juvenile Co-operators after refuting
charges he had hired white contractors to build his home, asserting he was a
"race man" who only employed "men of color" in personal and business deal-
ings.[36] Further, in addition to sustaining a cooperative economy, insurance
directors, undertakers, and surgeons were key civil rights leaders. Funeral car
drivers organized themselves and recruited embalmers into labor unions and
mutual aid associations, while also spurring the local NAACP's rebirth in the
1930s and '40s.[37]

Even more striking, benevolent associations ensured NAACP's integrationist legal challenges concretely benefitted black New Orleanians. Along
with eighteen other Creoles of color, prominent Roman Catholic fraternal
member and civil rights attorney Alexander Pierre Tureaud formed the New
Orleans Federation of Civic Leagues in 1929, an NAACP-affiliated voluntary association that united black and white city trade unions and community organizations dedicated to helping black New Orleanians "exercise their
prerogatives as citizens."[38] League men and women encouraged interracial
dialogue and cooperation as they convicted police officers for beating and
murdering black citizens; fought racist rezoning laws; opened playgrounds
and libraries; improved educational access by expanding curricula to include

black history and renovating deteriorating schools; and even pressured government officials into hiring more black employees rather than firing them during the Depression.

Finally, Creole of color mutual aid organizations provided the physical space in which racial justice activists convened to contest Jim Crow. Claiming their essential Americanness, mutual associations helped birth a politicized black public sphere whose discursive arena gave civil rights activists room to debate and enact African Americans' collective future.[39] For instance, the Knights of Peter Claver Building, home to a large Catholic black fraternal and service organization and itself once a cooperatively run hospital, leased office space to black enterprises as well as local and national civil rights activists.[40] Using the building as his base, Knights of Claver director Tureaud collaborated with national NAACP Legal Defense and Education Fund attorney Thurgood Marshall and his staff during the Orleans Parish school desegregation battles in the 1940s and '60s. For fifty years, Tureaud worked out of the Claver building, preparing legal suits that would eventually secure national equal voting rights and integrate schools and universities, public transportation, and public buildings.[41]

Yet while Creole of color benevolent associations were a magnet for black cooperation, Tremé's distinct cultural milieu and social justice organizing strategies left Dent cold. In fact, Dent's cultural aloofness became a sticking point for some Catholic Creoles, who, Dillard University trustees observed in 1940, "for the most part have not accepted him, feeling that he is an aristocrat."[42] Part of his disregard for New Orleanian mutual aid stemmed from class bias: Dent and his black professional contemporaries reviled social aid and pleasure clubs' jazz funerals and Mardi Gras parades as "grotesque" expressions of "lower-class hedonism." Even his friend A. P. Tureaud, a lifelong fraternal member, sneered that "parading and having men and women in the streets carrying on these body gyrations" was "not a good image of middle-class life." When combined with voodoo and spiritualist practices, street-level working-class social formation was symptomatic of the "credulity and faith of the ignorant."[43]

Institutionalizing and Internationalizing New Orleans Cooperatives

Instead, along with a growing number of black middle-class intellectuals and activists, Dent hailed the international Rochdale consumer cooperative movement as the ideal means to cultivate a self-reliant black populace capable of overturning legal and cultural barriers to racial integration, quality healthcare, and equitable economic opportunity. In tandem with social justice-oriented education and direct action, economic cooperation "develops attitudes in people, and . . . [the] impulse to do something about our attitudes."[44] Similarly, black teachers in the communistic Louisiana Farmers' Union believed cooperation would not only improve rural Louisianan economies, but instigate greater awareness of and pride in black accomplishments. Likewise, Dillard scholars proclaimed Rochdale cooperatives would "school" black consumers in egalitarian "co-operation and the realities of the social struggle."[45]

Looking specifically to democratize southern economies, Dent and his New Orleans colleagues closely followed the progress of black Rochdale cooperatives around the country. NAACP field secretary Ella Baker and Young Negroes' Co-operative League (YNCL) head George Schuyler created a host of national cooperative enterprises, including in New Orleans. Between 1930 and 1934, YNCL consumer cooperatives bought wholesale produce from white distributors to provision black consumers with low-cost food. New Orleanians also admired SCEA director Jacob Reddix's collaborations with Finnish Rochdale cooperatives in Gary, Indiana. In the Depression, he opened the Consumers' Cooperative Trading Company, which operated grocery stores, a gas station, and a credit union to employ black residents thrown out of work by steel mill closings. Operating alongside the NAACP's national "Don't Buy Where You Can't Work" campaigns against racial discrimination in stores, black cooperatives circumvented exploitative retail companies and circulated profits in their communities.[46]

Dent focused his cooperative mission on professionalizing New Orleans's informal system of medical and financial health services. To do so, he latched onto a burgeoning network of black middle-class fraternal organizations, churches, academics, and businesses he believed most capable of solving racialized political and economic disparity, effectively reorienting the city's cooperative economy away from Tremé to Dillard University, and outwards across rural Louisiana and the South. In 1932, Dent received a $4,500 Rosenwald Fund grant to initiate a "Penny-a-Day" cooperative hospital insurance plan, competing with established Creole benevolent associations. Modeled on Dallas hospital insurance and Atlanta life insurance companies, the cooperative sought to instill in poor African Americans the middle-class values of comportment and thrift, believing strict moral codes would ensure fiscal responsibility and eradicate poverty.[47] While such proscriptions often constricted black cultural expression, they were designed to liberate African Americans from their history as enslaved commodities.

The Flint-Goodridge medical insurance cooperative recruited impoverished New Orleanians as well as black middle-class and professional clients who formed the backbone of the city's civil rights movement: public school teachers, Pullman car porters, mail carriers, department store workers, hotel employees, nurses, church members, and medical society members. Paying a $7.50 to $9 annual fee, members could be admitted to any New Orleans hospital and received free care for three weeks of hospital care per year. The most destitute only paid $3.65 a year for full Flint-Goodridge services, including board, nursing care, interns, operating rooms, X-ray, routine medicines, and lab work. Dent used cooperative profits to reopen Dillard's nursing school and circulate graduates among underserved parishes to reach rural subscribers without access to black doctors. By 1943, when the cooperative was absorbed into the Hospital Service Association of New Orleans's comprehensive hospitalization insurance plan covering the entire city, over 5,000 patients had opted to use Dent's insurance cooperative.[48]

Finally, in conversation with African Americans' Depression-era campaign to build a national system of black-run cooperative enterprises "lift[ing] the burden of economic exploitation from their backs," Dent established resident-managed insurance cooperatives in public housing campuses in New Orleans and Atlanta.[49] Dent hailed federal slum clearance and public housing construction as improvements over decaying, disinvested black neighborhoods that endangered resident health and safety, an attitude shared by black social agencies and civil rights organizations pressuring federal officials to staff public housing complexes with black professionals and residents.[50]

After declining a position managing a Public Works Administration housing complex for black Atlantans in 1936, Dent proposed instead that its Atlanta University administrators institute his "Penny-a-Day" model. The public housing units would provide residents one day of free hospitalization and other essential medical services per month for a small fee, rather than forcing black tenants to visit largely inaccessible, segregated hospitals. Pulling from his experience with Flint-Goodridge's white medical advisors, Dent recommended that an integrated advisory committee of racial progressives hire a "few of the best qualified Negro physicians with some white physicians, probably teachers at Emory" to staff the complex.[51]

Dent's cooperatives helped establish public housing as an unlikely political lightning rod for working-class African Americans. First, by successfully negotiating with white power brokers to integrate the public housing administration, Dent multiplied sites of interracial exchange and cooperation. Second, joining New Orleanian and southern insurance cooperatives enabled black residents to secure their health, protect their finances, and embrace mutual aid and collective action.[52] By training members in formal resistance tactics, Depression-era public housing cooperatives foreshadowed the self-directed, oppositional economies black liberationist collectives like the FST would later foment at these sites.

After Dent became the president of Dillard University in 1941, he dedicated himself even more forcefully to molding a community-driven, regional cooperative economy that, in concert a global cooperative movement, would grant black businesses and consumers collective bargaining power and "serve as an organizing force in Negro life."[53] Doing so necessitated creating new modes of sociability that further shifted black economic development away from informal, neighborhood-specific benevolent associations to educational institutions enmeshed in multiracial professional networks across the South, nation, and world. Accordingly, in 1941, Dent joined the SCEA, whose roots in the Nova Scotian Catholic Antigonish movement had also inspired Henry Hermes to consider how having "a stake in the control over their economic life" would prevent southerners "from following the pied pipers of totalitarianism when they sweep across America." In concert with hundreds of black and white spiritual leaders, radical labor unionizers, socialists, New Deal agents, and social workers, Dent studied "people and conditions . . . that corresponded to our southern scene—fishermen, farmers, miners, and others who needed enlightenment in order to help themselves in a democratic way." Ultimately Dillard University would operate campus purchasing cooperatives and medical cooperatives within public housing projects and incorporated cooperative discussions into university curricula.[54]

However, like Dent, the SCEA's middle-class, often non-southern, organizers pronounced the "South . . . almost untouched by the growing Cooperative Movement[;] it lacks knowledge of its meaning, it lacks any coordination of effort among its few scattered Co-ops," a misapprehension that Dent did not correct. Asking "[h]ow can key people in churches, schools, community clubs, industrial and agricultural groups be reached, be interested, and become active as leavening influences," Dent and his SCEA compatriots reduced the decentralized mutual associations that had been the mainstays of working-class black life to recruiting pools for the "real" work Rochdale cooperatives would perform. Dent's participation in the SCEA became a simultaneous act of community assertion and erasure.[55]

Nonetheless, while his son would later spurn his politics as conservative and classist, the elder Dent joined radical Dillard faculty and staff in hailing the international Rochdale cooperative movement as a precursor to a new, cosmopolitan, and fundamentally socialistic world order grounded in black self-reliance and community uplift, as well as anti-capitalistic and anti-imperialist critique. Implicitly referencing Garvey, anthropologist and pan-Africanist John Gibbs St. Clair Drake conceded that mutual aid associations eased blacks' dependency on federal welfare and white businesses, but they were hobbled by personality-based leadership and "social disorganization." Instead, modern, professionalized cooperative institutions bound by clear, democratic principles expanded employment opportunities among the black working class. Because they neither "veil[ed] the brutalities of capitalism" nor tolerated "racial narrowness," formalized black cooperatives could foster interracial alliances resisting the "tribulations of a world-wide depression and Fascist and Communist co-ordinators."[56]

To that end, under Dent's leadership, Dillard University joined an international student movement to establish Rochdale cooperatives united in "brotherhood economics": by redistributing capital, the network would eliminate global capitalism's "selfish profiteering motives" and violent "class struggle."[57] Dent himself visited the Mississippi-based Delta Cooperative Farm to speak on health and community issues, and he also studied how the Christian socialist commune economically stabilized poor sharecroppers and promoted interracial equality. In conversation with ethicists around the world, founder Sherwood Eddy, a white pacifist and missionary, developed community service projects meant to shift society away from individualistic capitalism incompatible with Christianity.[58] Similarly, Dillard students eagerly participated in an integrated lecture in which Tokyo-based labor organizer, pacifist, and anti-fascist preacher Toyohiko Kagawa asserted that Christian socialism and cooperative development were "inseparable doctrines" propelling worldwide humanitarianism.[59]

Ultimately, Dent's faith in the transformative power of anti-imperialist cooperative economics reverberated throughout Dillard and Louisiana's cooperative movement for generations. The international Rochdale consumer cooperative movement continued to appeal to black radicals burned by the UNIA's failure to end diasporic Africans' continued political and economic exploitation. Cooperatives would form the cornerstone of the pan-Africanist UNIA-offshoot Nation of Islam's community economic development plan.[60] As Dillard graduate and music recording cooperative founder Harold Battiste recalls, "I'd been listening to speeches from . . . Elijah Muhammad, messages that often spoke to the need for our people to create wealth through ownership. It seemed that every ethnic group was identified with a product or service that they owned and controlled, and it seemed that the product generally attributed to us was music: jazz, blues, R&B, gospel."[61] On a larger scale, Dillard's coterie of communists theorized black New Orleanians would only achieve "complete liberation" by identifying their oppression as part of "the problems of the underprivileged peoples of the world" and joining "the organized efforts of the masses," whether they were from New Orleans,

Puerto Rico, or communist Poland. Eventually, anti-imperialist mass movements working in "larger and larger cooperating groups" would achieve "job
security, prosperity," and "enduring peace" for all.[62]

Finally, Father Albert McKnight, a black Catholic priest who would work
closely with the FST, translated Antigonish and black nationalist principles
into practice: the Rochdale model inspired him to "destroy racism and
humanize the face of capitalism by developing cooperatives with a human-
istic philosophy" across Louisiana from the 1960s to the '80s. United in their
understanding that "people are more important than money," politicized
insurance companies, credit unions, cooperative bus services, grocery stores,
and cooperative farms promulgated black liberationist ideology as they sold
low-cost, high quality goods and services to marginalized southern blacks.[63]
Tom Dent would join this new generation of cooperatives formalizing and
monetizing black production to foster neighborhood-responsive, regional
cooperative economies.

Thomas Dent and the Legacy of New Orleans on the Free Southern Theater

For the first thirty years of his life, Tom Dent had no intention of remaining
bound to New Orleans or its aesthetic traditions informed by racial hardship.
African Americans of Albert Dent's generation tried to help their children
"make the best of a restricted situation, and to overcome it via learning and
accommodation, not confrontation." Urging him to escape the segregated South
in search of better opportunities, his father's educational and professional contacts with national civil rights institutions not only provided Tom his earliest
jobs but later became critical avenues for establishing the FST's credibility on
a national scale. Albert arranged for Tom to work as a reporter for Houston's
Informer, a black weekly newspaper. There, he "obtained a much more realistic
sense of what life in the segregated world was like," as well as how the country's legacy of racial prejudice informed current events. Like his father, Dent
attended Atlanta's Morehouse College in the early 1950s before joining the navy.
Moving to New York City in 1959 to work as a Harlem newspaper reporter, his
father's friendship with Thurgood Marshall also secured Dent's position as press
attaché for the NAACP Legal Defense Fund between 1961 and 1963.[64]

However, it was within New York's black creative circles that Dent began
to meld his father's cooperative strategies and African diasporic cooperative
traditions into a lifelong career in creative arts and community development.
In 1962, he cofounded the writing workshop and magazine *Society of Umbra*,
with prominent black authors like Ishmael Reed and Amiri Bakara (LeRoi

Jones). Dent replicated the group's egalitarian artistic process and organizational structure in cooperative ventures that blended performance and politics.[65] Nor was he alone in pairing cooperative organization with creative production. Radical collectives like New York's Living Theater wrote plays together and lived communally to model an anarchist and pacifist philosophy at odds with hierarchical power structures. Similarly, the San Francisco Mime Troupe was a guerilla theater collective that practiced non-hierarchical social relationships and formed cooperative partnerships with like-minded organizations. Sacramento's El Teatro Campesino fervently believed that creative arts collectives would confront repressive political and economic institutions dominating marginalized populations.[66]

Yet meeting the integrated FST while volunteering in Mississippi's civil rights campaigns fully captured Dent's interest in fusing civil rights activism, working-class resistance tactics, and black theater. He relocated to New Orleans to join the collective in 1965. As the FST's chairman until 1967, its artistic director from 1966 to 1970, and an influential staff member until his departure in 1971, Dent fostered "a creatively nurturing environment for black youths" across the South. Just as his father synthesized New Orleans and southern mutual aid institutions, so did Dent and his colleagues transform the FST into a hybrid racial justice cooperative that embraced African diasporic, southern civil rights, and New Orleans-specific collective aesthetic production as a place-specific platform around which the global black working class could unite. The FST's relationship to Desire and Central City community organizations and the Episcopal Church's General Convention of Special Programs bridged multigenerational rural and urban black cooperative movements. By extension, this coalition forced the state to equitably integrate its constituents into the broader marketplace, spurring extensive regional community development.[67]

The FST's communitarian structure and egalitarian goals were directly informed by members' participation in the civil rights movement. In 1963, Student Nonviolent Coordinating Committee (SNCC) field directors Doris Derby, John O'Neal, and *Mississippi Free Press* reporter Gilbert Moses formed the collective out of Mississippi's Tougaloo College Drama Workshop and recruited "anyone who said 'We dig civil rights'" to act in its touring repertory group.[68] Early members like playwright Woodie King fashioned the collective after Detroit's Concept East Theater, a politically conscious project embracing African diasporic practices. The FST's permanent ensemble of eight to sixteen members practiced collective remediation, group writing sessions, and equitable distribution of roles. It selected actors for a repertory touring ensemble based on their commitment to cooperative principles and black civil rights.

However, it was 1964's Freedom Summer, and Mississippi's Freedom Schools in particular, that sharpened the FST's cooperative focus. Proposed by SNCC field secretary Charlie Cobb, Freedom Schools were alternative educational institutions that fostered black students' civic engagement and community activism. Presaging the quotidian setting of FST performances, classes were held in community spaces such as churches, homes, and parks.[69] One Lebanese American educator recalls students were "full of life, intelligent, and very creative" in a classroom in "a black church with a tin roof at the end of a dirt road." Most significantly, the volunteer-run schools rejected hierarchical instruction, instead promoting student-centered learning based on discussion, critical thinking, and leadership training. For young activists, movement-organized schools taught reciprocity and community belonging-ness: they "clearly illuminated that we had far more to learn from the poverty-stricken areas we were to be placed in than we would ever be able to give."[70]

Interested in wedding creative production with "the struggle of Black folk," Cobb championed the FST's political theatrics, and the collective became SNCC's cultural outlet. Freedom School staff used as the foundation for its curriculum FST's performance of white playwright Martin B. Duberman's 1963 documentary play *In White America*, a history of African Americans' fight for personhood, from slavery to desegregation battles. As John O'Neal recalls, "The whole curriculum of the Freedom School was built around the play, because the play was built around the struggle of African American peo-ple. . . . We'd read it and give a context to people who taught and organized the community that we were performing in."[71] Black and white FST actors reprised their experience as Freedom School volunteers. Touring Louisiana, Mississippi, Georgia, and Alabama, they lived among black families and per-formed to diverse audiences in untraditional theatrical spaces like stores, bars, churches, and schools. Black mutual aid networks sustained both the local civil rights movement and the FST. Shows drew SNCC and "CORE [Congress of Racial Equality] workers who have been in town, and others from neighboring towns," while the Deacons for Defense of Equality and Jus-tice, a militant black fraternal organization defending activists against white supremacist violence, "provide[d] a protective caravan of cars . . . when the company [left] for New Orleans."[72]

Training southern black residents to recognize and collectively resist their common exploitation required engaging audiences for whom theater and the "history of black people in America [were] absolutely foreign to their experience."[73] To that end, the collective merged egalitarian, participatory Popular Front theatrical genres and contemporary working-class musical and religious traditions, tying FST more firmly to Albert Dent's generation of cooperative activists. During the Depression, the city's communist-inspired Southern Negro Youth Congress hosted labor schools, registered voters, and organized a community theater to promote racial unity and grassroots political activism.[74] The New Orleans Group Theatre produced Lenox Antony's *Headlines in Review* as an anti-fascist Popular Front fundraiser with community members participating as actors and audience members, only for the FST to perform similar "living newspaper" productions thirty years later.[75] In a 1965 improvised documentary play about Bogalusa's civil rights demonstrations and subsequent racial violence, FST featured local high school students and demonstrators. Dent reported virtually "the entire Negro community" attended, "respond[ing] to the subtleties, humor, truth of every situation as it develops on the makeshift stage." Free-flowing post-performance conversations were just as important: audiences stayed behind to discuss with the FST "the determination of the Negro citizens . . . to fight for their rights, and to take action to insure their safety while protesting for their rights."[76]

Dent's 1968 play *Ritual Murder* also vividly represents the legacy of 1930s-era populism on the FST's fusion of national civil rights ideology and place-based cooperative action. Again, mining the Popular Front documentary genre, Dent fashioned the play as "an imaginative TV documentary" excavating two themes "unknown to the white world": the communal pleasures of black creativity and community belongingness, as well as structural racism and classism that drove violence in black neighborhoods.[77]

Speaking in rhythm to the strands of George Gershwin's 1934 song "Summertime," Ninth Ward characters deconstruct young black resident Joe Brown Jr.'s brutal stabbing of his friend, James Roberts. Gershwin, as part of the "Cultural Front," combined "philharmonic traditions and vernacular musics [to create] a musical renaissance in the United States," while imbuing his black musical simulacra with a politically radical consciousness, creating "music for use."[78] Fittingly, "Summertime" undergirds Dent's premise that systematic racial oppression drove the murder: "Something began to come loose in me, like my mind would float away from my body. . . . [M]y mind was trying to define me, to tell me who I was the way other people see me, only it couldn't because it didn't know where to begin." Further, Brown's homicidal act is "a form of group suicide." After years witnessing a grisly procession of black bodies "bleeding, blood seeping from the doors of the taxicabs . . . icepicks and knives," he theorizes, "When murder occurs for no apparent reason but happens all the time . . . it is ritual murder." Only militant grassroots action can overcome this self-defeating condition: "Friends kill each other all the time . . . unless you have an enemy you can both kill."[79] Drawing on cultural forms familiar to his father's generation of activists, Dent's *Ritual Murder* updated a Popular Front view that community-led protest and liberatory theater informed and inspired one another.[80]

Embedding black Baptist and Catholic cooperative elements into its plays, poetry, and music was another way the FST fostered politically conscious participation. Performance scholar Jan Cohen-Cruz argues that the civil rights movement's connection to the black church, central to southern black culture, "provided the Free Southern Theater with a particular moral and spiritual orientation" that inspired creative output while easily connecting to neighborhood community members.[81] New Orleans actor Karen Kaia Livers similarly describes communal religious ritual's leveling effect: "In community theater, the invisible wall [between performers and audience] was broken a long time ago. It excites us if somebody yells something from the audience.... [P]roductions are very much involved in pulling them up and bring them on stage."[82] As it drew on religious codes of conduct, the FST blurred the line between audience and performer to inspire civic engagement.

As it built a black theatrical community in line with Black Arts Movement objectives, cooperative principles became even more formally embedded within the FST's organizational structure, programming, and community partnerships. The movement adhered to a collectivist ideological framework, a flexible and idiosyncratic "conglomeration of local initiatives throughout the country that all worked from their own similar vision of Black Arts, while being influenced by the national movement."[83] For example, the FST performed nationally recognized plays such as Black Arts Movement founder Amiri Bakara's *Slave Ship* as well as original works inflected with political philosophy from the Nation of Islam, the black militant Revolutionary Action Movement, and Maulana Karenga's black nationalist US Organization. The FST was impressed by Karenga's *Nguzo Saba*, the Seven Principles of Kwanzaa, a "holistic value system" one practices daily to become spiritually whole. It formally incorporated collective work, unity, creativity, and cooperative economics into its political practice and revolutionary theater as it heightened local and national audiences' self-awareness as politicized, united black people.[84]

Cooperative Economics Spurs Ninth Ward Economic Redevelopment

Crucial to the FST's program of civil rights mobilization was urban economic development and community empowerment. In 1964, it moved to a disused New Orleans warehouse in the Lower Ninth Ward. While white FST member Murray Levy believed "gracious" residents "will give us a chance to earn our keep," the theater had a rocky start.[85] It suspended operations for five months as it scrambled for funding in the resource-poor neighborhood. Finally, in 1965 the FST set up headquarters in an abandoned Louisa Street supermarket near the Desire Housing Project, extending Albert Dent's vision of public housing as a channel for black economic autonomy and self-help.[86]

By operating in the Ninth Ward, the FST joined a high-stakes, citywide cooperative effort to buffer black New Orleanians against federally precipitated neighborhood disinvestment. In conjunction with proliferating life and health insurance plans that competed with mutual aid societies, federal slum clearance and infrastructure expansion rapidly dismantled cooperative sites that residents had traditionally relied upon as social safety nets.[87] Large-scale urban renewal projects were linked to a broader backlash against the civil rights movement; taking advantage of urban residents' lack of political clout, high-level transportation officials promoted public road and slum clearance projects as serving the social good, while decimating black communities across the country.[88]

For example, in 1956, the Department of Transportation and Bureau of Governmental Research and the New Orleans Central Area Committee proposed building a raised highway along the Mississippi River connecting the CBD to the outer suburbs. Officials argued that Interstate 10 would curb urban decay by demolishing pockets of inner-city black neighborhoods and promoting free-flowing transportation and commerce in and out of the city. Even though part of the highway would run along North Claiborne Avenue, bisecting and isolating the Sixth Ward, the city and developers began acquiring street property without consulting affected black Tremé citizens. Long-term construction closed off access to Claiborne's black-owned businesses, and residents were forced to shop at white Canal Street vendors after local businesses relocated or were shuttered for good.[89]

Worried that young, "world-class musicians" living in neighborhoods slotted for slum clearance would be displaced and, consequently, "might go unheard of among all the tasty flavors in the Gumbo," in 1961, prominent jazz musician and Nation of Islam adherent Harold Battiste opened two Tremé-based music cooperatives, All for One Records (AFO) and At Last Publishing. Like the FST, AFO's music was political: recording New Orleans luminaries like Barbara George and Prince Lala, Battiste also documented and popularized New Orleans second-line music, born of working-class neighborhood social aid clubs and collective jazz traditions. Preserving their oppositional sounds meant honoring the local, oppositional support networks that constituted "emotional ecosystems" binding residents to a shared space, place, and race.[90]

Battiste aimed to create a "conglomerate entertainment enterprise" that employed vulnerable residents while inspiring them to collectively achieve political liberation. Cooperative members waived payment for sessions but became co-owners of their recordings and received a percentage of the company's earnings. At Last Publishing also supervised recording sessions' musical arrangements, orchestrations, musicians, and studio set-up. Additionally, it acquired musical copyrights and composed piano scores and arrangements. The agency recorded performers' demos and circulated their material to other artists and publishers. Finally, like the FST, Battiste adhered to *Nguzo Saba*, professing that unity, self-determination, collective work, cooperative economics, purpose, creativity, and faith would improve the "economic state of . . . Black people in New Orleans."[91]

Nonetheless, Battiste's cooperatives could not stave off the economic devastation that neighborhood slum clearance generated. Between 1966 and 1968, city workers had uprooted 500 oak trees along Claiborne and 125 buildings had been demolished, displacing 170 residents and fifty businesses in the process. As former public housing resident Harvey Reed attests, as Tremé was "waiting for civil rights, [white officials] were cutting off communities for commerce." While national protest eventually led to the passage of the Federal Highway Act of 1968, which banned officials from evicting residents without providing replacement housing, their inability to divert the highway revealed to black New Orleanians the need for organized community action redressing systemic inequity.[92]

Into this combustive urban planning environment stepped the FST. One of the most dangerous and densely populated neighborhoods in New Orleans, rapid white flight and large-scale urban redevelopment projects displaced and concentrated 13,000 black Lower Ninth Ward residents in Desire's increasingly dilapidated housing. FST's Morris Levy labeled Desire "a forgotten ghetto," home to "thousands of imprisoned black people." Geographically isolated by railroads and canals, it lacked inadequate educational, occupational, and recreational opportunities. Flooding and structural damage from 1965's Hurricane Betsy accelerated the area's decline. The storm inflicted $1 billion in damages and eighty deaths on the low-lying, poorly drained Ninth Ward. Desire residents called on city administrators to let them plan and evaluate social services, and black mutual aid groups ranging from church groups, social aid and pleasure clubs, and medical and life insurance groups joined recovery efforts. Nonetheless, the housing project continued to suffer.[93]

Desire's young, black, and female residents experienced 1,000 percent higher jobless rates than did middle-class white suburbs like Lakeview. Additionally, juvenile delinquency rates in Desire were some of the highest in the city. In 1966, FST member Roscoe Orman described residents' "beauty in chains / Rumbling deep somewhere-between-the-stomach-and-the/brain," predicting that resident resentment over racialized poverty would ignite into violence. Four years later, the complex was caught in a shootout between police, Black Panthers, and Desire occupants.[94]

The FST's white and black members lobbied the city to reinvest in the Lower Ninth Ward before resident frustration became any "close[r] to exploding in the face of 'charming' New Orleans." Most notably, the collective exposed Desire's conditions to the national public in Look Up and Live, a 1966 CBS documentary about regional theaters. Its poetry program, Ghetto of Desire, excoriated the housing project as "dreamed up by a city planner at Auschwitz." While the show aired nationally, Mayor Victor Schiro, Police Chief Clarence Giarrusso, and HANO objected that Ghetto of Desire "engenders racial disharmony" and persuaded local media outlets to censor the documentary. Nonetheless, national positive reception cheered FST members, who began to use their productions to galvanize black audiences into demanding full participation in the city's economic life, while pressuring officials to rectify Desire's disinvestment.[95]

In the absence of satisfactory official response, the FST's free theater and cultural center created a politicized node of sociability that valorized black working-class cultural production as a driver of social upheaval. Believing that the "Afro-American has been divided for too long from his background and has been alienated from his great culture," the FST's cultural center strove to instill ethnic pride in public housing residents by educating them about the "art and science of the non-white races of the world."[96] Evening workshop attendees carving out time between school and work were exposed to local black luminaries like experimental psychedelic lightshow artists Warren Parker and Raymond DuVernay, Afrocentric fashion designer June Fields, and FST theater director Eluard Burt, best known for popularizing New Orleans's iteration of Afro-Cuban music and organizing the city's first African American arts festivals.[97]

Simultaneously, sustained resident participation enriched the collective: the neighborhood "brings ideas to [the theater], argues with it, and needs it." Accordingly, the FST performed original plays and hosted forums, poetry, song, improv, and film nights whose spontaneous after-show "bull sessions" included neighborhood residents. An outgrowth of the discussions was director John O'Neal's "story circle," in which residents and FST members exchanged creative ideas and collaborated on side projects.[98] Finally, workshops in acting, writing, and stagecraft were meant to cultivate community actors and playwrights and incorporate them into the FST.

Viewing the theater as a viable employer for local residents, FST productions increasingly drew on familiar New Orleanians "call-and-response" participatory aesthetics to turn black audiences into civic-minded performers. Tulane University drama professor Richard Schechner, the group's white producing director until 1967, observed that civil rights demonstrators channeled Mardi Gras street performance into protests over race riots and school board desegregation battles: collective, carnivalesque play transformed passive spectators into agents of democratic governance.[99] Symbolizing fierce neighborhood loyalty, fraternal organizations' second line parades were "the most democratic activity happening in America today." The low barrier between performer and audience encouraged improvisation and collective direct action. As historian George Lipsitz argues, black mutualistic traditions turn "segregation into congregation" by "fashioning ferocious attachments to place."[100] Schechner theorized that experimental drama involving audiences could also be personally liberating, inspiring politicized, participatory performances at Tulane and the FST.

Consequently, a growing body of local FST black writers and artists pushed the collective to more systematically wed traditional social aid and pleasure club resistance tactics to their Black Arts Movement-informed productions. Between 1965 and 1967, Tom Dent, Gilbert Moses, John O'Neal, and other, mostly New Orleanian members increasingly rejected middle-class production aesthetics, northern philanthropic organizations, and a moderate civil rights movement too focused on federal intervention and legislation. Why should the FST perform white-authored plays like *Waiting for Godot* and *In White America* to audiences unfamiliar with professional theatrical conventions and who needed few reminders of what it was like to be black? Moses proclaimed, the FST should be "a theater for the Black people established by Black people—and not a white liberal idea established for the good of the Black people." Consistent with SNCC's decision to bar white members to "determine our own destiny," in 1968, the FST ousted its white staffers and formally established itself as a community-based incubator for black creative writers and performers in New Orleans and the South.[101]

The FST's New Orleans-themed productions firmly reflected its new identity as a hybridized racial justice cooperative. For example, Ninth Ward resident Kalamu ya Salaam's poetry is infused with the improvisational and egalitarian imagery of brass bands and second line dancing. In 1969's "Leader," he questions the legitimacy of middle-class African American civil rights leaders who reject participatory working-class culture. Ya Salaam "saw a Negro at a dance / last nite who called himself / my leader & that nigger / couldn't dance to save his life / so how he gon lead me!"[102] Similarly, a 1967 touring poetry show featured Dent's manifesto poem, "Uncle Tom's Secondline Funeral," in which second line parades celebrate the death of black intellectual, spiritual, and political "race traitors" hindering the civil rights movement.[103] Dent asserts, "for the black public official who believes we have made enough progress . . . we bequeath lifted hats, three deep bows, a long, long memorial service replete with history of Harriet Tubman through Malcolm X." We "lay him to rest—then jump with jubilation that he is dead and gone." Communal performance, or the "tidal wave of us dancing in the street with brass bands" that ya Salaam envisions in "All in the Street" (1968) will lead to revolution: "the cities are next."[104] By integrating the second line into FST works, New Orleans performers transformed a neighborhood-based tool of defiance into a protest tool for all black southerners.

In addition to serving as an employer of local talent, by the late 1960s, the FST had resurrected Albert Dent's campaign to overturn white supremacist economic and political structures by constructing a sprawling regional economy rooted in neighborhood-based cooperative institutions. While Henry Hermes was networking with the Office of Economy Opportunity (OEO) to establish low income credit unions across Louisiana, the FST collaborated with the Ninth Ward's independent and War on Poverty administration-funded community economic development organizations to create new job opportunities for residents, reverse the neighborhood's continued disinvestment, and open new political channels to black citizens at the city, state, and federal level. It joined a host of OEO-funded Lower Ninth Ward cooperatives organized to "meet the immediate and long-range problems of residents," from the Desire Area Community Council and Total Community Action's (TCA) neighborhood tutoring programs, to the Urban League cooperative tenants' union run out of Desire.[105] Additionally, as part of their economic empowerment program, the Black Panthers, a militant black nationalist organization, established cooperative social services such as free clinics, community centers, and breakfast programs in the public housing complex.[106]

In turn, Ninth Ward cooperative organizations supported FST programming: TCA's neighborhood council watched middle school graduates from its community theater workshop perform Ron Milner's *The Warning: A Theme for Linda*. Since the play's portrait of urban poverty, neglect, and abuse could describe "any black neighborhood in any city in the country," FST urged residents to consider mobilizing tactics.[107] As Ronnie Moore, Louisiana's CORE cofounder and veteran of Freedom Summer voter registration campaigns, explained, neighborhood cultural, economic, and political cooperatives provided "minority groups" invaluable "experience, not only in local government, but in the sophisticated techniques of weaving channels of state and national government, corporations, and foundations" to solve the "besetting problems of the urban and rural ghettos."[108]

Cadre Organizing in Central City

When the FST relocated to Dryades Street in Central City in 1969, it deepened its partnership with anti-poverty agency TCA, training low-income citizens to secure gainful employment and improve their community in the process. Central City is a sprawling neighborhood, bordered by the downtown CBD, the Mississippi River, and affluent, white, Uptown communities. During the 1950s and '60s, Central City's demographics rapidly changed as white flight and manufacturing companies' suburban exodus concentrated low-income blacks within the neighborhood. Integration throughout the city drew black businesses away from Dryades Street to more profitable districts, so that what once had been a bustling commercial thoroughfare was now a decaying district. In 1968, nearly 7,000 families lived in poverty, the greatest number out of six most impoverished neighborhoods of New Orleans. With homeless rates at 10 percent, Central City residents demanded better job opportunities and public housing.[109]

When Tom Dent was hired to be TCA's public relations director from 1970 to 1974, a mutual partnership supported the theater's community-oriented educational goals and the TCA's self-help initiatives, with Central City as a prime beneficiary. TCA established Central City as one of six "target areas" to receive OEO-funded out-patient clinics and job training, youth leadership, and tutoring programs.[110] In tandem with TCA's cooperative stores, buying clubs, credit unions, and producer cooperatives stabilizing the neighborhood, FST-offshoots received funding for workshops and self-published anthologies redressing the "limited commercial possibilities for new writers, even if extremely talented."[111] Finally, both organizations developed local leaders: while TCA resident councils organized letter writing campaigns, marches, boycotts, and citywide coalitions to pressure New Orleans officials to address civic concerns, the collective also received TCA grants to fill its library with national, black-published creative works inspiring young writers to "attack the provinciality of black New Orleans."[112]

Despite antipoverty agencies' commitment to incorporate ordinary residents into community planning and development initiatives, Dent increasingly believed War on Poverty organizations were focused on individual gains and lacked the political will to transform exploitative capitalist systems. By 1969, the collective's cultural liberationist ethos had alienated its white, New York-based philanthropic donors accustomed to funding "a craft and techniques program" so African Americans "won't go out and riot and generally make trouble." Dent rejected further movement co-optation and manipulation by "the white financial establishment" unwilling to "accept the critical and militant work the professional theater should be doing."[113]

Similarly, as outlined in the last chapter, black radicals flatly rejected the OEO's fundamentally conservative view that "the only solution for poor folk was to [establish] co-ops with competent management": individual and community direct action alone were not curatives for deeply institutionalized inequality. For instance, Ronnie Moore was an FST ally and black nationalist who worked with the OEO-sponsored Southern Cooperative Development Fund to build a statewide cooperative economy. He conceded that despite "developing leadership and interpersonal communications skills in . . . young Black leaders of today," federally subsidized housing, food, health care, day care, and job training cooperatives "have not solved all the myriad problems created by a century of neglect."[114] Lloyd Medley's poem "Black Capitalism" underscored FST's fears that merely integrating African Americans into mainstream economic institutions would lead to a kind of slavery: the voracious logic of capitalism "[makes] Blackness a purchasable / Commodity. Yet we get none of / The profit and we remain the commodity." For real political access, Dent believed black New Orleanians needed leaders who "answer primarily to the interests of the community—not the power structure."[115]

To that end, when Illinois-born John O'Neal assumed FST leadership in the early 1970s, he steered the FST away from integrationist coalition-building, applying pan-Africanist, Marxist political theory to the theater's organizational structure and economic development initiatives linking Central City to a regional cooperative economy. Although the FST reopened its membership to all ethnicities after reorganizing in 1973, O'Neal remained focused on black social and political issues. He concurred with cultural nationalists like Amiri Bakara, who argued that as colonized African nations struggled for independence, a Marxist critique of Western capital would dismantle systems of economic and political oppression for Africans and people of African descent. As SNCC argued, "the broad masses of black people react to American society in the same manner as colonial peoples react to the West in Africa, and Latin America, and had the same relationship—that of the colonized toward the colonizer." Similarly, O'Neal tasked the FST with undermining corporate capitalism driving global economic disparity, racialized political disempowerment, economic recessions, and imperialist wars.[116]

To the FST, the Rochdale consumer cooperatives that black New Deal and War on Poverty civil rights activists embraced had failed to build black self-determination and community economic autonomy. Worse, they were complicit in maintaining a racist global economic and political order. After studying Federal Farm Bureau cooperative farms in the American South, the postwar British Labour Party imposed Rochdale cooperatives in Uganda and other African colonies as a paternalist means of transitioning to self-rule.

Centering on thrift and moral uplift, the nonpolitical cooperatives streamlined coffee production and distribution for British markets. Authorities raided and imprisoned oppositional indigenous cooperatives boycotting processing plants and mobilizing for price controls. Uganda's independent government would incorporate indigenous cooperatives into its democratic structure and rural development plan in the 1950s and '60s. Inspired by similar global decolonization movements, black liberationists like O'Neal envisioned a new, diasporic cooperative model freed from the "tentacles of the white power complex."[117]

Now heading a "cultural organization whose artistic work is thoroughly and consciously political in all aspects," O'Neal reorganized the theater along a Marxist cadre structure, propounding it as a model for other radical black theater cooperatives to emulate. As outlined in its 1976 "Basic Program Guidelines," the collective first required members to democratically discuss and agree upon a statement of purpose. For example, in the FST's evaluation sessions, core and supporting staff defined the organization's mission and philosophy. Second, cooperative ideals guided FST theatrical workshops and productions. The FST's permanent ensemble followed a collective labor model; roles were equitably distributed among members, and actors were hired based on their specific "utility to the group." The collective selected actors for its repertory touring ensemble based on demonstrated commitment to black liberation and the FST's revolutionary goals, as well as their ability to work with the collective and abide by its principles. Third, the FST's remediation policies were democratic. While members addressed concerns about individual policies to appropriate director heads, staff collectively assessed flaws in the group's overall directives and presented recommendations to the board of directors. If the Board rejected the proposal, it was required to explain its decision to the entire collective.[118]

Ironically, however, the cadre system's hierarchical decision-making process clashed with an egalitarian working-class "second-line epistemology" FST creative productions celebrated. Echoing Albert Dent and the SCEA's position that professionals should guide black advancement, the FST's inner circle of cultural nationalists contended that only activists who had attained revolutionary consciousness through dedicated work and study could "unify, educate, and inspire" audiences around a common diasporic culture born out of oppression and slavery. Like Albert Dent, who as Dillard president had hosted international dignitaries such as Ethiopia's Emperor Haile Selassie to connect New Orleanian students to a wider black intellectual and political world, Tom Dent brought African diasporic artists like Toni Morrison and Andrew Salkey, a Caribbean poet, essayist, and journalist, to forge aesthetic ties between New Orleans and the Global South.[119]

The collective was divided into two levels of membership: the central leadership and the Central City masses who would join its ranks once sufficiently educated. Because "all people are not at the same stage of development," residents were shepherded toward political resistance and economic self-determination. FST cofounder Gilbert Moses suggested, "We're grafting the idea [of socially conscious theater] onto a community. The graft will slowly heal and FST will become one with the community. Finally the community will change and create its own type of theatre."[120] Matt Robinson, a cooperative activist who worked with New Orleans Black Panther Malik Rahim after Hurricane Katrina, further describes the contradictions of cadre organizing:

> [To] the Black Panthers in the '60s, a "collective" meant a group of people that was outside of the social systems . . . with a very sturdy chain of command. . . . Everybody works for the collective good, and the collective good is . . . organized almost along hierarchical principles. . . . [W]hen Malik Rahim said, "We have a collective" . . . what he was really saying was, "We have a collective, and I am at the top, and you are collectively . . . granting me your power—or the power to act on your behalf."[121]

Despite its authoritarian overtones, the FST expanded career avenues for black activist-performers from impoverished communities by institutionalizing national black theater rooted in collective decision-making. The FST worked with black theater collectives around the country to ensure they produced cultural nationalist work "of the highest artistic quality possible." Operating as a cooperative consultant, O'Neal advised theaters from New York City's Olantunji's School of African Culture and National Black Theater to Atlanta's Blk Image Theater. He flew poets to the Cooperative College Center in Syracuse, New York to demonstrate the FST's performance style and cooperative principles and connected Miami's Theatre of Afro-Arts and Battle Creek, Michigan's Black Theatre to likeminded creative arts organizations. By sharing resources and socializing with other collectives, the FST "encourage[d] and support[ed] the revolutionary struggles of the Black Nation in America and oppressed people throughout the world," while popularizing black theater as an appealing means of employment.[122]

The FST cadre also guided economic development in Central City by supporting black creative endeavors. It collaborated with its New Orleans contemporary, the Ethiopian Theater, to supplement "urban social programs and educational programs" with dramatic workshops helping at-risk communities in the Sixth through Ninth Wards "deal more effectively" with "the debilitating effects of poverty" like high crime and low educational attainment.

Guided by professors and performers like Dent's mother, a classically trained pianist, its teenaged participants honed writing, acting, dancing, and musical skills for professional employment.[123] Similarly, the OEO-funded Dashiki Project Theatre, a Central City-based community theater, framed Black Arts Movement within a larger antipoverty agenda. Staging its productions in a Catholic bingo hall, its Dillard founders and benefactors gave residents "valid black images (as well as entertainment) through performance and production excellence," and hired the majority of its staff from the neighborhood. The FST thus became one link in a larger radical black economic chain reinventing the disinvested neighborhood as a test site for transforming the competitive marketplace into one that protected the "collective interests of the oppressed masses."[124]

In line with SNCC actively "[forming] our own institutions, credit unions, co-ops, political parties, write our own histories," the FST also partnered with black separatist cooperative institutions and traditional mutual aid associations reviving Central City's Dryades Street commercial hub.[125] By 1970, Dent recalls, "there was the bookstore down the street, the poetry journal, activist and political newspapers, the beginnings of a network of artists and activists. There was the Nation of Islam, which was attractive to many ex-Movement people because of its philosophy of economic self-determination." Despite police surveillance and a state congressional probe into its "subversive" activities, a chapter near the Magnolia Housing Project opened a cooperative bakery, fish market, and restaurant to foster neighborhood self-sufficiency. Central City was a "black world," a "small black cultural [center] . . . [that] helped provide a place where activities and interactions could take place."[126] Forging a communal identity based on anti-capitalism and political self-determination, the neighborhood reflected the Third World Left's "diffuse" grassroots movement, which historian George Mariscal argues targeted a "wide range of social projects, from ethnic separatism to socialist internationalism, from electoral politics to institutional reform and even armed insurrection."[127]

The General Convention of Special Programs: Funding a Southern Cooperative Society

Despite its separatist politics, the realities of the segregated South and a changing political landscape compelled the FST to nest its Central City development initiatives within a broader statewide cooperative economy connecting black rural and urban markets. It radicalized politically diverse black cooperatives, narrowing the gap between cultural nationalism and integrationist civil rights ideology and fundamentally upsetting white expectations for what

black economic and political equality should look like. While federal agricultural agencies and university cooperative extension services had been the cornerstone of the SCEA's Depression-era resource network, they now shunned
low-income, mostly black producers "not considered 'bankable' by traditional
financial institutions." Civil rights and antipoverty advocates saw independent cooperatives as "beacon[s] to the economically distressed who are confronted idly by an unrelenting stormy sea of unemployment, low incomes,
high prices, budget cuts, and loan sharks." Recognizing that "[m]oney can't
buy racial justice" yet it can "buy expertise, and credit," OEO-funded regional
cooperative leagues like the Federation of Southern Cooperatives provided
small cooperatives expertise, managerial training, and advocacy to confront
a rapidly industrializing agricultural system.[128] An emerging alliance of Deep
South agricultural cooperatives, stores, credit unions, and retraining centers
employed rank-and-file activists who had been fired for political activities or
abused by white employers and landowners to "counter-act [the] economic
pressure" scattering small farming communities westward and northward.[129]

The federation also worked closely with Albert Dent's fellow Antigonish cooperative convert, Father Albert McKnight, to disperse OEO funds to
cooperatives in some of the poorest Louisianan urban and rural communities.[130] Beginning in 1964, the Catholic priest created the Southern Consumers
Cooperative (SCC) and the Southern Cooperative Education Fund (SCEF),
umbrella organizations whose twenty low-income cooperatives and credit
unions gave its 2,000 member-owners political agency and "meaningful ownership opportunity in a growing financial institution."[131] To communicate the
concrete economic benefits of community self-help, affiliates like the Grand
Marie Vegetable Co-op used folksy analogies: one image compared its indi-
gent black sweet potato farmers to "hungry burros" bound by a restrictive
rope, while a grim photograph of "a fifteen year old boy with a mule on his
grandfather's farm . . . plowing a sweet potato field" was contrasted against
its hopeful logo, a black silhouette of a middle-class bungalow. As SCC manager Charles Prejean contended, a permanent, united body of black southern
cooperatives would "*tell* the government about [our] needs, just like other
major interest groups do. We shouldn't wait to have the government tell *us*
what to do."[132]

Along with strong partnerships among civil rights activists and antipoverty cooperatives, reliable OEO funding had helped "break through the
obstructionist tactics of Deep South politicians" to aid southern black farmers in need. As John Zippert, a northern CORE volunteer for both the federation and the SCC, recalls, local and state political elites hounded black
economic development organizations "trying to help people end various

kinds of economic exploitation and poor farmers get a fair price for their sweet potatoes."[133] In 1967, the Louisiana Joint Legislative Committee on Un-American Activities' denounced McKnight's organizations as communistic and stripped them of OEO funding, while angry whites shot at Grand Marie Co-op organizer Wilbert Guillory's house, and police and the FBI surveilled Zippert. Frustrated by "every sort of obstacle, bureaucratic delay, intimidation, mechanical difficulties and disappointment," Zippert was shocked by "the lengths to which the state would go to try to stop poor people from really working in their own interests."[134]

To make matters worse, by the early 1970s, President Richard Nixon worked in tandem with an influential congressional "Dixie bloc" to weaken Title II of the Equal Opportunity Act. Campaigning to restore the free market from the incursions of the welfare state, they restricted federal appropriations for black community development and returned control over antipoverty programs to white-dominated local and state agencies or private institutions.[135] The OEO demanded that the federation and the SCDF merge to receive sharply reduced funding renewals. Bitter infighting over the best course of action ensued, which was only exacerbated when government funding dried up by the mid-1970s. Finally, Zippert states, the partnership splintered, "caus[ing] a division on the state association and co-op level."[136]

Limping along, surviving black cooperatives turned to philanthropies and religious institutions still willing to grant "high-risk loans to experimental projects" across the South. The Ford Foundation alone granted $3.5 million to craft, cucumber, sweet potato, and shrimp cooperatives "struggling to gain an economic foothold in their communities."[137] Similarly, in 1970, the FST received funding from the General Convention of Special Programs (GCSP), an Episcopal Church initiative to financially "support the liberation struggles of oppressed people." It did not evaluate an applicant's political radicalness but the extent to which the organization would spur marginalized communities' economic growth and political empowerment. Granted a measure of financial stability, the FST continued its creative operations, while the GCSP hired O'Neal as its funding advisor, sending him to evaluate black credit unions and agricultural and consumer cooperative grant applicants throughout the South.[138]

O'Neal was initially reluctant to approve grant applications from mainstream antipoverty cooperatives, fearing that they were hamstrung by precarious funding and conservative political views. Reflecting a common feeling among radical urban activists of the 1970s, O'Neal had both "a respect for indigenous [rural] black culture . . . [and] a profound skepticism about the possibilities for meaningful political change" coming from institutionalized civil rights leadership.[139] For example, in 1971, he debated funding the Grand Marie Co-op.[140] While after five years in business, it was one of the oldest rural civil rights cooperatives operating in the state, O'Neal complained that white organizer Zippert had founded Grand Marie, rather than black farmers. After grudgingly conceding that his "influence did not appear detrimental to the project," O'Neal approved the cooperative's funding application. When the OEO-sponsored Southeast Alabama Self-Help Association at the Tuskegee Institute applied for GCSP monies, O'Neal sniped, "the operators are, in my judgment, off base 'politically.' In the jargon of the day they would be identified as 'negroes' rather than Black." Yet the association did register rural voters and opened community-driven cooperative businesses. Mollified, O'Neal approved the application because "their motive is a good one. Their continued involvement [in cooperative economics] will teach them" political consciousness.

Despite his ambivalence regarding what historian Doug Rossinow terms "cooperation with capitalism," O'Neal never joined contemporary white radicals despairing that countercultural cooperatives and rural communes pulled activists toward "private concerns" and were thus fundamentally incompatible with cadre structures and political revolution.[141] In fact, O'Neal ultimately recommended the GCSP aid any organization that fostered concrete community development and political engagement, particularly the federation and the SCEF's politicized network of rural and urban cooperatives. The FST subscribed to federation newsletters and attended its meetings. It also partnered with SCEF contacts in Opelousas to produce community theater celebrating rural folk culture and "The Black Experience" and hosted reciprocal tours of "sites of particular significance for Black people" for Opelousans visiting New Orleans. Now, the two organizations suffering from political smear campaigns and precarious funding gained a reliable grant source in the GCSP.[142]

Further, the FST emboldened Louisiana's antipoverty cooperatives to "create a political power vane," sloughing off the bonds of "White capitalism" eviscerating black communities.[143] For example, in 1974 Dent and ten other writers formed the FST-offshoot Congo Square Writers Association to economically support young black writers perpetuating the legacy of Congo Square, "the famous meeting place of slaves and free blacks . . . an important location in the history of jazz and black cultural survival." As it toured various southern towns in the early 1980s, the collective partnered with community organizations like the SCEF to perform plays that highlighted collective "mental and physical experiences [of] southern black folk," believing that "by doing so the awareness of blacks everywhere will be heightened."[144] Similarly, former FST member Mtumishi St. Julien served as Father McKnight's "mentor in Blackness." He introduced the priest to black nationalism and pan-African phi-losophy through the Ahidiana Co-operative, a black liberationist school and collective subscribing to "community control, self-reliance, self-determination, and self-defense." Consequently, McKnight applied the *Nguzo Saba* concept of "ujamaa," or African-inspired economic cooperation, to his traditional and faith-based cooperative model, as did other politicized black cooperatives.[145]

Indeed, by the 1980s, a black nationalist-infused worldview had funda-mentally reordered Louisiana's cooperative economy. SCEF and its joint ven-tures had contributed over $8 million into sixty-three different Louisianan cooperatives. Both it and the federation provided "day-to-day moral support, training, and technical assistance" to support the "full-scale economic devel-opment of [specific] needy communities," as well as "effect broad, permanent economic growth" across the South. Finally, recognizing that local markets were inextricable from global markets buffeted by climate change and politi-cal shifts, the southern cooperative movement argued that with federal assis-tance, the "small farmer" can "help *us* survive the worldwide food shortages expected in the nineteen-eighties."[146] Proclaiming "the right of all people to adequate, nutritious food," black agricultural cooperatives traveled abroad to exchange agricultural technologies with African, Asian, European, and Mid-dle Eastern farming communities.[147]

Ending at the Beginning, Beginning at the End

At the outset of *Southern Journey*, Thomas Dent's memoir and meditation on the civil rights movement, the playwright paints his youth as rooted to the physical and cultural geography of Louisiana that would simultaneously be the means of his liberation. Standing on the banks of the Mississippi River, the young Dent gazes into its "strange muddy currents," considering his "past hidden beyond the curve downriver, the future upriver. . . . It was a great highway out into the world beyond the street corners, beyond the limitations and boredoms of the world I was growing up into."[148] The Mississippi River represents the inexorable pull of modernity and the renunciation of the old, sweeping Dent away from his father's staid, black middle-class respectability politics toward vital black liberationist theatrical and political currents. Yet, the river also symbolizes an uninterrupted flow from past to present, carrying the flotsam of New Orleanian traditions, cultural production, and ideological currencies along with Dent into a promising future.

As the Mississippi ebbs and flows, so did New Orleans's intergenerational cooperative and civil rights currents speed resident-led neighborhood and regional economic growth. By reframing New Orleanian mutual aid traditions and aesthetics around radical pan-African cooperative principles, the FST pioneered a hybridized racial justice cooperative model that strengthened a cooperative Louisianan economy that not even Hurricane Katrina and attendant neoliberal redevelopment and recovery initiatives could permanently disrupt. As they reintegrated vulnerable Louisianans into a precarious post-Katrina economic landscape, our next chapter considers how neighborhood food cooperatives extended indigenous survival strategies and national and international resources that FST's regional cooperative network solidified. The government-community partnerships Albert and Tom Dent's racial justice cooperatives deployed would be tapped anew as another generation of cooperative activists campaigned to improve labor conditions for farmers and food service workers and guaranteed food security for impoverished consumers in New Orleans and Louisiana.

CHAPTER FIVE

The Louisiana Association of Cooperatives and Gathering Tree Growers' Collective: Rebuilding a Cooperative Food Economy in Katrina's Aftermath

On a suffocating July day in 2012, I was interviewing R.U.B.A.R.B. community bike collective member Liz Lichtman at her kitchen table when our conversation skittered to a halt. A call through her open window revealed New Orleans Free School Network staffer Aviva Rabins perched on the white shotgun house steps. Grabbing a bulging plastic bag from her counter, Lichtman reassured me, "I just want to share some blueberries with my friend [before resuming the interview]. There was a blueberry festival a few weeks ago . . . and for ten bucks you pick your own blueberries, and they were organic, delicious."[1] We ate blueberries drenched in lime juice and traded tidbits about ongoing cooperative initiatives. As blueberries plunked into bowls, Rabins breathlessly reported that the Free School had opened a bank account as a limited liability company. She handed me a flyer announcing an upcoming Solidarity Economy collective meeting, and Lichtman suggested I interview her as well. "People here need to know what's going on," Rabins declared, and outside researchers and on-the-ground activists provided two halves of the broader cooperative picture. The spontaneous interlude in an otherwise straightforward interview on bike advocacy underlines the central place food played in fostering social bonds and compelling action among post-Hurricane Katrina cooperative practitioners.

While Katrina dispersed many long-standing cooperatives when it careened into the Gulf Coast between August 23 and 31, 2005, hundreds of thousands of outside activists joined surviving cooperatives to provide urgently needed food, health care, housing construction, bioremediation, waste removal, and legal aid. In the first seven years after the hurricane, food sovereignty as a means of economic justice united the movement's disparate strands, particularly as urban land-use debates, the 2008 economic recession, and the 2010 Gulf Coast oil spill destabilized already vulnerable communities of color. During the city's long-term recovery period, from 2005 to 2012, two veteran activists dominated the food cooperative scene. Macon Fry's neighborhood community gardens and Harvey Reed's state agricultural cooperative network drew on personal experience and historical racial justice models like the Federation of Southern Cooperatives to resurrect an equitable regional food production and distribution system confronting large-scale government and market forces.

The tenacity of the state's post-Katrina cooperative economy stemmed from mutual aid organizations' definitional flexibility rooted in divergent geographic, class, and racial markers. Growing up in Sixth Ward public housing in the 1950s, black Louisiana Association of Cooperatives (LAC) director Harvey Reed observed how historical racial tensions among low-income populations hindered their mutually beneficial economic development. Seeking clear legal protections for marginalized producers and consumers, he worked closely with the international cooperative movement and federal agencies to institutionalize a statewide network of multicultural rural agricultural cooperatives and urban farms. In contrast, anarchist and other small grassroots collectives avoided incorporation, circumventing potential government interference but scrabbling for resources. White, Virginian-born community gardener Macon Fry blended both cooperative strands as he advocated sustainable horticulture methods. The Gathering Tree Growers Collective's mostly white, young, and culturally middle-class organizers mobilized black economic survival networks (in the form of community gardens and the sharing economy) to bridge the considerable cultural differences between post-Katrina transplants and the longtime black residents they served. In this way, Fry worked outward from the street-level to associate with cooperatives of various scales arguing for a more just food system. Examining the meaningful, sustained social interactions among both informal and formal activists and their ethnically diverse constituents and allies reveals how the post-Katrina cooperative movement mobilized Louisianans around far-reaching food policies democratizing the state economy.

Macon Fry: Citywide Community Gardening During the Louisiana Oil Bust

Long drawn to Louisiana's food and culture, in 1981, Macon Fry moved from southern Virginia to New Orleans, where he encountered the collective organizing tactics he and other activists would incorporate into post-Katrina cooperative networks twenty years later. Initially, Fry wrote about the region's music and food for various publications and worked with Orleans Parish Public Schools educating autistic young adults. Raised in a "homogeneous" suburban community, he was attracted to the city's "benign neglect," which warded off chain stores and large corporations. The city's independent restaurants, affordable housing, and "incredible old-school musicians" were given free reign. However, as the second largest producer of refined oil in the nation and the center of the petrochemical industry since 1945, Louisiana was dependent on an oil industry that heavily influenced state economic policies and legislation. When the oil industry "busted big time" in 1984, oil companies fled the city to invest in production abroad. The state's unemployment rate hit 13.2 percent, the highest in the country. Fry recalls that by 1985, "businesses closed, everything was for sale. . . . There were blighted cars—every block had three or four cars on it that were sitting there, dead. . . . And [blight is] progressive." Thousands of white and black middle-class New Orleanians fled to Jefferson Parish suburbs. In 1980, blacks constituted 45 percent of the city's 557,515 residents, but by 2000, they comprised over 60 percent of 484,674 residents and were concentrated in its impoverished urban core. The bust was so profound, Fry claims, that "on a small scale, and with much less repercussions, it was like a mini Katrina, because there were so many blighted properties in the city."[2]

The oil crisis forged Fry's interest in food justice and cooperative economics. He joined the Parkway Partners community garden program, part of a citywide effort to secure reinvestment by beautifying neutral grounds, playgrounds, and parks. Parkway founder Flo Schornstein established the nonprofit in 1982 to guide community economic development, primarily through educating citizen volunteers to "participate in the day-to-day functioning of this city" and environmental stewardship.[3] The public-private partnership converted abandoned lots into gardens "at a time when budgets were stretched really thin, and there was a huge amount of blight because of people leaving town from the oil bust."[4] Completing the program's master gardener training in the 1980s, Fry helped Parkway community gardens bloom in low-income communities across the city, his first taste of cooperative economics.

Staffed primarily by elderly African Americans who had migrated from rural communities during World War II, the community gardens guaranteed resident access to fresh food, cemented neighborhood identity, and transmitted foodways between generations. New Orleans food cultivation and preparation had long symbolized "scarcity and communality . . . deprivation and celebration." As Robert King Wilkerson, an Algiers-raised praline maker and prison reform advocate, remembers, "We had a lot of fruit trees when there wasn't a lot of food at home—like berries, pecans, peaches. It was sustainable. It had a variety of good things that nature provided, free."[5] Similarly, one community gardener remarked that in black working-class Gert Town, "people in this neighborhood have always known that this was a garden." Parkways professionalized black voluntary associations previously running informal, impermanent urban gardens by implementing a collective management structure. A staff horticulturalist collaborated with the community's head gardener to train residents and equitably distribute vegetable seeds, plants, and other resources, while democratic meetings decided garden activities. After twenty years in operation, Parkway Partners was one of the largest privately supported community garden systems in the nation and had cemented its role as an agent of community development by, in the words of one director, "working for the citizens with the citizens to connect them to the city."[6]

Yet undercutting Parkway Partners' ability to redress economic instability was the gardens' lack of land security. At the height of the oil bust, the city granted Parkway Partners permission to build community gardens on steadily accumulating "adjudicated properties," or private lots held for judgment on back taxes when owners defaulted on their loans and abandoned their property.[7] Fry states that the agreement placed Parkway Partners in a vulnerable and ambiguous legal position because the city had no "process to either collect the money or to get rid of the lots." Further, because municipal government did not technically own the adjudicated properties, the owners could return to reclaim their land at any time. As a result, "there was never a clear sense [that] those gardens would not be sold" by their original owners, making Parkway Partners and nearby residents vulnerable to the vagaries of private property owners and developers as the city regained its economic footing.

Consequently, when Fry was promoted to Parkway Partners' community garden coordinator in 2001, he discovered that of the organization's stable of 120 community gardens, only about twenty were adequately maintained. While the gardens' elderly black volunteers "brought their interest in gardening and their skills," those "very, very good gardeners . . . needed a lot of help because of their age." Surviving gardens were understaffed, resulting in "individuals brought in that may or may not have mutual interest . . . into a space where they're rubbing elbows." As contemporary urban gardeners explained, the general public was suspicious of "a city that would provide open spaces to those who wished to garden," dismissing community gardens variously as "private clubs" or evidence of government overreach. Consequently, the vast majority of plots were derelict. Fry either could not locate the gardens or "[found] that the sign had fallen down and was laying in the back . . . under a bunch of beer cans." On the eve of Hurricane Katrina, Fry had a clear-eyed look at these "time bombs" and vowed to avoid replicating community gardens' "fatal flaws" in future food cooperatives.[8]

Harvey Reed and Institutionalized National and International Cooperative Movements

While Fry struggled with land ownership rights, community disinterest, and conflicting program goals within the community garden movement, networking with state and federal farm agencies and agricultural corporations provided Harvey Reed more substantial institutional support for minority food cooperatives. Reed was familiar with the principles of mutual aid from a young age. Born in 1950, Reed grew up in Tremé's Lafitte Public Housing Projects and attended nearby public schools. Black neighborhood mutual aid associations, ranging from church groups, social aid and pleasure clubs, and medical and life insurance cooperatives, practiced economic resiliency stemming from racial oppression. "We knew how to survive" by pooling community resources, Reed says.[9]

Coming of age at the height of the civil rights movement, Reed's experiences with neighborhood mutualism highlighted the necessity of sustained community cooperation and self-reliance in the face of government apathy. He dedicated his career to combining civil rights activism and community organizing to agricultural production. In 1986, Reed was running a successful gardening business when he was tapped to serve as outreach coordinator for Delgado Community College's Horticulture Department. With the help of state agricultural agents, Reed taught Orleans Parish prisoners horticulture and implemented a high school summer program. Those same agents encouraged Reed to apply his gardening expertise to stabilize Orleans Parish and surrounding rural parish economies. He enrolled in Louisiana State University's (LSU) two-year Agricultural Leadership Development Program as its first black student. Initially Reed was hesitant, insisting that his "civil rights days are over. I'm tired of being the first [African American]." He was also the only horticultural expert in a program catering to wealthy white owners of large farming, ranching, and agricultural interests.[10]

Nonetheless, the two-year training course proved to be a formative one. Louisianan agricultural leaders attended lectures and travel seminars designed to strengthen rural economies by exposing state practitioners to national and global agricultural theories, methods, and resources. The class spent three weeks in Argentina and Brazil observing South American farming practices and attended a weeklong World Health Organization conference, during which Reed chaperoned international agricultural ministers, economic development agents, and financiers. Just as significant, the program connected him to powerful agricultural industries, while diverse global agricultural practices and policies provided models for Louisiana's marginalized farmers.[11]

Reed's openness to alternative agricultural organizing methods and practices primed him to consider cooperatives' potential to achieve food sovereignty, or community control over the means of agricultural production, distribution, and consumption. In the mid-1990s, he befriended Ben Burkett, a small farmer and the Mississippi coordinator for the Federation of Southern Cooperatives. In the 1970s, Burkett had cofounded the Indian Springs Farmers Association, a black-owned Mississippi cooperative encouraging black farmers to remain on the land by connecting them to markets in Chicago, New Orleans, and the greater South. This was particularly urgent because, as chairman of the federation board of directors and Louisiana's chapter director Charles Prejean bemoaned in the early 1980s, with the "formal legal abolition of 'Jim Crowism' . . . a more institutional approach is being used to frustrate and nullify our Black socio-economic initiatives."[12]

The USDA and other federal institutions' racial discrimination resulted in a dramatic decline in black-owned farmland from 15 million acres in the 1920s to only 3 or 4 million acres in the late 1990s. In 1999, the federation filed the *Pigford v. Glickman* lawsuit on behalf of 15,000 farmers of color whose USDA loans had been unfairly rejected between 1981 and 1996. The US District Court for the District of Columbia awarded the claimants $1 billion in reparations and demanded that the USDA revise racist and classist lending policies. Burkett and the federation helped remaining black producers recognize that "the one thing you have is all this land, but no one is buying your goods because you're black or another color . . . [so the] best thing is to come together as group." Cooperatively organized, "no one wanted to tackle with these farmers. . . . [White officials and large farmers] did not want to handle them wrong. If they handled one person wrong, the entire group was against them."[13]

Conversing with Burkett convinced Reed to join the federation in expanding the civil rights-era cooperative network it and Father Albert McKnight's Southern Cooperative Education Fund had established to develop poor black communities in Louisiana. To do so, the federation connected Reed to the international cooperative movement. Echoing the anti-imperialist objectives of black New Deal and War on Poverty cooperative activists, Burkett argued that globally informed, locally rooted cooperatives guaranteed "the right of every individual on earth to wholesome food, clean water, clean air, clean land, and the self-determination of a local community to grow and eat what they want."[14] He participated in an African diasporic historical recovery project that disseminated agricultural techniques that indigenous peoples, enslaved Africans, and black freedpeople perfected, while also training marginalized communities in current non-Western farming methods. Similarly, the federation sent Reed to Jamaica where the State Department and the large American cooperative Land O'Lakes were helping local Rochdale agricultural cooperatives grow and ship watermelons to the US. He learned about Jamaican cooperatives' environmentally sensitive and high-yield agricultural techniques, as well as their democratic organizational structure. Crucially, Reed would deploy the domestic and global networks culled through his work with the federation and LSU's Agricultural Leadership Program to incubate racial justice cooperatives helping Louisiana's devastated small, socially disadvantaged producers rebuild after Hurricane Katrina.[15]

Urban Redevelopment Debates after Hurricane Katrina

Fry's and Reed's parallel campaigns for food justice crystalized after Hurricane Katrina devastated the Gulf Coast in August 2005. In the wake of the hurricane and catastrophic levee failure, 1,800 people perished, 80 percent of the city's buildings were inundated, and citizen displacement shrank the population from 455,188 to 225,000. The federal government would invest $15 billion repairing 133 miles of Hurricane Katrina-damaged levees and floodwalls.[16]

As the city slowly turned from rescue operations to the mighty task of large-scale rebuilding, neighborhood activists charged that vulnerable residents' immediate needs were drowned out by multitudes of local and national stakeholders vying to control the city's future. Some developers, corporations, mainstream conservationists, and city administrators believed they could lure corporate investment and tourism by erecting a "smaller and more upscale" New Orleans as a laboratory for neoliberal reforms protecting private property rights, free markets, and free trade.[17] For example, the Urban Institute and Bring New Orleans Back Commission's first rebuilding plan was unveiled to the public in January 2006. It called for a smaller city footprint more resilient to flooding by rebuilding along natural levees and in the central city, historically the wealthiest and whitest part of New Orleans. Proposing that the flood-devastated Lower Ninth Ward be transformed into parkland, the commission offered no plan for rehousing displaced residents, essentially denying "right of return" to low-income black neighborhoods.[18]

When citizens vociferously rejected the proposal, the city's Democratic mayor, Ray Nagin, announced a new rebuilding policy based on free-market principles: if a critical mass of residents returned to a neighborhood, the city would extend services to the area. The plan dovetailed with inefficient, insufficient state and federal Road Home recovery funds that forced residents living outside of tourist destinations like the French Quarter and the Garden District to largely coordinate rebuilding efforts themselves. Simultaneously, the Nagin administration pursued "market-driven governance" by transferring government-supervised social and economic programs to individuals and the private sector, such as nonprofit charities, churches, and volunteers. City leaders focused instead on rebuilding the tourist and service industry by expanding shopping centers, rehabilitating highly trafficked tourist areas, and redeveloping the Mississippi riverfront. As city medical, housing, and educational systems rapidly privatized, poor black residents were slow to return four years after the storm, and those who did earned a 45 percent lower median income than their white counterparts.[19]

While New Orleans boosters celebrated the city's black cultural traditions, performing-artist advocate Sally Stevens claimed, the "city is reluctant to support indigenous musical forms except in highly contained, commodified ways," justifying black communities' "wholesale demolition and gentrification." First, shrinking public housing, a locus of musical and community identity, sped musicians' displacement. By 2008, unable to secure "basics like shelter and health care," 110 out of 300 Mardi Gras Indians had left New Orleans, threatening the generational transmission of collective traditions like sewing elaborate costumes and "masking" twice a year.[20]

Second, conflating practitioners with the "criminal underground economy" driving violence in New Orleans, officials often constricted low-income musicians' incomes by cracking down on neighborhood music and performance permits. For example, although the TBC Brass Band had played on the corner of Bourbon Street and Canal for nine years without incident, in 2010 officials barred their French Quarter performances, citing noise curfew violations. Band member Joseph Maize Jr. exclaimed, "[N]o one is in danger out here. Everyone is having fun." He connected French Quarter surveillance to policing at his St. Bernard Project home: "We are at war with ourselves." By repressing second line parades and Mardi Gras Indians, the city practiced blatant "aesthetic racism" that restricted black working-class creative expression, their livelihoods, and neighborhood integrity.[21]

A recovering tourist economy also excluded the city's 75,000 service and construction workers. Deregulating food service and construction, two of the largest sectors of the city's economy, disproportionately and adversely impacted immigrants and people of color. For the first five weeks after Katrina, federal authorities suspended occupational safety laws, eliminated affirmative-action policies and minimum wage standards, and opened competition for federal reconstruction contracts without requiring work authorization documentation for immigrant employees. The Department of Labor lacked funds to adequately supervise workplace standards, so temporary deregulation effectively became permanent. Consequently, in the years after Katrina, a third of restaurant workers made below-poverty wages, and many also had limited access to health insurance, paid vacations, or sick days. "Back-of-house" staff and fast food workers—75 percent of whom were immigrants, women, or people of color—received the lowest wages and experienced the worst working conditions. The same went for undocumented Latin American construction workers. Day laborers convening near the French Quarter faced constant police, National Guard, and Immigration and Customs Enforcement (ICE) harassment as tourists returned. Sociologists Aaron Schneider and Saru Jayaraman reported that employer "patterns of abuse and exploitation . . . harden[ed] and expand[ed] over time" to target construction and service industry workers more generally.[22]

Low-income workers suffering from stagnating wages also faced constricting affordable housing. While 60 to 70 percent of the city's housing stock was flooded, most of its public housing remained undamaged. Yet, in spite of skyrocketing rental prices, citywide housing shortages, and widespread racial discrimination, city officials, HANO, Housing and Urban Development (HUD), and developers razed four public housing complexes.[23] Mixed-use residential apartments with thousands fewer affordable units now stood in their place. Arguing that "density is good as long as you don't concentrate the poor," in 2013, prominent reconstruction architect Pres Kabacoff bulldozed 59 out of 75 Iberville Public Housing buildings in Mid-City. Yet only 227 of his promised 820 mixed-income new units were constructed on site and throughout New Orleans. Kabacoff blamed the affordable housing shortage on limited HUD funding for vouchers and incentives for private developers. Additionally, federal funding only ensured that housing was affordable for five or ten years before the property reverted to market-rate value.[24] Further contributing to the housing constriction was the 2008 recession, in which disproportionate numbers of unemployed, low-income, and minority homeowners lost their homes, jobs, and savings in the subprime mortgage loan crisis.[25]

Finally, white in-migration, subsequent gentrification, and black out-migration into surrounding suburbs enlarged historically white Uptown, Garden District, and the French Quarter neighborhoods, encroaching on black working-class communities close to tourist-friendly destinations and downtown amenities and displacing low-income renters. Kabacoff's development company, Historic Restoration Incorporated, completed a seventy-five-unit affordable housing apartment complex for artists in Bywater, anticipating thousands of newcomers seeking housing near the French Quarter's "authentic" culture and entertainment. Consequently, Bywater residents of color declined by as much as 64 percent over the course of the decade.[26] Nor were affluent whites the only agents of gentrification. In 2013, Xavier University, a Catholic University primarily serving African American students, rezoned a dozen adjacent properties in Gert Town to build dormitories. Rising property values pushed out some longtime residents. Across the city, redevelopment in low-income neighborhoods inflated property values by 30 to 60 percent between 2010 and 2013.[27]

Initial Cooperative Response to Katrina: Mapping a Cooperative Food Economy

The combined effect of neoliberal reconstruction policies restricted vulnerable New Orleanians and Louisianans' access to healthful foods, crippled when widespread flooding upended the city's food systems. Survivors' immediate needs were food and water as depopulated neighborhoods lacked a functioning grocery store. In the Lower Ninth Ward, grocer Burnell Cotlon had "to catch three buses just to get to a store—and the closest one is a Walmart in the next city." Two years after the storm, 84 percent of black communities still did without.[28] Similarly, Fry observed that Katrina "really put the whammy on [community] gardens," which were "already . . . decimated by poor planning, overdevelopment, lack of follow-up, [and] lack of community-building."[29] The low-lying, predominantly black Lower Ninth Ward and Gentilly suffered widespread flooding, and many elderly gardeners responsible for transmitting horticulture skills died or were evacuated during the storm. Consequently, "the number of gardens, the number of gardeners, there was nobody here . . . [it was a] tabula rasa."

A dispersed, decentralized cooperative movement composed of local residents and outside activists quickly emerged to redress survivors' continued food insecurity, tackling in the process gentrification, lack of affordable housing, deteriorating working conditions, and delayed rebuilding in communities of color. In the first six months after the storm, thousands of volunteers streamed into the city with stores of food and supplies. They collaborated with New Orleanian natives whose "French influence, Spanish influence, African influence, and Caribbean influence" and historical tendency to "[organize] themselves by neighborhoods and by proximity . . . because of racial tension" made them "more apt to be working together in a way that's community based."[30]

For example, immediately after the storm, Austin anarchist Scott Crow allied with New Orleans community organizer and former Black Panther

Malik Rahim to establish the Common Ground Collective, a radical, demo-cratic, and anti-oppressive organization serving mostly black neighborhoods in Algiers and the Lower Ninth Ward. The collective used Black Panther, Zapatista, and American anarchist survival tactics to craft an alternative to insufficient government relief efforts; volunteers staffed free medical treatment, food, and clothing distribution centers from sunrise until sunset, camping in founder Malik Rahim's yard and schlepping mounting food deliveries to the collective's "little distribution points" in flood-damaged parts of the city.[31] After raising $3 million in two years, it hoped to turn operations over to returning residents. The collective worked in concert with seventy community-led organizations formed to submit to city officials a formal neighborhood plan, access state and federal recovery funds, and independently begin rebuilding. Mapping the city's broader cooperative geography elucidates how a diverse mix of labor organiz-ers, immigrant advocates, anarchists, and progressives collaborated with local mutual aid networks to remake New Orleans and Louisiana into a "proving ground" for a more humane, participatory food economy.[32]

Producer Cooperatives: Latin American
Reconstruction Worker Advocacy in Central City

After Katrina, the city's Latin American population swelled from 3 to 5 per-cent to handle its mounting reconstruction contracts. While Hondurans, Guatemalans, and Mexicans were already steeped in collective action and mutual aid traditions, they often lacked family support networks to pool assets to purchase food, vehicles, homes, and health insurance or negotiate regular police and ICE harassment. Undocumented day laborers joined a "family" of immigrant rights organizations countering food insecurity, wage theft, poor working conditions, and state surveillance. Although Schneider and Jayaraman contend that traditional "working class organization [had not] taken hold in New Orleans," food cooperatives offered a flexible organiza-tional structure and "contextually specific and extra-class identities around which workers can organize."[33]

For example, since 2008, the Latino Farmers Cooperative of Louisiana served as a service clearinghouse for undocumented and documented immi-grant recovery workers from New Orleans, as well as outlying suburbs of Metai-rie, Kenner, Gretna, and Westwego. Costa Rican founder Kathia Duran and her staff ran a food pantry and helped documented residents acquire food stamps out of their sea-foam green shotgun house in Mid-City. Taking advantage of the fact that between 75 and 85 percent of Lower Ninth Ward lots remained vacant in 2012, Duran's community gardens and community land trusts also promoted immediate and long-term economic development among Spanish-speaking families.[34] Community land trusts are resident-led, nonprofit trusts that purchase an empty lot or city block to cooperatively farm.[35]

Likewise, the cooperative's first *huerta* (or "micro sustainable farm"), the Oretha Castle Haley Community Garden, harnessed Central City high school student labor, as well as local, state, national, and global farming organization resources, and rural immigrants' expertise with gardening and animal husbandry. For instance, twenty-two-year-old co-op member Girasol Romero parlayed her "household farming" skills that were "always part of her culture" into a directorship, pairing food cultivation with nonprofit management. Garden produce and dairy improved residents' nutrition and built "entrepreneurial skills for long-term self-sufficiency" by marketing at city farmers' markets. As Romero affirms, the cooperative "gives me a sense of more purpose than just being a Latino woman in the United States or just being a housewife at home. . . . I feel useful in the world. [It's] having a sense of pride and being able to help out my community and help my family at the same time."[36]

Food Service Industry: Central City Cooperatives Revitalize the Labor Movement

Since many of the city's low-income residents worked in the exploitative food service sector, the Restaurant Opportunities Center of New Orleans (ROC) and Rhythm Conspiracy organized them into restaurant cooperatives, following the example of Albert Dent's Depression-era public housing-based cooperatives. They faced fierce neoliberal opposition from city agencies and businesses casting cooperative economics as "too socialistic" to help food industry workers and consumers. Mimicking the anti-communist rhetoric that had besieged cooperatives from the Brotherhood of Co-operative Commonwealth to the Free Southern Theater, critics like *Times-Picayune* journalist James Varney decried food cooperatives as a "hard-left union front" serving a tiny subset of the population. They would misuse public funds, instead conspiring to foment labor unrest and minimum wage increases. The Pelican Institute for Public Policy, a Louisianan free-market think tank, agreed: "We already have an industry characterized by innovation, service, diversity, value and opportunity. Owners, employees and customers benefit from this flexibility and we should be wary of union advocates who seek to restrict it."[37]

Despite opposition, in 2006, Sally Stevens, a white northeastern cultural preservationist, cofounded Central City-based Rhythm Conspiracy to serve mostly black food and hospitality workers, musicians, and social aid and

pleasure club members living in Magnolia, St. Thomas, and Calliope Projects.[38] As Stevens observed, the worker cooperative appealed to service industry workers "[dreaming] to get out of the hotel; they know what they want
to do . . . and who they want to do it with. That's what cooperation is all
about." Defending members as essential to New Orleans's tourism industry,
Rhythm Conspiracy helped performers secure prestigious local gigs and set
up international tours. It liaised with citizens, businesses, and economic and
workforce development organizations to expand Central City government
services, equitable neighborhood reinvestment, and job opportunities. Ultimately, if "significant cultural services and products are coming out of the
most marginalized neighborhoods," greater wealth would prevent them from
"[becoming] gentrified in ways that similar neighborhoods are being gentrified in cities around the country."

Similarly, in 2012, ROC organizer Reese Chenault announced the national
nonprofit would counteract poor nutrition, as well as "labor abuse and wage-
theft" among St. Roch food industry workers by opening Colors, a cooperative restaurant.[39] Receiving a $200,000 Centers for Disease Control grant, the
national nonprofit provided job training and professionalization programs
to help racially diverse worker-owners receive a living wage, create "healthful
menu options," and grow food on site. Further, in a right-to-work state that had
eviscerated labor unions and collective bargaining, ROC aimed to unionize
the food service industry to secure living wages and safe working conditions.[40]

At the same time, Chenault and Stevens realized that while their respec-
tive cooperatives admirably served Central City and St. Roch, their geographic
dispersal impeded generalized economic development. Isolated cooperatives
operated as lonely buoys floating in an ocean of citizens often unaware of or
hostile to cooperative goals, organizational structure, and ideology. Accordingly, they joined Solidarity Economy, a Loyola University-based cooperative
think tank and study group that emerged alongside the legions of under-
employed and unemployed citizens forming alternative economic organizations to counteract the Great Recession's economic fallout. Many of Solidarity
Economy's twenty veteran and newcomer activists had participated in Occupy
Wall Street in 2011, protesting national corporate malfeasance and the prison-
industrial system, as well as the city's own history of police brutality, political
corruption, and neoliberal rebuilding plans perpetuating racial disparity.[41]

Aligning with the international solidarity economy movement, Solidary
Economy collaborated with city and state activists on a range of cooperative projects, from worker cooperatives and farmers' markets to community
gardens and land trusts, to build a citywide network of neighborhood cooperatives challenging capitalistic political and economic systems. For example,

volunteers trained ROC's St. Roch restaurant cooperative members in cooperative principles and connected Chenault to regional cooperative produce suppliers. Likewise, Rhythm Conspiracy asked for assistance seeding service worker cooperatives in public housing complexes in order to stabilize gentrifying neighborhoods. In this way, Stevens argued, Solidary Economy's decentralized system of food "cooperatives [would] mitigate abuses of the private market and expand the commons."[42]

Consumer Cooperatives and Gentrification in the Ninth Ward

Rhythm Conspiracy and ROC's campaign to mobilize restaurant workers for workplace justice complemented consumer cooperatives' efforts to provide reliably sourced, affordable, and nutritious food in the city's poorest neighborhoods. Food justice activists decried the Ninth Ward's pervasive food deserts, and St. Roch residents complained that nearby conventional grocery stores so often sold rotten vegetables that they purchased packaged junk food at St. Claude Avenue's plethora of fast food chains and gas stations instead. In response, community advocates erected a patchwork of cooperative buying clubs and grocery cooperatives around the Ninth Ward. Drawing on his experience running a 1970s food cooperative, Solidarity Economy cofounder John Clark recommended applying member dues to fund low-income cooperative buying clubs' weekly bulk produce excursions to the French Market. Similarly, recalling Egleston's and Hermes's grocery cooperative delivery trucks, the New Orleans Food Co-op operated a mobile food market in conjunction with nonprofit organizations Market Umbrella and the Second Harvest Food Bank to provide fresh produce to underserved populations.[43]

To further expand the local cooperative economy while improving black residents' nutrition, in 2011, the New Orleans Food Co-op opened a storefront along St. Claude Avenue dividing disinvested St. Roch from the gentrifying Marigny. Viewing fresh produce access as a social justice issue, the cooperative educated patrons about environmental and health issues and sold organic foods from a city network of farmers' markets, local farms, and community-supported agriculture organizations.[44] Some residents hailed its slogan, "100% owned by the 99%" and fair prices as "far more in keeping" with the Marigny's "eccentric . . . cultural fabric" than its upscale grocery competitors.[45]

However, other New Orleanians decried the New Orleans Food Co-op's decision to open within the New Orleans Healing Center, a community space and small business hub at the heart of contentious debates around St. Roch gentrification. Between 2000 and 2010, rising rental prices in the bohemian

Marigny enclave pushed young artists north of St. Claude Avenue into St. Roch. Developer Pres Kabacoff began building the Healing Center in 2008 as an anchor for his corporation's sprawling St. Claude Avenue redevelopment plan, itself predicated on demolishing public housing and dispersing renters across the city.[46] St. Claude Avenue area residents charged that the complex's cafés, yoga studios, galleries, and juice bars targeted young, middle-class consumers and heralded racially and class-specific "sub-cities, separate communities that happen to abut each other, but otherwise do not interact." In fact, few working-class people of color initially patronized the center or the co-op because their products were too expensive and unfamiliar.[47]

Yet food advocates saw in the New Orleans Food Co-op the potential to stabilize gentrifying neighborhoods, especially when aligned with citywide labor and cooperative organizing. ROC's Chenault spent the summer of 2012 working with St. Roch churches to encourage congregants to join the co-op. At the same time, the cooperative began offering residents who had a Section 8 voucher, food stamps, a fixed Social Security income, or disability benefit a $25 limited-income membership fee, a quarter of its individual member dues. Eventually, advocates hoped, by circulating money within the community, reducing crime, and providing healthful food to residents, a critical mass of community-run cooperative restaurants and grocery stores would democratically revive stagnating neighborhood economies.[48]

Neighborhood Cooperative Rebuilding: Gathering Tree Growers Collective

Seven years after Katrina, New Orleans's producer, consumer, and worker cooperatives shifted from addressing specific neighborhood needs to studying city and regional food equity.[49] Repeatedly bumping into each other at conferences, workshops, lectures, and protests, activists constructed a loose coalition of food cooperatives with broadly interlocking agendas. As veterans of the local food movement, Fry and Reed emerged as prominent power brokers wrangling neighborhood cooperatives into a vibrant city and state food network.

After Katrina, Fry parlayed his work with Parkway Partners into a position as mentor farmer at the Mid-City Hollygrove Market and Farm, a community-supported agriculture organization, and as farm advisor and mentor farmer at Grow Dat Youth Farm, a nonprofit City Park organization that teaches socioeconomically diverse teens to cultivate and sell or donate produce to neighborhoods with limited access to fresh foods. He was also inspired by the legions of "guerrilla gardeners" from Common Ground and other grassroots groups that, in the early days after Katrina, performed bioremediation on contaminated abandoned lots and "beautif[ied] unoccupied and derelict spaces that gathered garbage even before the storm." Community gardens gave underserved, flood-ravaged communities of color access to fresh produce, improved resident health, and spurred community redevelopment.[50] Revitalized gardens would generate "gathering places for conversation" essential for community self-advocacy. Common Ground's Matt Robinson describes volunteers' pervasive optimism: the "chessboard was empty . . . it seemed like anything was possible. You just take a piece of land, start growing stuff on it, and boom! You have a community garden. Irrespective of who owns the property, where they are, what are they going to do with it, what the condition of the property is, and all that."[51]

Yet while he commended outside activists' resolve, Fry watched as new community gardens "became highly politicized," particularly those located in the un-flooded, and therefore commercially desirable, strip of high ground in Uptown New Orleans. Pre-Katrina gentrification and property development resumed as increasing numbers of wealthy, well-educated, white migrants settled in this historic area. Uptown community gardens "that had survived the development of the early 2000s . . . and hadn't been developed, were suddenly really valuable" to investors. Their ownership contested, the properties "simply became . . . too valuable" to use for community gardening. Fry warned, "if you're trying to do community building around the garden, it's a non-starter to not have land security." So, he embarked on permanent cooperative gardening project that would preserve local foodways, revive communities, and expand food access to needy residents. A democratic urban gardening model would transform conventional food distribution into a community-centered, citywide environmentally sustainable system.[52]

After establishing demonstration market gardens at Mid-City's Hollygrove Market and Farm, Fry replicated the experiment in a flood-damaged Parkway Partners community plot in Gert Town, near Xavier University. In 2005, the scrappy neighborhood had been severely damaged in the storm and was depopulated. Reflecting the legacy of black neighborhood self-sufficiency, returning Gert Town residents clamored to rehabilitate their old community garden. As Fry recalls, 100 housing reconstruction volunteers "cleaned this garden down to the bones. I mean, by hand got out every bit of grass," eventually transforming the "total junkyard" back into a working garden. Fry gave Iola and Leola, two elderly but ardent community gardeners, their old plots. He turned the remaining parcel of land into the Gathering Tree Growers Collective, a sustainable farming experiment station and collective farm staffed by dedicated Hollygrove volunteers. As a demonstration garden, its larger mission was to promote community-driven sustainable agriculture to make productive the city's abandoned lots, contaminated by residue in Katrina's floodwaters. Collective members planted crops to eat themselves or donate to the neighborhood, selling only the remaining produce at local farmers' markets.[53]

The result was a scruffy but productive garden plot along Gert Town's Telemachus Street. When I visited Gathering Tree in the summer of 2012, the demonstration garden measured about 150 feet by 50 feet and was sandwiched between lines of neat, unassuming houses on an owner-occupied block within spitting distance of Xavier University. Gardening was seasonal: sweet potatoes crowded the chain-link fence, partially obscured by what collective member Jocine Velasco described as "poorly tended blackberry bushes."[54] Collective members harvested rows of exuberant summer and winter squash, basil "in the back that smells really good whenever somebody walks by it," heirloom tomatoes, and trellises of fat Christmas lima beans. A wooden sign labeled "The Gathering Tree Collective" in pink curlicue script hung over a small shed in the garden corner.

Gathering Tree replicated the qualities Fry admired in the most successful Parkway Partners community gardens: a strong leader, resident participation, land security, and sustained institutional support. As owner of the garden, Fry mentored the collective's thirteen young transplants looking to the urban farm movement to provide a sense of community in their new home. For example, Filipino American Velasco grew up in Florida. A few years after graduating from college, she moved to New Orleans to pursue a career in urban and sustainable agriculture in 2011. Velasco first volunteered at the New Orleans Food Co-op, inspired by its mission to make nutritious food accessible to black St. Roch community members. Her desire to eventually run her own urban farm led her to volunteer with Hollygrove and then Gathering Tree.[55]

While Fry joked that he serves as "benevolent dictator," training all members, outlining their tasks, and supervising their work, the garden operated along a modified consensus model that supported an egalitarian, cooperative organizational structure. Velasco relished the group's democratic nature and collective decision-making: because everyone "has a complete stake" in maintaining the lot, "it's really important that we ask every single person . . . what we want to grow, and when we're going to help out." Each week, the collective divvied up labor tasks among themselves: "We make a calendar, and see what everybody's availability are. And we just decide from there." When Fry fled New Orleans to escape the oppressive summer heat, Gathering Tree elected Velasco to manage the garden, with each individual responsible for completing one shift a week, such as watering, irrigating, or harvesting. If the members failed to maintain the garden by neglecting to coordinate vacations or forgetting to water and weed, "we have to take ownership of the problems ... and try to alleviate [them] together."[56]

Fry and Velasco contended that the collective's democratic structure nurtured close social relationships in ways absent in other urban agricultural projects. As Fry noted, "It's really neat that there's been a sense of community generated around this garden that I ... seldom was able to generate in a community garden space, where people ... tended to their own little plot." Rather than perpetuating the city's reputation as being "sort of a lone wolf, no club type place," Gathering Tree cemented social ties among gardeners. Velasco elaborated, "Everybody is a myriad of really funny people coming together really for the sake of being curious and wanting to learn how to urban farm.... It's really fun getting to meet people I wouldn't otherwise get to meet before." Members bonded through weekly communal workdays, which mixed labor with socializing. Sundays "feel more like a collective, I guess," explained Velasco, when members spent the early morning first volunteering at Hollygrove before driving or biking to Gathering Tree to "tackle a lot of really big garden issues," like weeding. They usually ate lunch together after gardening shifts and often invited each other to parties.[57]

As the collective fostered a tight-knit community among its members, it slowly forged social ties with Gert Town's working-class residents. Velasco says that black residents were initially curious about the garden's staff of mostly white volunteers because they were "a) not from here [New Orleans], and b) don't [live] ... in the same neighborhood." Yet Sunday harvest days soon became a neighborhood social affair, as collective members filled wheelbarrows with greens and root vegetables. Passersby took as much produce as they wished, or, "if we have too much, we ... just knock on doors."[58] As one New Orleanian explained, "[I]f you have extra [food], you wouldn't think of not calling your neighbors. Sharing food is thus a crucial form of communication in New Orleans." Gathering Tree's acts of non-commodified social solidarity facilitated its assimilation into New Orleans culture and transmitted food traditions across race and class.[59]

Regular mixing with neighbors was important, because cooperatives comprised of idealistic, middle-class, educated members can perpetuate inequality and gentrification in the transitional neighborhoods they seek to serve. Gathering Tree concurred with environmental justice activists that sustainable agriculture must "include consciousness about gentrification and class to be truly effective." It aligned with national sustainable agriculture advocates who declared, "working-class neighborhoods deserve community gardens, green spaces, and easy access to healthy food, transportation, and services." Urban gardens would create a sense of community identity and economic resiliency necessary to resist urban renewal, over-consumption, and dependence on large companies and agencies for residents' basic needs.[60]

To appeal to neighborhood residents, the collective blended permaculture ideals with New Orleans foodways. Permaculture, or the practice of "closed loop" living, rejects large-scale food production exploiting non-renewable resources and human and non-human animals.[61] Gathering Tree taught New Orleanians to intensively cultivate seasonal produce specific to coastal southern Louisiana by "reusing materials . . . making your own potting mix, say, and reusing that potting mix. A lot of seed saving. Using as little of our precious resources as possible." After bioremediation, Velasco believed vacant lots would be "perfect places to grow food, as community gardens, for personal use, or . . . to sell to markets." By no longer relying on expensive, poor quality supermarkets, "you're feeding yourself, and you're feeding a lot of people with [the garden] in a very small space." Gathering Tree echoed regional food activists who felt a "collective responsibility" to preserve "imperiled culinary traditions" after Katrina's floodwaters dislocated practitioners and destroyed their businesses.[62]

While Gathering Tree served the Gert Town community, Fry's sustainable agriculture methods and cooperative organizing structure exerted an outsized influence on citywide urban farming initiatives. As social geographers Patricia Allen and Clare Hinrichs argue, the local food movement rapidly gained momentum across large segments of the public during the first decade of the 2000's as community gardens and other grassroots urban agricultural projects were increasingly "seen as fostering direct democratic participation in the local food economy and cultivating caring relationships among people in a community."[63] In post-Katrina New Orleans, "locavores" ranging from vegan activists and farmers' market directors to inner-city community organizers preserved Louisiana's indigenous foods while fostering a local food economy accessible to all New Orleanians. Vegetarian and vegan restaurants spread across the city, and as Velasco observes, by 2012 there were "pop-ups and speakeasies and restaurants opening all the time that [had] those alternatives." Restaurants like Maurepas Foods in Bywater advertised a "farm-to-table mentality about their food" by procuring locally sourced ingredients. Also, beginning in 2010, NOLA Locavores organized the annual "Eat Local Challenge," sponsored by over forty restaurants and food purveyors, which encouraged New Orleanians to consume foods grown or raised within 100 miles of the city for one month.[64]

Local food movement organizations served as middlemen resource providers for Gathering Tree's urban gardeners. For instance, Hollygrove and Baker Creek farms donated heirloom seeds, while the police department supplied the farm with its horse manure for free "because we're technically . . . just taking their garbage." Additionally, Fry was part of the New Orleans Food and Farm Network, which connects "neighborhood food clusters" of residents, nonprofits, institutions, and businesses to empower local citizen-activists to direct urban food policy. In 2012, the network's executive director, Sanjay Kharod, urged sustained collaboration among white food activists, policymakers, and vulnerable communities of color to advance a nuanced understanding of the city's racial and class dynamics necessary for true food justice. The Network supervised Fry's work with Hollygrove and Grow Dat Youth Farm, outlets for African Americans to produce and consume environmentally sustainable foods.[65]

Finally, collective members disseminated permaculture methods throughout the city, reflecting Fry's belief that "showing people success is a good thing." A Hong Kong architect incorporated her urban farming interests into her job as restaurant manager, while Fry's connections at Hollygrove secured Velasco a position as farm supervisor at Vintage Garden Farms, a new urban farm in Chalmette. Community gardens began to effectively integrate marginalized residents into an ecologically sustainable, permanent food justice movement.[66]

Regional Organizing: Louisiana Association of Cooperatives

While Fry's Gathering Tree addressed specific block-level food security needs, Harvey Reed's Louisiana Association of Cooperatives (LAC) adapted the international cooperative movement to develop an institutionalized community redevelopment plan after Hurricanes Katrina and Rita and the Gulf Coast oil spill devastated Louisiana's small producers. It reknit the urban-rural partnership between the Free Southern Theater (FST) and the federation to connect Louisiana's marginalized growers to the city's disadvantaged consumers. As a crucial intermediary between government agencies and underserved urban farmers' markets, community gardens, and rural agricultural cooperatives, the LAC reconstructed vulnerable communities and sparked interracial, cross-class cooperative formation across the state.

Reed was recovering from cancer when Hurricanes Katrina and Rita slammed into the Gulf Coast states in the late summer and fall of 2005. He felt "the need to do something [positive] without having a pity party," so he rejoined the federation to help flood victims apply for federal relief programs. He also organized cooperative and credit union workshops to rebuild marginalized communities. Reed traveled across Louisiana, meeting with small fishermen and farmers to identify their most pressing needs. Cameron Parish fishermen were "wiped out" after Hurricane Rita.[67] In the Cajun agricultural community of Delcambre, a ten-foot storm surge flooded virtually all structures, crops, infrastructure, and its fishing industry. At the opposite end of the state, Plaquemines Parish lost 80 percent of its commercial fleet and its docks, equipment, and coastal businesses.[68]

The hurricanes exacerbated the unequal marketing and distribution systems long plaguing independent, marginalized seafood businesses. First, in both Cameron and Plaquemines parishes, low-income fishers were forced to use expensive commercial docks for processing seafood hauls, which significantly reduced already meager profits.[69] Cameron Parish fisher Susan Meaux sighed, "in such a small community like ours . . . it's hard to get resources . . . You can spend 19 hours a day on the water, spinning your wheels for nothing." While interracial cooperatives could have pooled black, Native American, Southeast Asian immigrant, and white independent fishers' resources to build their own docks, historical racial and cultural antagonism discouraged collaboration.[70]

Second, Governor Kathleen Blanco's Louisiana Recovery Authority (LRA) sometimes ineffectively distributed its $10 billion in federal recovery funding to Louisiana's devastated communities and legitimized the privatization of housing, workforce development, and health care services.[71] It also overlooked small commercial outfits by directing recovery monies to the Louisiana Fishing Community Recovery Coalition, a well-organized advocacy group for large fishing corporations and recreational boaters. Additionally, outreach centers initially had no mechanism for holding frequent, bilingual public meetings in immigrant fishing communities to explain how residents could receive recovery funds and assist with application processing. Without adequate government support, independent seafood workers would not be able to resume their livelihood: fishing "brings us tourists, it helps the economy, it's everything to this area." After being repeatedly denied insurance claims, one black oysterman despaired, "now I'm living off of $200 a month in food stamps." Others faced homelessness, describing government neglect as a "poison" in their communities. In response, Reed demanded government officials directly engage with underrepresented groups "that have never been approached [for policy input] in the past" to democratically dispense recovery funds to rebuild houses and businesses.[72]

To recover their losses, Reed and the federation helped marginalized Plaquemines and Cameron Parish fishing communities form marketing cooperatives. The South Plaquemines United Fisheries Cooperative was incorporated in 2007, a racially diverse marketing cooperative whose fifty members sold shrimp, crab, and oysters. A bumpy approval process delayed their rebuilding plans, however, largely because the Louisiana Secretary of State had to be reminded what cooperatives were. The federal government had recognized the legal status of fishing cooperatives in its Fishermen's Collective Marketing Act of 1934, yet it still took three weeks for Louisiana to approve the South Plaquemines charter.[73] Similarly, cooperatives across the state and country reported regularly diverting time and energy from their daily operations to educate public officials about their status as legal entities and their protections under the law. Nonetheless, Reed's persistence was rewarded, and he used the Plaquemines charter as a template to rapidly incorporate federation-affiliated cooperatives across Louisiana. As Susan Meaux, a charter member of a federation-affiliated Cameron Parish fishing cooperative, explains, Reed "helped us be heard and be seen."[74]

In December 2007 Reed officially incorporated the LAC, a state organization independent from, though it worked alongside, the federation. It served two major purposes: 1) to aid individual cooperatives, and 2) integrate them into the international cooperative economy. To that end, it educated the public about cooperatives, organized cooperative affiliates, collaborated with other cooperative organizations and government agencies, and advocated for cooperatives at the local, state, and federal level. Run out of a small office in Gretna, a suburb outside of New Orleans, the LAC's nine employees deployed covert black working-class survival strategies to mobilize grassroots cooperatives against a host of "adversaries": the legacy of state repression of social justice organizations, widespread "disaster capitalism," rancorous cooperative competition, and government corruption. Maintaining a policy of protective secrecy, the organization had no website or public relations staffer, only a weekly e-newsletter that outlined government policies and agricultural issues. Reed carefully guarded LAC initiatives until he was ready to implement them, and he did not publish "what area we cover, who we're working with."[75] Instead, he publicized small producers' concerns at innumerable policy workshops, government recovery meetings, and conferences across the country.[76]

Philosophically, the cooperative bound distressed Louisianan communities to a transnational, anti-imperialist network of marginalized agricultural cooperatives in Spain, Costa Rica, and the Pacific Islands also striving for "self-help, self-responsibility, democracy, equality, equity, and solidarity." Reed dismissed nonpolitical and Eurocentric Rochdale cooperatives that "pigeon-hole based on cultures." Like the federation, the LAC adhered to the International Cooperative Alliance's (ICA) updated Rochdale cooperative principles, that, since 1995, had enshrined the pursuit of anti-discrimination and social justice as its purpose for fostering "jointly-owned and democratically-controlled enterprises" in developing countries. Holding a common stake in community development at home and abroad while retaining their individual autonomy, affiliates understood that "wherever they go, they know they're part of the international cooperative movement."[77]

To that end, Reed initiated an extensive training program whose consciousness-raising exercises exposed new members to the legacy of imperialism and the benefits of global solidarity. He first appealed to communities' familiarity with bartering and mutual aid. As Vietnamese cooperative organizer Daniel Nguyen explains, "If you're a shrimp boat captain and you harvest 100 pounds of shrimp, you would sell 75 pounds to the market and 25 pounds you would keep to feed your family or barter with other community members. . . . A [shrimp] farmer may . . . pay a carpenter to fix his house in the form of seafood." Accordingly, Reed encouraged the New Orleans East-based VEGGI Farmers Cooperative, established after the Gulf Coast oil spill threw Vietnamese fishers and farmers out of work, to "integrate what you've been doing in home country" with the ICA's ethos as well as "how we do things culturally [and legally] here." Continuing members attended periodic sessions to refresh their commitment to the ICA's democratic leadership and cooperative principles.[78]

However, the LAC's critique of self-serving global capitalism was difficult for early affiliates to understand. Like Father Albert McKnight, who faulted "capitalistic personalities" for allowing civil rights-era cooperatives "to be destroyed as long as they gain financially," Reed confronted a common "quick profit" mentality at odds with cooperative ethics. Some members grew impatient with the logistics of running a cooperative and its slow investment return. Others disbanded or reverted to private associations after trying to inflate profits by acting as middlemen brokers for producers or otherwise engaging in "impropriety or cutting deals or propositions."[79] Reed cautioned new cooperatives, "if you agree [to work with me], you must promise me that you will stand right next to me, not behind me. And not in front of me because you don't know what you're doing."[80] He emphasized his point by gesturing to a wall crowded with framed pictures of LAC members. Then he threw open a desk drawer full of discarded photographs, a "graveyard" for the "bad apples," or former affiliates who had discredited cooperation.

Goal One: Using Cooperatives to Rebuild Local Communities

Beyond persuasively communicating its collective ethos to members, the LAC's most pressing challenge was to convey producers' needs to large funding bodies to immediately start small communities' rebuilding efforts. Like generations of working-class cooperatives organizing vulnerable populations on a tiny budget, the LAC hustled to secure often unpredictable financial support from nonprofit organizations and government agencies such as the Cooperative Development Foundation, the USDA Office of Rural Development, and Oxfam.[81] Reed wrote grant applications and expedited funding "so that a cooperative member does not have to put up their house or farm [to provide collateral for bank loans]. . . . People lose their land and homes because they didn't have adequate advice." So needed were its technical and advocacy services that Reed, the only paid staffer, temporarily closed the LAC to streamline operations: "there were too many calls, and not enough manpower to work with everyone."[82]

Despite limited resources, Reed waded into Louisiana's recovery fund gladiatorial ring to secure small producers a say in state rebuilding initiatives. He accused LRA's Baton Rouge Infrastructure Task Force of "[holding] meetings in all these outlying places so people couldn't get to them. [But] we would go to the meetings. We didn't care where. We were speaking for the fishing co-ops." Armed with fishers' personal accounts, state Department of Wildlife and Fisheries data, and LAC research, Reed scolded the LRA for funding recreational boats and large commercial fishing outfits and "forgetting about the small fishermen." At one meeting, he pointedly asked, "'Between recreational boating and the fishing industry, which generates the most tax dollars?' They couldn't answer. Recreational boating generates zero tax dollars, while fishing boats generate $54 billion in taxes. They were rescuing recreational boats without putting their tax dollars to work."[83]

The LRA yielded to Reed's persuasive powers. In January 2007, it allocated $20 million to spur sustainable economic development in marginalized communities through the Small Firm Loan and Grant Program. Cameron Parish's Gulf Coast United Fisheries Cooperative received $1.1 million in direct aid, which it used, along with nonprofit funds, to purchase seafood-processing equipment and construct its own dock.[84] More successes followed: in February 2007, Reed argued that LRA should allocate its $20 million Community Development Block Grant to provide storm-affected fishers, processors, suppliers, and dock owners "start-up capital, replacement or repair of boats, inventory, docks and 'gap collateral' for borrowing money from other financial institutions."[85] Accordingly, South Plaquemines Cooperative received an LRA grant to build a docking facility, while federation and USDA technical assistance enabled members to locate better markets and increase profits. Republican Governor Bobby Jindal also promoted grant-funded shrimper and processor-owned and-controlled cooperatives throughout Louisiana. Susan Meaux contends that if "we hadn't formed a co-op, experiences could have passed us by," and damage from subsequent environmental disasters Hurricane Ike and the Gulf Coast oil spill could have been irreparable.[86] Instead, Reed's unrelenting advocacy cultivated a far-reaching coalition of citizens, powerful agricultural cooperatives, and state and federal agencies transforming how economic and political power was distributed in Louisiana.

Goal Two: Integrating Cooperatives into the Metropolitan Regional Equity Movement

Beyond aiding individual communities, Reed strove to revive McKnight and the federation's statewide cooperative economy that, until Katrina, had countered generations of inequitable city development patterns and national social, economic, and political trends driving concentrated poverty, racial isolation, depopulation, and disinvestment. Between the 1970s and 2000, cities like New Orleans experienced a profound outmigration of white residents, and with them, thousands of jobs. Subjected to largely undeveloped regional transit, poor blacks living in deteriorating urban cores were cut off from high paying suburban jobs. Slowly, though, low-income urban families began to move to parish suburbs to find work. Without access to educational services or professional development, suburbs reproduced inner cities' unequal economic and social conditions.[87]

Yet in the 1970s and '80s, "innumerable and decentralized small units" of cooperatives steeped in church-based voluntarism sprang up in places like New Orleans to counteract the "central city poverty and inequality . . . [stifling] a whole region's development."[88] Subscribing to Murray Bookchin's theory of social ecology, countercultural food cooperatives and buying clubs posited that cities should balance individual autonomy with an egalitarian, ecologically sound, and community-centered system of governance. On weekend supply trips, volunteers purchased vegetables in bulk from French Market farmer stalls or Esplanade Avenue's Community Co-op Food Store to reduce struggling families' grocery bills, improve nutrition, advance ecological principles, and ultimately, reform capitalist employer, worker, and consumer relations.[89] They worked alongside a state system of rural and urban community banks that "recognized the dire need for financial [and technical] assistance by consumer groups" beset by federal fiscal policies favoring corporate growth and slashed funding. Credit unions extended low-interest loans so that electric utility, grocery, housing, and agricultural cooperatives covering large swaths of Louisiana could supply tens of thousands of residents low-cost services and employment options while returning hundreds of millions of dollars in profits back into community infrastructure.[90]

After Katrina, however, the state's cooperative system lay in shambles, unable to help rebuild an environmentally just and sustainable region. Instead, under the sway of wealthier, whiter, and less populated parishes like Plaquemines Parish, regional land use plans and state and federal reconstruction allocations accelerated "suburbanization, decentralization, and low-density development."[91] Fighting this trend, the LAC participated in a "metropolitan regional equity" movement in which broad partnerships of community members, labor unions, urban planners, and social justice activists collaborated with government officials and developers to spur sustainable regional economic development. Movement adherents encouraged tax credits, developer incentives, and fair housing laws to create interlocking communities marked by strong schools, affordable housing, parks, grocery stores, public services, and easy access to good jobs both within and beyond the neighborhood. Ultimately, by reducing regional economic disparity and raising local governments' tax bases, regional "smart growth" would mitigate the effects of natural disasters, curb environmentally unsustainable suburban sprawl, and halt gentrification in vulnerable suburban and urban communities.[92]

Like metropolitan regional equity advocates, the LAC contended that unequal conditions for small farmers of color adversely impacted Louisiana's agricultural economy and eroded marginalized communities' food and land security. Board member James Brady held up community food production as "the new Mother of sustainability" because it fostered "Social, Health, Environmental, and . . . economic development measures."[93] The LAC's expanding cooperative network reflected Robert Bullard's "community based regionalism," in that regional and national cooperatives and agricultural agencies provided training, education, and technical and financial support to independent cooperatives directing community rebuilding. Individual cooperatives would then be integrated into an egalitarian "hub-and-spoke" regional food system driving wider job development and economic growth. As food advocate James McWilliams theorizes, the hub-and-spoke model equitably reorients food production by selecting central nodes most conducive to environmentally sensitive, high-yield agriculture and then distributing low-cost food from these centers to distant markets.[94]

One example of a burgeoning food hub is New Orleans. Reed took advantage of city efforts to expand infrastructure for urban farms and community gardens, recommend urban farming policy, and include farmers and cooperatives in the New Orleans Master Plan and Comprehensive Zoning Ordinance. Working with New Orleans community development and social justice organizations like Crescent City Farmers Market, Solidarity Economy, and the New Orleans Cooperative Development Project, the LAC implemented urban farming and other job training programs for impoverished New Orleanians. Both urban and rural cooperatives' produce is sold at New Orleans farmers' markets and other, more creative, venues.[95] For instance, the LAC pressed large agricultural conferences to source catered food from local cooperatives. Reed explains, "If your conference is on farmers, then farmers should bring their bounty to share. What you're doing is taking a dollar out of their pocket and putting it in someone else's who doesn't even care about you. . . . Now the first thing [my hosts] tell me is, 'Harvey, this came from so and so'" cooperative.[96]

The LAC cemented regional food hubs through sustained socializing among its grassroots affiliates and allies. As James Brady argues, only strong community fellowship could combat members' geographic isolation and competitiveness and grow a statewide food production and distribution system that "ensures quality and sustainability of the environment, provides adequate levels of economic and social development while assuring social relationships that are respected and supported."[97] For example, in a show of "structural solidarity," the LAC and the federation's Mississippi chapter celebrated the organization's fortieth anniversary by hosting a cross-state fish fry for affiliated members. Sociologist Daina Harvey suggests that such performative meals united various hurricane recovery organizations addressing the same issues.[98] Centered on culturally resonant foods such as gumbo or jambalaya, nonprofit-sponsored dinners ignored cultural, racial, or class differences to "convey a shared sense of identity . . . and purpose" and manifest a "future community to be built by participants."

Reed also urged communities of color to professionally associate with politically connected state and national producer cooperatives to receive vital government representation, job contracts, and support services. Observing the racial and class divides between the mainstream agricultural cooperative movement and the LAC's disadvantaged affiliates, in 2007, he joined the prominent Louisiana Council of Farmers Cooperatives, whose white farmer-members cultivated vast tracts of land. As the Louisiana Council's first black board member, Reed represented small producers at the state level. The limits of interracial cooperative solidarity within the context of lingering racial discrimination, finite government resources, and pervasive poverty could be stark. Reed contended, "There's a subtle point about civil rights in Louisiana. It's not that you're going in [to white cooperatives] as a sell-out; it's that you're . . . saying, this need has to be met [or] it will affect . . . the whole industry."[99] For example, preferring to sell large lots of rice by the tons, powerful rice cooperatives ignored ethnic businesses catering to Louisiana's Asian, Greek, and Latin American communities. Reed advised these white "old liners" "to start dealing with the small minority farmers and buyers." If white rice farmers "don't want to [listen to me] because I'm black, fine," but in the meantime corporations might corner specialty markets and destabilize the entire cooperative rice industry.

Further, as state representative to the National Council of Farmers Cooperatives and National Conference of State Councils, Reed discovered new opportunities to network with prominent cooperative businesses and craft federal laws shielding cooperatives from corporate competition.[100] Yet here, too, the legacy of institutionalized racism threatened to sabotage marginalized producers' long-term economic security. When the LAC contracted with national cooperative ConAgra to sell northeastern Louisianan sweet potatoes, the local cooperative mistrusted the white-dominated, mainstream cooperative and "talked themselves out of cooperation."[101] Dissecting the stalled project, Reed sighed that national cooperatives were eager to work with them, but "you don't invest millions in something that won't work."

However, Reed acknowledged that black communities had strong historical cause to be suspicious of dominant white agricultural institutions and agencies. He pointed specifically to a second *Pigford* settlement in October 2011 that allowed thousands of farmers to apply for a $1.25 billion claim redressing USDA racial discrimination. The same year, the consulting firm Jackson Lewis Corporate Diversity Counseling Group published a comprehensive study recommending key changes to the USDA's technical and financial aid programs to ensure "fair access for all USDA customers."[102] While Obama administration Agriculture Secretary Tom Vilsack hailed a "New Civil Rights Era" in which "[USDA] assistance programs are administered equitably and in full compliance with civil rights and equal opportunity laws," Reed maintained that "nine times out of ten [USDA staff] in the field ignore the [Jackson Lewis] report." For example, one LAC member forgot to list his place of employment on a USDA loan application. The agency denied the loan instead of informing the member of the error.[103]

To circumvent local agencies' racialized resistance and enforce its compliance with civil rights court rulings, the LAC worked directly with state USDA directors. In the case of the LAC farmer, Reed called the Louisiana agency head, who ordered the local field office to inform the producer what paperwork he needed to complete. Reed exclaimed, "[T]he field officer didn't like it, but I didn't care. It's our tax dollars that are keeping you employed." He collaborated with a legal team to assist black farmers sorting through their *Pigford* claims, hosting educational meetings at Southern University and Louisiana State University. Referring to the LAC's e-newsletter, which had a worldwide readership of 20,000, Reed warned recalcitrant local agents, "we'll put [the story] out; don't threaten us. Don't say you can't [provide a loan]. . . . We know that the Secretary of Agriculture pumps a lot of money into Louisiana and Mississippi for rural economic development. The money can't stop in Baton Rouge."[104]

Largely due to Reed's tenacity and the USDA's efforts to remediate discriminatory rural funding programs, the LAC obtained consistent agency support for its food-oriented metropolitan regional equity plan. The USDA's Business and Industry Guaranteed Loan Program and Rural Cooperative Development Grant Program provided start-up loans and funds for cooperative training. The LAC was also one of the first Louisianan organizations to receive a Small and Socially Disadvantaged Producer Grant, which increased job opportunities in rural black communities by developing businesses and cooperatives. A $200,000 grant enabled the LAC to purchase furniture, equipment, and supplies for its affiliate cooperatives. A subsequent award provided essential training and salaries for employees. Reliable government funding allowed the LAC to train over 200 cooperative members a month, host events and workshops for target communities, and tackle organizing all sixty-four state parishes.[105] In line with the metropolitan regional equity movement, it advanced the USDA's mission to "connect our rural communities to each other, to our nation's metropolitan areas, and to the world." Consequently, by 2012, USDA officials credited the LAC with revitalizing the state's small producer cooperative movement. Reflecting the solid foundation the LAC had built, one director assured Reed, "if you die today, it won't stop the cooperative movement; people are now moving in that direction."[106]

Conclusion

Taking advantage of a post-hurricane groundswell of grassroots organizing, Harvey Reed and Macon Fry integrated flood-damaged communities and neighborhood-based food cooperatives into a sweeping regional agricultural network that strengthened the economic standing of the state's disadvantaged producers and consumers. Their firsthand experience and research on local and international food justice cooperatives informed how both men's recovery efforts reversed entrenched racialized, classed food inequality aggravated by neoliberal deregulation and development. Generative ideological, strategic, and social exchanges among recent transplants, returning residents, and veteran cooperative activists unified Louisiana's storm-scattered cooperative movement to direct regional economic development. Today, cooperatives apply these hard-won lessons to confront government-sanctioned global climate change and resource depletion.

CONCLUSION

Hope for a Cooperative Life:
Forecasting Cooperative Trends

On a sunny day in June 2012, community bike workshop organizer Matt Robinson gazed out onto the Marigny's eclectic mix of cafés, galleries, and painstakingly rehabilitated townhomes. He reflected, "Hurricane Katrina shifted . . . the debate on everything from collective organizing to . . . how a federal government responds and fails to respond."[1] Instead, recovery was driven by "the organizational power of people acting empowered for themselves and determining what they're going to do" in the absence of effective government action.

Peering simultaneously into the past and future, Robinson predicted, "[i]t's not difficult to see that in the near future there might be something that fails us in such a way that we are suddenly dependent on those around us. . . . And if and when the next huge event that calls upon FEMA to come and save the day and they fail to do so, that's going to be one more instance where people are . . . going to spontaneously come together."[2] Guiding community support should be time-tested cooperative models: "if we have a leg up on knowing how to organize, . . . when the next big shock comes, more people who are acquainted with [cooperative histories] and who are conversant with that language are going to make sure that more people are going to be able to survive . . . and come out better on the other side."

Indeed, while cooperatives have thrived throughout New Orleans's history, certain conditions made cooperative economics more fertile at different moments than at others. Recognizing these factors can facilitate future democratic economic development. For instance, integrated social spaces within the Seventh Ward and CBD hosted crucial Brotherhood of Co-operative Commonwealth meetings in which members weighed how various international political and economic programs might transform New Orleans into a more equitable society for all citizens. Their synthesis of French republicanism and utopian socialism with Caribbean and African diasporic survival politics created a flexible, cosmopolitan cooperative model responsive to diverse working-class concerns. Equally important, members' experience as veteran union, benevolent association, and political organizers made them adept at translating the brotherhood's agenda to appeal to skittish government, corporate, and union stakeholders. At the same time, suffering an uncertain economy, yellow fever epidemic, and frequent flooding made New Orleans administrators more open to experimenting with alternative routes to urban growth than those provided by industrial capitalism. However, the brotherhood's demand for a government-funded unemployment program, expansive flood protection plan, and improved working conditions for laborers was circumscribed by a creeping xenophobia that excluded non-citizens, and eventually African Americans, from the fruits of a modernized urban landscape.

Similarly, women's economic precarity and social exclusion birthed the Housewives' League Co-operative Store. Drawing on their observations of other societal configurations during domestic and international travel for school, vacation, and work, the league's non-Louisianan, Jewish, and first-generation members debated how best to enfranchise women and integrate them into a global marketplace. Like the brotherhood, the league was made up of veteran activists who expertly rallied progressive, union, and farmer allies. Under the guise of wartime patriotism and postwar boosterism, members proffered material feminist and socialist solutions to a stagnating southern economy, disparities in regional produce distribution, and the high cost of living for laborers and consumers. Yet in the midst of a Red Scare that conflated leftist activism with treacherous communism, the league tempered its vision of a statewide Rochdale cooperative network ushering the South toward a gradual socialist evolution. Instead, it appealed to investors by casting cooperative farmers' markets, public kitchens, and grocery stores as agents of a modern, humane capitalist system. This strategy successfully incubated cooperatives across the state, but by excluding black domestic servants, white immigrants, and Creole women from a new woman-centered economy, the league demonstrates the ethical shortcomings of a feminist socialist ideology lacking an intersectional racial and class analysis.

Like the HLCS, the New Orleans Consumers' Co-operative Union used the Rochdale consumer cooperative model to integrate formerly excluded consumers into financial markets and facilitate neighborhood and regional economic growth. Inspired by a global anti-fascist movement, the cooperative's Latin American, black, and white ethnic Popular Front directors pushed the residents of the Freret neighborhood who were fed up with the lingering Depression and state government corruption to envision a socialist society supported by community cooperatives. Henry Hermes's cooperative mission dovetailed with New Deal agencies' faith that cooperatives would cultivate self-sufficiency among small producers and consumers. Partnering with SCEA and CLUSA also provided the CCU vital educational resources and technical services, national government and institutional contacts, and access to a progressive cooperative network battling racialized poverty across the South, as well as a global cooperative movement aiming to establish peace, democracy, and economic justice worldwide after World War II.

Although the CCU won substantial municipal investment transforming Freret into a modern shopping and residential district, vicious desegregation battles, white flight, and the rise of suburban supermarkets crippled the neighborhood economy by the mid-1950s. The CCU collapsed when its white directors chose to protect white members' economic interests rather than collaborating with growing numbers of black residents. However, Hermes redoubled his commitment to helping all New Orleanians, regardless of race: in the 1960s, he worked with old New Deal partners now active within the state's War on Poverty agencies to construct a network of credit unions extending low-interest loans to more than 200,000 ordinary Louisianans, a significant aspect of grassroots economic development civil rights activists would also harness.

While Flint-Goodridge Hospital administrator and Dillard University president Albert Dent's medical insurance cooperatives drew on the same partnerships that buoyed the CCU, cooperative economics had different implications for African Americans. Like Hermes, Dent expanded the SCEA's regional Rochdale cooperative network by working with interracial southern government officials, academics, and professionals seeking to include black citizens in sweeping New Deal economic reforms. However, he was driven by the need to demonstrate black economic self-sufficiency and civic fitness. To do so, Dent institutionalized and modernized the mutual aid traditions of New Orleans by applying global anti-fascist and socialist ideology to middle-class southern black civil rights institutions.

Even as Tom Dent would take up the mantle of cooperative activism in the 1960s and '70s, he and the FST criticized the Rochdale cooperative model as mired in imperialist machinations. Instead, they wed New Orleans's working-class black participatory aesthetic traditions and street-level survival tactics to a pan-Africanist political ideology. Despite perennial attacks on members' "Americanness," the FST collaborated with black liberationist theater collectives and antipoverty cooperatives marshalling War on Poverty funds and philanthropic monies to stimulate job growth and resident activism in disinvested Louisianan communities.

Finally, riding a wave of residents and urban planners' optimism that Hurricanes Katrina and Rita had handed municipalities an unprecedented opportunity to correct long-ingrained mistakes, Harvey Reed and Macon Fry participated in a metropolitan regional equity movement integrating multiracial, marginalized populations into a democratized regional food production and distribution system. By working with state, national, and international government agencies, cooperative leagues, and agricultural practitioners, Reed and Fry accrued technical expertise and professional contacts they deployed to equitably rebuild flood-ravaged Louisianan communities and expand consumer and producer protections even in the midst of large-scale public service deregulation. Most significantly, they avoided imposing a top-down economic development model by studying local stakeholders' needs, incorporating past and present neighborhood mutual aid traditions, and, most importantly, training communities in self-advocacy.

Collectively, then, what do these seven case studies say about the viability of cooperative economics as a whole? Catastrophes such as economic depressions or ecological disasters reveal the constructed, fragile nature of capitalism and make people willing to experiment with different social arrangements. However, the fact that New Orleanian cooperatives have remained a constant presence demonstrates the enduring appeal of this economic model, even without a crisis as impetus. Rooted in specific neighborhoods and organized by longtime community activists, cooperatives intimately understand resident needs and draw on a common community identity and mutual aid traditions to recruit members. At the same time, cooperatives work best when born out of fluid social boundaries and spaces in which diverse people freely socialize and exchange ideas about alternative ways of organizing economic structures. The confluence of international cooperative theory and local mutual aid creates a dynamic cooperative model that avoids the pitfalls of parochialism or an outsider-imposed, "one-size-fits all" approach unresponsive to local conditions.

Just as important, coalition-building among likeminded city and regional organizations, as well as institutional allies, provides cooperatives technical expertise, funding, and communication channels to integrate dispersed neighborhoods into a cohesive cooperative economy without sacrificing their autonomy. Broad cooperative networks comprised of producer, consumer, and financial cooperatives can thus transcend affiliates' original purpose for organizing and survive individual closings to permanently transform regional landscapes.

Ultimately, the city's internationally inspired cooperatives can be models for other marginalized communities seeking democratic alternatives to both free-market globalism and solipsistic "America First" protectionism. As we enter what some commentators call the "Age of Localism," the David and Goliath story of New Orleans's motley neighborhood cooperatives resonates with segments of the public disenchanted with "business-as-usual" politicians and corporations. As already discussed, the Great Recession of 2008 popularized the national cooperative movement as ordinary citizens who had lost jobs, savings, and homes formed neighborhood cooperatives and opened credit union accounts.[3] Frustrated by sluggish economic recovery and systemic inequality that neoliberal policies like post-2008 home foreclosure measures had exacerbated, the 2011 Occupy Wall Street Movement also spurred interest in the "sharing economy" as a community-driven solution to global economic instability.

Under the umbrella of the solidarity economy movement, coalitions of anti-globalization and anti-capitalist worker cooperatives, intentional communities, farmers' markets, time banks, and other alternative economic institutions identified residents' needs and guided public reinvestment programs to ensure equitable neighborhood growth.[4] Many of these radical collectives were unaffiliated with institutionalized cooperative networks and eschewed the formal marketplace and politics. Matt Robinson, a member of a Ninth Ward community bicycle workshop, observed in 2012 that there was a "strong undercurrent among folks who are anarchist-minded to not engage with the government in any way."[5] Applying for federal nonprofit status "was just pulling teeth, because folks would be like, 'we don't need to do that. We're not here to be part of the government; we're just here to work with kids and fix bikes.'"

Donald Trump's 2016 presidential campaign tapped into the groundswell of populist sentiment, adopting policy measures long championed by community-oriented cooperatives. Some leftist "localists" initially, if cautiously, welcomed Trump's anti-globalization platform, in which he decried corporate outsourcing of manufacturing jobs and free-falling hourly wages of domestic workers competing with foreign laborers.[6] For their part, rural electric cooperatives, representing over 42 million members, endorsed Trump's promise to repeal onerous Obama-era environmental regulations. Similarly, the Credit Union National Association was a major donor to Vice President Mike Pence's congressional campaign, hoping he could repeal the Great Recession-era Dodd-Frank Wall Street Reform and Consumer Protection Act on the grounds that it would "kill jobs, raise taxes and restrict the flow of credit" for the 109 million credit union members staggering under higher compliance costs.[7]

However, an increasingly inward-looking political landscape had major ramifications for the nation's environmental and economic policies. After President Trump's election, localist cooperatives joined a deregulatory, localist movement pressuring a new Republican administration to repeal former President Barack Obama's federal environmental regulations and international climate change agreements. For instance, the Cooler Heads Coalition, a collection of libertarian and conservative nonprofit organizations, spent two decades discrediting climate change research and funding political campaigns. Rural electric cooperatives representing over 42 million members echoed the coalition's mission to stall the "regulatory onslaught" of federal policies they deemed harmful to the national economy and citizens' autonomy.[8] In response, congressional Republicans threatened to defund the Department of Interior's twenty-two conservation cooperatives and eight regional climate centers that, under Obama, had enabled university and government scientists to collaboratively study how global warming impacts water quality and supply, species health, and weather patterns across broad regions.[9] By June 1, 2017, these vociferous lobbyists had also successfully persuaded Trump to back out of the Paris Accords, international guidelines for drastically reducing nations' greenhouse gas emissions.

Yet cooperatives have become increasingly aware of how populist rhetoric on both sides of the political spectrum can celebrate cooperation without integrating citizens into an institutional process capable of redressing exploitative economic structures. For example, Republican politicians often praised the "real" white rural and urban working-class Americans who constituted their voting base. However, over the course of 2017, they quietly eliminated federal funding for community-based cooperatives and government aid programs serving these same constituents, actions ironically first initiated by the decidedly globalist president Bill Clinton in the 1990s.[10] The National Farmers Union, a cooperative incubator, protested President Trump's 2017 proposal to slash the USDA's budget, agricultural and federal conservation programs, crop insurance, healthcare, and Supplemental Nutrition Assistant Program subsidies. It worried cuts would stymie rural economic development, conservation, and research and disproportionately harm low-income farmers and ranchers already reeling from a "drastic, four-year slide in farm prices and a 50 percent drop in net farm income."[11]

Similarly, the National Cooperative Business Association claimed reducing domestic discretionary funding and foreign aid would hurt "over 120 million members of cooperatives and 40,000 cooperative businesses throughout the nation that inject over $600 billion back into the economy," upending the economic stability of "families and communities, both domestically and internationally."[12] Cooperatives from diverse political ideologies contended that populists denied America's complicity in world affairs and climate change while enacting policies that favored national corporations exploiting global workers, people of color, immigrants, women, and the environment.

The visceral economic and human costs of political tribalism and environmental and economic deregulation were laid bare on August 25 through September 1, 2017, when Hurricane Harvey inundated coastal Texas and Louisiana with fifty-two inches of rain. Thirty percent of Houston was underwater. Partially to blame were Democratic administrators' lax zoning laws that permitted construction in flood-prone areas and shrank wetland recharge zones, making the city increasingly vulnerable to climate change-related weather events. Ineffective flood management policies disproportionately impacted low-income areas, like Houston's public housing complexes located in floodplains and contaminated exurbs bordering storm-compromised chemical and oil plants. As environmental justice advocate Robert Bullard contends, neighborhoods' "pre-existing condition of inequality" hampered "how people are able to address [disasters] because of [their] vulnerability," slowing marginalized communities' recovery. For instance, just before the storm, the president had revoked laws mandating that federally funded construction projects account for global warming-caused flooding and sea-level rise.[13]

Further validating Robinson's prediction that grassroots cooperatives would rebuild stricken communities in the absence of effective government supervision, crisis responders overwhelmed by the historic magnitude of Harvey's rainfall and a cascade of rescue requests turned to an outpouring of citizen-organized relief. Harris County, Texas, police and firefighters welcomed "an armada of citizen bass boats and Jet Skis" from across Louisiana and Texas to locate trapped flood victims.[14] Visiting Corpus Christi on August 29, First Lady Melania Trump praised individual rescue efforts from helpful neighbors to the Cajun Navy, applauding "not only the strength and resilience of the people of Texas, but the compassion and sense of community that has taken over the State."[15] Cooperatives were also on the frontlines. Because the "nature of our business" is to "always [look] for a way to help folks," Kentwood Co-op, a Louisianan farm supply store, fueled Cajun Navy vessels.[16] When the Texas energy company Entergy lost five substations, the Washington-St. Tammany Electric Cooperative braved flooded, traffic-choked roads to erect a mobile substation powering thousands of Texas homes.[17]

However, scattered, uncoordinated community crisis responses only underlined the need for cooperative-government partnerships to construct comprehensive, science-driven state and federal resource management programs mitigating global climate change's devastating repercussions for

American municipalities. Even staunchly conservative cooperatives increasingly confront the boundaries of localism as natural disasters expose how inextricably tied Americans are to both global markets and shifting climate patterns. For instance, the National Rural Electric Cooperative Association tacked cautiously between affirming President Trump's populist "America First" messaging and committing to renewable energy research. It assured its 900 affiliated cooperatives that it can put "the needs of members first" and still take "aggressive steps to reduce our carbon footprint."[18] Nationally, electric cooperatives representing some of the poorest, most rural states have invested in "solar gardens," in which underserved members invest in and lease utility-run, shared solar panels connected to the local power grid. These "community solar" cooperatives provide fixed-cost, ten-year energy plans to rural consumers at odds with mainstream conservatives' fossil fuel-oriented infrastructure initiatives.[19] Citizens, as well as their elected officials, must prioritize sustainability and safety for all residents, while considering the global context of their efforts. This requires fundamentally revising the technocratic assumption that cities can simply engineer their way out of environmental change.

Thirteen years after Hurricane Katrina, locally responsive, internationally inspired New Orleanian cooperative-city partnerships provide a model of "equitable bioregionalism" promoting economic and environmental sustainability.[20] In line with their predecessors, "glocalized" urban cooperatives continue to apply proven neighborhood and global strategies to confront both globalized neoliberalism and knee-jerk economic protectionism.[21] For instance, on August 2017, a powerful rainstorm dumped between five and ten inches of rain on New Orleans in three hours, overwhelming the Sewerage and Water Board's hundred-year-old pump system and inundating vehicles, homes, and businesses in low-lying areas.[22] While administrators shrugged that flooding would be the new normal "in an era of climate change," residents urged the city to recommit to the 2013 Greater New Orleans Urban Water Plan.[23] Partially written by Central City co-working collective founder and urban planner Aron Chang, the plan embraces climatic and geographical particularities and encourages community participation. The Dutch-inspired proposal reconfigures flood-prone neighborhoods to store and slowly absorb rather than immediately drain storm water.[24]

Additionally, the Louisiana Association of Cooperatives (LAC) and other cooperative advocates see democratic technological innovation and government investment as bulwarks against competition from vast multinational agricultural and forestry corporations.[25] Pointing to the $212 billion in total gross business volume that American agricultural marketing, supplies, and service cooperatives generate per year, New Orleans cooperatives have developed a multifaceted approach to safeguarding southern agricultural communities' public health and economic growth. First, the LAC pressures state and federal governments to invest in "social infrastructure," such as rural utilities and modern ports and waterways, to connect small cooperatives to regional and global markets.[26] Simultaneously, believing that access to improved, resilient infrastructure can transform vulnerable communities into economic powerhouses, Propeller, a Gert Town nonprofit incubator and co-working space, helps minority-owned businesses to implement flood prevention systems like wetland preservation to protect Louisiana's poor coastal and urban areas at greatest risk of flood damage.[27]

Second, the LAC calls on an international network of cooperatives and scientists to equitably disseminate technology and expertise to southern cooperatives so they can produce diverse, higher yield crops for a wide range of consumers. For example, Latin American farmers and operators in Mississippi and Louisiana otherwise excluded from government rural assistance programs receive educational services, technological assistance, and leadership training.[28] Similarly, biotech company director Kaleb Hill is a "PROUD third generational agriculturalist living in the Deep [S]outh" who helps black farmers secure grants and markets for their products.[29] When he discovered that his Holly Grove neighborhood farmers' market was too expensive for low-income residents, Hill opened Oko Vue Produce Company, an all-natural cooperative farmers' market that battles food insecurity by extending hours, lowering prices, and accepting food stamps.[30] Honoring the "sacrifices my [black and indigenous farmer] ancestors made so that I could live," Hill applies current USDA and African diasporic agricultural methods to improve poor New Orleanians' nutrition and economic well-being.[31]

Third, the LAC urges "traditional [agriculture] co-ops" to deploy online communication and support services that can connect them to local and international "digital agribusiness marketplaces."[32] Rather than succumbing to totalizing global economic forces, cooperatives can create an "open-source," data-driven culture that improves communication, information and services exchange, and governance among farmers while cultivating a "fair value-driven marketplace." For example, LAC board member James Brady envisions small urban producers using "internet enabled application [that] . . . standardize agricultural technology platforms" to predict preferable growing conditions and deliver nutritious, inexpensive foods to inner-city populations suffering from a host of poverty-related public health woes.[33] Similarly, in 2018, Propeller provided technical assistance and mentorship to FASOLEAF, Ulrick Yameogo's New Orleans-based online company that sells moringa that female cooperative farmers, artists, educators, and food activists in Burkina-Faso sustainably harvest and process into nutritional supplements. Yameogo uses a digital platform to combat a "diabetic and cholesterol epidemic," which he describes as a "global challenge, especially in the Black community."[34]

New Orleanian cooperatives' mix of historical and contemporary, indigenous and cosmopolitan organizing models can be a way forward for small communities desiring democratic economic growth while remaining engaged in ethical issues impacting the nation and world. As Matt Robinson concludes, "It's good to document [the New Orleans cooperative movement]. Because I'll tell you, 100 years from now, people are going to be looking back and be like, 'Wow, where did this amazing cooperative urge in America come from, to where they could survive *this* [next disaster]?' Hopefully, that's going to be the way [laughs] . . . and not, 'Wow, where did America go wrong?'"[35] Fellow organizer John Clark concurs, "[Local cooperatives offer] the hope that people can live [a better] life. Let's show what we could have."[36]

NOTES

Introduction

1. Melissa Hoover, interviewed by Steven Dubb, "C-W Interview," *Community Wealth* (June 2010), http://community-wealth.org/content/melissa-hoover.

2. Cedric Johnson, "Introduction," in *The Neoliberal Deluge: Hurricane Katrina, Late Capitalism, and the Remaking of New Orleans*, ed. Cedric Johnson (Minneapolis: University of Minnesota Press, 2011), xx–xxi, xxxvi; John Arena, "Black, White, Unite and Fight?" in ibid., 152–73; Kent E. Portney, *Taking Sustainable Cities Seriously: Economic Development, the Environment, and Quality of Life in American Cities* (Cambridge: MIT Press, 2003), vii; Gary Rivlin, *Katrina: After the Flood* (New York: Simon & Schuster Paperbacks, 2015), 402; "Locations," Urban Strategies, accessed on July 9, 2014, http://urbanstrategiesinc.org/by-location/; Joel Dinerstein, "Second Lining Post-Katrina," *American Quarterly* 61, no. 3 (September 2009): 615–16.

3. Clyde Woods, "Katrina's World: Blues, Bourbon, and the Return to the Source" *American Quarterly* 61, no. 3 (September 2009): 446.

4. Hoover, quoted in Dubb, "C-W Interview."

5. Jessica Gordon Nembhard, "Uplifting and Strengthening Our Community: A Showcase of Cooperatives in New Orleans," Grassroots Economic Organizing, accessed on October 19, 2014, http://www.geo.coop/node/356.

6. Erin Rice, "The USFWC Work Week: Post Conference Event in New Orleans, June 2008," Grassroots Economic Organizing, http://geo.coop/node/355, accessed on September 9, 2017.

7. Jeff Brite, quoted in Ajowa Nzinga Ifateyo, "USFWC: Ten Years of Achievement, Part 2 of 2," Grassroots Economic Organizing, http://www.geo.coop/story/usfwc-ten-years-achieve ment-2, accessed on July 25, 2017.

8. Ruth A. Morton to Ed Yeomans, November 28, 1940, 3, Box 1, Folder 2, Southeastern Cooperative League Records, 1939–1952, Louis Round Wilson Special Collections Library, University of North Carolina at Chapel Hill.

9. Harvey Reed, interview with author, June 26, 2012, Cooperative Oral History Project.

10. Harvey Reed, "Welcome, Cooperatives in New Orleans and Louisiana: Ted Quant, Harvey Reed," speech given at the US Federation of Worker Cooperatives Conference, New Orleans, Louisiana, June 21, 2008, http://www.pdfio.com/k-2694397.html#; Greta de Jong, *Invisible Enemy: The African American Freedom Struggle After 1965* (West Sussex: John Wiley & Sons, 2010), 163; Greta de Jong, "'From Votes to Vegetables': Civil Rights Activism and the Low-Income Cooperative Movement in Louisiana after 1965," in *Louisiana Beyond Black and White: New Interpretations of Twentieth-Century Race and Race Relations*, ed.

Michael S. Martin (Lafayette: University of Louisiana at Lafayette Press, 2011), 145–61; Albert J. McKnight, C.S.Sp., *Whistling in the Wind: The Autobiography of The Reverend A. J. McKnight, C.S.Sp.* (Opelousas: Southern Development Foundation, 1994), 75, 110–12.

11. Reed, interview with author; Anne Todd, "Disasters Spur Co-op Formations: Louisiana Co-op Association Helps Farmers, Fishermen Recover Following Hurricanes and Oil Spill," *Rural Cooperatives* (July 1, 2012): 6, https://www.rd.usda.gov/files/RuralCoop_July Aug12.pdf; Beverly Bell, "A Future for Agriculture, a Future for Haiti," *Louisiana Association of Cooperatives* e-newsletter, no. 161 (January 2018): 1.

12. Sally Stevens, interview with author, June 27, 2012, Cooperative Oral History Project; Reed, interview with author; "New Orleans Police Attack Peaceful March at St. Bernard" (December 16, 2007), YouTube, https://www.youtube.com/watch?v=9GPjNhVUzqk; Doug Parker, "Photos: Housing Debate Heats Up," *Times-Picayune*, December 20, 2007, http://www.nola.com/news/index.ssf/2007/12/photo_council_debates_housing.html.

13. Arena, "Black, White, Unite and Fight?" 172–73; Vincanne Adams, *Labors of Faith, Markets of Sorrow: New Orleans in the Wake of Katrina* (Durham: Duke University Press, 2013), 5–6.

14. "The Cooperative Economy: A Conversation with Gar Alperovitz," *Orion* (May/June–July/August 2014), http://www.orionmagazine.org/index.php/articles/article/8163; Diane K. Levy, Jennifer Comey, and Sandra Padilla, *Keeping the Neighborhood Affordable: A Handbook of Housing Strategies for Gentrifying Areas* (Washington, DC: Urban Institute, 2006), 38–39; Myungshik Choi, "The Impact of Community Land Trusts on Gentrification" (PhD diss., Texas A&M University, 2015), 150–55.

15. Fredric Jameson, *Archaeologies of the Future: The Desire Called Utopia and Other Fictions* (London: Verso, 2007), xii; David Harvey, *Spaces of Hope* (Berkeley: University of California Press, 2000), 154.

16. Robin D. G. Kelley, *Race Rebel: Culture, Politics, and the Black Working Class* (New York: Free Press, 1994), 3–4.

17. Arena, "Black, White, Unite and Fight?" 172–73; Adams, *Labors of Faith*, 5–6.

18. Paula Giese, "How the Old Coops Went Wrong," in *Workplace Democracy and Social Change*, eds. Frank Lindenfeld and Joyce Rothschild-Whitt (Boston: Porter Sargent Publishers, 1982), 315.

19. Pierre Bourdieu, "Utopia of Endless Exploitation: The Essence of Neoliberalism," *Le Monde Diplomatique* (December 1998), http://mondediplo.com/1998/12/08bourdieu.

20. Harvey, *Spaces of Hope*, 159.

21. Henri Lefebvre, *The Production of Space*, trans. Donald Nicholson-Smith (Oxford: Blackwell, 1991), 26.

22. Robin D. G. Kelley, *Hammer and Hoe: Alabama Communists during the Great Depression* (Chapel Hill: University of North Carolina Press, 1990), xi.

23. Richard Campanella, *Bienville's Dilemma: A Historical Geography of New Orleans* (Lafayette: University of Louisiana, 2008), 185–87.

24. Shirley Thompson, *Exiles at Home* (Cambridge: Harvard University Press, 2009), 82.

25. Campanella, *Bienville's Dilemma*, 152, 185–86; Warner, "Freret's Century," 343.

26. Thompson, *Exiles at Home*, 6.

27. Justin A. Nystrom, *New Orleans After the Civil War: Race, Politics, and a New Birth of Freedom* (Baltimore: Johns Hopkins University Press, 2010), 213.

28. Vincent Brown, *The Reaper's Garden: Death and Power in the World of Atlantic Slavery* (Cambridge: Harvard University Press 2008), 69.

29. Thompson, *Exiles at Home*, 74–78, 81–82.

30. George Sanchez, *Becoming Mexican American: Ethnicity, Culture and Identity in Chicano Los Angeles, 1900–1945* (New York and Oxford: Oxford University Press, 1993), 8.

31. "Mishaps and Misdeeds," *Daily Picayune*, May 19, 1884, 8, Advance Local Media; "Mishaps and Misdeeds," ibid., August 25, 1890, 2.

32. "Bacarisse Resigns from Laboring Men," *Daily Picayune*, August 30, 1897, 3, Advance Local Media.

33. "Officer Fredericks is Accused of Murder," *Daily Picayune*, December 16, 1905, 4, Advance Local Media; "Policeman Who Shot Harmless Negro," ibid., January 11, 1906, 5; "Trenchard Fined and Transferred," ibid, January 30, 1906, 4; "Grand Jury," ibid., February 21, 1906, 4.

34. Pierre Nora, "Between Memory and History: Les Lieux de Mémoire," *Representations* 26 (Spring 1989): 13.

35. Macon Fry, interview with author, June 10, 2012, Cooperative Oral History Project; Julia Africa, "Community Gardens as Healing Spaces," Harvard University Graduate School of Design, last updated 2011, http://isites.harvard.edu/icb/icb.do?keyword=k94076&pageid=icb.page577179; Leonard N. Moore, *Black Rage in New Orleans: Police Brutality and African American Activism* (Baton Rouge: Louisiana State University Press, 2010), 10–11.

36. Jocine Velasco, interview with author, June 24, 2012, Cooperative Oral History Project.

37. Reed, interview with author.

38. John W. Blassingame, *Black New Orleans, 1860–1880* (Chicago: University of Chicago Press, 1973), 139–47, 151, 164–69; Jessica Gordon Nembhard, *Collective Courage: A History of African American Cooperative Economic Thought and Practice* (University Park: Pennsylvania State University Press, 2014), 42, 101; Woods, "Katrina's World," 446; Hasan Kwame Jeffries, *Bloody Lowndes: Civil Rights and Black Power in Alabama's Black Belt* (New York: New York University, 2009), 40–41, 72–73; Kent B. Germany, *New Orleans After the Promises* (Athens and London: University of Georgia Press, 2007), 31.

39. Michel de Certeau, *The Practice of Everyday Life*, trans. Steven Randall (Berkeley: University of California Press, 1984).

40. Kelley, *Hammer and Hoe*, xi; Kelley, *Race Rebels*, 2–5.

41. Thompson, *Exiles at Home*, 114–33.

42. Gilles Vandal, "Black Utopia in Early Reconstruction New Orleans: The People's Bakery," *Louisiana History* 38, no. 4 (Autumn 1997); 444; Giese, "How the Old Coops Went Wrong," 322; Jonathan Garlock, *Guide to the Local Assemblies of the Knights of Labor* (Westport: Greenwood Press, 1982), xi.

43. Covington Hall, *Labor Struggles in the Deep South and Other Writings*, ed. David R. Roediger (Chicago: Charles H. Kerr Publishing Company, 1999), 24.

44. Joanna Brooks, *American Lazarus: Religion and the Rise of African-American and Native American Literatures* (Oxford: Oxford University Press, 2003), 116; Adam Fairclough, *Race and Democracy; The Civil Rights Struggle in Louisiana, 1915–1972* (Athens: University of Georgia Press, 1999), 69–71; Thompson, *Exiles at Home*, 109; Vandal, "Black Utopia," 437–39.

45. Germany, *New Orleans After the Promises*, 28, 29; "Historical Scope and Notes," 1, Box 1, New Orleans Black Benevolent Associations Collection, 1872–1950, Xavier University Archives and Special Collections, Xavier University.

46. David Elliot Draper, *Mardi Gras Indians: The Ethnomusicology of Black Association in New Orleans* (PhD diss., Tulane University, 1973), 31.

47. Rachel Lorraine Emanuel and Alexander P. Tureaud, *A More Noble Cause: A. P. Tureaud and the Struggle for Civil Rights in Louisiana* (Baton Rouge: Louisiana State University Press, 2011), 123; Joel Dinerstein, interview with author, July 1, 2012.

48. Germany, *New Orleans After the Promises*, 31.

49. Thompson, *Exiles at Home*, 100–101.

50. Dr. Ernest Cherrie to JCFBMAA President, Officers and Members, September 6, 1933, Box 1, Folder 1, Juvenile Co-operators Fraternals Benevolent Mutual Aid Association Records, Xavier University Archives and Special Collections, Xavier University. Hereafter cited as JCFBMAA Records.

51. Rebecca Scott, *Degrees of Freedom: Louisiana and Cuba after Slavery* (Cambridge: President and Fellows of Harvard College, 2005), 76, 88, 200; Vandal, "Black Utopia," 441–48; Fairclough, *Race and Democracy*, 69–71.

52. Giese, "How the Old Coops Went Wrong."

53. Mrs. Howard Egleston, "The Co-operative Movement in New Orleans and the South," in *Proceedings of the National Conference of Social Work, at the Forty-Seventh Annual Session Held in New Orleans, Louisiana*, April 14–21, 1920 (Chicago, 1920), 306.

54. Lizabeth Cohen, *A Consumers' Republic: The Politics of Mass Consumption in Postwar America* (New York, 2003), 25; de Jong, "From Votes to Vegetables," 145–46; Rivlin, *Katrina: After the Flood*, 148.

55. Glenda Elizabeth Gilmore, *Defying Dixie: The Radical Roots of Civil Rights, 1919–1950* (New York: W. W. Norton and Company, 2009), 11.

56. Vandal, "Black Utopia," 440.

57. Ibid., 440–44; Ellen C. Merrill, *Germans of Louisiana* (Gretna: Pelican Publishing Company, 2005, 91).

58. Lafcadio Hearn, "Jewish Emigrants for Louisiana," in *Inventing New Orleans: Writings of Lafcadio Hearn*, ed. S. Frederick Starr (Jackson: University Press of Mississippi, 2001), 162–64; Robert P. Sutton, *Communal Utopias and the American Experience: Religious Communities, 1732–2000* (Westport: Praeger, 2003), 105–108.

59. Egleston, "Co-operative Movement in New Orleans and the South," 305–306; Giese, "How the Old Coops Went Wrong," 317–19; Florence E. Parker, *The First 125 Years: A History of Distributive and Service Cooperation in the United States, 1829–1954* (Superior: CLUSA, 1956), 66; J. G. St. Clair Drake, "Why Not 'Co-operate'?" *Opportunity: Journal of Negro Life* 14, no. 8 (August 1936): 231, 234, 251.

60. "Cooperative Stores," *Daily Picayune*, August 27, 1879, 1, Advance Local Media.

61. Giese, "How the Old Co-ops Went Wrong," 327.

62. Ibid., 320, 327–29; Victoria Baiamonte, "New Orleans, the New South, and the Fight for the Panama Exposition" (MA thesis, University of New Orleans, 2011), iv.

63. Giese, "How the Old Co-ops Went Wrong," 320, 323.

64. Ibid., 320, 330; Daniel Zwerdling, "The Uncertain Revival of Food Cooperatives," in *Co-ops, Communes and Collectives: Experiments in Social Change in the 1960s and 1970s*, eds. John Case and Rosemary C. R. Taylor (New York: Pantheon Books, 1979), 104, 108; Drake, "Why Not 'Co-operate'?" 231; John Curl, *For All the People: Uncovering the Hidden History of Cooperation, Cooperative Movements, and Communalism in America* (Oakland: PM Press, 2009), 165; Cohen, *A Consumer's Republic*, 25.

65. Giese, "How the Old Co-ops Went Wrong," 328.

66. Beverly Hendrix Wright, "New Orleans: A City that Care Forgot," in *In Search of the New South: The Black Urban Experience in the 1970s and 1980s*, ed. Robert D. Bullard (Tuscaloosa: University of Alabama Press, 1989), 51, 56–60.

67. Robert Sommer, Deborah Schlanger, Robert Hackman, and Steven Smith, "Consumer Cooperatives and Worker Collectives: A Comparison," *Pacific Sociological Association* 27, no. 2 (April 1984): 139–40; "Differences Between Worker Cooperatives and Collectives," Cultivate.coop, last modified on February 24, 2016, http://cultivate.coop/wiki/Differences_Between_Worker_Cooperatives_and_Collectives.

68. Asante Salaam, "Griot House, Draft 2," November 1997, Box 188, Folder 2, Tom Dent Papers, 1861–1998, Amistad Research Center, Tulane University. Hereafter cited as Tom Dent Papers.

69. Giese, "How the Old Co-ops Went Wrong," 328.

70. Curl, *For All the People*, 248, 254.

71. Jameson, *Archaeologies of the Future*, xvi.

72. George Lewis and the Nameless Sound / Shepherd School Ensemble perform George Lewis's Creative Construction Set, October 18, 2018, Rice University, Houston, Texas.

73. James C. Scott, *Domination and the Arts of Resistance: Hidden Transcripts* (New Haven: Yale University Press, 1990), 183.

74. John Clark, interview with author, June 28, 2012, Cooperative Oral History Project.

75. Kelley, *Race Rebels*, 8–9.

Chapter One

1. "Ready to Solve the Great Problem of Finding Work for All the City's Unemployed," *Daily Picayune*, July 16, 1897, 3, Advance Local Media; "Coxey's Army: To Have an Imitation in a Parade and Meeting Here," ibid., June 3, 1897, 12.

2. "Ready to Solve," 3.

3. Ibid., 3.

4. Eric Arnesen, *Waterfront Workers of New Orleans: Race, Class, and Politics, 1863–1923* (New York: Oxford University Press, 1991), 121, 147; Donald D. Devore, *Defying Jim Crow: African American Community Development and the Struggle for Racial Equality in New Orleans, 1900–1960* (Baton Rouge: Louisiana State University Press, 2015), 27–28; Thompson, *Exiles at Home*, 269.

5. Arnesen, *Waterfront Workers*, 25, 121, 147; Devore, *Defying Jim Crow*, 27–28, Scott, *Degrees of Freedom*, 76, 88, 200.

6. Quoted in Thompson, *Exiles at Home*, 269.

7. Eric Arnesen, "The Peculiar Waterfront: The Crescent City and the Rewriting of the History of Race and Labor in the United States," in *Working in the Big Easy: The History and Politics of Labor in New Orleans*, ed. Thomas J. Adams (Lafayette: University of Louisiana at Lafayette Press, 2014), 28–31.

8. "Bacarisse Resigns," 3.

9. Tim Craig, "It Wasn't Even a Hurricane, But Heavy Rains Flooded New Orleans as Pumps Falter," *Washington Post*, August 9, 2017, https://www.washingtonpost.com/national/it-wasnt-even-a-hurricane-but-heavy-rains-flooded-new-orleans-as-pumps-faltered/2017/08/09/b3b7506a-7d37-11e7-9d08-b79f191668ed_story.html?utm_term=.2fa42cf20d3e; Carolyn Kolb, "At the Confluence of Science and Power: Water Struggles of New Orleans in the Nineteenth Century (PhD diss., University of New Orleans, 2006), 240; John Kendall, *History of New Orleans* (Chicago: Lewis Publishing Company, 1922), 530, http://penelope.uchicago.edu/Thayer/E/Gazetteer/Places/America/United_States/Louisiana/New_Orleans/_Texts/KENHNO/33*.html.

10. Benjamin F. Alexander, *Coxey's Army: Popular Protest in the Gilded Age* (Baltimore: Johns Hopkins University Press, 2015), 47; Hallie Flanagan, "The Federal Theatre Project," in *An Ideal Theater: Founding a New American Art*, ed. Todd London (New York: Theatre Communications Group, 2013), 42.

11. 1870 United States Census, s.v. "Eugene Bacarise," New Orleans, Orleans Parish, Louisiana, Ancestry.com; "Bacarisse" (February 2, 1839), Passenger Lists of Vessels Arriving at New Orleans, Louisiana, 1820–1902, Ancestry.com; Amadee Ducatel, "Bacarisse, Lise Augustin Cohen," Notarial Act Index 3 (June–December 1867): 2, http://www.notarialarchives.org/aducatelindexes/ducatel_amedee_vol_90.pdf; 1900 United States Census, s.v. "Augustine Bacarisse," New Orleans, Orleans Parish, Louisiana, Ancestry.com.

12. "Bacarisse, Charles (C. Bacarisse & Co.)," *Soard's New Orleans City Directory* (New Orleans: L. Soards & Co., 1876), 114.

13. José Cantón Navarro, *History of Cuba: The Challenge of the Yoke and the Star* (Havana: Union Nacional de Juristas, 2000), 43–44; John D. Ribó, "Cubans and Cuban Americans, 1870–1940," in *Immigrants in American History: Arrival, Adaptation, and Integration*, ed. Elliott Robert Barkan (Santa Barbara: ABC-CIO, LLC, 2013), 309; Evan Matthew Daniel, "Cubans," in *Encyclopedia of U.S. Labor and Working-Class History*, ed. Eric Arnesen (New York: Routledge, 2007), 1, 332.

14. 1870 United States Census, s.v. "Eugene Bacarise"; David M. Pletcher, *The Diplomacy of Trade and Investment: American Economic Expansion in the Hemisphere, 1865–1900* (Columbia: University of Missouri Press, 1998), 178–79; Henry A. Kmen, "Remember the Virginius: New Orleans and Cuba in 1873," *Louisiana History* 11, no. 4 (Fall 1970): 313–30.

15. Ribó, "Cubans and Cuban Americans," 309; Otto Olivera, "Jose Marti, Cuba y Nueva Orleans," *Guaracabuya*, http://www.amigospais-guaracabuya.org/oago0002.php.

16. Max Henríquez Ureña, "Poetas Cubanos de Expresion Francesa," *Inicio* 3, no. 6 (May 1941): 6, http://revista-iberoamericana.pitt.edu/ojs/index.php/Iberoamericana/article/view/1031/1265; *French Newspapers of Louisiana* (1932), 304, http://www.americanantiquarian.org/proceedings/44817365.pdf; J. G. Hava, "La Propaganda Política," in Los Habitantes de Cuba. La Indemnización [pamphlet] (New Orleans, 1870), cited in Gerald E. Poyo, *With All, and for the Good of All: The Emergence of Popular Nationalism in the Cuban Communities of the United States, 1848–1898* (Durham: Duke University, 1989), 37.

17. Matthew Frye Jacobson, *Whiteness of a Different Color* (Cambridge: Harvard University Press, 1998), 206; Matthew Frye Jacobson, *Barbarian Virtues: The United States Encounters Foreign Peoples at Home and Abroad, 1876–1917* (New York: Hill and Wang, 2000), 41, 43; Daniel, "Cubans," 333.

18. 1870 United States Census, s.v. "Eugene Bacaris"; 1880 United States Census, s.v. "Charles Bacarrisse," New Orleans, Orleans Parish, Louisiana, accessed through Ancestry.com.

19. "The City," *The Crusader* 2, no. 23 (July 19, 1890): 3; Daniel Hardie, *Exploring Early Jazz: The Origins and Evolution of the New Orleans Style* (Lincoln: Writers Club Press, 2002), 26; "At Loeper's Park," *Daily Picayune*, June 27, 1887, 2, Advance Local Media; "Notes About Town," *Weekly Pelican*, November 16, 1889, 3.

20. "The Late Post-Office Robbery Case," *New Orleans Daily Crescent*, September 27, 1861, 1. Chronicling America; Orleans Parish Civil District Court, "Amadeé Praderes," *Louisiana, Orleans Parish Will Books* 19 (New Orleans: Orleans Parish Civil District Court, 1877–1878), 390–91; "Eugene Bacarisse," *Soards' New Orleans City Directory* (New Orleans: Soards' Directory Co, 1898), 86.

21. Blassingame, *Black New Orleans*, 167–68; Nembhard, *Collective Courage*; "Notes About Town" 1889, 3; "Scope Notes," Box 1, JCFBMA Records.

22. J. B. Prados to JCFBMA board of directors, February 12, 1918, Box 1, Folder 1, JCFBMA Records.

23. "Strikers Fill Exchange Alley," *Daily Picayune*, July 26, 1901, 3, Advance Local Media; Daniel," Cubans," 333–34.

24. Thompson, *Exiles at Home*, 267; Norman R. Smith, *Footprints of Black Louisiana* (www.Xlibris.com: Xlibris Corporation, 2010), 54; Jack Rummel, *African-American Social Leaders and Activists* (New York: Fact on File, 2003), 55; Turry Flucker and Phoenix Savage, *African Americans of New Orleans* (Charleston: Arcadia Publishing, 2010), 28; "Alpizar, Andrew," *Soards' New Orleans City Directory* (New Orleans, Soards' City Directory, 1895), 72; Arnesen, *Waterfront Workers*, 34–35; Daniel Rosenberg, *New Orleans Dockworkers: Race, Labor, and Unionism, 1892–1923* (Albany: State University of New York Press, 1988), 6–8.

25. Scott, *Degrees of Freedom*, 75–77; Joseph Logsdon and Caryn Cossé Bell, "The Americanization of Black New Orleans," in *Creole New Orleans: Race and Americanization*, eds. Arnold R. Hirsch and Joseph Logsdon (Baton Rouge: Louisiana State University Press, 1992), 255–56.

26. Louis Martinet, *The Violation of a Constitutional Right* (New Orleans: Citizens' Committee, 1893), 17.

27. Jazmin Smith, "l'Athénée Louisianais Records, 1834–1987: Collection Overview," Louisiana Research Collection, Howard-Tilton Memorial Library, Tulane University. Hereafter cited as LaRC.

28. "Personal and General Notes," *Daily Picayune*, March 20, 1892, 6, Advance Local Media; Graeme Pente, "From Paris to Texas: French Fourierists in Power and in Exile, 1848–1857," paper presented at Society for Utopian Studies Annual Conference, Berkeley, California, November 2, 2018.

29. Scott, *Degrees of Freedom*, 88, 200; Vandal, "Black Utopia"; Jossianna Arroyo, *Writing Secrecy in Caribbean Freemasonry* (New York: Palgrave MacMillan, 2013); Thompson, *Exiles at Home*, 267; "Louis A. Martinet Records," New Orleans Notarial Archives, available at http://www.notarialarchives.org/martinet.htm.

30. Helena Blavatsky, *The Key to Theosophy* (Pasadena: Theosophical University Press [1946, 1889]), 39.

31. John Thorn, *Baseball in the Garden of Eden* (New York: Simon and Schuster, 2012), 264; "The Theosophists," *Daily Picayune*, February 28, 1897, 11, Advance Local Media; Theosophists to Make a Crusade," ibid., November 22, 1896, 20; "The Theosophists," ibid., May 27, 1892, 3; "Banquet to Cuban Guests," *New Century* 6, no. 3 (November 13, 1902): 19.

32. "The Unemployed Organized Now, But Call Themselves the Laboring Men's Protective Association," *Daily Picayune*, July 26, 1897, 7, Advance Local Media.

33. "Bacarisse Will Resign: Neither Capital nor Labor Will Give Him Food," *Daily Picayune*, August 14, 1897, 3, Advance Local Media.

34. "Eugene Bacarisse," *Soards' New Orleans City Directory* (New Orleans: Soards' Directory Co., 1893); "Eugene Bacarisse," ibid. (New Orleans: Soards' Directory Co., 1894); "Eugene Bacarisse," 1898, 86; Richard Campanella, *Geographies of New Orleans* (Lafayette: Center for Louisiana Studies, 2006), 215.

35. "Bacarisse, Antone" and "Bacarisse, Charles," *Soards' New Orleans City Directory* (New Orleans: Soards Directory Co, 1890), 132.

36. "People's Party," *Daily Picayune*, November 30, 1897, 7, Advance Local Media; Woods, "Katrina's World," 436; William Ivy Hair, *Bourbonism and Agrarian Protest: Louisiana Politics, 1877–1900* (Baton Rouge: Louisiana State University Press, 1969), 155–56, 215–17, 274; Matthew Hild, *Greenbackers, Knights of Labor, and Populists: Farmer-Labor Insurgency in the Late-Nineteenth-Century South* (Athens: University of Georgia Press, 2007), 151; Charles Postel, *The Populist Vision* (Oxford: Oxford University Press, 2009), 121–22.

37. Charles Pierce LeWarne, *Utopias on Puget Sound, 1885–1915* (Seattle: University of Washington Press, 1995), 6; Sue Eakin and Manie Culbertson, *Louisiana: The Land and Its People* (Gretna: Pelican Company, 1998), 361.

38. LeWarne, *Utopias on Puget Sound*, 55–61; Charles L. Easton, "A Backward Look at a Utopian Plan: Equality Colony Near Bow, 1896–1906," *Seattle Times*, November 25, 1962, http://www.skagitriverjournal.com/WestCounty/NW/Colony/EastonCL3-Equality1962.html.

39. John Frederick Nau, *The German People of New Orleans, 1650–1900* (Hattiesburg: Mississippi Southern College, 1958), 55, 63, 68; Campanella, *Bienville's Dilemma*, 38, 373; Rosenberg, *New Orleans Dockworkers*, 17.

40. Rosenberg, *New Orleans Dockworkers*, 213.

41. LeWarne, *Utopias on Puget Sound*, 92.

42. Ad, "A Young German," *Daily Picayune*, May 30, 1896, 6, Advance Local Media; "German-American Republicans," ibid., September 30, 1896, 9.

43. "The Unemployed Miss Their Dinners," *Daily Picayune*, August 9, 1897, 3, Advance Local Media; "Mayor and Unemployed," ibid., September 18, 1897, 3; "Local Populists," ibid., October 3, 1897, 12.

44. "Co-operative Commonwealth," *Daily Picayune*, February 13, 1897, 3; Eugene Bacarisse, "Socialism Set Forth by a Socialist," ibid., June 6, 1897, 16.

45. LeWarne, *Utopias on Puget Sound*, 60–61, 92.

46. Blavatsky, *The Key to Theosophy*, 39–41; Eugene Bacarisse, "The Problems of Industrial Life," *Daily Picayune*, June 30, 1897, 6, Advance Local Media; "The Unemployed Miss," 3.

47. "Theosophists to Make a Crusade," 20.

48. Bacarisse, "The Problems of Industrial Life," 6.

49. Ibid.

50. Matthew Wilson, "Republican Spaces: An Intellectual History of Positivist Urban Sociology in Britain, 1855–1920" (PhD diss., Royal Holloway, University of London, 2015), 168; Matthew Wilson, "Victorian Sociology, Trade Unionism, and Utopia: A Social Programme for an Ideal Republic: The Positivist Sociology of Frederic Harrison," paper presented at the Society of Utopian Studies Annual Conference, Memphis, Tennessee, November 10, 2017.

51. "Bishop Sessums Called Upon by the Co-operative Commonwealth," *Daily Picayune*, March 12, 1897, 11, Advance Local Media.

52. Curl, *For All the People*, 121.

53. Bacarisse, "The Problems of Industrial Life," 6.

54. Germany, *New Orleans After the Promises*, 39; "Coxey Talks to the Co-operative Commonwealth and Its Guests," *Daily Picayune*, February 27, 1897, 10, Advance Local Media; Alexander, *Coxey's Army*, 98.

55. H. W. Brands, *The Reckless Decade: American in the 1890s* (Chicago: University of Chicago Press, 1995), 162; Jacob S. Coxey, *The Coxey Plan* (Massillon: Jacob S. Coxey, 1914), 62.

56. "Coxey to Talk," *Daily Picayune*, February 28, 1897, 10, Advance Local Media.

57. Joy J. Jackson, *New Orleans in the Gilded Age: Politics and Urban Progress* (Baton Rouge: Louisiana State University Press, 1969), 53–54.

58. Michinard, "Floods and Overflows in New Orleans During the 1890s," Works Progress Administration (1930), 1. State Library of Louisiana, http://cdm16313.contentdm.oclc.org/cdm/ref/collection/LWP/id/8833.

59. Kendall, *History of New Orleans*, 529.

60. Ibid., 529–30; Jackson, *New Orleans in the Gilded Age*, 37–44; Donald W. Davis, "Historical Perspective on Crevasses, Levees, and the Mississippi," in *Transforming New Orleans and Its Environs: Centuries of Change*, ed. Craig E. Colten (Pittsburgh: University of Pittsburgh Press, 2000), 92.

61. Robert M. Brown, "The Mississippi River Flood of 1912," *American Geographical Society of New York Bulletin* 44, part 2, no. 9 (1912): 652.

62. "The Unemployed Organized," 7.

63. "The Picayune's Telephone," *Daily Picayune*, June 2, 1897, 6. Advance Local Media.

64. "Coxey's Army," 12.

65. Freddi Williams Evans, *Congo Square: African Roots in New Orleans* (Lafayette: University of Louisiana at Lafayette Press, 2011), 19, 30, 35–36, 73–74.

66. Keith Weldon Medley, *We as Freemen: Plessy v. Ferguson* (Gretna: Pelican Publishing, 2003), 34; Humbert S. Nelli, *The Business of Crime: Italians and Syndicate Crime in the United States* (Chicago: University of Chicago Press, 1981), 62.

67. "Coxey's Army," 12.

68. "That Mass Meeting" *Daily Picayune*, June 8, 1897, 3, Advance Local Media.

69. "Graf Acts Coxey Just for One Day," *Daily Picayune*, June 4, 1897, 3, Advance Local Media.

70. "That Mass Meeting," 3.

71. "Unemployed Organized," 7; "Ready to Solve," 3.

72. "Graf Acts Coxey," 3.

73. Bacarisse, "Socialism Set Forth," 16.

74. "Bacarisse Resigns," 3.

75. "Unemployed Organized," 7.

76. The LMPA's black members included Rudolph Charles, sergeant-of-arms; Albert J. Holmes first vice president and president; Victor Joachim, finance committee; and J. W. White, ways, means, and employment committee. Caleb Yancey and Henry Desalles both served on a committee to meet with Mayor Flower. Lafayette Tharpe and R. W. B. Gould, black dockworker unionists, spoke at a LMPA meeting. LMPA's platform intersected black union, political party, and cooperative activism, as well. Colored Laboringmen's Alliance head Tharpe convened a series of conferences in August and September 1896 in which white and black cotton screwmen and longshoremen agreed to boycott companies if they refused to hire black union men. More biographical information about black LMPA members available at: Scott, *Degrees of Freedom*, 88, 153–65; "The Republican State Convention," *Daily Picayune*, January 30, 1896, 8, Advance Local Media; "Colored Democrats," ibid., May 16, 1897, 15; "The Ebony Brother as a Statesman," ibid., August 16, 1896, 10; "The Suffrage Committee," ibid., February 25, 1898, 14; "Levee Labor," ibid., August 17, 1896, 3; R. B. W. Gould, *Official Journal of the Proceedings of the Senate of the State of Louisiana at the Regular Session* (Baton Rouge: General Assembly, 1888), 341–42; Arnesen, *Waterfront Workers of New Orleans*, 159.

77. "Unemployed Miss," 3; Scott, *Degrees of Freedom*, 88, 153–65; Nystrom, *New Orleans After the Civil War*, 202.

78. Rosenberg, *New Orleans Dockworkers*, 14–15, 97.

79. David Roediger, introduction to Hall, *Labor Struggles in the Deep South*, 22; James R. Green, *Grass-Roots Socialism: Radical Movements in the Southwest, 1895–1943* (Baton Rouge: Louisiana State University Press, 1978), 95.

80. American Federation of Labor, *Report of the Proceedings of the Fourteenth Annual Convention of the American Federation of Labor* held in Denver, Colorado, December 10–18, 1894, 25.

81. "Bacarisse Resigns," 3.

82. Scott, *Degrees of Freedom*, 76, 88, 200; "Unemployed Miss," 3; "Unemployed Organized," 7; Martinet, *The Violation of a Constitutional Right*, 9; Medley, *We as Freemen*, 33;

83. "A Labor Meeting," *Daily Picayune*, September 23, 1897, 6, Advance Local Media.

84. Richard White, *The Middle Ground: Indians, Empires, and Republics in the Great Lakes Region, 1650–1815* (Cambridge: Cambridge University Press, 1991), x.

85. "Bacarisse, Eugene," *Soards' New Orleans City Directory* (New Orleans: Soards' Directory Co., 1898), 86; "Mathieu, Louis H.," *Soards' New Orleans City Directory* (New Orleans: Soards' Directory Co., 1895).

86. "Supervisors of Election," *Daily Picayune*, October 27, 1888, 8, Advance Local Media; "Some of Our Patrons," *The Crusader* 2, no. 23, July 19, 1890, 3.

87. "An Act," *Weekly Louisianan*, July 6, 1871, 3; "Advertisement," *New Orleans Tribune*, December 24, 1867, 1; "Attorney Rene Calvin Metoyer (1858–1937)," CreoleGen, http://www.creolegen.org/2012/09/15/attorney-rene-calvin-metoyer-1858–1937/.

88. "Scope Notes," "Historical Notes," 2–3, and "Journal of Minutes" (January 22, 1895), 10, Box 1, Folder 2, JCFBMAA Records; Scott, *Degrees of Freedom*, 75; "Louis A. Martinet Records."

89. Rosenberg, *New Orleans Dockworkers*, 17.

90. "Unemployed Organized," 7.

91. "Unemployed Miss," 3.

92. Ibid.; first through third quotes: "Unemployed Organized," 7.

93. "Custom House Notes," *Daily Picayune*, October 27, 1892, 3; "Colored Meeting," *Times-Democrat*, June 8, 1898, 6; Nystrom, *New Orleans After the Civil War*, 230; Flucker and Savage, *African Americans of New Orleans*, 28; Smith, *Footprints of Black Louisiana*, 54.

94. "Sensations in the Levee Riot Trial," *Daily Picayune*, July 26, 1895, 3, Advance Local Media; "Levee Riot Case a Record Breaker," ibid., June 21, 1895, 3.

95. "Bacarisse Resigns," 3; Hild, *Greenbackers, Knights of Labor, and Populists*, 151.

96. "Graf Gets a Hall and an Audience" *Daily Picayune*, July 18, 1897, 16, Advance Local Media; "The Conference on Wages," ibid., July 23, 1897, 7; "Unemployed Organized," 7; "Local Populists," 12.

97. "Unemployed Organized," 7.

98. "Unemployed Miss," 3.

99. Scott, *Degrees of Freedom*, 156–59; Kendall, *History of New Orleans*, 521; "To Try to Keep Out Italians," *The Sun*, August 20, 1897, 9; Frank A. Fetter, *Economics in Two Volumes* (New York: Century Co., 1922), 11, 220.

100. Joseph Maselli and Dominic Candeloro, *Italians in New Orleans* (Charleston: Arcadia Publishing, 2004), 13; Donna R. Gabaccia, *We Are What We Eat: Ethnic Food and the Making of Americans* (Cambridge: Harvard University Press, 1998), 152–54.

101. "The American Federation of Labor," *Forest Republican*, October 6, 1897, 1.

102. "To Try to Keep Out Italians," 9; Scott, *Degrees of Freedom*, 156–58.

103. "Graf Gets a Hall," 16.

104. "Home Labor's Plea," *Daily Picayune*, July 19, 1897, 10, Advance Local Media.

105. United States Bureau of Labor Statistics, *History of Wages in the United States from Colonial Times to 1928* (Washington, DC: US Government Printing Office, 1934), 260, https://babel.hathitrust.org/cgi/pt?id=uc1.32106007458745;view=1up;seq=276; "The Conference on Wages," *Daily Picayune*, July 23, 1897, 7, Advance Local Media.

106. "Unemployed Organized Now," 7.

107. "Bacarisse Resigns," 3.

108. "Ninety Cases, Eight Deaths," *Daily Picayune*, October 1, 1897, 1, 8, Advance Local Media; Margaret Humphreys, *Yellow Fever in the South* (Baltimore: Johns Hopkins University Press, 1999), 115, 137, 145.

109. "Laboring Men Call a Conference to Urge Quarantine Modification," *Daily Picayune*, October 1, 1897, 8, Advance Local Media; "The Governor Asked to Appeal for a Modification of Quarantine Rigors," ibid., September 25, 1897, 7, Advance Local Media; Robert H. Zieger, *For Jobs and Freedom: Race and Labor in America Since 1865* (Lexington: University Press of Kentucky, 2007), 40; Charles B. Hersch, *Subversive Sounds: Race and the Birth of Jazz* (Chicago: University of Chicago Press, 2008), 18.

110. Kendall, *History of New Orleans*, 768; "Laboring Men Call," 7.

111. "Drainage Board Nearing the Work of Building the First Section of the System," *Daily Picayune*, July 30, 1987, 8, Advance Local Media; "Engineering Society," ibid., November 6, 1898, 8; 1900 US Census, s.v. "Henry L. Zander," New Orleans, Orleans Parish, Louisiana, Ancestry.com; "Bacarisse Resigns," 3.

112. Arnesen, *Waterfront Workers of New Orleans*, 148; "Administrations of the Mayors of New Orleans: Walter Chew Flower (1850–1900)," Louisiana Division New Orleans Public Library, http://www.neworleanspubliclibrary.org/~nopl/info/louinfo/admins/flower.htm.

113. "Unemployed Organized," 7; "Bacarisse Resigns," 3.

114. Rosenberg, *New Orleans Dockworkers*, 15.

115. "Local Populists," 12.

116. "A Mysterious Orator," *Daily Picayune*, October 24, 1897, 8, Advance Local Media.

117. Quoted in "Colored Meeting," *Times-Democrat*, June 8, 1898, 6, Advance Local Media; Scott, *Degrees of Freedom*, 166–72; Amy Kaplan, "Black and Blue on San Juan Hill," in *Cultures of U.S. Imperialism*, eds. Amy Kaplan and Donald E. Pease (Durham: Duke University Press, 1993), 232.

118. Michael E. Crutcher, *Tremé: Race and Place in a New Orleans Neighborhood* (Athens: University of Georgia Press, 2010), 52; "Notes About Town," 3; Thomas J. Ward Jr., *Black Physicians in the Jim Crow South* (Fayetteville: University of Arkansas Press, 2003), 140–41; "Scope Notes," Box 1, Folder 2, JCFBMAA Records; Nembhard, *Collective Courage*, 149; Scott, *Degrees of Freedom*, 167, 267; William Hilary Coston, *The Spanish-American War Volunteer* (Freeport: Books for Libraries Press, 1899), 102; "Case of the Steamship Agents Against the Screwmen," *Daily Picayune*, May 10, 1903, 40, Advance Local Media; "A Fair for the Poor," ibid., March 20, 1899, 3.

119. Jacobson, *Whiteness of a Different Color*, 209–210.

120. "The Unemployed Miss," 3.

121. Kaplan, "Black and Blue on San Juan Hill," 225.

122. "Graf, August," *Soards' New Orleans City Directory* (New Orleans: Soards Directory Co., 1894), 388; Orleans Parish (La.) Registrar of Voters, "Index to Registration of Foreign Born Persons, Vol 2: 1891–1896," New Orleans Public Library City Archives, accessed on November 30, 2017, http://nutrias.org/~nopl/inv/vx/vx100g2.htm.

123. "German-American Republicans," 9.

124. "Laboring Men: Draw up a Memorial with Reference to City Emergency Employ," *Daily Picayune*, October 25, 1897, 3, Advance Local Media; "German-American Republicans," 9; Campanella, *Geographies of New Orleans*, 257.

125. Nau, *The German People of New Orleans*, 55; "August Graf Dead," *Times-Picayune*, December 29, 1915, 9, Advance Local Media; Pamela Tyler, *Silk Stockings and Ballot Boxes: Women & Politics in New Orleans, 1920–1963* (Athens and London: University of Georgia Press, 1996), 11.

126. Matthew Josephson, *Union House, Union Bar: The History of the Hotel and Restaurant Employees and Bartenders International Union, AFL-CIO* (New York: Random House, 1956), 173; "Bartenders' Union," *Times-Picayune*, February 17, 1907, 2, Advance Local Media; "Co-operative Commonwealth," 3.

127. "Laboring Men: Approve the Mayor-Mullen-McGary Plan of Relief," *Daily Picayune*, October 31, 1897, 3, Advance Local Media.

128. "Laboring Men: Draw," 3.

129. "Laboring Men: Approve," 3; "Quarantine's Farewell," *Daily Picayune*, November 5, 1897, 1, Advance Local Media; "Labor's Indorsement," ibid., November 5, 1897, 1.

130. Campanella, *Bienville's Dilemma*, 49, 151.

131. "Getting Work: The Unemployed Meeting Success Now," *Daily Picayune*, November 29, 1897, 5, Advance Local Media; "White Laboring Men," ibid., November 25, 1897, 3.

132. "Thanksgiving in Shorthand," *Daily Picayune*, November 25, 1892, 3, Advance Local Media; Kolb, "At the Confluence of Science and Power," 234.

133. Eugene Bacarisse, "The Lesson of the Flood," *Daily Picayune*, April 21, 1897, 9, Advance Local Media.

134. Tyler, *Silk Stockings and Ballot Boxes*, 184–85; Sara M. Evans, *Born for Liberty: A History of Women in America* (New York, 1989), 157, 191; Kolb, "At the Confluence of Science and Power," 236–37; "The Committee on City Sewerage," *Daily Picayune*, August 6, 1897, 7, Advance Local Media; "Sewerage as the Private Prerequisite," ibid., October 7, 1898, 9; "A Mysterious Orator," 88; "Laboring Men: Draw," 3; "Laboring Men: Approve," 3.

135. Henry E. Chambers, *A History of Louisiana* (Chicago: American Historical Society, 1925), 2, 101–102; Jackson, *New Orleans in the Gilded Age*, 54; Kolb, "At the Confluence of Science and Power," 234–40.

136. Kolb, "At the Confluence of Science and Power," 239.

Chapter Two

1. Harvey A. Levenstein, *Revolution at the Table: The Transformation of the American Diet* (New York, 1988), 109–112. Funding for this research was provided by the Louann Atkins Temple Endowed Presidential Fellowship and the Graduate School Continuing Fellowship from the University of Texas at Austin.

2. "Housewives Still Successful with New Curb Market," *Times-Picayune*, January 16, 1916, 6, Advance Local Media.

3. "Curb Market Is So Successful," *Times-Picayune*, January 6, 1916, 10, Advance Local Media.

4. Egleston, "The Co-operative Movement in New Orleans and the South," 305–308.

5. "Farmers Flock to Curb Market of Housewives," *Times-Picayune*, January 20, 1916, 8, Advance Local Media; "Municipal Curb Markets Opened in Carrollton," ibid., July 14, 1917, 4.

6. Anne Firor Scott, *The Southern Lady: From Pedestal to Politics, 1830–1930* (Charlottesville: University Press of Virginia, 1970), 150; Levenstein, *Revolution at the Table*, 109–110; Anne Meis Knupfer, *Food Co-ops in America: Communities, Consumption, and Economic Democracy* (Ithaca: Cornell University Press, 2013), 18–19.

7. "City Federation of Woman Clubs Forms," *Daily Picayune*, November 27, 1912, 5, Advance Local Media.

8. Landon R. Y. Storrs, *Civilizing Capitalism: The National Consumers' League, Women's Activism, and Labor Standards in the New Deal Era* (Chapel Hill: University of North Carolina Press, 2000), 145; Tracey Deutsch, *Building a Housewife's Paradise: Gender, Politics, and American Grocery Stores in the Twentieth Century* (Chapel Hill: University of North Carolina Press, 2010), 106.

9. Storrs, *Civilizing Capitalism*, 16, 140; Tyler, *Silk Stockings and Ballot Boxes*, 5–6.

10. Campanella, *Bienville's Dilemma*, 185–87.

11. Corrine M. McConnaughy, *The Woman Suffrage Movement in America: A Reassessment* (New York: Cambridge University Press, 2013), 186; Tyler, *Silk Stockings and Ballot Boxes*, 11; Arnesen, *Waterfront Workers of New Orleans*, 146–47, 211.

12. Victor Zarnowitz, *Business Cycles: Theory, History, Indicators, and Forecasting* (Chicago: University of Chicago Press, 1992), 226–29; Mrs. Julian Heath, "Work of the Housewives League," *Annals of the American Academy of Political and Social Science* 48, no. 1 (July 1913): 121; Levenstein, *Revolution at the Table*, 109.

13. Anthony J. Stanonis, *Creating the Big Easy: New Orleans and the Emergence of Modern Tourism, 1918–1945* (Athens: University of Georgia Press, 2006), 7–8, 41–43; Campanella, *Bienville's Dilemma*, 203; "Buyers Welcome!" *Daily Picayune*, August 18, 1913, 1, Advance Local Media; Arnesen, *Waterfront Workers of New Orleans*, 205; Kevin Fox Gotham, *Authentic New Orleans: Tourism, Culture, and Race in the Big Easy* (New York: New York University Press, 2007), 76.

14. Manuscript Census Returns, Ninth Census of the United States, 1870, Rock Island County, Illinois, Ward 1, National Archives Microfilm Series (NAMS) M-593, reel 273 ("John McMartin," Ancestry.com); Manuscript Census Returns, Twelfth Census of the United States, 1900 (hereafter cited as 1900 US Census), Calcasieu Parish, Louisiana, Jennings, District 24, p. 9A, NAMS T-623, reel 561 ("John J. Martin," Ancestry.com); "Home Happenings," *Daily Record*, August 16, 1902, 8; "Society," *Daily Picayune*, December 18, 1887, 12, Advance Local Media; Cleveland Sessums, "Quits Sorting Mail, Turns to Pictures of Postoffices," ibid., April 3, 1938, 10; "Meyers," *Soards' New Orleans City Directory for 1914* (New Orleans: Soards' Directory Co., 1914), 848.

15. Manuscript Census Returns, Thirteenth Census of the United States, 1910 (hereafter cited as 1910 US Census), Orleans Parish, Louisiana, Ward 3, District 27, p. 14B, NAMS T-624, reel 520 ("Inez Mayers," Ancestry.com); "Funeral Today for Mrs. Myers, Woman Leader," *Times-Picayune*, November 3, 1923, 3, Advance Local Media; "Parents Condemn Movie Thrillers," ibid., June 26, 1921, 12; Effie Leese Scott, "Activity in Women's Clubs," *Daily Star*, January 11, 1914, Women's Section, 8 (quotation).

16. Bill Brown, "Science Fiction, the World's Fair, and the Prosthetics of Empire," in *Cultures of United States Imperialism*, 139; "The Woman's Club," *Daily Picayune*, November 7, 1905, 5, Advance Local Media; "Suffrage to Seek Working Women," ibid., January 18, 1914, 7; "Howard Egleston Dies of Pneumonia," ibid., February 6, 1926, 2; Elna C. Green, *Southern Strategies: Southern Women and the Woman Suffrage Question* (Chapel Hill: University of North Carolina Press, 1997), xv–xvi; Dr. E. L. McGehee Sr., "A Report from the

Anti-Tuberculosis League to the State Medical Society," *New Orleans Medical and Surgical Journal* 60, no. 9 (March 1908): 725; "Great American Ports: New Orleans," *Railway and Marine News* 15 (August 1917): 19–22; "New Orleans Building Greater Trade with South American Ports," *New Orleans Item*, May 8, 1920, 16.

17. John E. Land, *Pen Illustrations of New Orleans, 1881–1882* (New Orleans, 1882), http://nutrias.org/exhibits/gateway/mercur.htm.

18. Scott, *Southern Lady*, 190.

19. Ray L. Bellande, "Newspapers and Research," Ocean Springs Archives, http://oceanspringsarchives.net/node/213/contact; "Winifred Dabney," New Orleans, Passenger Lists, 1813–1963 (Ancestry.com database, compiling source data from Records of the Immigration and Naturalization Service, Record Group 85 [National Archives and Records Administration, Washington, DC]); "Mrs. L. B. Elliot," *Times-Picayune*, March 14, 1915, 36, Advance Local Media.

20. "Women of City Show Admiration for Russ Sisters," *Times-Picayune*, August 7, 1917, 12, Advance Local Media; "Organization Chronicles," ibid., July 7, 1918, 44; "A Talent for Cooperation," ibid., May 21, 1922, sec. 2, 6; "Homestead News of Interest Here," ibid., October 15, 1911, sec. 2, 10; "Co-op Store Has Big Future, Mrs. Egleston Says," *New Orleans Item*, April 4, 1920, 13.

21. Karen Trahan Leathem, "Ida Weis Friend, 1868–1963," Jewish Women: A Comprehensive Historical Encyclopedia, Jewish Women's Archive, http://jwa.org/encyclopedia/article/friend-ida-weis; Campanella, *Geographies of New Orleans*, 269, 276, 282; Storrs, *Civilizing Capitalism*, 144–45; Germany, *New Orleans After the Promises*, 30.

22. Linda Gordon Kuzmack, *Woman's Cause: The Jewish Woman's Movement in England and the United States, 1881–1933* (Columbus: Ohio State University Press, 1990), 3; Scott, *Southern Lady*, 161.

23. Tyler, *Silk Stockings and Ballot Boxes*, 24; McConnaughy, *Woman Suffrage Movement in America*, 185, 190–93; "Says Husbands, 'Ring' Followers, Keep Wives Away," *Times-Picayune*, November 22, 1919, 12, Advance Local Media.

24. "Moving Picture Peace," *Daily Picayune*, September 14, 1912, 4, Advance Local Media; Harriet C. Barton, *Report of the Sanitation Committee of the Woman's League* (1910), Woman's League Papers, Louisiana Division, New Orleans Public Library; Tyler, *Silk Stockings and Ballot Boxes*, 18–26; Elna C. Green, "The Rest of the Story: Kate Gordon and the Opposition to the Nineteenth Amendment in the South," *Louisiana History* 33, no. 2 (Spring 1992): 176–77.

25. "Suffrage to Seek," 7.

26. "Suffrage Rally at City Park," *Daily Picayune*, August 31, 1913, 7, Advance Local Media.

27. Scott, "Activity in Women's Clubs," 8; "City Federation of Woman Clubs Forms," *New Orleans Daily Picayune*, November 27, 1912, 5; Ellen Foley, "New Orleans Federation Will Mark Silver Anniversary," *Times-Picayune*, November 21, 1937, sec. 3, 15, Advance Local Media.

28. "Mrs. Graham Heads City Federation of Women's Clubs," *Times-Picayune*, May 25, 1915, 4, Advance Local Media.

29. Scott, *Southern Lady*, 161–62.

30. "City Federation of Women's Clubs," *New Orleans Times-Democrat*, November 28, 1912, 8.

31. Germany, *New Orleans After the Promises*, 39; Storrs, *Civilizing Capitalism*, 16–18.

32. Grace Julian Clarke, "Activities of Woman's Clubs," *Indianapolis Star*, July 13, 1913, 36.

33. "WCTU Gets New Members," *Times-Picayune*, January 29, 1915, 6, Advance Local Media.

34. "Questions and Answers," *Times-Picayune*, April 30, 1922, sec. 4, 8, Advance Local Media; Ellen Blue, *St. Mark's and the Social Gospel: Methodist Women and Civil Rights in New Orleans, 1895–1965* (Knoxville: University of Tennessee Press, 2011), 12; Mrs. R. W. Mac-Donell, "Home Mission Work, Woman's Department," *Missionary Voice* 1 (July 1911), 53.

35. Trinity Episcopal Church, "History of the Church," accessed on November 20, 2018, http://www.trinitynola.com/page.aspx? pid=797; Isabelle Dubroca, *Good Neighbor: Eleanor McMain of Kingsley House* (New Orleans: Pelican Publishing Co., 1955); "Howard Egleston Dies of Pneumonia," *New Orleans Times-Picayune*, February 6, 1926, 2; "Consumers' League," *Daily Picayune*, February 19, 1913, 9, Advance Local Media; Ethel Hutson, "Housewives' Body Active to Better Living Conditions," ibid., March 13, 1921, sec. 3, 4; Margaret Leonard, "Kingsley House: A Great Dynamic Community Force," *Social Service Review* 5, no. 6 (July 1917): 15; Blue, *St. Mark's and the Social Gospel*, 66; James B. Bennett, *Religion and the Rise of Jim Crow in New Orleans* (Princeton: Princeton University Press, 2005), 234; Laura Shapiro, *Perfection Salad: Women and Cooking at the Turn of the Century* (New York: University of California Press, 1986), 120–59.

36. Dolores Hayden, *The Grand Domestic Revolution: A History of Feminist Designs for American Homes, Neighborhoods, and Cities* (Cambridge: MIT Press, 1981), 3, 151–79; "Mrs. Porter's Memorial," *Daily Picayune*, February 15, 1911, 6, Advance Local Media; "Era Club," ibid., December 13, 1908, 5; Storrs, *Civilizing Capitalism*, 15–18; Charlotte Perkins Gilman, *Women and Economics: A Study of the Economic Relation Between Men and Women as a Factor in Social Evolution* (Boston: Small, Maynard & Company, 1898).

37. Mrs. George H. Williams, "Of Interest to Housekeepers," *Times-Picayune*, April 19, 1914, Advance Local Media.

38. "Mrs. Gilman's Lecture," *Daily Picayune*, January 21, 1911, 4, Advance Local Media; "Co-operative Plan Shown in Detail," ibid., April 16, 1920, 14; "Important Event to Take Place in April," *New Orleans Item*, April 2, 1920, 21; "Kelley is to Speak to Wives and Consumers," ibid., April 20, 1920, 15.

39. Cullom, "Description and History of the Athenaeum or the Young Men's Hebrew Association in New Orleans, Louisiana" (New Orleans: Works Progress Association, 193?), 1, Louisiana Works Progress Administration Digital Collection, State Library of Louisiana, http://louisianadigitallibrary.org/islandora/object/state-lwp:6768.

40. Rosenberg, *New Orleans Dockworkers*, 97; David R. Roediger, "Introduction," in Hall, *Labor Struggles in the Deep South*, 13; "The Socialists," *Daily Picayune*, September 20, 1903, 5, Advance Local Media.

41. "A Socialist Kick," *Daily Picayune*, September 11, 1904, sec. 2, 7, Advance Local Media (first and third quotations); "Mrs. Alvin Porter," ibid., January 27, 1911, 10 (second quotation); Eakin and Culbertson, *Louisiana: The Land and Its People*, 361.

42. Deutsch, *Building a Housewife's Paradise*, 106–107; Storrs, *Civilizing Capitalism*, 15, 19–23; Levenstein, *Revolution at the Table*, 109.

43. Mrs. H. B. Myers, "Housewives League of Orleans, La.," *Housewives Magazine* 11, no. 2 (February 1918): 32.

44. "Consumers' League," *Daily Picayune*, February 19, 1913, 9, Advance Local Media; "City Federation of Women's Clubs," ibid., February 19, 1913, 9; "Housewives Seek to Sever League from Federation," ibid., June 5, 1915, 5.

45. "Women Work for Humanity Cause," *Daily Picayune*, September 1, 1913, sec. 2, 14, Advance Local Media (first quotation); "Housewives' League Branch Organized," ibid., June 12, 1915, 5 (second quotation).

46. Heath, "Work of the Housewives League," 121.

47. Zarnowitz, *Business Cycles*, 226–29; "Co-op Store Has Big Future, Mrs. Egleston Says," *New Orleans Item*, April 4, 1920, 13 (first quotation); "Price 'Outrageous,' Says League Head," *Times-Picayune*, May 10, 1919, 10, Advance Local Media (second quotation).

48. Evans, *Born for Liberty*, 15; "Consumers' League," *Daily Picayune*, March 27, 1914, 11, Advance Local Media; "Consumers' League Opposes Opening Stores at Night," ibid., December 1, 1917, 6.

49. "Price 'Outrageous,'" 10.

50. Julia Truitt Bishop, "To Cut the Cost of Living Women Must Learn How to Buy," *Times-Picayune*, May 16, 1915, sec. 2, 2, Advance Local Media.

51. "State Farmers' Union to Hold Annual Meeting," *Times-Picayune*, May 15, 1915, 7; Mrs. H. B. Myers, "Marketing Problems in New Orleans," *Housewives League Magazine* 6 (October 1915): 46, 48; Egleston, "Co-operative Movement in New Orleans and the South," 306.

52. Joseph G. Knapp, *The Rise of American Cooperative Enterprise: 1620–1920* (Danville: Interstate, 1969), 176–82; Curl, *For All the People*, 131.

53. "The Farmers' Union and the City," *Times-Picayune*, July 13, 1915, 8, Advance Local Media.

54. "What America's Society Women of Wealth Are Doing to Correct Wastefulness," *Ogden Standard*, June 30, 1917, 5.

55. "Farmers Flock to Curb Market of Housewives," *Times-Picayune*, January 20, 1916, 8, Advance Local Media.

56. "Housewives Sell Products Despite Great Handicaps," *Times-Picayune*, December 23, 1915, Advance Local Media.

57. Quoted in "Housewives Lose," 11; "Prof. Wilkinson to Help Organize the Curb Market," *Times-Picayune*, January 3, 1916, 13, Advance Local Media.

58. Julia Truitt Bishop, "Personal Visit to the Great Port of New Orleans," *Times-Picayune*, July 4, 1915, Magazine, 1, Advance Local Media.

59. Arnesen, *Waterfront Workers of New Orleans*, 212–13; Evans, *Born for Liberty*, 145; Storrs, *Civilizing Capitalism*, 144; "Matrons to Decide on Store Monday," *Times-Picayune*, October 30, 1921, 6, Advance Local Media; "Plan Entertainment of Spring Buyers," ibid., March 5, 1915, 3; "Housewives' League Branch Organized," 5; "Buyers Welcome!" 1.

60. "Housewives Lose" 11.

61. "Farmers Flock," 8; "Members of the Housewives' League to Try Operating Stalls in the Public Markets," *Daily Picayune*, July 21, 1915, 5, Advance Local Media; "Housewives Gain Low Prices from Dealers," ibid., February 27, 1916, 6B; Julia Truitt Bishop, "Housewives' League Factor in Fight on High Living Cost," ibid., December 10, 1916, 17A; Levenstein, *Revolution at the Table*, 109.

62. Collection Overview, Market Committee Records, LaRC; Egleston, "Co-operative Movement in New Orleans and the South."

63. Bishop, "Housewives' League Factor," 17A.

64. Evans, *Born for Liberty*, 171–73; Susan H. Godson, *Serving Proudly: A History of Women in the U.S. Navy* (Annapolis: Naval Institute Press, 2001), 60.

65. "Dr. Shaw Comes to Organize War Work for Women," *Times-Picayune*, April 1, 1918, 9, Advance Local Media.

66. Carmen Meriwether Lindig, "The Woman's Movement in Louisiana: 1897–1920" (PhD diss., North Texas State University, 1982), 199; Levenstein, *Revolution at the Table*, 138; "Patriotic Talks Mark School's End," *Times-Picayune*, July 21, 1918, 4A, Advance Local Media; "What America's Society," *Ogden Standard*, June 30, 1917, 5.

67. "Dr. Shaw Comes," 9; "Defense Council Hears Dr. Scherer on Work to Do," *Times-Picayune*, July 22, 1917, 1A, 12A, Advance Local Media; "Women's Meetings," ibid., March 19, 1918, 7; "The Women's Committee," *Bulletin* 6, no. 17, 1, Folder "Council of National Defense, Field Division," Box 2J384, Texas War Records Collection, Dolph Briscoe Center for American History, University of Texas at Austin; Women in Industry Committee, Council of National Defense, New Orleans Division and Louisiana State Division, *Conditions of Women's Labor in Louisiana: New Orleans and Louisiana Industrial Survey* (New Orleans, Tulane University Press, 1919).

68. Ida M. Tarbell, "Mobilizing the Women," *Harper's Monthly Magazine* 135 (November 1917): 841–47 (first and second quotations on 847; fifth quotation on 844); "Societies and Institutions," *Catholic Charities Review* 1 (May 1917): 150; "Hope Haven Farm Wins General Approval," *Times-Picayune*, January 25, 1918, 15, Advance Local Media (third quotation); "'Hope Haven Day' Feb. 9," ibid., January 20, 1918, 9A (fourth quotation); Egleston, "Cooperative Movement in New Orleans and the South," 307 (sixth quotation).

69. Tyler, *Silk Stockings and Ballot Boxes*, 21; Glenda Elizabeth Gilmore, *Gender and Jim Crow: Women and the Politics of White Supremacy in North Carolina, 1896–1920* (Chapel Hill: University of North Carolina, 1996), 199; Lee Sartain, *Invisible Activists: Women of the Louisiana NAACP and the Struggle for Civil Rights, 1915–1945* (Baton Rouge: Louisiana State University Press, 2007), 55; Leathem, "Ida Weis Friend"; Nikki Brown, *Private Politics and Public Voices: Black Women's Activism from World War I to the New Deal* (Bloomington: Indiana University Press, 2006), 43 (quotation); DeVore, *Defying Jim Crow*, 145–47; "Mrs. Wilkinson's Last Rites Today," *Times-Picayune*, December 3, 1951, 2, Advance Local Media; Podine Schoenberger, "Homemaking Art Taught to Women at Night Classes," ibid., May 31, 1936, sec. 2, 7; Nicolle Dunnaway, "Flowers in Their Beauty: The Phyllis Wheatley Club of New Orleans," MA thesis, Southeastern Louisiana University, 2011, 10, 73.

70. "Instruction in Canning," *Times-Picayune*, August 12, 1917, 9A, Advance Local Media.

71. "Strike 'Male' from Utilities Bill, Housewives League Asks," *New Orleans Item*, May 16, 1920, 13.

72. "Negro School Says City Has Law Keeping H.C.L. at Zenith," *New Orleans Item*, April 25, 1920, 4.

73. Maurine Weiner Greenwald, *Women, War, and Work: The Impact of World War I on Women Workers in the United States* (Westport: Greenwood Press, 1980), 41; Brown, *Private Politics and Public Voices*, 45; Matthew Reonas, "World War I," in *Know Louisiana: Digital Encyclopedia of Louisiana History and Culture*, ed. David Johnson, http://www.knowlouisiana.org/entry/world-war-i/; Hayden, *The Grand Domestic Revolution*, 21–22; "Housewives Call Meet to Discuss Dearth of Labor," *Times-Picayune*, July 16, 1918, 1, Advance Local Media (quotations); "Homemakers' Meeting," ibid., July 22, 1918, 12.

74. "Supplemental Report of Committee on Credentials," *Report of Proceedings of the Thirty-Ninth Annual Convention of the American Federation of Labor* (Washington, DC: AFL, 1919), 185; Brown, *Private Politics and Public Voices*, 44–45; Elizabeth Ross Haynes, "Negroes in Domestic Service in the United States," *Journal of Negro History* 8, no. 4 (October 1923): 435–36; "Three Hundred Negro Servants in Union for More Pay, Less Work," *Times-Picayune*, May 9, 1918, 3, Advance Local Media; "Negroes Criticize Objections Urged to Cooks' Union," ibid., May 21, 1918, 14.

75. Stephen J. Ochs, *A Black Patriot and a White Priest: André Cailloux and Claude Paschal Maistre in Civil War New Orleans* (Baton Rouge, Louisiana State University Press, 2000), 77; Seymour Alcorn, 74th US Colored Infantry, Compiled Military Service Records of Volunteer Union Soldiers Who Served the United States Colored Troops (USCT): 56th–138th USCT Infantry, 1864–1866, Record Group 94, NAMS M-594, reel 213 (Ancestry.com); 1900 US Census, Orleans Parish, La., New Orleans Ward 11, District 114, 195A, NAMS T-623, reel 574 ("Elenora Alchorn," Ancestry.com); Arnesen, *Waterfront Workers of New Orleans*, 229–33.

76. "Deaths: Sylvester Peete," *Times-Picayune*, July 15, 1959, sec. 1, 2, Advance Local Media; Mrs. Greg, "The Servant Problem," ibid., July 21, 1918, 10A (quotation); "Household Labor Finds New Orleans Homemakers Calm," ibid., July 23, 1918, 12; "Three Hundred Negro Servants," 3; Lee Sartain, "'It's Worth One Dollar to Get Rid of Us': Middle-Class Persistence and the NAACP in Louisiana, 1915–1945," in *Long Is the Way and Hard: One Hundred Years of the National Association for the Advancement of Colored People (NAACP)*, eds. Kevern Verney and Lee Sartain (Fayetteville: University of Arkansas Press, 2009), 121–34; "Brooks, Rev. Charles Edward," in *Centennial Encyclopaedia of the African Methodist Episcopal Church*, eds. Richard R. Wright Jr. and John R. Hawkins (Philadelphia: AME Church, 1916), 44.

77. Arnesen, *Waterfront Workers of New Orleans*, 176, 220, 229, 242; "Household Labor Finds," 12 (first and fifth quotations); "Cooks' Union Slogan Brings Protests from Housewives," *Times-Picayune*, May 19, 1918, 11A, Advance Local Media (second quotation); "Cooks Must Toe Line Under Rule of Women's Body," ibid., July 17, 1918, 4; "Servant Problem Occupies Meeting of Women's Clubs," ibid., October 29, 1920, 1, 27 (third and fourth quotations on 1); Storrs, *Civilizing Capitalism*, 16, 19; Hayden, *Grand Domestic Revolution*, 21–22.

78. "Homemakers' Meeting," *Times-Picayune*, July 22, 1918, 12, Advance Local Media; "Home Makers Organized at Suffrage House Tuesday," ibid., July 21, 1918, magazine, 4; "Reception Planned [for] Oldest Clubwoman," ibid., February 28, 1918, 7; "Parties and Events," ibid., May 16, 1926, 53; "New Orleans Society Moves to Gulf Coast for Week-End," ibid., July 4, 1925, 13; "Suffrage House to Give Service Dances," ibid., August 23, 1918, 7.

79. "Household Labor Finds," 12 (quotations); "Committees Named to Serve at Tombs Confederate Memorial Day, Wednesday," *Times-Picayune*, June 1, 1914, 3, Advance Local Media; "Confederate Daughters," ibid., October 22, 1913, 14; "James E. Hart," ibid., November 19, 1912, 13.

80. "New Orleans Society Moves to Gulf Coast for Week-End," *Times-Picayune*, July 4, 1925, 13, Advance Local Media (quotation); "Memorial Rites Set for Leader," ibid., December 13, 1963, sec. 1, 12; "Over Thirty-Two Thousand Babies Weighed in City," ibid., May 5, 1918, 3. On the "Better Baby" movement, see Tamsen Wolff, *Mendel's Theatre: Heredity, Eugenics, and Early Twentieth-Century American Drama* (New York: Palgrave Macmillan, 2009), 95–98 and Judith Daar, *The New Eugenics: Selective Breeding in an Era of Reproductive Technologies* (New Haven: Yale University Press, 2017), 50–52.

81. *Minutes of the Twenty-Third Annual Convention of the United Daughters of the Confederacy* (Raleigh: United Daughters of the Confederacy, 1917), 51, 55, 173; "Cooks' Union Slogan Brings Protests from Housewives," *Times-Picayune*, May 19, 1918, 11A, Advance Local Media (first and second quotations); "Practical Domestic Science Taught to Increase Efficiency and Number of Colored Cooks," ibid., January 27, 1918, magazine, 1; "Urge Home Economics," ibid., May 25, 1919, 11C (third and fourth quotations); "Negroes Criticize Objections Urged to Cooks' Union," ibid., May 21, 1918, 14 (fifth quotation); Michele Alishahi, "'For Peace and Civic Righteousness': Blanche Armwood and the Struggle for Freedom and Racial

Equality in Tampa, Florida, 1890–1939," (MA thesis, University of South Florida, 2003), 63, 94, 115; Mary Burke, "The Success of Blanche Armwood (1890–1939)," *Sunland Tribune* 15 (November 1989): 38–43.

82. "Cooks Must Toe Line," 4 (first quotation); "Household Labor Finds," 12 (second quotation); "Home-Makers Organized at Suffrage House Tuesday," *Times-Picayune*, July 21, 1918, magazine, 4, Advance Local Media (third and fourth quotations); Brown, *Private Politics and Public Voices*, 45; "Memorial Rites Set," 12; Evans, *Born for Liberty*, 190; Storrs, *Civilizing Capitalism*, 17–18.

83. Sarah P. Williams, "'The Servant Problem,'" *Times-Picayune*, July 28, 1918, 10A, Advance Local Media (first, second, and fourth quotations); Women in Industry Committee, *Conditions of Women's Labor in Louisiana*, 128 (third quotation); "Women in Industry: Plans for Improvement of Domestic Service," *Monthly Labor Review* 10, no. 5 (May 1920): 116 (fifth and sixth quotations on 116); Nikki Brown, "Domestic Work," in *The Jim Crow Encyclopedia*, eds. Nikki L. M. Brown and Barry M. Stentiford (2 vols.; Westport: Greenwood, 2008), 1, 242–44; Haynes, "Negroes in Domestic Service in the United States," 435–36.

84. "Women Give Assistance to Food Control Department," *Times-Picayune*, July 21, 1918, magazine, 4, Advance Local Media; "Will Open Canning Clubs This Week," ibid., July 21, 1918, 8C; "Training School for Servants May Hold Husbands," ibid., December 31, 1918, 6 (quotations).

85. *Soards' New Orleans City Directory for 1917* (New Orleans: Soards' Directory Co., 1917), 894; 1910 US Census, Orleans Parish, La., Ward 12, District 195, 11A, NAMS T-624, reel 524 ("Jeannette M. Moser," Ancestry.com); Lindig, "Woman's Movement in Louisiana," 191; "New Orleans Gives Thanks for Various Good Reasons," ibid., November 27, 1919, 9.

86. Levenstein, *Revolution at the Table*, 111; Hayden, *Grand Domestic Revolution*, 178, 224; "Give First Exhibit of Cooking Today," *Times-Picayune*, April 10, 1918, 16; Mrs. Herbert Moser Complimented," *Times-Picayune*, January 17, 1918, 5, Advance Local Media (quotations); 1900 US Census, Orleans Parish, La., New Orleans Ward 2, District 12, 15A, NAMS T-623, reel 570 ("Thomas Hayes," Ancestry.com); 1920 US Census, Orleans Parish, Louisiana, New Orleans Ward 2, District 19, 2A, NAMS T-625, reel 619 ("Thomas Hays," Ancestry.com).

87. Shapiro, *Perfection Salad*, 212; Gabaccia, *We Are What We Eat*, 131; "Ask Labels Show Weight of Bread," *Times-Picayune*, January 15, 1921, 11, Advance Local Media; "Housewives, Here Are Ways to Utilize All That Bacon," ibid., August 7, 1919, 12; "Servant Problem Occupies Meeting of Women's Clubs," *New Orleans Times-Picayune*, October 29, 1920, 1 (quotation); "Rosa Michaelis," JewishGen Online Worldwide Burial Registry (Ancestry.com); 1900 US Census, Orleans Parish, La., New Orleans Ward 1, District 4, p. 60B, NAMS T-632, reel 570 ("Rosa F. Michaelis," Ancestry.com).

88. Hayden, *Grand Domestic Revolution*, 207–227; "Cooks' Union Slogan," 11A; Catherine C. Van Meter, "What Women Are Doing," *Times-Picayune*, September 15, 1918, 13A; "How to Manage With a Servant and Without One," ibid., April 20, 1919, 6A (first and second quotations); Edward Bellamy, "A Vital Domestic Problem: Household Service Reform," *Good Housekeeping* 10, no. 4 (December 21, 1889): 76 (third quotation); Levenstein, *Revolution at the Table*, 66 (fourth quotation).

89. "How to Manage with a Servant and without One," *Times-Picayune*, April 20, 1919, 6A, Advance Local Media; "To Show Electric Appliances Tuesday," ibid., April 14, 1919, 7 (first quotation); "Housework Minus Servants, Subject," ibid., April 9, 1919, 5 (second quotation); "Let Women Make Survey of Duties Daily, is Urged," ibid., November 24, 1918, 9C (third quotation).

90. Hayden, *Grand Domestic Revolution*, 21–22.

91. Curl, *For All the People*, 152–53; Arnesen, *Waterfront Workers of New Orleans*, 228–44; Deutsch, *Building a Housewife's Paradise*, 45.

92. "Business Men Ask City to Enlarge Food Sale," *Times-Picayune*, August 13, 1919, 1 (first quotation); "Co-operative Store Rouses Interest in Big Territory," ibid., February 19, 1920, 1; "Co-operative Plan Enthusiasts Not Afraid of Jobbers," ibid., February 24, 1920, 2; "Co-op Store Plan Begins to Sweep Southern States," ibid., March 11, 1920, 1; Arnesen, *Waterfront Workers of New Orleans*, 230; "Cooperation," in *The New International Year Book: A Compendium of the World's Progress for the Year 1916*, ed. Frank Moore Colby (New York: Dodd, Mead, and Co., 1917), 164; Cohen, *A Consumers' Republic*, 25.

93. "Labor Considering Co-operative Plan," *Times-Picayune*, February 22, 1920, 12, Advance Local Media; "Housewives' Store Boosted by Unions," ibid., May 23, 1920, sec. 5, 16; "Union Men Open Their Own Shop," *New Orleans Item*, May 10, 1920, 11; Deutsch, *Building a Housewife's Paradise*, 52, 107.

94. Deutsch, *Building a Housewife's Paradise*, 50, 107; Knupfer, *Food Co-ops in America*, 18–21; "Housewives' League Plan to Establish Co-operative Store," *Times-Picayune*, June 29, 1919, 4A; "Cost of Living to Be Attacked by Housewives," ibid., March 12, 1920, 1; "Milk Price Goes Up, Consumption Goes Down, Today," ibid., October 1, 1919, 4 (quotation); "Says Husbands," November 22, 1919, 12; 1920 US Census, Jefferson Parish, La., Ward 8, District 11, p. 4B, NAMS T-625, reel 615 ("Edna M. Egleston," Ancestry.com); "Urges Co-operative Grocery Store Plan," ibid., June 21, 1919, 16.

95. "Housewives' League Plan," 4A (first and second quotations); "Co-op Store Has Big Future," 13 (fourth and fifth quotations).

96. "Committee to Set Store Opening Date," *Times-Picayune*, March 3, 1920, 1, Advance Local Media; "Cost of Living," 1; "Says Husbands," 12; "Funeral Today for Mrs. Myers," 3.

97. Tracey Deutsch, "Untangling Alliances: Social Tensions Surrounding Independent Grocery Stores and the Rise of Mass Retailing," in *Food Nations: Selling Taste in Consumer Societies*, eds. Warren Belasco and Philip Scranton (New York: Routledge, 2002), 158; "Business Men Ask," 1, 5; "Housewives' Store Hits $5000 Mark," *Times-Picayune*, March 20, 1920, 4 (first quotation); "Housewives Await Letter from Dupre," ibid., February 23, 1920, 14; "Co-operative Stores Become Vital Issue in City's H.C.L. Fight," ibid., February 22, 1920, 1; "Thompson States Claim of Grocers," ibid., February 22, 1920, 1, 6; "Cost of Living," 1.

98. "Labor Considering Co-operative Plan," *Times-Picayune*, February 22, 1920, 12, Advance Local Media; "Ex-Service Men Beneficiaries of Army Sales, Legion Shows," ibid., February 22, 1920, 1, 2; "Co-operative Stores Become Vital Issue," 1, 12; "Housewives' League Outlines Plan for Co-operative Stores," ibid., February 22, 1920, pp. 1, 6 (quotation); "Co-operative Store Rouses," 157; Giese, "How the Old Coops Went Wrong," 315–35.

99. Egleston, "Co-operative Movement in New Orleans and the South," 305–306; LeWarne, *Utopias on Puget Sound*, 117; Giese, "How the Old Coops Went Wrong," 317–19; Parker, *The First 125 Years*, 66; "Co-op Store Plan," 1 (quotation); Aaron Windel, "Co-operatives and the Technocrats, or 'The Fabian Agony' Revisited," in *Brave New World: Imperial and Democratic Nation-Building in Britain Between the Wars*, eds. Laura Beers and Geraint Thomas (London: Institute of Historical Research, 2011), 250–53.

100. "Co-op Store Has Big Future," 13; Curl, *For All the People*, 144–45, 154–59; Parker, *First 125 Years*, 56–58; Kathleen Donohue, "From Cooperative Commonwealth to Cooperative Democracy: The American Cooperative Ideal, 1880–1940," in *Consumers Against Capitalism?: Consumer Cooperation in Europe, North America, and Japan, 1840–1990*, eds.

Ellen Furlough and Carl Strikwerda (Lanham: Rowman and Littlefield, 1999), 121; "Many Food Buyers Back Housewives' Co-operative Plan," *Times-Picayune*, February 29, 1920, 12, Advance Local Media; "Housewives' League Plan," 4A (second quotation).

101. "Many Food Buyers," 1 (first quotation); "Housewives' League Plan," 4A; "Housewives' Store Boosted," 155–56; "Housewives' Grocery in Operation," *New Orleans Item*, April 17, 1921, 2; "Co-op Store Has Big Future," 13 (second quotation); "Funeral Today" 3 (third quotation).

102. Michael Mizell-Nelson, "Interracial Unionism Meets the Open Shop Drive: African American Membership in the Carmen's Union, 1918–1926," in *Working in the Big Easy*, 69–97; "Co-op Store Has Big Future," 13; Louis C. Hennick and E. Harper Charlton, *The Streetcars of New Orleans* (Gretna: Jackson Square Press, 2005), 36; "Laundry Prices and Food Costs Held Excessive," *Times-Picayune*, June 11, 1921, 17, Advance Local Media; "Organized Labor Proposes Battle on Living Costs," ibid., May 7, 1921, 1; "Labor Indorses Co-op Stores," *New Orleans Item*, May 7, 1921, 12; "Says Husbands" 12.

103. Curl, *For All the People*, 147–56; "More Hopeful Strike Status in N.O. Is Seen," *New Orleans Item*, April 11, 1920, 1 (quotation).

104. Julia L. Mickenberg, "Suffragettes and Soviets: American Feminists and the Specter of Revolutionary Russia," *Journal of American History* 100, no. 4 (March 2014), 1022, 1044–45; Storrs, *Civilizing Capitalism*, 17–18, 38; US Senate Committee on the Judiciary, *Bolshevik Propaganda: Hearings before a Subcommittee of the Committee on the Judiciary, United States Senate, Sixty-Fifth Congress, Third Session and Thereafter, Pursuant to S. Res. 439 and 469, February 11, 1919, to March 10, 1919* (Washington, DC: US Senate, 1919), 699 (first and second quotations).

105. Tyler, *Silk Stockings and Ballot Boxes*, 23–26; Lindig, "Woman's Movement in Louisiana," 209–215; "Says Husbands," 12 (quotations).

106. Hutson, "Housewives' Body Active," 4; Frederick John Harper, "The Anti-Chain Store Movement in the United States, 1927–1940" (PhD diss., University of Warwick, 1981), 53, 69; "Mrs. Egleston Objects to Fixed Retail Prices," *New Orleans Item*, April 10, 1920, 4 (first and second quotations); "Co-operative Stores Become Vital," 1, 12; "Eve Up-to-Date," *Times-Picayune*, August 28, 1920, 7, Advance Local Media (third quotation).

107. Egleston, "Co-operative Movement in New Orleans and the South," 307 (first quotation); "Housewives' Store Hits $5000 Mark," 4; "Army Store Head to Lecture Women," *Times-Picayune*, March 19, 1920, 5, Advance Local Media; "Women Appeal to Men to Subscribe for Balance of Co-operative Stock," *New Orleans Item*, April 2, 1920, 22 (second and third quotations).

108. "Urges Co-operative Grocery," 16; "Housewives' League Outlines Plan," 1, 6; "Housewives Open Subscription List for Joint Store," *Times-Picayune*, March 6, 1920, 1, 5, Advance Local Media; Hutson, "Housewives' Body Active," 4; "Housewives' Grocery," 2; "Eve Up-to-Date," 7 (second quotation).

109. "Shober Rites This Morning," *Times-Picayune*, August 27, 1959, sec. 1, 6, Advance Local Media; "Liquidators' Sale of People's Co-operative Laundry, Inc.," advertisement, ibid., October 30, 1924, 30; "Good Business and Elections in Homesteads," ibid., January 16, 1916, 47; 1920 US Census, Orleans Parish, La., New Orleans Ward 13, District 229, p. 10A, NAMS T-625, reel 624 ("E. W. Vacher," Ancestry.com); "Housewives Open Subscription," 1, 5 (first quotation); "Co-op Store Plan," 1 (second quotation); Chambers, *A History of Louisiana* 2: 7–8; "Eve Up-to-Date," 7; Kendall, *History of New Orleans* 3: 1042; "Army Store Head," 5.

110. "Housewives Open Subscription," 1 (first, second, and third quotations); "Committee to Set Store," 1; "Housewives' Grocery in Operation," 2; "Housewives Report Big Trade at

Co-operative Store," *Times-Picayune*, May 3, 1921, 5 (fourth quotation); "Housewives' Body Enters Politics at June Meeting," ibid., June 12, 1921, sec. 3, 5 (fifth, sixth, and seventh quotations); Windel, "Co-operatives and the Technocrats," 254.

111. "Co-operative Stores Become Vital," 12 (first quotation); Stephen Maloney, "Heritage Club Reception Honors Members on October 20." Preservation Resource Center of New Orleans, last updated on October 9, 2015, http://www.prcno.org/news-and-media/ 1144; "Housewives' Store Program Indorsed," *Times-Picayune*, March 4, 1920, 9, Advance Local Media (second quotation); "Housewives Find Co-operative Plan Not Money Maker," ibid., October 28, 1921, 15 (third and fourth quotations); Egleston, "Co-operative Movement in New Orleans and the South," 308; "Co-op Store Plan Begins," 1; "Housewives' Store Reports," 24.

112. "Temporary Site for Store Found," *Times-Picayune*, January 29, 1921, 2, Advance Local Media; Alice Rightor, "Housewives' League to Open Co-operative Store This Week," ibid., February 20, 1921, sec. 2, 8 (first, second, and third quotations); "Housewives' Store is Reality," ibid., February 26, 1921, 7; "Housewives Find Co-operative Plan," 15 (fourth quotation); "Housewives' Grocery in Operation," *New Orleans Item*, April 17, 1921, 2.

113. Rightor, "Housewives' League to Open," 8 (quotations); "Committee to Set Store," 1; "Housewives Report," 5; "Cabbages Are In, Fish Out as Summer Time Arrives," *Times-Picayune*, April 29, 1921, Homestead sec., 13, Advance Local Media; "Housewives Co-operative Stores, Inc.," advertisement, ibid., September 17, 1921, 12; "Housewives' Co-operative Stores, Inc.," advertisement, ibid., October 8, 1921, 17; Hutson, "Housewives' Body Active," 4.

114. "Over 100 Women Buying Groceries from Own Store," *Times-Picayune*, May 8, 1921, sec. 3, 4, Advance Local Media; Egleston, "Co-operative Movement in New Orleans and the South," 305.

115. Rightor, "Housewives' League to Open," 8 (first, second, and third quotations); "Housewives Co-operative Stores, Inc.," 17; "Housewives' Co-operative Stores, Inc.," 10; "Housewives Co-operative Stores, Inc.," 12; Levenstein, *Revolution at the Table*, 189 (fourth quotation).

116. Knupfer, *Food Co-ops in America*, 20; Deutsch, *Building a Housewife's Paradise*, 11–72; "Housewives Open Subscription List," 1 (quotation).

117. "Co-op Store Has Big Future," 13 (first quotation); Egleston, "Co-operative Movement in New Orleans and the South," 307 (second quotation), 306 (third quotation); "Co-operative Plan Shown," 14 (fourth and fifth quotations).

118. Egleston, "Co-operative Movement in New Orleans and the South," 306 (first quotation); "Housewives' League Outlines Plan," 1 (second quotation).

119. Egleston, "Co-operative Movement in New Orleans and the South," 305 (first quotation), Jonathan M. Hansen, *The Lost Promise of Patriotism: Debating American Identity, 1890–1920* (Chicago: University of Chicago Press, 2003), 186; Matthew Anderson, *A History of Fair Trade in Contemporary Britain: From Civil Society Campaigns to Corporate Compliance* (New York: Palgrave Macmillan, 2015), 70–71; Windel, "Co-operatives and the Technocrats," 255.

120. Egleston, "Co-operative Movement in New Orleans and the South," 306 (first quotation); "Housewives Find," 15 (second and third quotations); "Over 100 Women," 4; Blue, *St. Mark's and the Social Gospel*, 66–69; "By Way of Comment," *Times-Picayune*, November 6, 1921, sec. 3, 8, Advance Local Media (fourth through eighth quotations).

121. Campanella, *Bienville's Dilemma*, 150–52, 190–91; "Housewives Find," 15 (first quotation); "Give First Exhibit of Cooking Today," *Times-Picayune*, April 10, 1918, 16, Advance Local Media; "Suffrage to Seek Working Women," ibid., January 18, 1914, 7 (second

quotation); "By Way of Comment," ibid., November 6, 1921, sec. 3, 8 (third quotation); "Housewives' Store Assets Inventoried at $1540.35," *Times-Picayune*, January 11, 1922, 3, Advance Local Media.

122. Arnesen, *Waterfront Workers of New Orleans*, 243; "Housewives Find," 15; "House-wives' Body Enters Politics," 5; Harper, "Anti-Chain Store Movement," 53, 69; Curl, *For All the People*, 151–57.

123. "Farm-to-Table Garden Marketing Looms After Price Exposed," *New Orleans Item*, May 5, 1921, 11 (first quotation); "The Former Customers of the Housewives' Co-operative Stores, Inc.," advertisement, *Times-Picayune*, November 12, 1921, 17, Advance Local Media (second quotation); Kendall, *History of New Orleans* 3: 1042.

124. "List of Original Members of the LLPCR" (1937), 1, Vertical File: "Political Organizations, Louisiana League for the Preservation of Constitutional Rights," LaRC; Gilmore, *Defying Dixie*, 19–21; Storrs, *Civilizing Capitalism*, 17–18, 38; "Decrease Shown in Tuberculosis, Auxiliary Told," *Times-Picayune*, April 2, 1931, 22, Advance Local Media; "History of State to Be Theme at Luncheon Friday," ibid., April 28, 1933, 20; "Clubs Are Oiling Machinery for Year's Program," ibid., October 9, 1921, sec. 3, 5.

125. League for Industrial Democracy, "What Is the L.I.D.?" n.d.; and League for Industrial Democracy, *Democracy in Action: Six Discussion Lectures. Fifth Annual Series Through the New Orleans Committee for LID Lectures* (New Orleans, 1938), 4, both in Vertical File: "Political Organizations, League for Industrial Democracy" (LaRC); "Institute to Hear Brooklyn Minister," *Times-Picayune*, February 20, 1933, 12, Advance Local Media; "House-wives' League Plan," 4A (quotation).

Chapter Three

1. "Facts Concerning the Arrest of Henry Hermes," August 1937, Box 1, Folder 5, Harold Newton Lee Papers, 1917–1970, LaRC. Hereafter cited as Lee Papers.

2. "$10,000 Damages Asked of Grosch by Local Barber," *Times-Picayune*, July 14, 1938, 4, Advance Local Media (first through third quotations); Sidney A. Mitchell to George A. Dreyfous, August 26, 1937, Box 3, Folder 2, Mathilde Dreyfous (Mrs. Geo. A) Papers, 1937–1989, LaRC. Hereafter cited as Dreyfous Papers (fourth quotation).

3. League for Industrial Democracy, pamphlet, "Democracy in Action" (n.d.): 4, Vertical File: Political Organizations, League for Industrial Democracy, LaRC. Hereafter cited as LID Vertical File; "$10,000 Damages," 4; George A. Dreyfous to Isaac S. Heller, September 11, 1937, Box 3, Folder 2, Dreyfous Papers (first quotation); "False Arrest Suit Filed," *Middlesboro Daily News*, July 13, 1938, 1 (second quotation).

4. "Hermes Announces Senate Candidacy," *Times-Picayune*, October 30, 1943, 2; "Tonight—WNOE," ibid., January 10, 1944, 18; "The 'New Orleans Co-operator,'" *New Orleans Co-operator* (January–February 1944), 2–3, Folder 2, Box 1, Herman Lazard Midlo Collection, Earl K. Long Library, University of New Orleans. Hereafter cited as Midlo Collection.

5. Passenger Record, s.v. "Heinrich Hermes" (October 27, 1913) accessed through The Statue of Liberty-Ellis Island Foundation; 1925 New York State Census, s.v. "Henry W. Hermes," Brooklyn, Kings County, New York, accessed through Ancestry.com; 1920 United States Census, s.v. "Amelia Mendez," New Orleans, Orleans Parish, Louisiana, accessed through Ancestry.com; 1930 United States Census, s.v. "Albert E. Mendez Sr.," New Orleans, Orleans Parish, Louisiana, accessed through Ancestry.com; 1930 United States Census, s.v. "Henry Hermes," New Orleans, Orleans Parish, Louisiana, accessed through Ancestry.com;

1940 United States Census, s.v. "Albert E. Mendez Sr.," New Orleans, Orleans Parish, Louisiana, accessed through Ancestry.com; Coleman Warner, "Freret's Century: Growth, Identity, and Loss in a New Orleans Neighborhood," *Louisiana History* 42, no. 3 (2001): 324.

6. Warner, "Freret's Century," 340, 343; "Freret Street Has Switched to Trolley Coaches Because Trolley Coaches Are MODERN," *Times-Picayune*, September 3, 1947, 21, Advance Local Media; "Freret Carnival Club Picks LaMont," ibid., April 30, 1952, 36 (quotation); *Stanonis, Creating the Big Easy*, 172.

7. Warner, "Freret's Century," 335 (quotation); Lizabeth Cohen, *Making a New Deal: Industrial Workers in Chicago, 1919–1939* (Cambridge: Cambridge University Press, 1990), 2–3, 261–62; "Foes of Fascism Fined $5 Each for Picketing Theater," *Times-Picayune*, March 19, 1935, 13, Advance Local Media; "Assail Congress for Passing Cut in Relief Budget," ibid., January 29, 1939, 4.

8. Garry Boulard, *Huey Long Invades New Orleans: The Siege of a City, 1934–36* (Gretna: Pelican Publishing, 1998), 36, 75, 199; Alan Brinkley, *Voices of Protest: Huey Long, Father Coughlin, and the Great Depression* (New York: Vintage Books, 1983), 31, 201–203.

9. Edward F. Haas, "New Orleans on the Half-Shell: The Maestri Era, 1936–1946," *Louisiana History* 13, no. 3 (Summer 1972): 284.

10. Cohen, *Making a New Deal*, 253; "Lotto Party Announced," *Times-Picayune*, April 14, 1932, 5, Advance Local Media; "Barber Band to Play," ibid., June 5, 1931, 24.

11. Maselli and Candeloro, *Italians in New Orleans*, 43; "Boat Ride is Set," *Times-Picayune*, October 15, 1941, 11, Advance Local Media; "Flag Present by VFW Auxiliary," ibid., September 20, 1959, 8; "Consumers' Union to Install Staff," ibid., January 5, 1947, 18; "Consumer Group Elects Officers," ibid., December 13, 1945, 29.

12. "Bootblack Jailed as Barber, Freed," *Times-Picayune*, October 5, 1932, 3, Advance Local Media (first quotation); "Officers Installed by Master Barbers," ibid., January 4, 1934, 4; "Long Chief Issue in City Election," ibid., January 9, 1934, 1 (second and third quotation).

13. "Socialists to Meet," *Times-Picayune*, March 9, 1934, 8, Advance Local Media (quotation); Gilmore, *Defying Dixie*, 185–86, 211; Germany, *New Orleans After the Promises*, 13; James E. Fickle, *The New South and the "New Competition": Trade Association Development in the Southern Pine Industry* (Urbana: University of Illinois Press, 1980), 315; Cohen, *Making a New Deal*, 262; Communist Party, District 24, "An Open Letter!" (New Orleans: Trades Council Allied Printing, n.d.): 1, University of Michigan Special Collections Library, http://quod.lib.umich.edu/s/sclradic.

14. Haas, "New Orleans on the Half-Shell," 284, 287–88, 293, 297–98; Stanonis, *Creating the Big Easy*, 71, 86; Germany, *New Orleans After the Promises*, 28.

15. Fairclough, *Race and Democracy*, 34.

16. Boulard, *Huey Long Invades New Orleans*, 36; "Arrests, Permit Fee Ordinance Draw Fire," *Times-Picayune*, October 8, 1936, 4, Advance Local Media.

17. S. R. McCulloch, "Civic and Social Societies Unite to Combat 'Subversive Activities,'" *St. Louis-Post Dispatch*, November 22, 1936, 1. Vertical File: Communist Party, New Orleans Public Library.

18. Harold Lee to Morris Langley, March 7, 1938, Box 1, Folder 5, Lee Papers (quotation); Louisiana Coalition of Patriotic Societies, Inc. Newsletter [1937], 1, Box 3, Folder 2, Dreyfous Papers.

19. Dreyfous, letter, September 11, 1937; Louisiana Coalition of Patriotic Societies, Inc. Newsletter, 1; "Workers Will Hear Frank McCallister," *Times-Picayune*, March 3, 1938, 11, Advance Local Media; "Norman Thomas Urges Increases in Civil Liberties," ibid., September 11, 1937, 15 (quotation); "Weil Social Center Dedication Today," ibid., January 4, 1925, 4, 13;

The Workers Defense League Collection Papers, 1935–1971, Walter P. Reuther Library, Wayne State University; Socialist Party of America, New Orleans Chapter, pamphlet, "An Open Letter to the People of New Orleans," 1937, Box 1, Folder 1, Midlo Collection.

20. Eric Smith, *American Relief Aid and the Spanish Civil War* (Columbia: University of Missouri Press, 2013), 71–72; Ana Maria Varela-Lago, "Conquerors, Immigrants, Exiles: The Spanish Diaspora in the United States (1848–1948)" (PhD diss., University of California, San Diego, 2008), 14–15.

21. North American Committee to Aid Spanish Democracy, Louisiana Division (NACASD), Newsletter (April 25, 1937), 1, Vertical File: Organizations, North American Committee to Aid Spanish Democracy, LaRC.

22. "Garment Workers Hear Labor Chiefs," *Times-Picayune*, July 30, 1933, 5, Advance Local Media; "Union Leader Will Address Socialists," ibid., August 19, 1936, 22; "Arrest of Seven Pickets of Film Arouses Protest" ibid., December 16, 1935, 8; "Socialist Leader Will Speak Here," ibid., September 2, 1934, 12; "Arrests, Permit Fee Ordinance Draw Fire," 4; Lillian Muniz, "Defends Position of Coal Miners," ibid., November 7, 1943, 40 (first and second quotation).

23. "China Aid Group Sets Boycott on Japanese Goods," *Times-Picayune*, April 4, 1938, 9, Advance Local Media, emphasis mine (quotation); Earl F. Wegmann, "'Rebel,' 'Invader' Scored in Films," ibid., July 10, 1938, 6.

24. NACASD, Newsletter, 1.

25. Knupfer, *Food Co-ops in America*, 36; John H. Dietrich, "The Cooperative Movement," *The Humanist Pulpit Series 16* (Minneapolis: First Unitarian Society, 1933), 94–95; Curl, *For All the People*, 180–84.

26. League for Industrial Democracy, pamphlet, "What is the L.I.D.?" (n.d.): 2, LID Vertical File (quotation).

27. Dr. Walter Siegmeister, "The Downfall of Capitalism and the Birth of the New Cooperative System," *Llano Colonist* (April 1, 1933) (first and second quotation); "Anti-War Summer School Planned for Southerners," *Fortnightly* 13, no. 13 (July 1, 1936): 1; William H. Cobb, *Radical Education in the Rural South: Commonwealth College, 1922–1940* (Detroit: Wayne State University Press, 2000), 15–26; "Socialists to Hear of New Llano Plan," *Times-Picayune*, December 14, 1934, 15, Advance Local Media; "Norman Thomas Would Organize 'Useful Workers,'" ibid., March 9, 1936, 13 (third and fourth quotation).

28. Socialist Party of New Orleans, *Two Packs of Cigarettes a Month* (1934), 1, Williams Research Collection, Historic New Orleans Collection (quotation); Gary Alan Donaldson, "A History of Louisiana's Rural Electric Cooperatives, 1937–1983" (PhD diss., Louisiana State University and Agricultural and Mechanical College, 1983), vii, ix, LaRC; "Hermes Announces Senate Candidacy," ibid., October 30, 1943, 2.

29. Raymond F. Gregory, *Norman Thomas: The Great Dissenter* (United States: Algora Publishing, 2008), 177, 186; "13th Ward Group Backs Candidates," *Times-Picayune*, October 12, 1939, 6, Advance Local Media; "Independents Set Rally for Monday," ibid., December 10, 1939, 11; "Why Jones, Noe Joined Forces in Drive Explained," ibid., January 25, 1940, 3.

30. Deutsch, *Building a Housewife's Paradise*, 117 (first quotation); Dietrich, "The Cooperative Movement," 94–95 (second and third quotations).

31. Deutsch, *Building a Housewife's Paradise*, 64, 117; Campanella, *Bienville's Dilemma*, 50; Curl, *For All the People*, 189; "Our Store," *New Orleans Co-operator* (January–February 1944): 1, Box 1, Folder 2, Midlo Collection; "Improved Garbage Collection Asked," *Times-Picayune*, April 4, 1945, 24, Advance Local Media; Anwarul Hoque and Leroy Davis, *Survey of Cooperatives in Louisiana* (Baton Rouge: Southern University and A&M College, 1980), 4; Louisiana

Grocers' Cooperative, *Annual Report* (January 28, 1983), 1, Business Vertical File: Louisiana Grocers Co-op Inc., New Orleans Public Library; "Julia Street," *New Orleans Magazine* (December 2008), accessed on April 27, 2014, http://www.myneworleans.com/New-Orleans-Magazine/December-2008/Julia-Street/; Maggie H. Richardson, "A Grocer and a Gentleman," *Greater Baton Rouge Business Report*, April 6, 2009, accessed on September 21, 2012, http://www.businessreport.com/article/20090406/BUSINESSREPORT01/304069956/0/businessreport0403.

32. "Consumers Cooperative Union, Inc. Joins SCEA," 3; *Southeastern Cooperator* 1, no. 7 (October 1941): 3, Box 2, Folder 43, SCL Records (first quotation); Deutsch, *Building a Housewife's Paradise*, 105 (second through fourth quotation) and 122.

33. J. Mark Souther, *New Orleans on Parade: Tourism and the Transformation of the Crescent City* (Baton Rouge: Louisiana State University Press, 2006), 9; Michael Denning, *The Cultural Front: The Laboring of American Culture in the Twentieth Century* (London: Verso, 1996), 36 (quotation); Dennis Rader, *Learning Redefined: Changing Images that Guide the Process* (Frankfort: Building Democracy Press, 2010).

34. "The 'New Orleans Co-operator,'" 2–3, emphasis mine (quotation); Amy Bentley, *Eating for Victory: Food Rationing and the Politics of Domesticity* (Urbana: University of Illinois Press, 1998), 15.

35. Sisters Angelina Prior and Mary LaBurthe, mother Amelia and daughter Marion Hermes, as well as Catherine Pazos, Carmen Dade, Mary McDermott and Lillian Muniz, were of Latin American or Spanish extraction.

36. Cohen, *A Consumers' Republic*, 8, 19, 40; Mrs. A. Prior, "Greetings to the Co-op on its Second Anniversary," *New Orleans Co-operator* (January–February 1944), 4; Shannon Lee Frystak, *Our Minds on Freedom: Women and the Struggle for Black Equality in Louisiana* (Baton Rouge: Louisiana State University Press, 2009), 39; Helen Godfrey-Smith, "Oral History Tour Stop 3: Helen Godfrey Smith and Martha Morris of Shreveport FCU," Credit Union History, http://cuhistory.blogspot.com/2014/03/oral-history-tour-stop-3-helen-godfrey.html, last modified on March 10, 2014; "Union Leader Will Address," 22; Henry W. Hermes to Herman Midlo, 26 December 1942, Box 1, Folder 2, Midlo Collection.

37. Lee Brooks, letter to Southeastern Cooperative Educational Association, February 21, 1941, Box 1, Folder 4, SCL Records; SCEA Membership List, 1942, Box 2, Folder 51, SCL Records; 1920 United States Census, s.v. "Lillian Muniz," New Orleans, Orleans Parish, Louisiana, accessed through Ancestry.com.

38. Scott, *The Southern Lady*, 192; Dorothea Browder, "A 'Christian Solution of the Labor Situation': How Workingwomen Reshaped the YWCA's Religious Mission and Politics," *Journal of Women's History* 19, no. 2 (2007): 103–105 (first and second quotation); Landon Storrs, "Left-Feminism, The Consumer Movement, and Red Scare Politics in the United States, 1935–1960," *Journal of Women's History* 18, no. 3 (2006): 52; Frystak, *Our Minds on Freedom*, 38; "Consumers Cooperative Union, Inc. Joins SCEA," 3; "Leaders in State Student Conference," *Times-Picayune*, November 9, 1934, 34, Advance Local Media; "'Tomorrow' Film to be Exhibited," ibid., April 4, 1943, 24; "Consumers' Union to Install Staff," ibid., January 5, 1947, 18; Gilmore, *Defying Dixie*, 269.

39. Mrs. Cordella A. Winn to Mrs. Elizabeth S. Thompson, May 20, 1935, Box 41, Folder 4, New Orleans YWCA Records, LaRC (first through third quotation); "Findings—Southern Regional Conference, April 17–20, 1939, Box 39, Folder 3, New Orleans YWCA Records (fourth quotation).

40. 1930 United States Census, s.v. "Fletcher Sherrod," New Orleans, Orleans Parish, Louisiana, accessed through Ancestry.com; "J. W. Mason Heads Postal Relief Body"

Times-Picayune, April 10, 1938, 12, Advance Local Media; "Consumers' Group Plans Celebration," ibid., January 5, 1945, 16.

41. Jeffries, *Bloody Lowndes*, 41; Fairclough, *Race and Democracy*, 57, 81–82; "Deaths," *Times-Picayune*, February 12, 1950, 10, Advance Local Media; "Win the War and Win the Peace," *New Orleans Co-operator* (January–February 1944): 2–3, Box 1, Folder 2, Midlo Collection; Gilmore, *Defying Dixie*, 269; The Cooperative League, press release, "Southeastern Cooperative Education Association," May 16, 1940, Box 2, Folder 46, SCL Records.

42. Benedict Anderson, *Imagined Communities: Reflections on the Origin and Spread of Nationalism* (London: Verso, 1983); Jerry Purvis Sanson, *Louisiana During World War II: Politics and Society, 1939–1945* (Baton Rouge: Louisiana State University Press, 1999), 245; Cohen, *A Consumers' Republic*, 26; Deutsch, *Building a Housewife's Paradise*, 166; "Our Store," June–July 1942, 1 (first quotation); "Our Store," January–February 1944, 1 (second and third quotations).

43. Sanson, *Louisiana During World War II*, 251–53; "Bond Buyer Signs," *Times-Picayune*, May 19, 1942, 2; "Gossip," *New Orleans Co-operator* (January–February 1944): 7.

44. "Our Store," June–July 1942, 1 (first quotation); Sanson, *Louisiana During World War II*, 259; "Grocers Blamed for Point Losses," *Times-Picayune*, July 29, 1945, 11, Advance Local Media (second quotation); Storrs, *Civilizing Capitalism*, 246.

45. Mary Rizzo, "Revolution in a Can: Food, Class, and Radicalism in the Minneapolis Co-op Wars of the 1970s," in *Eating in Eden: Food and American Utopias*, eds. Etta M. Madden and Martha L. Finch (Lincoln: University of Nebraska, 2006), 220–21; Jeffrey Charles, "Searching for Gold in Guacamole," in *Food Nations*, 143, 146 (first quotation); "Our Store," June–July 1942, 1 (second quotation).

46. Charles McGovern, *Sold American: Consumption and Citizenship, 1890–1945* (Chapel Hill: University of North Carolina Press, 2006), 302; Deutsch, *Building a Housewife's Paradise*, 166; "Our Store," January–February 1944, 1; Bentley, *Eating for Victory*, 115.

47. Gabaccia, *We Are What We Eat*, 144–47; Sanson, *Louisiana During World War II*, 257; Elizabeth M. Williams, *New Orleans: A Food Biography* (Lanham: AltaMira Press 2012), 92; Bentley, *Eating for Victory*, 64; "Our Store," June–July 1942, 1; "Our Store," January–February 1944, 1; "These Dealers are Featuring Swift's Premium Ham," *Times-Picayune*, April 7, 1950, 18, Advance Local Media; "R.O. Peace Meat Markets," ibid., February 27, 1949, 14; "Grand Opening," ibid., January 7, 1949, 38.

48. Greta de Jong, "'With the Aid of God and the F.S.A.' The Louisiana Farmers' Union and the African American Freedom Struggle in the New Deal Era," *Journal of Social History* 34, no. 1 (Autumn 2000): 111; Curl, *For All the People*, 122–23; "Assail Congress for Passing," 4.

49. "Centennial!!! 1844–1944," *New Orleans Co-operator* (January–February 1944): 6.

50. Moses Coady, *Masters of Their Own Destiny: The Story of the Antigonish Movement of Adult Education Through Economic Cooperation* (New York: Harper and Brothers Publishers, 1939); Lee M. Brooks to Edward Yeomans, October 17, 1940, Box 1, Folder 2, SCL Records; Southeastern Cooperative Education Association, newsletter, February 8, 1941, Box 2, Folder 46, ibid.; Lee M. Brooks, "The South, Our Problem in Cooperative Democracy," radio transcript, 28 September 1942, Box 2, Folder 46, ibid.; Ruth A. Morton to Ed Yeomans, November 28, 1940, 3, Box 1, Folder 2, ibid. (quotation).

51. Advertisement, "R.O. Peace Meat Markets," *Times-Picayune*, February 10, 1949, 8; "Consumers' Co-operative Ice Cream Parlor," *Polks' New Orleans City Directory* (New Orleans: R. L. Polk and Co., 1949); "Co-operative Laundry and Linen Service, Inc.," Louisiana Companies, accessed on August 21, 2014, available at http://labusiness.us/co-operati

.list-of-louisiana-companies.az; Peter N. Biewer, "Our Credit Union," *New Orleans Co-operator* (January–February 1944), 3–4.

52. "Mrs. Ruth Braniff Wins Freret Contest," *Times-Picayune*, October 5, 1945, 22, Advance Local Media; "Improved Garbage," 24; "Freret Street has Switched" 21; "Trolley Busses" 1, 9 (quotations).

53. David M. Potter, *People of Plenty: Economic Abundance and the American Character* (Chicago: University of Chicago Press, 1954), 79 (first quotation); "Cooperatives and Their Promotion to be Studied in Louisiana," *Southeastern Cooperator* (April 1942): 1, Box 2, Folder 46, SCL Records; "Win the War and Win the Peace!" 2–3 (second and third quotation).

54. "Centennial" 6.

55. Ibid. (first quotation); Jack Shaffer, *Historical Dictionary of the Cooperative Movement* (Lanham: Scarecrow Press, 1999), 18; Jerry Voorhis, *American Cooperatives: Where They Come From, What They Do, Where They Are Going* (New York: Harper, 1961), 3–10, 217 (second quotation); Curl, *For All the People*, 190.

56. Jameson, *Archaeologies of the Future*, xi; Jay Winter, *Dreams of Peace and Freedom: Utopian Moments in the Twentieth Century* (New Haven: Yale University Press, 2006), 99–116; Michael Bess, *Realism, Utopia, and the Mushroom Cloud: Four Activist Intellectuals and Their Strategies for Peace, 1945–1989* (Chicago: University of Chicago Press, 1993), 42–86.

57. "Centennial," 6.

58. Jeff Woods, *Black Struggle, Red Scare: Segregation and Anti-Communism in the South, 1949–1968* (Baton Rouge: Louisiana State University Press, 2004), 26–27.

59. F. W. Sinclair Sr. to Hale Boggs, February 28, 1950, Box 530, Folder 9, Hale Boggs and Lindy Boggs Papers, 1914–1998, Louisiana Research Collection, Tulane University. Hereafter cited as Boggs Papers.

60. E. H. Murphy, letter to Hale Boggs, January 17, 1950, Folder 9, Box 530, Boggs Papers.

61. "Italy Lifts Expulsion Order Against Former FAO Officer," Associated Press, February 18, 1956, Box 9, Folder 1938–1956, Clyde Johnson Papers, 1930–1990, Louis Round Wilson Special Collections Library, University of North Carolina at Chapel Hill, Chapel Hill, North Carolina. Hereafter cited as Johnson Papers.

62. Gordon McIntire to Clyde and Anne Johnson, April 14, 1956, Box 9, Folder 1938–1956, Johnson Papers.

63. "Testimony of Jerry Voorhis, Executive Secretary of the Cooperative League of the USA, Before the Ways and Means Committee-House of Representatives, February 23, 1950," cited in Jerry Voorhis to Hale Boggs, March 4, 1950, Box 530, Folder 9, Boggs Papers.

64. Curl, *For All the People*, 191; Giese, "How the Old Co-ops Went Wrong," 320; "Consumers' Union to Install Staff," 18; "Hermes Renamed by District Group," *Times-Picayune*, March 17, 1955, 7, 80, Advance Local Media.

65. Warner, "Freret's Century," 348; Campanella, *Bienville's Dilemma*, 50; Curl, *For All the People*, 189; "These Dealers Are Featuring," 18; "Legal Notices," *Times-Picayune*, October 3, 1965, 108, Advance Local Media.

66. Biewer, "Our Credit Union," 3–4 (esp. 4, first quotation); Gunnar Trumbull, *Consumer Lending and America: Credit and Welfare* (Cambridge: Cambridge University Press, 2014), 19–20; Edgar Wallace Wood, "Credit Union Development in Louisiana" (PhD diss., Louisiana State University, 1967), 5–19; Lee Brooks, letter to SCEA Office, February 2, 1941, Folder 4, Box 1, SCL Records (second quotation).

67. Wood, "Credit Union Development," 3–7; Biewer, "Our Credit Union," 4 (quotations).

68. Cohen, *Consumers' Republic*, 160–61; Wood, "Credit Union Development," 5; Biewer, "Our Credit Union," 4.

69. Godfrey-Smith, "Oral History Tour Stop 3" (quotation); Germany, *New Orleans After the Promises*, 31; "Negro Housing Steps Planned," *Times-Picayune*, April 2, 1953, 26, Advance Local Media.

70. Thomas Sugrue, *Origins of the Urban Crisis: Race and Inequality in Postwar Detroit* (Princeton: Princeton University Press, 1996), 60, 196; Cohen, *Consumers' Republic*, 170–71; "Cooperative Project Began with Eviction," *Washington Post*, January 18, 1953, R5; "Legion Oaks Will Get First Church," ibid., July 6, 1952, 65; Germany, *New Orleans After the Promises*, 3.

71. Nembhard, *Collective Courage*, 101; Godfrey-Smith, "Oral History Tour Stop 3."

72. "Improved Garbage Collection Asked," 24; Barreca, quoted in Warner, "Freret's Century," 342.

73. Wood, "Credit Union Development in Louisiana," 54.

74. "Freret Credit Union Re-elects Barreca," *Times-Picayune*, January 16, 1952, 24, Advance Local Media; "Merrick School Restraint Asked," ibid., June 21, 1952, 10; "School Location Policy Defended," ibid., April 17, 1951, 3 (quotation); Justin Poché, "Separate but Sinful: The Desegregation of Louisiana Catholicism, 1938–1962," in *Louisiana Beyond Black and White*, 35–36; Warner, "Freret's Century," 346–51.

75. Germany, *New Orleans After the Promises*, 23, 30; Campanella, *Bienville's Dilemma*, 187; "Local's Credit Union to Meet," *Times-Picayune*, January 23, 1963, 8, Advance Local Media; "Meeting Planned for Credit Union," ibid., January 5, 1957, 15; "Magnolia Room in Frank's Steak House Caters to All Organizations," ibid., November 10, 1955, 49; "Freret Credit Union Re-elects Barreca," 24; Warner, "Freret's Century," 344–46.

76. Ed Yeomans to Lee M. Brooks, September 27, 1940, Box 1, Folder 1, SCL Records; Godfrey-Smith, "Oral History Tour Stop 3"; "Headline News," Louisiana Credit Union League, accessed on August 20, 2014, http://www.lcul.com/Headline_News_102.html?article_id =2667; Warner, "Freret's Century," 352.

77. "Hermes Renamed by District Group," 80; Photograph, "International Credit Union Day, New Orleans, 1967, 'A Happy Occasion,'" October 17, 1967, Box 114, Folder 56, Victor Schiro Papers, 1904–1995, LaRC (hereafter cited as Schiro Papers); "Credit Union Heads to Meet," *Times-Picayune*, March 3, 1966, 40, Advance Local Media; "Deaths: Henry W. Hermes," ibid., June 1, 1987, 19; "Henry W. Hermes," ibid., March 18, 1955, 7; Wood, "Credit Union Development," 36–41, 47–51; "Credit Unions Will Celebrate: Editor of International Publication to Speak," *Times-Picayune*, October 15, 1951, 18; "About the League," Louisiana Credit Union League, accessed on September 18, 2012, http://www.lcul.com/Chapter_Information_210. html; Cohen, *A Consumers' Republic*, 160–61.

78. "Credit Unions Will Celebrate," 18; Lee M. Brooks to the Right Reverend John L. Jackson, February 2, 1941, Box 1, Folder 4, SCL Records; "Consumers' Union to Install Staff," 18 (quotation).

79. Louisiana Credit Union League, "34th Annual Meeting and Convention Program, Jung Hotel, New Orleans," June 1, 1968, Folder 11, Box 1008, Boggs Papers; Louisiana Credit Union League, photograph, "39th Annual Meeting and Convention, June 22–24," June 22–24, 1973, Folder 14, Box 2096, Boggs Papers; Edgar L. Fontaine, letter to Lindy Boggs, October 9, 1973, Folder 19, Box 2682, Boggs Papers; Lindy Boggs, letter to Edgar L. Fontaine, October 16, 1973, Folder 19, Box 2682, Boggs Papers.

80. Julia Mickenberg, *Learning from the Left: Children's Literature, the Cold War, and Radical Politics in the United States* (New York: Oxford University Press, 2006), 4–5; "Officers Installed at Meeting of Freret Business Men's Group," *Times-Picayune*, June 19, 1958, 54, Advance Local Media.

81. "Credit Unions Will Celebrate," 18; "Day Dedicated to Credit Union," *Times-Picayune*, October 16, 1957, 39, Advance Local Media; "Credit Unions in Poverty War," ibid., May 23,

1965, 6 (first quotation); US Public Law 88–452, 88th Congress, the Economic Opportunity Act of 1964, 1, 9 (second and third quotation).

82. Rebecca Tiger, "A Bitter Pill Indeed: The War on Poverty and Community Action in New Orleans, 1964–1970" (MA thesis, University of New Orleans, 1997), 5; Charles D. Tansey, "Community Development Credit Unions: An Emerging Player in Low Income Communities," Brookings Institute, September 2001, http://www.brookings.edu/research/articles/2001/09/metropolitanpolicy-tansey; US Public Law 88–452, 1.

83. Germany, *New Orleans After the Promises*, 111; Martin E. Segal, "Senior Citizens Trained in Consumer Education," *Times-Picayune*, June 24, 1968, 10, Advance Local Media; Cohen, *A Consumers' Republic*, 355; F. J. Tellez and E. P. Roy, "Economic and Socio-Economic Relationships Between Farmer Cooperatives and Low-Income Farmers in Louisiana," *Department of Agricultural Economics and Agribusiness Research Report*, no. 359 (December 1966): 34; Terse Boasberg to Fred Hayes, et al., memorandum, March 8, 1966, 4, file "Admin. Confidential," Box 34A, Records of the Community Services Administration, National Archives.

84. "4 Areas to Get Credit Unions," *Times-Picayune*, February 26, 1966, 22, Advance Local Media; "Consumer Credit Session Today," ibid., October 16, 1966, 16; Quick Facts: TCA Target Areas (n.d.): 2, Vertical Files, Organization Total Community Action, LaRC; Tiger, "A Bitter Pill Indeed," 2.

85. "History of SSA During the Johnson Administration 1963–1968," Social Security Administration, accessed on August 20, 2014, http://www.socialsecurity.gov/history/ssa/lbjoper7.html (first and second quotations); "Credit Unions to Have Program," *Times-Picayune*, January 6, 1967, 16, Advance Local Media (fourth through sixth quotations).

86. "Credit Unions to Have Program," 16; "Credit Union Heads to Meet," 40; "Credit Union League Meets," *Times-Picayune*, May 29, 1966, 13, Advance Local Media.

87. "Hermes Renamed by District Group," 80; Hale Boggs, speech, "Remarks of US Rep. Hale Boggs Before the Louisiana Credit Union League, New Orleans, Louisiana" (June 8, 1968), 1, Box 1008, Folder 11, Boggs Papers (quotations).

88. De Jong, *Invisible Enemy*, 163; Tiger, "A Bitter Pill Indeed," 1; John Wofford, "The Politics of Local Responsibility: Administration of the Community Action Program, 1965–1966," in *On Fighting Poverty*, ed. James L. Sundquist (New York: Basic Books, 1969), 71; Michael L. Gillette, *Launching the War on Poverty: An Oral History* (Oxford: Oxford University Press, 2010), 308 (quotation).

89. "N.O. Moneywise Project Begins," *Times-Picayune*, January 10, 1967, 35, Advance Local Media (first and second quotations); "Four Areas to Get Credit Unions," ibid., February 26, 1966, 22 (third quotation); Cohen, *A Consumers' Republic*, 356–57; Germany, *New Orleans After the Promises*, 112–13.

90. Godfrey-Smith, "Oral History Tour Stop 3" (quotation); "NCUA Share Insurance Fund Information, Reports, and Statements," National Credit Union Administration, accessed on August 22, 2014, http://www.ncua.gov/dataapps/pages/si-ncua.aspx.

91. Fairclough, *Race and Democracy*, 393; Germany, *New Orleans After the Promises*, 120; de Jong, *Invisible Enemy*, 36.

92. "Neighborhood Activist of Lower 9th Ward Dies," *Times-Picayune*, December 28, 1996, http://files.usgwarchives.net/la/orleans/newspapers/00000161.txt; "Mrs. George Ethel Warren," ibid., October 7, 1971, 60, Advance Local Media (quotation); Germany, *New Orleans After the Promises*, 75–76.

93. Warner, "Freret's Century," 349, 351, 353; "August Weber Garden Center," *Times-Picayune*, October 24, 1971, 79; "Freret Street is Wearing a New Look," *Times-Picayune*, November

7, 1981, Advance Local Media; August Weber, quoted in Lovell Beaulieu, "Friendly Service Makes Nursery a Success," *Times-Picayune*, October 7, 1984, 15.

94. Richard Campanella, "A Glorious Mess: A Perceptual History of New Orleans Neighborhoods," *New Orleans Magazine*, last modified on June 2014, http://www.myneworleans.com/new-orleans-magazine/june-2014/a-glorious-mess/; "HUD History," US Department of Housing and Urban Development, accessed on July 8, 2014, http://portal.hud.gov/hudportal/HUD?src=/about/hud_history; Fry, interview with author (quotation); Neil Smith, *The New Urban Frontier: Gentrification and the Revanchist City* (London and New York: Routledge, 1996), 38.

95. Wright, "New Orleans: A City That Care Forgot," 56; Lawrence Knopp, "Some Theoretical Implications of Gay Involvement in an Urban Land Market," *Political Geography Quarterly* 9, no. 4 (October 1990): 337–52; Mark Gottdiener and Leslie Budd, *Key Concepts in Urban Studies* (London: Sage Publications, 2005), 33–34; Richard Campanella, interview with author, July 9, 2012; Chava Nachmias and J. John Palen, "Membership in Voluntary Neighborhood Associations and Urban Revitalization" *Policy Sciences* 14, no. 2 (April 1982): 191.

96. Wright, "New Orleans: A City That Care Forgot," 51, 56–60; Warner, "Freret's Century," 353; "Freret Street is Wearing a New Look," 13; Ed Anderson, "Holman Center Ready to Move into Ex-Grocery," *Times-Picayune*, May 4, 1985, 7, Advance Local Media.

97. August Weber, quoted in Joan Kent, "Closing of Freret Street Canal Villere Upsets Revitalization Boosters," *Times-Picayune*, August 14, 1984, 10, Advance Local Media (first quotation); Nachmias and Palen, "Membership in Voluntary Neighborhood Associations," 179; Robert Morris, "The Redevelopment of Freret Street," *The Gambit*, August 13, 2013, http://www.bestofneworleans.com/gambit/the-redevelopment-of-freret-street/Content?oid=2238586 (second quotation).

Chapter Four

1. SCEA, *Digest of The Baton Rouge Conference*, April 25, 1941, 1, Box 1, Folder 5, SCL Records (first quotation); Ed Yeomans to Dr. Lee M. Brooks, September 27, 1940, 1, Box 1, Folder 1, ibid. (second through fourth quotation).

2. SCEA, *Digest of The Baton Rouge Conference*, 1 (first, second, and fourth quotations); Ed Yeomans to Dr. Lee M. Brooks, October 13, 1940, 1, Box 1, Folder 2, SCL Records (third quotation); Lee Brooks to SCEA officials, April 17, 1941, 2, ibid. (fifth quotation).

3. SCEA, "Memorandum and Report Number 2: On Activities for Summer, 1941," to SCEA Directors and the Julius Rosenwald Fund, 2, Box 2, Folder 53, SCL Records.

4. Letter, Albon L. Holsey, Executive Director, the National Negro Business League, to SCEA, September 16, 1940, Box 1, Folder 1, SCL Records (first quotation); Michele Mitchell, *Righteous Propagation: African Americans and the Politics of Racial Destiny after Reconstruction* (Chapel Hill: University of North Carolina Press, 2004), 242–46 (second quotation on 245); Robert E. Weems, *Desegregating the Dollar, African American Consumerism in the Twentieth Century* (New York: New York University Press, 1998), 60.

5. Drake, "Why Not 'Co-operate'?" 234, 251.

6. Free Southern Theater, "Basic Program Guidelines" (December 1976): 17–18, Box 26, Folder 42, O'Neal Papers, 1927–1999, Amistad Research Center, Tulane University. Hereafter cited as O'Neal Papers.

7. Tom Dent, "Black Theater in the South: Report and Reflections," in *The Theater of Black Americans: A Collection of Critical Essays*, ed. Errol Hill (New York: Applause Theatre and Cinema Books, 1987), 261.

8. Ibid.

9. Tom Dent, *Southern Journey: A Return to the Civil Rights Movement* (New York: William Morrow and Company, 1997), 35–36; Fairclough, *Race and Democracy*, 143; Annemarie Bean, "The Free Southern Theater: Mythology and the Moving Between Movements," and Jan Cohen-Cruz, "'Comforting the Afflicted and Afflicting the Comfortable': The Legacy of the Free Southern Theater," in *Restaging the Sixties*, eds. James M. Harding and Cindy Rosenthal (Ann Arbor: University of Michigan Press, 2006); James Smethurst, *The Black Arts Movement: Literary Nationalism in the 1960s and 1970s* (Chapel Hill: University of North Carolina Press, 2005); Ellen Louise Tripp, "Free Southern Theater: There is Always a Message" (PhD diss., University of North Carolina at Greensboro, 1986); Samori Sekou Camara, "'There are Some Bad Brothers and Sisters in New Orleans': The Black Power Movement in the Crescent City from 1964–1977" (PhD diss., University of Texas at Austin, 2011).

10. Cynthia Young, *Soul Power: Culture, Radicalism, and the Making of a U.S. Third World Left* (Durham: Duke University Press, 2006), 4.

11. De Jong, "'With the Aid of God and the F.S.A.'"; de Jong, *Invisible Enemy*; Fairclough, *Race and Democracy*; Jeffries, *Bloody Lowndes*, 41–48 (quotation).

12. Dent, *Southern Journey*, 35 (quotation); Joe M. Richardson, "Albert W. Dent: A Black New Orleans Hospital and University Administrator," *Louisiana History* 37, no. 3 (Summer 1996): 309.

13. Shirley Thompson, "Adventures in Black Life Insurance," April 14, 2014, invited talk at the University of Texas at Austin; Angela Jones, *African American Civil Rights: Early Activism and the Niagara Movement* (Santa Barbara: Praeger, 2011), 22; Devore, *Defying Jim Crow*, 152–53; Jim Jones, "The Legacy of Toyohiko Kagawa," Cooperative Development Foundation, last modified on March 15, 2011, https://www.cdf.coop/wp/wp-content/uploads/2014/09/Kagawa-article.pdf.

14. Lee M. Brooks to Miss Elizabeth K. Lynch, November 1, 1940, 3, Box 1, Folder 2, SCL Records; Richardson, "Albert W. Dent," 311.

15. Donald Holley, *Uncle Sam's Farmers: The New Deal Communities in Lower Mississippi Valley* (Urbana: University of Illinois Press, 1975), 183, Fairclough, *Race and Democracy*, 38–39; Devore, *Defying Jim Crow*, 51; Richardson, "Albert W. Dent," 310.

16. Germany, *New Orleans After the Promises*, 6.

17. Wright, "New Orleans: A City That Care Forgot," 48–49; Campanella, *Bienville's Dilemma*, 44.

18. Wright, "New Orleans: A City That Care Forgot," 48–49, 56; Campanella, *Bienville's Dilemma*, 183.

19. Germany, *New Orleans After the Promises*, 6, 40; Claire and George Sessions Perry, "Penny-A-Day Hospital," *Saturday Evening Post*, September 2, 1939, 30, 67, Box 2, Folder 2, Albert Walter and Ernestine Jessie Covington Dent Family Papers, Amistad Research Center. Hereafter cited as Dent Family Papers; Raymond P. Sloan, "Five Years of Negro Health Activities," reprinted from *The Modern Hospital* 48, no. 4 (April 1937): 3, ibid; Ward, *Black Physicians in the Jim Crow South*, 123–24, 179.

20. Reed, interview with author.

21. Mitchell, *Righteous Propagation*, 245; Fairclough, *Race and Democracy*, 81–82; Germany, *New Orleans Beyond the Promises*, 11, 31.

22. Mitchell, *Righteous Propagation*, 70, 219–25, 233 (quotation).

23. Germany, *New Orleans Beyond the Promises*, 31; Fairclough, *Race and Democracy*, 54, 72.

24. Darlene Hine, "Flint-Goodridge Hospital of Dillard University: The Development of Black Collegiate Nursing, 1932–1950," Box 2, Folder 2, Perry, "Penny-A-Day Hospital," 67–68 (quotation on 30); Sloan, "Five Years of Negro Health Activities," 6; Ward, *Black Physicians in the Jim Crow South*, 30, 67–68.

25. Richardson, "Albert W. Dent," 313–14 (quotation on 312); Devore, *Defying Jim Crow*, 116.

26. Dent, *Southern Journey*, 1; Ward, *Black Physicians in the Jim Crow South*, 174.

27. A. W. Dent, "The Need for Public Understanding and Support," *Public Health Reports* 67, no. 4 (April 1952): 327 (quotation); Beverly W. Jones, "Mary Church Terrell and the National Association of Colored Women, 1896–1901," *Journal of Negro History* 67, no. 1 (Spring 1982): 27; Devore, *Defying Jim Crow*, 115.

28. Hine, "Flint-Goodridge Hospital of Dillard University," 178.

29. Jones, "Mary Church Terrell," 28.

30. Mitchell, Righteous Propagation, 244, 247.

31. George Lipsitz, *The Possessive Investment in Whiteness: How White People Profit from Identity Politics* (Philadelphia: Temple University Press, 2006), 243.

32. Reed, interview with author.

33. Emile Labat to JCFBMAA, January 10, 1934, Box 1, Folder 1, JCFBMAA Records; New Orleans Embalmers Association Records, *By-laws* (1984), 3, Box 1, Folder 5, New Orleans Embalmers Association Records, 1952–1996 (first quotation), Amistad Research Collection. Hereafter cited as NOEA Records; Dent, *Southern Journey*, 15 (second quotation).

34. Fairclough, *Race and Democracy*, 37.

35. Justin Poché, "Separate but Sinful: The Desegregation of Louisiana Catholicism, 1938–1962," in *Louisiana Beyond Black and White*, 35–36; McKnight, *Whistling in the Wind*.

36. Dr. Ernest Cherrie to JCFBMAA President, Officers and Members, September 6, 1933, Box 1, Folder 1, JCFBMAA Records.

37. Germany, *New Orleans After the Promises*, 48, 69; NOEA, "A Half-Century of Serving the Community and the Funeral Industry," 50th Anniversary Program and Certificate (1995): 2, Box 2, Folder 2, NOEA Records.

38. F. J. Dejoie, "The Origin, Development and Achievements of the N.O. Federation of Civic Leagues" (1929): 2–6 (esp. 3), Box 77, Folder 46, A. P. Tureaud Papers, 1798–1977. Amistad Research Center.

39. Jones, *African American Civil Rights*, 3; Mitchell, *Righteous Propagation*, 245.

40. Smith, *Footprints of Black Louisiana*, 23; "Civic Worker is Taken by Death," *Times-Picayune*, May 29, 1970, 20, Advance Local Media; "Dejoie Funeral Rites Planned," ibid., April 3, 1967, 7; Vice President to Officers and Members of JCFBMAA board of directors, February 23, 1919, Box 1, Folder 1, JCFBMAA Records; "Journal of Minutes" (April 23, 1944), 264, Box 1, Folder 5, ibid.; "Journal of Minutes" (April 23, 1961), 74, Box 2, Folder 1, ibid.

41. Fairclough, *Race and Democracy*, xii; Emanuel and Tureaud, *A More Noble Cause*, 124.

42. Fred L. Brownlee to Mr. Phillips Bradley, September 20, 1940, Box 1, Folder 3, Dent Family Papers.

43. Fairclough, *Race and Democracy*, 49 (first and second quotations); Emanuel and Tureaud, *A More Noble Cause*, 123 (third and fourth quotations).

44. A. W. Dent, quoted in John LaFarge, "The Development of Cooperative Acceptance of Racial Integration," *The Journal of Negro Education* 21, no. 3 (Summer 1952): 436; Dent, *A Southern Journey*, 35–36.

45. Gordon McIntire, "Statement on Farm-Tenancy," Sharecroppers Union Newsletter (n.d.), Box 2, Folder 3, Clyde Johnson Papers, 1930–1990, Louis Round Wilson Special Collections Library, University of North Carolina Chapel Hill; Drake, "Why Not 'Co-operate'?" 231, 234 (quotations).

46. Charles M. Payne, *I've Got the Light of Freedom: The Organizing Tradition and the Mississippi* (Berkeley: University of California Press, 1995), 83; Nembhard, *Collective Courage*, 114, 232; Oscar Renal Williams, *George S. Schuyler: Portrait of a Black Conservative* (Knoxville: University of Tennessee Press, 2007), 84; Melinda Chateauvert, *Marching Together: Women and the Brotherhood of Sleeping Car Porters* (Champaign: University of Illinois Press, 1997), 142; Deutsch, *Building a Housewife's Paradise*, 109, 129.

47. Thompson, "Adventures in Black Life Insurance"; Perry, "Penny-A-Day Hospital," 67.

48. "Hospital Insurance," *Negro Star* (December 9, 1932): 1; Perry, "Penny-A-Day Hospital," 67–68; Hine, "Flint Goodridge Hospital of Dillard University," 182–83, 188.

49. Jacob L. Reddix, *A Voice Crying in the Wilderness: The Memoirs of Jacob L. Reddix* (Jackson: University of Mississippi Press, 1974), 119.

50. Fairclough, *Race and Democracy*, 61; Campanella, *Bienville's Dilemma*, 183.

51. Quote from A. W. Dent to Miss Read, memorandum, May 23, 1936, 1, Box 1, Folder 2, Dent Family Papers; Miss Elizabeth Logan to Mr. Albert Dent, October 23, 1935, 1, Box 1, Folder 1, ibid.

52. SCEA, "Memorandum and Report Number 2: On Activities for Summer, 1941," 2.

53. Drake, "Why Not 'Co-operate'?" 233–34.

54. Cooperative League of the United States of America, "Southeastern Cooperative Education Association," bulletin (May 16, 1940): 3, Box 2, Folder 46, SCL Records (first quotation); "Sketch of the Development of the SCEA," *Southeastern Cooperative Education Association Newsletter* (February 8, 1941): 1, ibid. (second quotation).

55. "Sketch of the Development of the SCEA," 1 (quotations).

56. Drake, "Why Not 'Co-operate'?" 231 (first quotation), 234 (second and third quotation), and 232 (fourth quotation).

57. Jones, *African American Civil Rights*, 1–2.

58. Fred L. Brownlee to Miss Fannie C. Williams, September 23, 1940, Box 1, Folder 3, Dent Family Papers; "Delta and Providence Cooperative Farms Papers, 1925–1963 (Bulk 1936–1943) Finding Aid," the Southern Historical Collection at the Louis Round Wilson Special Collections Library, http://finding-aids.lib.unc.edu/03474/, accessed on January 16, 2018; Ronald H. Stone, *Professor Reinhold Niebuhr: A Mentor to the Twentieth Century* (Louisville: Westminister John Knox Press), 115; Brian Stanley, "The Legacy of George Sherwood Eddy," *International Bulletin of Missionary Research* 24, no. 3 (2000): 130–31.

59. "Drop in Japanese Divorces Cited by Christian Leader," *Times-Picayune*, March 17, 1936, 3, Advance Local Media; Wayne Flynt, *Southern Religion and Christian Diversity in the Twentieth Century* (Tuscaloosa: University of Alabama Press, 2016), 21; R. H. Erbes Jr., "Union of Church and Economics is Dramatized as Co-ops Reveal Rapid Progress," *Printers' Ink: A Journal for Advertisers* (n.d.): 1, Series 4, Folder 1, Herman Midlo Records (quotations).

60. Judith Stein, *The World of Marcus Garvey: Race and Class in Modern Society* (Baton Rouge: Louisiana State University Press, 1991), 256; Mitchell, *Righteous Propagation*, 244.

61. Harold Battiste, *Unfinished Blues: Memories of a New Orleans Music Man* (New Orleans: Historic New Orleans Collection, 2010), 58.

62. Berlin C. Plummer, "Ideas for Enduring Peace," *Courtbouillon* 14, no. 1 (New Orleans, Dillard University, 1949): 4, 6, https://archive.org/stream/CourtbouillonV0114No1/court bouillon_v0114_n01009_djvu.txt (quotations); Arthur Zebbs, "Know Your Place," ibid.

63. McKnight, *Whistling in the Wind*, 5 (quotations).

64. Dent, *Southern Journey*, 13 (first quotation) and 224 (second quotation).

65. Michna, "Hearing the Hurricane Coming," 76.

66. Sally Banes, *Greenwich Village 1963: Avant-Garde Performance and the Effervescent Body* (Raleigh: Duke University Press, 1993), 173; Michael William Doyle, "Staging the Revolution: Guerrilla Theater as a Countercultural Practice, 1965–1968," in *Imagine Nation: The American Counterculture of the 1960s and '70s*, eds. Michael William Doyle and Peter Braunstein (New York: Routledge, 2002), 72; Yolanda Broyles-Gonzalez, "Reconstructing Collective Dynamics: El Teatro Campesino from a Twenty-First-Century Perspective," in *Restaging the Sixties*, 220.

67. Kalamu ya Salaam, "Enriching the Paper Trail: An Interview with Tom Dent," *African American Review* 27, no. 2 (Summer 1993): 327–45 (quotations); Dent, *Southern Journey*, 1–2; John O'Neal to Dr. Samuel Hay, May 12, 1980, 2, Box 2, Folder 7, O'Neal Papers.

68. William Glover, "A Squad of Actors is Taking Special Training for a Back-Roads Tour of Dixie This Summer" (April 5, 1965): 1, Box 26, Folder 40, O'Neal Papers (quotation); Free Southern Theater, "Basic Program Guidelines," 17–18; John O'Neal to Dr. Samuel Hay, 1; Jan Cohen-Cruz, "'Comforting the Afflicted," 288; "The Free Southern Theater: Historical Overview," *Restaging the Sixties*, 263; "Mississippi Free Press," Mississippi Civil Rights Project, accessed on October 21, 2014, http://mscivilrightsproject.org/index.php?option=com_conte nt&view=article&id=499:mississippi-free-press&catid=295:organization&Itemid=33.

69. Glover, "A Squad of Actors," 1.

70. Robert M. Ferris, *Flood of Conflict: The New Orleans Free School Story* (Roslyn Heights: Alternative Education Resource Organization, 2012), 17 (first and second quotations) and 24 (third quotation).

71. O'Neal to Hay (first quotation); Cohen-Cruz, "Comforting the Afflicting," 288 (second quotation); Shani Jamila, "Creative Resistance: A Study of the Free Southern Theater," *Huffington Post*, last updated on September 14, 2014, http://www.huffingtonpost.com/shani -jamila/creative-resistance_b_5586443.html (third quotation).

72. Doris Derby, Gilbert Moses, and John O'Neal, "The Free Southern Theater," in *An Ideal Theater: Founding Visions for a New American Art*, ed. Todd London (New York: Theatre Communications Group, 2013), 128; Tom Dent, Report, "The Free Southern Theater: An Evaluation," *Freedomways* (First Quarter, 1966), Box 188, Folder 15, Tom Dent Papers (quotations).

73. Dent, "The Free Southern Theater: An Evaluation," 4.

74. Germany, *New Orleans After the Promises*, 54.

75. Rachel Breunlin, "The Legacy of the Free Southern Theater in New Orleans: Interviews with Karen-Kaia Livers and Chakula Cha Jua," ChickenBones, accessed on October 2, 2013, http://www.nathanielturner.com/legacyfreesouttheater.htm; Free Southern Theater, "Basic Program Guidelines," 17; Mass mailer, "The New Orleans Medical Bureau and Spanish-American Ladies' Committee of the North American Committee to Aid Spanish Democracy" (n.d.), Vertical File: Organizations, North American Committee to Aid Spanish Democracy, LaRC.

76. Dent, "The Free Southern Theater: An Evaluation," 2.

77. Congo Square Writers Union, "Congo Square Theater: Summer" (1979), 2, Box 188, Folder 3, Tom Dent Papers (first quotation); Tom Dent, "Ritual Murder," in *New Orleans Noir: The Classics*, ed. Julie Smith (New York: Akashic Books, 2016), 159 (second quotation); Michna, "Hearing the Hurricane," 126.

78. Denning, *The Cultural Front*, 287–88.

79. First quote, Dent, "Ritual Murder," 164; second through fourth quote, ibid., 173; fifth quote, ibid. 171.

80. Tom Dent, "Beyond Rhetoric: Toward a Blk Southern Theater," 13, Box 37, Folder 6, Tom Dent Papers; Tom Dent, "The Black Arts Movement in the South: Black Consciousness through Reality Mirrors," in *Free Southern Theater by the Free Southern Theater: A Documentary of the South's Radical Black Theater with Journals, Letters, Poetry, and Essays, and a Play Written by Those Who Built It* (New York: Bobbs-Merrill, 1969), 5.

81. Cohen-Cruz, "Comforting the Afflicted," 290, 293.

82. Breunlin, "The Legacy of the Free Southern Theater in New Orleans."

83. Kalamu ya Salaam, "Historical Overviews of the Black Arts Movement," accessed on October 7, 2013, http://www.nathanielturner.com/kalamuessay.htm.

84. Free Southern Theater, "Basic Program Guidelines," 3; Camara, "'There are Some Bad Brothers and Sisters," 46; McKnight, *Whistling in the Wind*, 112 (quotation).

85. Murray Levy, "Free Southern Theater Plans Afro-American Emphasis," *New Orleans Freedom Press* 1, no. 1 (May 1966): 7.

86. Camara, "There are Some Bad Brothers and Sisters," 60; Dent, "The Free Southern Theater: An Evaluation."

87. "Historical Notes," 3, Box 1, JCFBMA Records; Germany, *New Orleans After the Promises*, 23..ermany, New Orleans After the Promises, owerful challenge to d in 1982. cooperation:orking-class cultural production.y eras

88. Crutcher, *Tremé*, 50–58.

89. Ibid., 59–60; Ari Kelman, *A River and Its City: The Nature of Landscape of New Orleans* (Berkeley: University of California Press, 2003), 201–210.

90. A.F.O. Records (All for One), Promotional Materials (n.d.), 1, Box 4, Folder 17, Harold Battiste Papers, Amistad Research Center, Tulane University (first and second quotations); Battiste, *Unfinished Blues*, 72; Mindy Thompson Fullilove, *Root Shock: How Tearing Up City Neighborhoods Hurts America, and What We Can Do About It* (New York: Ballantine Books, 2004), 17 (third quotation).

91. Brian Ward, *Just My Soul Responding: Rhythm and Blues, Black Consciousness and Race Relations* (London: UCL Press, 1998), 255–56 (first quotation); "Tentative Brochure," October 17, 1961, 1, Box 4, Folder 10, Harold Battiste Papers; Battiste, *Unfinished Blues*, 70.

92. Crutcher, *Tremé*, 59–64; Kelman, *A River and Its City*, 201–210; Reed, interview with author (quotation).

93. Levy, "Free Southern Theater Plans Afro-American Emphasis," 7 (quotations); Breunlin, "The Legacy of the Free Southern Theater in New Orleans"; Woods, "Katrina's World," 442; Germany, *New Orleans After the Promises*, 3–5; Economic Opportunity Committee, Desire Area Community Council, letter to Victor Schiro, March 16, 1966, Box S66–7, Folder: Economic Opportunity-1966, Victor Schiro Papers, 1904–1995, LaRC. Hereafter cited as Schiro Papers.

94. Department of Program Development, *Profile of Poverty in New Orleans* (New Orleans: Department of Program Development, April 1973), 20, 32; Roscoe Orman, quoted

in Breunlin, "The Legacy of the Free Southern Theater"; Orissa Arend, *Showdown in Desire: The Black Panthers Take a Stand in New Orleans* (Fayetteville: University of Arkansas Press, 2009), 69.

95. Levy, "Free Southern Theater Plans Afro-American Emphasis," 7 (first quotation); Allen Dowling to Tom Dent, July 1, 1966, in *Free Southern Theater by the Free Southern Theater*, 126 (second and third quotation).

96. Levy, "Free Southern Theater Plans Afro-American Emphasis," 7.

97. Thomas Dent to members, board of directors, contributors, friends, "Current Activities of FST," *Free Southern Theater Newsletter* (March 18, 1968): 2; Folder 22, Box 188, Tom Dent Papers.

98. Cohen-Cruz, "Comforting the Afflicted," 299.

99. Christina Larocco, "Participatory Drama": The New Left, the Vietnam War, and the Emergence of Performance Studies," conference talk at the American Studies Association Annual Meeting, November 6, 2014; Helen A. Regis, "Keeping Jazz Funerals Alive': Blackness and the Politics of Memory in New Orleans," in *Southern Heritage on Display: Public Ritual and Ethnic Diversity within Southern Regionalism*, ed. Celeste Ray (Tuscaloosa: University of Alabama Press, 2003).

100. Stevens, interview with author (first quotation); Lipsitz, *The Possessive Investment in Whiteness*, 243 (second and third quotation).

101. Michna, "Hearing the Hurricane Coming," 102–103; Glover, "A Squad of Actors," 1–2; "Letter from Gilbert Moses to John O'Neal on March 1967," *Free Southern Theater by the Free Southern Theater*, 101 (first quotation); SNCC, "Position Paper on Black Power," in *Modern Black Nationalism: From Marcus Garvey to Louis Farrakhan, Issue 2*, ed. William L. Van Deburg (New York: New York University Press, 1997), 120–26.

102. Kalamu ya Salaam, "Art for Life: My Story, My Song," *Chickenbones*, accessed on January 1, 2015, http://www.nathanielturner.com/artforlife7.htm.

103. Tom Dent, quoted in Michna, "Hearing the Hurricane," 113–14.

104. ya Salaam, "Art for Life."

105. "Calendar of Events," *New Orleans Coalition Newsletter* 1, no. 9 (March 1, 1969), Vertical File: Organizations, New Orleans Coalition, Jones Hall Special Collections; "Calendar of Events," *New Orleans Coalition Newsletter* 1, no. 10 (April 1, 1969): 2, ibid.; "Tutoring and Enrichment Programs for Young Children in New Orleans," *New Orleans Coalition Newsletter* 1, no. 11 (May 1, 1969): 2–3, 6, ibid.; "What's Happening Where?" *New Orleans Coalition Newsletter* 1, no. 7 (January 1, 1969): 1, ibid.

106. Arend, *Showdown in Desire*; Rosemary C. R. Taylor, "Free Medicine," in *Co-ops, Communes and Collectives*, 21.

107. Ronald Milner, "The Warning," *Negro Digest* 18, no. 6 (April 1969): 53 (quotation); "FST: Strong Black Hands . . . To Break the Shackles of the Mind," 1972, Box 4, Folder 28, Nkombo Publications Records, 1968–1974, Amistad Research Center, Tulane University. Hereafter cited as Nkombo Records.

108. Ronnie Moore and Marvin Rich, "When Blacks Take Office," *The Progressive* 36, no. 5 (May 1972): 30 (first and second quotations) and 33 (third quotation), Box 1, Folder 4, Ronnie Moore Papers, Amistad Research Center, Tulane University.

109. Amy Liu and Bruce Katz, "Katrina is Everywhere: Lessons from the Gulf Coast," in *Breakthrough Communities: Sustainability and Justice in the Next American Metropolis*, eds. Carl Anthony and M. Paloma Pavel (Boston: Massachusetts Institute of Technology, 2009),

81–94; Social Welfare Planning Council, *Community Organization in Low-Income Neighborhoods in New Orleans* (New Orleans: Social Welfare Planning Council, December 1968), 19, 27, 31; Woods, "Katrina's World," 442.

110. Tiger, "A Bitter Pill Indeed," 54–56; Social Welfare Planning Council, *Community Organization*, 15.

111. Tom Dent to Rev. Milton Upton, "Subject: Summary of Activities and Request for Support," January 10, 1975, 2, Box 188, Folder 6, Tom Dent Papers (quotation); "Suggested Guidelines New Orleans Committee on Economic Opportunity Program," September 16, 1964, Box S64-10, Folder: Economic Opportunity Program-1964, Schiro Papers; Marilyn Jane Celestine, "Volunteer in Service to America, VISTA as Agent for Social Change (A Case Study of VISTA in New Orleans)" (MA thesis, University of New Orleans, 1976), 18; "Hopeful Signs of New Social Action in the Irish Channel," *New Orleans Coalition Newsletter* 1, no. 12 (June 1, 1969): 2, New Orleans Coalition; Total Community Action, *Quick Facts: TCA Target Areas* (n.d.): 2, Vertical Files: Organization Total Community Action, LaRC.

112. Broadside Press Receipt, Detroit Michigan, October 20, 1976, Box 188, Folder 6, Tom Dent Papers; Tom Dent to Rev. Milton Upton, "Summary of Activities and Request for Support," 3 (quotation).

113. Tiger, "A Bitter Pill Indeed," 65; Tom Dent, quoted in Clarissa Myrick Harris, "Mirror of the Movement: The History of the Free Southern Theater as a Microcosm of the Civil Rights and Black Power Movements, 1963–1978" (PhD diss., Emory University, 1988), 92.

114. John Baker, in Gillette, *Launching the War on Poverty*, 308 (first quotation); SNCC, "Position Paper on Black Power, 123; Angela Young, "Making the Best of Me: 1987 Black Youth Congress," Box 1, Folder 2, Ronnie Moore Papers (second quotation); Moore and Rich, "When Blacks Take Office," 32 (third quotation).

115. Lloyd Medley, "Black Capitalism," *Bamboula Publication* (1976), Box 188, Folder 5, Tom Dent Papers; Thomas Dent, "New Orleans Versus Atlanta," *Southern Exposure* 7, no. 1 (1979): 68.

116. Michna, "Hearing the Hurricane," 152; Dent, *Southern Journey*, 52; Camara, "There are Some Bad Brothers and Sisters," 73; SNCC, "Position Paper on Black Power, 126 (quotation); Free Southern Theater, "Basic Program Guidelines," 5–7.

117. Aaron Windel, "Decolonizing the Cooperative Movement," paper presented at Society for Utopian Studies Annual Conference, Berkeley, CA, November 2, 2018; SNCC, "Position Paper on Black Power," 123 (quotation).

118. Free Southern Theater, "Basic Program Guidelines," 5–7.

119. Camara, "There are Some Bad Brothers and Sisters," 73 (first quotation); Dent, *Southern Journey*, 52 (second quotation); Walter N. Vernon, *Becoming One People: The History of Louisiana Methodism* (Bossier City: Everett Publishing Company, 1987), 271.

120. Free Southern Theater, "Basic Program Guidelines," 6 (first quotation); "Gilbert Moses Commentary," *Free Southern Theater by The Free Southern Theater*, 33 (second quotation).

121. Matt Robinson, interview with author, June 5, 2012, Cooperative Oral History Project.

122. Free Southern Theater, "Basic Program Guidelines," iv (quotations); Joe Stevens, "Black Theater Study Tour Report," Parts 1 and 2 (n.d.), Box 4, Folder 28, Nkombo Records.

123. "A Brief History of the Ethiopian Theater" (n.d.), 1, Box 188, Folder 12, Tom Dent Papers (quotations).

124. Dashiki Project Theatre, Background Info (1972): 1; Box 188, Folder 10, Tom Dent Papers (first quotation); Stanley R. Coleman, "Dashiki Project Theatre: Black Identity and

Beyond" (PhD diss., Louisiana State University, 2003), 10; Free Southern Theater, "Basic Program Guidelines," 7 (second quotation).

125. SNCC, "Position Paper on Black Power," 122.

126. Dent, *Southern Journey*, 45 (quotations); The Joint Legislative Committee on Un-American Activities, State of Louisiana, *Report No. 3: Activities of "The Nation of Islam" or the Muslim Cult of Islam, in Louisiana* (January 9, 1963), 84; Priscilla McCutcheon, "Community Food Security 'For Us, By Us': The Nation of Islam and the Pan African Orthodox Christian Church," in *Food and Culture: A Reader*, eds. Carole Counihan and Penny Van Esterik (New York: Routledge 2013), 574; "The History of the Nation of Islam in New Orleans," NOI New Orleans, accessed on October 1, 2014, http://noineworleans.org/news/back_issues/history.html.

127. George Mariscal, *Brown Eyed Children of the Sun: Lessons from the Chicano Movement, 1965–1975* (Albuquerque: University of New Mexico Press, 2005), 3–9.

128. SCDF, *Southern Cooperative Development Fund Annual Report* (1987): 9, Box 13, Folder 1, George Jr. Esser Papers, Louis Round Wilson Special Collections Library, University of North Carolina Chapel Hill (first and second quotations); Billy E. Barnes to Tom Johnson, "R.E.: Ford Foundation Supported Farm Co-ops" (n.d.) 4, Box 5, Folder: Billy Barnes, ibid. (third quotations).

129. Greta de Jong, *You Can't Eat Freedom: Southerners and Social Justice After the Civil Rights Movement* (Chapel Hill: University of North Carolina Press, 2016), 89, 91.

130. Cecilia A. Moore, "Writing Black Catholic Lives: Black Catholic Biographies and Autobiographies," *U.S. Catholic Historian* 29, no. 3 (Summer 2011): 52; Charles Prejean, "Louisiana State Association of Cooperatives: Articles and Bylaws" (Lafayette: LSAC, 1967).

131. SCDF, *Southern Cooperative Development Fund Annual Report*, 9 (first quotation); de Jong, "'From Votes to Vegetables,'" 146–47; de Jong, *You Can't Eat Freedom*, 97–98.

132. Photographs, Grand Marie Co-op, Opelousas, LA (1966), Box 4, Folder 6, Ronnie Moore Papers (first and second quotations); SCDF, *Southern Cooperative Development Fund Annual Report* (1987): 6 (emphasis in the original) (third quotation).

133. Billy E. Barnes to Tom Johnson, "R. E.: Ford Foundation Supported Farm Co-ops," 2 (first quotation); John Zippert, interview by Greta de Jong (June 28, 1998); transcript, 34–40, Louisiana State University Libraries, Louisiana State University (second quotation).

134. Joint Legislative Committee on Un-American Activities, State of Louisiana, *Report No. 8: Aspects of the Poverty Program in South Louisiana* (April 14, 1967); de Jong, *You Can't Eat Freedom*, 101, 104 (first quotation); Zippert, interview by Greta de Jong (second quotation).

135. Billy E. Barnes to Tom Johnson, "R.E.: Ford Foundation Supported Farm Co-ops" (quotation); de Jong, *You Can't Eat Freedom*, 116, 119, 127.

136. McKnight, *Whistling in the Wind*, 36–38.

137. Billy E. Barnes to Tom Johnson, "R.E.: Ford Foundation Supported Farm Co-ops," 2 (first quotation); SCDF, *Southern Cooperative Development Fund Annual Report*, 9 (second quotation).

138. Federation of Southern Cooperatives, memorandum, June 4, 1971, Box 2, Folder 5, O'Neal Papers; Jim Lee to Mrs. Roberta Jones, July 13, 1970, Box 2, Folder 2, ibid. (quotation); John O'Neal, memorandum to Herb Callender, May 18, 1970, ibid.; Dent, *Southern Journey*, 43; "History," North Carolina Association of Community Development Corporations, accessed on October 15, 2013, http://ncacdc.org/history.cfm.

139. Kim Lacy Rogers, *Righteous Lives: Narratives of the New Orleans Civil Rights Movement* (New York: New York University Press, 1993), 111.

140. O'Neal, memorandum to Herbert Callender, 1.

141. Doug Rossinow, *The Politics of Authenticity: Liberalism, Christianity, and the New Left in America* (New York: Columbia University Press, 1998), 118.

142. Rev. A. J. McKnight to John O'Neal, April 21, 1971, Box 2, Folder 5, O'Neal Papers; Federation of Southern Cooperatives, memorandum, June 4, 1971; "The Treasures of Opelousas Project Presents the Congo Square Players," flier, Box 188, Folder 7, Tom Dent Papers (quotation).

143. O'Neal, memorandum to Herbert Callender, 1 (first quotation); McKnight, *Whistling in the Wind*, 75 (second quotation).

144. Walter Isaacson, "Foreword," Scott Cowen with Betsy Seifer, *The Inevitable City: The Resurgence of New Orleans and the Future of Urban America* (New York: Palgrave MacMillan, 2014), viii (first quotation); "The Congo Square Writer's Workshop," Box 188, Folder 3, Tom Dent Papers (second and third quotation).

145. McKnight, *Whistling in the Wind*, 110–12 (first quotation) and 75 (second quotation); Mtumishi St. Julien, *Upon the Shoulders of Elephants We Reach the Sky: A Parent's Farewell to a Collegian* (New Orleans: Runagate Press, 1995).

146. Billy E. Barnes to Tom Johnson, "R.E.: Ford Foundation Supported Farm Co-ops," 9 (first quotation), 10 (emphasis in the original) (fourth quotation); SCDF, *Southern Cooperative Development Fund Annual Report*, 9, 26 (second and third quotations).

147. De Jong, *You Can't Eat Freedom*, 150.

148. Dent, *Southern Journey*, 1–2.

Chapter Five

1. Liz Lichtman, interview with author, July 2, 2012, Cooperative Oral History Project.

2. Fry, interview with author (quotations); Beverly Wright, "Race, Politics, and Pollution: Environmental Justice in the Mississippi River Chemical Corridor," in *Just Sustainabilities: Development in an Unequal World*, eds. Julian Agyeman, Robert Bullard, and Bob Evans (London: Earthscan Publications, 2003), 125–45; Kimberly Quillen, "The Oil Bust," *Times-Picayune*, January 29, 2012, http://www.nola.com/175years/index.ssf/2012/01/the_oil_bust_the_times-picayun.html; Campanella, interview with author; "Louisiana: Race and Hispanic Origin for Selected Cities and Other Places: Earliest Census to 1990," US Census Bureau, accessed on August 13, 2014, http://www.census.gov/population/www/documentation/twps0076/twps0076.html.

3. Sarah Andert, "Relief Through ReLeaf," *The Advocate*, March 10, 2008, https://www.theadvocate.com/gambit/new_orleans/news/article_1036719–1b41–529b–99ff-7aab90fbd9f9.html.

4. Fry, interview with author.

5. Julia Africa, "Community Gardens as Healing Spaces: Addressing the Aftermath of Hurricane Katrina in New Orleans," Harvard University Graduate School of Design, last updated on 2011, http://isites.harvard.edu/icb/icb.do?keyword=k94076&pageid=icb.page577179; Daina Cheyenne Harvey, "'Gimme a Pigfoot and a Bottle of Beer': Food as Cultural Performance in the Aftermath of Hurricane Katrina," *Symbolic Interaction* 40, no. 4 (2017): 511 (first quotation); Robert King Wilkerson quoted in "King's Candy: A New Orleans Kitchen Vision," *Fugitive Waves* (August 25, 2015), http://www.kitchensisters.org/2015/08/25/fugitive-waves-kings-candy-a-new-orleans-kitchen-vision/ (second quotation).

6. Velasco, interview with author (first quotation); Jeffrey Hou, "Making and Supporting Community Gardens as Informal Urban Landscapes," in *The Informal American City: Beyond Taco Trucks and Day Laborers*, eds. Vinit Mukhija and Anastasia Loukaitou-Sideris (Cambridge: MIT Press, 2014), 83; Aya Hoffman, "Seeds of Renewal," Ithaca College, last modified on April 24, 2012, https://www.ithaca.edu/parkscholars/blogs/park_scholars_in _service/seeds_of_renewal:_community_gardens_in_new_orleans/; R. Stephanie Bruno, "Parkway Partners of New Orleans Marks its 30th Year of Fostering Urban Horticulture," *Times-Picayune*, October 19, 2012, https://www.nola.com/homegarden/index.ssf/2012/10/ parkway_partners_of_new_orlean.html; Sarah Andert, "Relief Through ReLeaf" (second quotation).

7. Fry, interview with author.

8. Ibid. (first through third and fifth through seven quotation); Hou, "Making and Supporting Community Gardens as Informal Urban Landscapes," 82 (fourth quotation).

9. Reed, interview with author.

10. Ibid. (quotation); African Scientific Research Institute, "Panel and Bio," Inaugural International African Diaspora Heritage Trail Promiseland Symposium last modified on October 12, 2013, http://asrip.org/index.php/inaugural-cultural-heritage-symposium/ panelists.

11. Reed, interview with author; "Agricultural Leadership Development Program," LSU AgCenter, accessed on July 17, 2014, http://www.lsuagcenter.com/en/community/leadership/ ag_leadership/Agricultural+Leadership+Development+Program/.

12. Reed, interview with author; Donna F. Abernathy, "Cooperative Update: A Legacy Lives On," Rural Cooperatives: USDA/Rural Development, last modified on May 1998, http://www.rurdev.usda.gov/rbs/pub/may98/legacy.html; Federation of Southern Cooperatives, *The Ben Burkett Story: The Unlikely Journey of a Small Farmer*, video, April 4, 2013, https://www.youtube.com/watch?v=JM7zHWey3DQ#t=168; Tony Field and Beverly Bell, "The Consumer's Got to Change the System," Other Worlds, last modified on March 15, 2013, http://www.otherworldsarepossible.org/consumers-got-change-system-farmer-ben-burkett-racism-and-corporate-control-agriculture; de Jong, *You Can't Eat Freedom*, 150, 172 (quotation).

13. Adrian Sainz, "Thousands of Black Farmers File Claims in USDA Discrimination Settlement," CNS News, last modified on March 28, 2012, http://cnsnews.com/news/article/ thousands-black-farmers-file-claims-usda-discrimination-settlement; Jackson Lewis, United States Department of Agriculture: Independent Assessment of the Delivery of Technical and Financial Assistance "Civil Rights Assessment" Final Report (March 31, 2011), USDA, http:// www.usda.gov/documents/Civil_Rights_Assessment-Final_Report.pdf; Reed, interview with author (quotations).

14. De Jong, *You Can't Eat Freedom*, 223.

15. "Louisiana," African Scientific Research Institute, accessed on February 26, 2018, https://asrip.org/events-and-activities/haiti-america-cultural-economic-connection/louisi anna-natives/?v=dc91aeca51b5; Reed, interview with author.

16. Aaron Schneider and Saru Jayaraman, "Ascriptive Segmentation Between Good and Bad Jobs: New Orleans Restaurant and Construction Workers," in *Working in the Big Easy*, 234; Craig, "It Wasn't Even a Hurricane"; Warren, "New Orleans Flooding."

17. Thomas and Campo Flores, quoted in Beverly Wright and Robert D. Bullard, "Washed Away by Hurricane Katrina: Rebuilding a 'New' New Orleans," in *Growing Smarter: Achieving Livable Communities, Environmental Justice, and Regional Equity*, ed. Robert D. Bullard

(Boston: MIT Press, 2007), 193; Cedric Johnson, "Introduction," in *The Neoliberal Deluge*, xx–xxiv; Kent E. Portney, *Taking Sustainable Cities Seriously*, vii; Swearingen, *Environmental City*, 215–17.

18. Campanella, *Bienville's Dilemma*, 244; Arena, "Black, White, Unite and Fight?" 152–73; Kristina Ford, *The Trouble with City Planning: What New Orleans Can Teach Us* (New Haven: Yale University Press, 2010), 31.

19. Ford, *The Trouble with City Planning*, 33; Adams, *Labors of Faith*, 5–6 (quotation); Schneider and Jayaraman, "Ascriptive Segmentation Between Good and Bad Jobs," 234.

20. Stevens, interview with author (first and second quotations); Eric Porter and Lewis Watts, *New Orleans Suite: Music and Culture in Transition* (Berkeley: University of California Press, 2013), 28; Rick Jervis, "Mardi Gras Tribes Still Follow Suit," *USA TODAY*, January 11, 2008, 3A (third and fourth quotations).

21. *Gambit Weekly*, "TBC Brass Band Protest" (June 16, 2010), YouTube, https://www.you tube.com/watch?v=sn2gESJMGuc (first and second quotations); Dinerstein, "Second Lining Post-Katrina," 615–16 (third quotation).

22. Schneider and Jayaraman, "Ascriptive Segmentation," 229–31, 236–46, 251; Aurelia Lorena Murga, "Organizing and Rebuilding a Nuevo Orleans: Day Labor Organizing in the Big Easy," *Working in the Big Easy*, 212, 219, 223.

23. Arena, "Black, White, Unite and Fight?" 152–73; Cedric Johnson, "Charming Accommodations," in *Neoliberal Deluge*, 191; Wright and Bullard, "Washed Away by Hurricane Katrina," 199.

24. Richard A. Webster, "Demolition of Iberville Housing Development Beings," *Times-Picayune*, September 10, 2013, http://www.nola.com/politics/index.ssf/2013/09/demolition_of_iberville_housin.html; Tyler Bridges, "Pres Kabacoff Outlines $1 Billion Vision to Redevelop New Orleans' Urban Core," *The Lens* (September 24, 2013), http://thelensnola.org/2013/09/24/pres-kabacoff-outlines-1-billion-vision-to-redevelop-new-orleans-urban-core/ (quotation); Brentin Mock, "New Orleans' Leading Affordable-Housing Developer Explains its Lack of Affordable Housing," City Lab (September 3, 2015), https://www.citylab.com/equity/2015/09/new-orleans-leading-affordable-housing-developer-explains-its-lack-of-affordable-housing/403351/; Eve Abrams, "Crescent City Community Land Trust Helps Mid-City Create Affordable Rental Units," WWNO, last modified on November 5, 2013, http://wwno.org/post/crescent-city-community-land-trust-helps-mid-city-create-afford able-rental-units.

25. Arena, "Black, White, Unite and Fight?" 159; Johnson, "Charming Accommodations," 191; Wright and Bullard, "Washed Away by Hurricane Katrina," 199; Solidarity Economy meeting, Loyola University, June 27, 2012.

26. Campanella, interview with author; Maureen O'Hagan, "Post-Katrina: Will New Orleans Still Be New Orleans?" Institute for Southern Studies (April 10, 2014), accessed on July 9, 2014, http://www.equalvoiceforfamilies.org/post-katrina-will-new-orleans-still-be -new-orleans/; Doug MacCash, "St. Claude Avenue May Roll Into the 21st Century Aboard a Streetcar," *Times-Picayune*, January 13, 2013, http://www.nola.com/arts/index.ssf/2013/01/st_claude_avenue_neighborhoods_1.html.

27. Susan Buchanan, "Gert Town Overlooked as New Orleans Redevelops," *Huffington Post* (October 17, 2012), http://www.huffingtonpost.com/susan-buchanan/gert-town-over looked-as-n_b_1973777.html; Bruce Eggler, "Xavier University Rezoning Request OK'd By New Orleans City Council," *Times-Picayune*, April 20, 2013, http://www.nola.com/politics/

index.ssf/2013/04/xavier_university_rezoning_req_1.html; Bridges, "Pres Kabacoff Outlines $1 Billion Vision."

28. Dave Isay and Maya Millett, eds., *Callings: The Purpose and Passion of Work* (New York: Penguin Press, 2016), 149 (quotation); Donald Rose, J. Nicholas Bodor, Janet C. Rice, et al., "The Effects of Hurricane Katrina on Food Access Disparities in New Orleans," *American Journal of Public Health* 101, no. 3 (March 2011): 482–84.

29. Fry, interview with author.

30. Lichtman, interview with author.

31. Clark, interview with author; Scott Crow, interview with author, January 29, 2012, ibid.; Robinson, interview with author (quotation).

32. Sue Hilderbrand, Scott Crow, and Lisa Fithian, "Common Ground Relief," in *What Lies Beneath: Katrina, Race, and the State of the Nation*, ed. South End Press Collective (Cambridge: South End Press Collective, 2007), 81–88; Arend, *Showdown in Desire*, 192–94; Campanella, *Bienville's Dilemma*, 347; Stevens, interview with author.

33. Murga, "Organizing and Rebuilding a Nuevo Orleans, 212–25; Schneider and Jayaraman, "Ascriptive Segmentation," 234, 251, 258 (first quotation), 261 (second quotation).

34. "The Latino Farmers Cooperative of Louisiana," Urban Ministry, last accessed on March 3, 2018, www.urbanministry.org/org/latino-farmers-cooperative-louisiana; Levy, Comey, and Padilla, *Keeping the Neighborhood Affordable*, 38–39; Reed, interview with author; Sally Golub, interview with author, July 11, 2012, Cooperative Oral History Project.

35. Scott Kellogg and Stacy Pettigrew, *Toolbox for Sustainable City Living* (Cambridge: South End Press, 2008), 212; Solidarity Economy meeting.

36. "The Latino Farmers Cooperative of Louisiana," National Immigrant Farming Initiative, accessed on October 31, 2014, http://www.immigrantfarming.org/project-profiles/the-latino-farmers-cooperative-of-louisiana; Ian McNulty, "Community Impact Series: Latino Farmers Cooperative," WWNO, accessed on March 3, 2018, http://wwno.org/post/community-impact-series-latino-farmers-cooperative (first, second, and fourth quotation); "The Latino Farmers Cooperative of Louisiana," Urban Ministry (third quotation).

37. James Varney, "A Dubious Grant for a Dubious Outfit," *Times-Picayune*, June 16, 2013, http://www.nola.com/opinions/index.ssf/2013/06/a_dubious_grant_for_a_dubious.html.

38. Stevens, interview with author.

39. Solidarity Economy meeting; Sally Stevens, June 18, 2013, comment on James Varney, "A Dubious Grant for a Dubious Outfit," *Times-Picayune*, June 16, 2013, http://www.nola.com/opinions/index.ssf/2013/06/a_dubious_grant_for_a_dubious.html (quotation).

40. "New Orleans," Restaurant Opportunities Centers United, accessed on July 8, 2014, http://rocunited.org/nola/.

41. Solidarity Economy meeting; Brendan McCarthy, "About 400 Marches Join 'Occupy New Orleans' Protest," *Times-Picayune*, October 6, 2011, http://www.nola.com/politics/index.ssf/2011/10/about_400_marchers_join_occupy.html; Mike Howells, "On the Plunder of Post-Isaac Rebuilding," Occupy New Orleans, last modified on September 6, 2012, http://onola.wordpress.com/2012/09/06/on-the-plunder-of-post-isaac-rebuilding-onola/; Knupfer, *Food Co-ops in America*, 191; Gordon Russell, "New Orleans City Council Meets This Morning; Occupy NOLA Protest Expected at 11," *Times-Picayune*, November 17, 2011, http://www.nola.com/politics/index.ssf/2011/11/city_council_meeting_this_morn.html.

42. Erin Rice, e-mail message to the author, June 26, 2012; Solidarity Economy meeting; Stevens, interview with author (quotation).

43. Solidarity Economy meeting; Keelia O'Malley, Jeanette Gustat, Janet Rice, and Carolyn C. Johnson, "Feasibility of Increasing Access to Healthy Foods in Neighborhood Corner Stores," *Journal of Community Health* 38, no. 4 (August 2013): 741–49; "NOFC History," New Orleans Food Co-op, accessed on July 24, 2014, http://www.nolafood.coop/about-nofc/beginnings/.

44. Knopp, "Some Theoretical Implications," 337–52; Knupfer, *Food Co-ops in America*, 191–92; "Our Mission, Ends, and Goals," New Orleans Food Co-op, accessed on July 24, 2014, http://www.nolafood.coop/about-nofc/mission/; "Our Farmers and Producers," New Orleans Food Co-op, accessed on July 24, 2014, http://www.nolafood.coop/shopping-at-nofc/meet-our-farmers/.

45. C. W. Cannon, "Call Me a Sentimental Old Fool, But I Miss My Schwegmans— And I Got a Right To," *The Lens*, last modified on August 20, 2014, https://thelensnola.org/2014/08/20/call-me-a-sentimental-old-fool-but-i-miss-my-schwegmanns-and-i-got-a-right-to/.

46. Richard Campanella, "Gentrification and its Discontents: Notes from New Orleans," New Geography, last modified on March 1, 2013, http://www.newgeography.com/content/003526-gentrification-and-its-discontents-notes-new-orleans; Doug MacCash, "Gentrification of Bywater and St. Claude Avenue Was Sped Up by Flood and 2008 Economic Slump," *Times-Picayune*, January 25, 2013, http://www.nola.com/arts/index.ssf/2013/01/the_long_term_gentrification_0.html; Richard Webster, "St. Claude Neighbors Wary of Healing Center Plans," *New Orleans City Business*, June 17, 2011, http://neworleanscitybusiness.com/blog/author/richardwebster; "Healing Center Attacked for Role in Gentrification," NOLA Anarcha (blog), September 11, 2011, http://nolaanarcha.blogspot.com/2011/09/healing-center-attacked-for-role-in.html.

47. Solidarity Economy meeting; Campanella, *Bienville's Dilemma*, 187 (quotation).

48. Solidarity Economy meeting; Knupfer, *Food Co-ops in America*, 191; "Invest— Co-OWN It!" New Orleans Food Co-op, accessed on March 4, 2018, http://www.nolafood.coop/ownership/become-a-member/.

49. Reed, interview with author, June 26, 2012.

50. "Our Farm," Grow Dat Youth Farm, accessed on July 10, 2014, http://growdatyouthfarm.org/what-we-do/our-farm/; Fry, interview with author; Scott Crow, *Black Flags and Windmills* (Oakland: PM Press 2011), 156 (quotations); Lichtman, interview with author; "Lower Ninth Ward 18," Sustain the Nine, accessed on August 11, 2014, http://www.sustainthenine.org/sites/default/files/uploaded-documents/L9W%20CSED%20Food%20Action%20Plan%20FINAL_sm_0.pdf.

51. Robinson, interview with author.

52. Fry, interview with author (quotations); Velasco, interview with author; Campanella *Bienville's Dilemma*, 272.

53. Fry, interview with author (quotations); Velasco, interview with author.

54. Velasco, interview with author.

55. Ibid.; Fry, interview with author.

56. Fry, interview with author (first quotation); Velasco, interview with author (second through fifth quotation).

57. Fry, interview with author (first quotation); Velasco, interview with author (second through fourth quotation).

58. Velasco, interview with author (first and second quotation).

59. Harvey, "Gimme a Pigfoot and a Bottle of Beer," 513 (quotation); Susan Tucker, *New Orleans Cuisine: Fourteen Signature Dishes and Their Histories* (Jackson: University Press of Mississippi, 2009).

60. Daniel Mottola, "Bringing Urban Living in Harmony with Nature," *Austin Chronicle*, January 20, 2006, http://www.austinchronicle.com/news/2006-01-20/325865/ (first quotation); Kellogg and Pettigrew, *Toolbox for Sustainable City Living*, 211.

61. "Take the Virtual Tour," Rhizome Collective, accessed on October 17, 2011, http://www.rhizomecollective.org/node/7.

62. Velasco, interview with author (first through third quotations); *The Southern Foodways Alliance Community Cookbook*, eds. Sara Roahen and John T. Edge (Athens: University of Georgia Press, 2015), 72.

63. Patricia Allen and Clare Hinrichs, "Buying into 'Buy Local': Engagements of United States Local Food Initiatives," in *Alternative Food Geographies: Representation and Practice*, eds. Damian Maye, Lewis Holloway, and Moya Kneafsey (New York: Elsevier, 2007), 255–60.

64. Ibid. Velasco, interview with author (first and second quotation); "About Us," The New Orleans 4th Annual Eat Local Challenge, accessed on July 13, 2014, http://www.nolalocavore.org/nola-locavores/ (third quotation).

65. Velasco, interview with author (quotation); "Finding Common Ground in NOLA Through Food Justice," NOLA Food and Farm Network News, last modified on April 3, 2012, http://noffn.tumblr.com/post/20426706499/finding-common-ground-in-nola-through-food-justice; Fry, interview with author.

66. Fry, interview with author (quotation); Velasco, interview with author.

67. Reed, interview with author.

68. Rod E. Emmer, Jim Wiggins, Wendell Verret, and Thomas Hymel, "Louisiana Sea Grant Assists Delcambre, LA, During Hurricane Recovery," Sea Grant Louisiana (2007), http://www.laseagrant.org/wp-content/uploads/A-Town-Too-Smart-Delcambre.pdf; De Jong, *Invisible Enemy*, 164; Nembhard, *Collective Courage*, 210; "Cooperative Support for New Post-Katrina Fishing Co-op in Louisiana," Federation of Southern Cooperatives, last updated on February 27, 2007, http://www.federationsoutherncoop.com/press/feb2707.htm.

69. Reed, interview with author; Nembhard, *Collective Courage*, 210; Louisiana Disaster Recovery Foundation, "Initiating Change for a Sustainable Louisiana," *Initiate Change: 2009 Annual Report* (2009): 12, http://www.foundationforlouisiana.org/docs/news_reports/ldr_09ar_final.pdf.

70. Todd, "Disasters Spur Co-op Formations," 7. https://www.rd.usda.gov/files/Rural Coop_JulyAug12.pdf (quotation); Jane Livingston, "Miracle on the Bayou," *Rural Cooperatives* 74, no. 2 (March–April 2007), http://www.rurdev.usda.gov/rbs/pub/mar07/miracle.htm.

71. Reed, interview with author; Mtangulizi Sankiya, "Katrina and the Condition of Black New Orleans: The Struggle to Justice, Equality, and Democracy," in *Race, Place, and Environmental Justice after Hurricane Katrina*, eds. Robert D. Bullard and Beverly Wright (Philadelphia: Perseus Books Group, 2009), 106; Sheila J. Webb, "Investing in Human Capital and Healthy Rebuilding in the Aftermath of Hurricane Katrina," in ibid., 147–48; Robert K. Whelan and Denise Strong, "Rebuilding Lives Post-Katrina: Choices and Challenges in New Orleans's Economic Development," in ibid., 195–96.

72. Jeremy Alford, "Board Develops Plan to Help Fishermen with Storm Recovery," *Houma Today*, January 13, 2007, http://www.houmatoday.com/article/20070113/NEWS/701130305; (Jefferson 2014); Nailah Jefferson, "Vanishing Pearls: Trailer," YouTube, last modified on March 18, 2014, video, 2:29, https://www.youtube.com/watch?time_continue=56&v=wBLkLOG5MwA (first through third quotations); Reed, interview with author (fourth quotation).

73. Reed, interview with author; Federation of Southern Cooperatives, "Cooperative Support"; Nembhard, *Collective Courage*, 210; Andrew W. Kitts and Steven F. Edwards,

"Cooperatives in US Fisheries: Realizing the Potential of the Fishermen's Collective Marketing Act," *Marine Policy* (April 4, 2003): 1, http://www.uwcc.wisc.edu/info/fishery/kitts.pdf.

74. Stevens, interview with author; "What We're Working On," Austin Cooperative Think Tank, accessed on August 14, 2014, http://www.thinktank.coop/what-we-do; Susan Meaux, quoted in Todd, "Disasters Spur Co-op Formations," 7.

75. Todd, "Disasters Spur Co-op Formations"; Reed, interview with author (quotations); Kelley, *Race Rebels*, 2–5.

76. Nembhard, "Uplifting and Strengthening Our Community"; "Interactive Session II," National Association of Black Journalists, accessed on March 15, 2018, http://www.nabj.org/?page=InterSessionII; Ben Burkett, "From the President," *Family Farm Agenda* (December 2009): 1, https://www.nffc.net/Pressroom/Newsletters/2009%20December.pdf; Ben Burkett, "From the Desk of State Coordinator Ben F. Burkett," *The Quiet Movement* 2 (April, May, June 2007): 3; http://federationsoutherncoop.com/coopnews/mac2.pdf.

77. Curl, *For All the People*, 254 (first quotation); Reed, interview with author (second and fourth quotations); "Cooperative Identity, Values, and Principles," International Co-operative Alliance, accessed on July 15, 2014, http://ica.coop/en/whats-co-op/co-operative-identity-values-principles.

78. Nina Feldman, "How Anti-Communist Vietnamese Refugees Signed Up for a Cooperative Farm," PRI, last modified on May 20, 2015, https://www.pri.org/stories/2015–05–20/how-anti-communist-vietnamese-refugees-signed-cooperative-farm (first quotation); Reed, interview (second quotation); "Who We Are," VEGGI Farmers Cooperative, accessed on August 14, 2014, http://www.veggifarmcoop.com/.

79. McKnight, *Whistling in the Wind*, 32.

80. Reed, interview with author.

81. Federation of Southern Cooperatives, "Cooperative Support."

82. Reed, interview with author.

83. Ibid.

84. Nembhard, *Collective Courage*, 210; Louisiana Disaster Recovery Foundation, "Initiating Change for a Sustainable Louisiana"; Alford, "Board Develops Plan"; Louisiana Recovery Authority board of directors meeting minutes (March 14, 2006): 11, accessed on July 19, 2014, http://lra.louisiana.gov/assets/other/by_month/march07/LRAMinutes031407.pdf; Louisiana Recovery Authority board of directors meeting minutes (January 12, 2007): 15, accessed on July 19, 2014, http://www.lra.louisiana.gov/assets/other/by_month/jan07/LRAMinutes011207.pdf.

85. Press release, "Crowe Supports Funding Assistance for Our Louisiana Fishing Industry," A. G. Crowe: Louisiana Senate, last modified on February 25, 2007, http://www.agcrowe.com/pg-51–15-pressviewer.aspx?pressid=6.

86. Nembhard, *Collective Courage*, 210–11; Susan Meaux, quoted in Todd, "Disasters Spur Co-op Formations," 7; Louisiana Shrimp Harvester Advisory Panel, Minutes, Baton Rouge, Louisiana (September 21, 2009): 6, 8, accessed on March 15, 2018, http://www.wlf.louisiana.gov/sites/default/files/pdf/shrimp_task_force/6591-Shrimp%20Harvester%20Advisory%20Board%20Meeting%20-%20MONDAY,%20SEPTEMBER%2021,%202009/Draft_Minutes_Shrimp_Harvestors_Advisory_Panel_9–21–09.pdf.

87. Harvey, *Spaces of Hope*, 148; Liu and Katz, "Katrina is Everywhere," 81–94.

88. Rossinow, *The Politics of Authenticity*, 280–82 (first quotation); Bullard, Introduction, *Growing Smarter*, 7–10 (second quotation).

89. Murray Bookchin, *Social Ecology and Communalism* (Oakland: AK Press, 2007), 19; "The Benefits of Cooperation," *Social Ecology Newsletter* 1, no. 2 (March 1983): 2; "Broadway Co-op Seeks New Members," ibid. 4; "Bookchin Speaks in New Orleans," ibid. 1, no. 1 (January 1983): 4; "New Businesses in New Orleans," *Times-Picayune*, February 2, 1975, 90, Advance Local Media; "Co-op Store is Being Formed," *Times-Picayune*, November 14, 1974, 62; Clark, interview with author.

90. Hoque and Davis, *Survey of Cooperatives in Louisiana*, 1; Curl, *For All the People*, 282.

91. Bullard, "Introduction," 1–5, 14.

92. Liu and Katz, "Katrina is Everywhere," 81–94; Carl Anthony, "Forward," *Growing Smarter*, vii–vi, xi; Bullard, "Introduction," 7–10.

93. James Brady, "EcoBro," *Louisiana Association of Cooperatives* e-newsletter (May 15, 2017): 8, https://www.501c3koggrants.com/uploads/6/4/6/9/64693481/louisiana_enewsletter_-_may_15_2017_1_.pdf.

94. Bullard, "Introduction," 7 (quotation); James E. McWilliams, *Just Food: Where Locavores Get It Wrong and How We Can Truly Eat Responsibly* (New York: Little, Brown and Company, 2009), 49.

95. "Food Production," New Orleans Food Policy Advisory Committee, accessed on March 15, 2018, http://www.nolafoodpolicy.org/index.php?page=food-production; Solidarity Economy meeting; Fry, interview with author; Initiative for a Competitive Inner City, "ICIC Summit: Urban Innovation No. 4: New Orleans Cooperative Development Project," last updated on October 27, 2013, http://www.icic.org/connection/blog-entry/blog-icicsummit-urban-innovation-no.-4-new-orleans-cooperative-development.

96. Reed, interview with author.

97. James Brady, "What's Growing On!" Con10u2Farm L3Cm, last modified on February 22, 2017, https://www.con10u2farm.com/2017/02/22/eco-bro-speaks/.

98. Harvey, "Gimme a Pigfoot and a Bottle of Beer," 512–13.

99. Reed, interview with author.

100. "LCFC Board," LA Council of Farmer Co-ops, accessed on July 19, 2014, http://www.lafarmercoops.org/lcfc_board_5.html; Curl, *For All the People*, 252.

101. Reed, interview with author.

102. Jackson Lewis, United States Department of Agriculture: Independent Assessment of the Delivery of Technical and Financial Assistance "Civil Rights Assessment" Final Report (March 31, 2011), USDA, http://www.usda.gov/documents/Civil_Rights_Assessment-Final_Report.pdf.

103. "New Civil Rights Era at USDA Continues with Service Contract to Assist Program Administration," Jackson Lewis, last modified on October 9, 2009, http://www.jacksonlewis.com/legalupdates/article.cfm?aid=1874 (first quotation); Reed, interview with author (second quotation).

104. Reed, interview with author (quotations); "Farmers Get Assistance with Pigford Claims," Southern University Agricultural Research and Extension Center, last updated on April 5, 2010, https://suagcenter.blogspot.com/2010/04/.

105. "Funding for Cooperatives," USDA, accessed on July 19, 2014, http://www.rurdev.usda.gov/BCP_FundingForCoops.html; Reed, interview with author; "USDA Support for Historically Black Colleges and Small Agricultural Producers," North Carolina Agribusiness Council (September 20, 2010), https://www.ciclt.net/sn/new/n_detail.aspx?ClientCode=ncagbc&N_ID=23740; John Patrick Jordan, et al., *Leadership in Agriculture: Case Studies for a New Generation* (College Station: Texas A&M University Press, 2013), 95.

106. Sonny Perdue, "Social Infrastructure," *Louisiana Association of Cooperatives* e-newsletter, no. 163 (March 2018): 1 (first quotation); Reed, interview with author (second quotation).

Conclusion

1. Robinson, interview with author.

2. Ibid.

3. Knupfer, *Food Co-ops in America*, 191.

4. Howells, "On the Plunder of Post-Isaac Rebuilding"; McCarthy, "About 400 Marches Join 'Occupy New Orleans' Protest"; Russell, "New Orleans City Council Meets."

5. Robinson, interview with author.

6. US Bureau of Labor Statistics, "The Recession of 2007–2009," 2012, https://www.bls .gov/spotlight/2012/recession/pdf/recession_bls_spotlight.pdf; Richard Heinberg, "Localism in the Age of Trump," Post Carbon Institute, last modified on December 9, 2016, http://www .postcarbon.org/localism-in-the-age-of-trump/; Media Relations, "NRECA Statement on President Trump's Paris Decision," America's Electric Cooperatives, last updated on June 1, 2017, https://www.electric.coop/nreca-statement-on-president-trumps-paris-decision/.

7. Anca Voinea, "What Will Donald Trump Do for Co-operatives? Co-op News, November 10, 2016, https://www.thenews.coop/110987/sector/banking-and-insurance/will-donald-trump-co-operatives/ (quotation); Credit Union National Association, "U.S. Credit Union Profit Profile" (2017), 8, file:///Users/annegessler/Downloads/NationalProfile-M17-Final.pdf.

8. Voinea, "What Will Donald Trump Do for Co-operatives?" (quotation); Robert O'Harrow Jr., "A Two-Decade Crusade by Conservative Charities Fueled Trump's Exit from Paris Climate Accord," *Washington Post*, September 5, 2017, https://www.washingtonpost. com/investigations/a-two-decade-crusade-by-conservative-charities-fueled-trumps-exit -from-paris-climate-accord/2017/09/05/fcb8d9fe-6726–11e7–9928–22d00a47778f_story. html?utm_term=.9e22a2c3a3ac.

9. Elizabeth Shogren, "Obama's Climate Legacy will be Harder to Undo Than Trump Thinks," *Mother Jones*, January 7, 2017, http://www.motherjones.com/environment/2017/01/ obama-climate-change-legacy-west/; Gavin Shire, "President Proposes $1.3 Billion FY 2018 Budget for U.S. Fish and Wildlife Service," US Fish and Wildlife Service, May 23, 2017, https://www.fws.gov/news/ShowNews.cfm?ref=president-proposes-$1.3-billion-fy-2018 -budget-for—u.s.-fish-and-w&_ID=36050.

10. Nathan Schneider, "Economic Democracy and the Billion-Dollar Co-op," *The Nation*, May 8, 2017, https://www.thenation.com/article/economic-democracy-and-the-billion -dollar-co-op/.

11. Andrew Jerome, "President Trump's Budget is an Assault on the Farm Safety-Net, NFU Says," National Farmers Union, last updated on May 23, 2017, https://nfu.org/2017/ 05/23/president-trumps-budget-is-an-assault-on-the-farm-safety-net-and-rural-communi ties-nfu-says/.

12. "NCBA CLUSA Defends Co-ops, Responds to Trump Administration's Budget Blue-print," National Cooperative Business Association CLUSA, last updated on March 16, 2017, http://ncba.coop/ncba-advocacy/1754-ncba-clusa-defends-co-ops-responds-to-trump -administration-s-budget-blueprint.

13. "Dr. Robert Bullard: Houston's 'Unrestrained Capitalism' Made Harvey 'Catastrophe Waiting to Happen,'" *Democracy Now* interview with Robert Bullard (August 29, 2017),

https://www.democracynow.org/2017/8/29/dr_robert_bullard_houston_s_unrestrained (quotation); Jon Penndorf, "Hurricane Harvey Reinforces Need for Cities to Plan for Disaster Resiliency," *Washington Post*, August 29, 2017, https://www.washingtonpost.com/news/where-we-live/wp/2017/08/29/hurricane-harvey-reinforces-need-for-cities-to-plan-for-disaster-resiliency/?utm_term=.ef69819a7ac7; Eliza Relman, "Trump Reversed Regulations to Protect Infrastructure Against Flooding Just Days Before Hurricane Harvey," *Business Insider*, August 28, 2017, http://www.businessinsider.com/trump-reversed-obama-flooding-regulations-before-hurricane-harvey-2017–8; Donald J. Trump, "Presidential Executive Order on Establishing Discipline and Accountability in the Environmental Review and Permitting Process for Infrastructure," Executive Order, Office of the Press Secretary, August 15, 2017, https://www.whitehouse.gov/the-press-office/2017/08/15/presidential-executive-order-establishing-discipline-and-accountability.

14. Dave Phillips, "Trucks with Aid Roll into FEMA Hub," *New York Times*, August 30, 2017, https://www.nytimes.com/2017/08/30/us/fema-aid-storm-victims-harvey.html?action=click&pgtype=Homepage&clickSource=story-heading&module=span-abc-region&region=span-abc-region&WT.nav=span-abc-region.

15. Patrick Svitek, "Trump Visits Corpus Christi, Austin to See Harvey Recovery," *Texas Tribune*, August 29, 2017, https://www.texastribune.org/2017/08/29/trump-visit-corpus-christi-austin-see-harvey-recovery/ (quotation).

16. Louisiana Department of Agriculture and Forestry, "Who You Gonna Call"? Facebook post (March 1, 2018), https://www.facebook.com/LouisianaDepartmentofAgriculture-andForestry/videos/10155372379518181/?q=kentwood%20co-op, accessed on April 6, 2018.

17. Derrill Holly, "Louisiana Co-op Helps Entergy with Harvey Recovery," America's Electric Cooperatives, last modified on September 7, 2017, https://www.electric.coop/washington-st-tammany-electric-entergy-substation/.

18. Media Relations, "NRECA Statement."

19. Associated Press, "U.S. Utilities Seek Solar Power as Trump Sides with Coal, Fossil Fuels," *Los Angeles Times*, February 4, 2017, http://www.latimes.com/business/la-fi-solar-power-20170204-story.html; Schneider, "Economic Democracy"; O'Harrow Jr., "A Two-Decade Crusade."

20. Heinberg, "Localism in the Age of Trump."

21. Krishan Kumar, "The Ends of Utopia," *New Literary History* 41, no. 3 (Summer 2010): 549–69.

22. Craig, "It Wasn't Even a Hurricane."

23. Warren, "New Orleans Flooding."

24. "Aron Chang," Tulane School of Architecture, accessed on August 26, 2017, http://architecture.tulane.edu/people/aron-chang; Richard Rainey, "'We Can't Pump Our Way Out': Rethinking New Orleans' Approach to Flood Control," *Times-Picayune*, August 11, 2017, https://www.nola.com/weather/2017/08/new_orleans_flooding_living_wi.html; Shreya Subramni, "New Orleans's Gentilly Resilience District," Princeton H2o, last updated on October 15, 2016, https://princetonh2o.wordpress.com/pane13/http://www.nola.com/weather/index.ssf/2017/08/new_orleans_flooding_living_wi.html.

25. Thiago Terzi, "With Virtual Coops on the Rise, Will Tradition Ag Coops Go Virtual?" *Louisiana Association of Cooperatives* e-newsletter, no. 163 (March 2018): 8. Pdf; Steven Jay Schiffer, "'Glocalized' Utopia, Community-Building, and the Limits of Imagination" *Utopian Studies* 29, no. 1 (March 2018): 67–87.

26. "Social Infrastructure," *Louisiana Association of Cooperatives* e-newsletter, no. 163 (March 2018): 1. PDF.

27. "Water," *Propeller*, last accessed on August 2, 2017, http://gopropeller.org/sectors/water/.

28. "Farmers Program of Mississippi and Louisiana," *Louisiana Association of Cooperatives* e-Newsletter, no. 162 (February 2018): 13. PDF.

29. Kaleb J. Hill, Twitter post, February 23, 2018, 4:37 p.m., https://twitter.com/KalebJHill/status/967196804998713344. Emphasis in the original.

30. Kaleb J. Hill, Twitter post, April 14, 2017, 8:04 a.m., https://twitter.com/KalebJHill/status/852900470557376512; Kaleb J. Hill, Twitter post, February 24, 2018, 6:40 p.m., https://twitter.com/KalebJHill/status/967590196266102785.

31. Hill, February 23, 2018.

32. Terzi, "With Virtual Coops," 8–10.

33. James Brady, "EcoBro," *Louisiana Association of Cooperatives* e-newsletter, May 15, 2017. PDF.

34. "FASOLEAF," Propeller, accessed on January 1, 2019, http://gopropeller.org/ventures/fasoleaf/.

35. Robinson, interview with author.

36. Clark, interview with author.

REFERENCE LIST

"13th Ward Group Backs Candidates." *Times-Picayune*, October 12, 1939. Advance Local Media.

1870 United States Census, s.v. "Eugene Bacarise," New Orleans, Orleans Parish, Louisiana. Ancestry.com.

1870 United States Census, s.v. "John McMartin," Ward 1, Rock Island County, Illinois, Ward 1. Ancestry.com.

1880 United States Census, s.v. "Charles Bacarrisse," New Orleans, Orleans Parish, Louisiana. Ancestry.com.

1900 United States Census, s.v. "Augustine Bacarisse," New Orleans, Orleans Parish, Louisiana. Ancestry.com.

1900 United States Census, s.v. "Elenora Alchorn," New Orleans, Orleans Parish, Louisiana. Ancestry.com.

1900 United States Census, s.v. "Henry L. Zander," New Orleans, Orleans Parish, Louisiana. Ancestry.com.

1900 United States Census, s.v. "John J. Martin," Jennings, Calcasieu Parish, Louisiana. Ancestry.com.

1900 United States Census, s.v. "Rosa F. Michaelis," New Orleans, Orleans Parish, Louisiana. Ancestry.com.

1900 United States Census, s.v. "Thomas Hayes," New Orleans, Orleans Parish, Louisiana. Ancestry.com.

1910 United States Census, s.v. "Inez Mayers," New Orleans, Orleans Parish, Louisiana. Ancestry.com.

1910 United States Census, s.v. "Jeannette M. Moser," New Orleans, Orleans Parish, Louisiana. Ancestry.com.

1920 United States Census, s.v. "Amelia Mendez," New Orleans, Orleans Parish, Louisiana. Ancestry.com.

1920 United States Census, s.v. "Edna M. Egleston," Metairie, Jefferson Parish, Louisiana. Ancestry.com.

1920 United States Census, s.v. "E. W. Vacher," New Orleans, Orleans Parish, Louisiana. Ancestry.com.

1920 United States Census, s.v. "Lillian Muniz," New Orleans, Orleans Parish, Louisiana. Ancestry.com.

1920 United States Census, s.v. "Thomas Hays," New Orleans, Orleans Parish, Louisiana. Ancestry.com.

1925 New York State Census, s.v. "Henry W. Hermes," Brooklyn, Kings County, New York. Ancestry.com.

1930 United States Census, s.v. "Albert E. Mendez Sr.," New Orleans, Orleans Parish, Louisiana. Ancestry.com.

1930 United States Census, s.v. "Henry Hermes," New Orleans, Orleans Parish, Louisiana. Ancestry.com.

1930 United States Census, s.v. "Fletcher Sherrod," New Orleans, Orleans Parish, Louisiana. Ancestry.com.

1940 United States Census, s.v. "Albert E. Mendez Sr.," New Orleans, Orleans Parish, Louisiana. Ancestry.com.

1940 United States Census, s.v. "Henry Hermes," New Orleans, Orleans Parish, Louisiana. Ancestry.com.

"$10,000 Damages Asked of Grosch by Local Barber." *Times-Picayune*, July 14, 1938. Ancestry.com.

"A Fair for the Poor." *Daily Picayune*, March 20, 1899. Advance Local Media.

"A Labor Meeting." *Daily Picayune*, September 23, 1897. Advance Local Media.

"A Mysterious Orator." *Daily Picayune*, October 24, 1897. Advance Local Media.

"A Socialist Kick." *Daily Picayune*, September 11, 1904. Advance Local Media.

"A Talent for Cooperation." *Times-Picayune*, May 21, 1922. Advance Local Media.

"A Young German." *Daily Picayune*, May 30, 1896. Advance Local Media.

Abernathy, Donna F. "Cooperative Update: A Legacy Lives On." Rural Cooperatives: USDA/ Rural Development. Last modified on May 1998. http://www.rurdev.usda.gov/rbs/pub/ may98/legacy.html.

"About the League." Louisiana Credit Union League. Accessed on September 18, 2012. http:// www.lcul.com/Chapter_Information_210.html.

Abrams, Eve. "Crescent City Community Land Trust Helps Mid-City Create Affordable Rental Units." WWNO. Last modified on November 5, 2013. http://wwno.org/post/ crescent-city-community-land-trust-helps-mid-city-create-affordable-rental-units.

"An Act." *Weekly Louisianan*, July 6, 1871.

Adams, Thomas J., ed. *Working in the Big Easy: The History and Politics of Labor in New Orleans*. Lafayette: University of Louisiana at Lafayette Press, 2014.

Adams, Vincanne. *Labors of Faith, Markets of Sorrow: New Orleans in the Wake of Katrina*. Durham: Duke University Press, 2013.

"Administrations of the Mayors of New Orleans: Walter Chew Flower (1850–1900)." n.d. Louisiana Division New Orleans Public Library. Accessed on January 1, 2015. http://www .neworleanspubliclibrary.org/~nopl/info/louinfo/admins/flower.htm.

"Advertisement." *New Orleans Tribune*, December 24, 1867.

Africa, Julia. "Community Gardens as Healing Spaces: Addressing the Aftermath of Hurricane Katrina in New Orleans." Harvard University Graduate School of Design. Last updated 2011. http://isites.harvard.edu/icb/icb.do?keyword=k94076&pageid=icb .page577179.

African Scientific Research Institute. "Panel and Bio." Inaugural International African Diaspora Heritage Trail Promiseland Symposium. Last modified on October 12, 2013. *http://asrip.org/index.php/inaugural-cultural-heritage-symposium/panelists*.

A. G. Crowe: Louisiana Senate. "Crowe Supports Funding Assistance for Our Louisiana Fishing Industry." Last modified on February 25, 2007. http://www.agcrowe.com/pg-51 –15-pressviewer.aspx?pressid=6.

"Agricultural Leadership Development Program." LSU AgCenter. Accessed on July 17, 2014. http://www.lsuagcenter.com/en/community/leadership/ag_leadership/Agricultural+Lea dership+Development+Program/.

Albert Walter and Ernestine Jessie Covington Dent Family Papers. Amistad Research Center. Tulane University, New Orleans, Louisiana.

Alexander, Benjamin F. *Coxey's Army: Popular Protest in the Gilded Age*. Baltimore: Johns Hopkins University Press, 2015.

Alford, Jeremy. "Board Develops Plan to Help Fishermen with Storm Recovery." *Houma Today*, January 13, 2007. http://www.houmatoday.com/article/20070113/NEWS/701130305.

Alishahi, Michele. "'For Peace and Civic Righteousness': Blanche Armwood and the Struggle for Freedom and Racial Equality in Tampa, Florida, 1890–1939." MA thesis, University of South Florida, 2003.

Allen, Patricia, and Clare Hinrichs. "Buying into 'Buy Local': Engagements of United States Local Food Initiatives." In *Alternative Food Geographies: Representation and Practice*, eds. Damian Maye, Lewis Holloway, and Moya Kneafsey, 255–72. New York: Elsevier, 2007.

Alperovitz, Gar. "The Cooperative Economy. *Orion*, May/June–July/August 2014. http://www.orionmagazine.org/index.php/articles/article/8163.

"Alpizar, Andrew." *Soards' New Orleans City Directory*. New Orleans, Soards' City Directory, 1895. Ancestry.com.

American Antiquarian Society. *French Newspapers of Louisiana*, October 1932. Accessed on November 28, 2018. http://www.americanantiquarian.org/proceedings/44817365.pdf.

American Federation of Labor. *Report of the Proceedings of the Fourteenth Annual Convention of the American Federation of Labor*. Denver: AFL, 1894.

American Federation of Labor. "Supplemental Report of Committee on Credentials." *Report of Proceedings of the Thirty-Ninth Annual Convention of the American Federation of Labor*. Washington, DC: AFL, 1919.

"The American Federation of Labor." *Forest Republican*, October 6, 1897.

Anderson, Benedict. *Imagined Communities: Reflections on the Origin and Spread of Nationalism*. London: Verso, 1983.

Anderson, Ed. "Holman Center Ready to Move into Ex-Grocery." *Times-Picayune*, May 4, 1985. Advance Local Media.

Anderson, Matthew. *A History of Fair Trade in Contemporary Britain: From Civil Society Campaigns to Corporate Compliance*. New York: Palgrave Macmillan, 2015.

Andert, Sarah. "Relief Through ReLeaf." *The Advocate*, March 10, 2008. https://www.theadvocate.com/gambit/new_orleans/news/article_10367129-1b41-529b-99ff-7aab90fbd9f9.html.

"Anti-War Summer School Planned for Southerners." *Fortnightly* 13, no. 13 (July 1, 1936): 1.

Arend, Orissa. *Showdown in Desire: The Black Panthers Take a Stand in New Orleans*. Fayetteville: University of Arkansas Press, 2009.

"Army Store Head to Lecture Women." *Times-Picayune*, March 19, 1920. Advance Local Media.

Arnesen, Eric. *Waterfront Workers of New Orleans: Race, Class, and Politics, 1863–1923*. New York: Oxford University Press, 1991.

"Aron Chang." Tulane School of Architecture. Accessed on August 26, 2017. http://architecture.tulane.edu/people/aron-chang.

"Arrest of Seven Pickets of Film Arouses Protest." *Times-Picayune*, December 16, 1935. Advance Local Media.

"Arrests, Permit Fee Ordinance Draw Fire." *Times-Picayune*, October 8, 1936. Advance Local Media.

Arroyo, Jossianna. *Writing Secrecy in Caribbean Freemasonry*. New York: Palgrave MacMillan, 2013.

"Ask Labels Show Weight of Bread." *Times-Picayune*, January 15, 1921. Advance Local Media.

"Assail Congress for Passing Cut in Relief Budget." *Times-Picayune*, January 29, 1939. Advance Local Media.

Associated Press. "U.S. Utilities Seek Solar Power as Trump Sides with Coal, Fossil Fuels." *Los Angeles Times*, February 4, 2017. http://www.latimes.com/business/la-fi-solar-power-20170204-story.html.

"At Loeper's Park." *Daily Picayune*, June 27, 1887. Advance Local Media.

"Attorney Rene Calvin Metoyer (1858–1937)." CreoleGen, 2012. Accessed on January 1, 2015. http://www.creolegen.org/2012/09/15/attorney-rene-calvin-metoyer-1858-1937/.

"August Graf Dead." *Times-Picayune*, December 29, 1915. Advance Local Media.

"August Weber Garden Center." *Times-Picayune*, October 24, 1971. Advance Local Media.

"Bacarisse." Passenger Lists of Vessels Arriving at New Orleans, Louisiana, 1820–1902, February 2, 1839. Ancestry.com.

"Bacarisse, Antone." *Soards' New Orleans City Directory*. New Orleans: Soards Directory Co., 1890. Ancestry.com.

"Bacarisse, Charles (C. Bacarisse & Co.)." *Soard's New Orleans City Directory*. New Orleans: L. Soards & Co., 1876. Ancestry.com.

"Bacarisse, Charles." *Soards' New Orleans City Directory*. New Orleans: Soards Directory Co., 1890. Ancestry.com.

Bacarisse, Eugene. "The Lesson of the Flood." *Daily Picayune*, April 21, 1897. Advance Local Media.

Bacarisse, Eugene. "The Problems of Industrial Life." *Daily Picayune*, June 30, 1897. Advance Local Media.

Bacarisse, Eugene. "Socialism Set Forth by a Socialist." *Daily Picayune*, June 6, 1897. Advance Local Media.

"Bacarisse Resigns from Laboring Men, And the Association Actually Lets Him Go." *Daily Picayune*, August 30, 1897. Advance Local Media.

"Bacarisse Will Resign: Neither Capital nor Labor Will Give Him Food." *Daily Picayune*, August 14, 1897. Advance Local Media.

Baiamonte, Victoria. "New Orleans, the New South, and the Fight for the Panama Exposition." MA thesis, University of New Orleans, 2011.

Banes, Sally. *Greenwich Village 1963: Avant-Garde Performance and the Effervescent Body*. Raleigh: Duke University Press, 1993.

"Banquet to Cuban Guests." *New Century* 6, no. 3 (November 13, 1902).

"Barber Band to Play." *Times-Picayune*, June 5, 1931. Advance Local Media.

"Bartenders' Union." *Times-Picayune*, February 17, 1907. Advance Local Media.

Barton, Harriet C. *Report of the Sanitation Committee of the Woman's League* (1910). Woman's League Papers. New Orleans Public Library, New Orleans, Louisiana.

Battiste, Harold. *Unfinished Blues: Memories of a New Orleans Music Man*. New Orleans: Historic New Orleans Collection, 2010.

Belasco, Warren. *Appetite for Change: How the Counterculture Took on the Food Industry, 1966–1988*. New York: Pantheon Books, 1989.

Belasco, Warren, and Philip Scranton, eds. *Food Nations: Selling Taste in Consumer Societies*. New York: Routledge, 2002.

Bell, Beverly. "A Future for Agriculture, a Future for Haiti." *Louisiana Association of Cooperatives* e-newsletter, no. 161 (January 2018): 1.

Bellamy, Edward. "A Vital Domestic Problem: Household Service Reform." *Good Housekeeping* 10, no. 4 (December 21, 1889): 74–77.

Bellande, Ray L. "Newspapers and Research." Ocean Springs Archives. Accessed on January 1, 2015. http://oceanspringsarchives.net/node/213/contact.

Bennett, James B. *Religion and the Rise of Jim Crow in New Orleans*. Princeton: Princeton University Press, 2005.

Bentley, Amy. *Eating for Victory: Food Rationing and the Politics of Domesticity*. Urbana: University of Illinois Press, 1998.

Bess, Michael. *Realism, Utopia, and the Mushroom Cloud: Four Activist Intellectuals and Their Strategies for Peace, 1945–1989*. Chicago: University of Chicago Press, 1993.

Bishop, Julia Truitt. "Housewives' League Factor in Fight on High Living Cost." *Times-Picayune*, December 10, 1916. Advance Local Media.

Bishop, Julia Truitt. "Personal Visit to the Great Port of New Orleans." *Times-Picayune*, July 4, 1915. Advance Local Media.

Bishop, Julia Truitt. "To Cut the Cost of Living Women Must Learn How to Buy." *Times-Picayune*, May 16, 1915. Advance Local Media.

"Bishop Sessums Called Upon by the Co-operative Commonwealth." *Daily Picayune*, March 12, 1897. Advance Local Media.

Blassingame, John W. *Black New Orleans, 1860–1880*. Chicago: University of Chicago Press, 1973.

Blavatsky, Helena. *The Key to Theosophy*. Pasadena: Theosophical University Press, 1946.

Blue, Ellen. *St. Mark's and the Social Gospel: Methodist Women and Civil Rights in New Orleans, 1895–1965*. Knoxville: University of Tennessee Press, 2011.

Boasberg, Terse to Fred Hayes, et al. Memorandum, March 8, 1966, 4. File "Admin. Confidential." Box 34A, Local Problem Area File, 1966. Records of the Office of the Director, Office of Economic Opportunity. Records of the Community Services Administration, RG 381, National Archives, Washington, DC (RG 381).

"Boat Ride is Set." *Times-Picayune*, October 15, 1941. Advance Local Media.

"Bond Buyer Signs." *Times-Picayune*, May 19, 1942. Advance Local Media.

Bookchin, Murray. *Social Ecology and Communalism*. Oakland: AK Press, 2007.

"Bookchin Speaks in New Orleans." *Social Ecology Newsletter* 1, no. 1 (January 1983): 4.

"Bootblack Jailed as Barber, Freed." *Times-Picayune*, October 5, 1932. Advance Local Media.

Boulard, Garry. *Huey Long Invades New Orleans: The Siege of a City, 1934–36*. Gretna: Pelican Publishing, 1998.

Bourdieu, Pierre. "Utopia of Endless Exploitation: The Essence of Neoliberalism." *Le Monde Diplomatique*, December 1998. http://mondediplo.com/1998/12/08bourdieu.

Brady, James. "EcoBro." *Louisiana Association of Cooperatives* e-newsletter, May 15, 2017. https://www.501c3koggrants.com/uploads/6/4/6/9/64693481/louisiana_enewsletter_-_may_15_2017_1_.pdf.

Brady, James. "What's Growing On!" Con1ou2Farm L3Cm. Last modified on February 22, 2017. https://www.con1ou2farm.com/2017/02/22/eco-bro-speaks/.

Brands, H. W. *The Reckless Decade: American in the 1890s*. Chicago: University of Chicago Press, 1995.

Breunlin, Rachel. "The Legacy of the Free Southern Theater in New Orleans: Interviews with Karen-Kaia Livers and Chakula Cha Jua." *ChickenBones: A Journal*, February 4, 2015. http://www.blackacademypress.com/2015/02/legacyfreesouttheater/.

Bridges, Tyler. "Pres Kabacoff Outlines $1 Billion Vision to Redevelop New Orleans' Urban Core." *The Lens*, September 24, 2013. http://thelensnola.org/2013/09/24/pres-kabacoff-outlines-1-billion-vision-to-redevelop-new-orleans-urban-core/.

Brinkley, Alan. *Voices of Protest: Huey Long, Father Coughlin, and the Great Depression.* New York: Vintage Books, 1983.

Brooks, Joanna. *American Lazarus: Religion and the Rise of African-American and Native American Literatures.* Oxford: Oxford University Press, 2003.

Browder, Dorothea. "A 'Christian Solution of the Labor Situation': How Workingwomen Reshaped the YWCA's Religious Mission and Politics." *Journal of Women's History* 19, no. 2 (Summer 2007): 85–110.

Brown, Nikki. "Domestic Work." In *The Jim Crow Encyclopedia* 1, eds. Nikki L. M. Brown and Barry M. Stentiford, 240–45. Westport: Greenwood, 2008.

Brown, Nikki. *Private Politics and Public Voices: Black Women's Activism from World War I to the New Deal.* Bloomington: Indiana University Press, 2006.

Brown, Robert M. "The Mississippi River Flood of 1912." *American Geographical Society of New York Bulletin* 44, no. 9 (1912): 642–57.

Brown, Vincent. *The Reaper's Garden: Death and Power in the World of Atlantic Slavery.* Cambridge: Harvard University Press, 2008.

Bruno, R. Stephanie. "Parkway Partners of New Orleans Marks its 30th Year of Fostering Urban Horticulture." *Times-Picayune*, October 19, 2012. https://www.nola.com/home garden/index.ssf/2012/10/parkway_partners_of_new_orlean.html.

Buchanan, Susan. "Gert Town Overlooked as New Orleans Redevelops." *Huffington Post*, October 17, 2012. http://www.huffingtonpost.com/susan-buchanan/gert-town -overlooked-as-n_b_1973777.html.

Bullard, Robert D., ed. *Growing Smarter: Achieving Livable Communities, Environmental Justice, and Regional Equity.* Boston: MIT Press, 2007.

Bullard, Robert D., and Beverly Wright, eds. *Race, Place, and Environmental Justice after Hurricane Katrina.* Philadelphia: Perseus Books Group, 2009.

Burke, Mary. "The Success of Blanche Armwood (1890–1939)." *Sunland Tribune* 15 (November 1989): 38–43.

Burkett, Ben. "From the Desk of State Coordinator Ben F. Burkett." *The Quiet Movement* 2 (April–June 2007): 3. http://federationsoutherncoop.com/coopnews/mac2.pdf.

Burkett, Ben. "From the President." *Family Farm Agenda* (December 2009): 1. https://www .nffc.net/Pressroom/Newsletters/2009%20December.pdf;

Burkett, Randall K. *Garveyism as a Religious Movement: The Institutionalization of a Black Civil Religion.* Lanham: Scarecrow Press, 1978.

"Business Men Ask City to Enlarge Food Sale." *Times-Picayune*, August 13, 1919. Advance Local Media.

"Buyers Welcome! Buy-at-Home, Too." *Daily Picayune*, August 18, 1913. Advance Local Media.

"By Way of Comment." *Times-Picayune*, November 6, 1921. Advance Local Media.

"Cabbages are In, Fish Out as Summer Time Arrives." *Times-Picayune*, April 29, 1921. Advance Local Media.

Camara, Samori Sekou. "'There are Some Bad Brothers and Sisters in New Orleans:' The Black Power Movement in the Crescent City from 1964–1977." PhD diss., University of Texas at Austin, 2011.

Campanella, Richard. *Bienville's Dilemma: A Historical Geography of New Orleans.* Lafayette: Center for Louisiana Studies, 2008.

Campanella, Richard. *Geographies of New Orleans*. Lafayette: Center for Louisiana Studies, 2006.

Campanella, Richard. "Gentrification and its Discontents: Notes from New Orleans." New Geography, 2013. Last modified on March 1, 2013. http://www.newgeography.com/content/003526-gentrification-and-its-discontents-notes-new-orleans.

Campanella, Richard. "A Glorious Mess: A Perceptual History of New Orleans Neighborhoods." *New Orleans Magazine* (2014). Last modified on June 2014. http://www.myneworleans.com/new-orleans-magazine/june-2014/a-glorious-mess/.

Cannon, C. W. "Call Me a Sentimental Old Fool, But I Miss My Schwegmans—And I Got a Right To." *The Lens* (2014). Last modified on August 20, 2014. https://thelensnola.org/2014/08/20/call-me-a-sentimental-old-fool-but-i-miss-my-schwegmanns-and-i-got-a-right-to/.

Case, John, and Rosemary C. R. Taylor, eds. *Co-ops, Communes and Collectives: Experiments in Social Change in the 1960s and 1970s*. New York: Pantheon Books, 1979.

"Case of the Steamship Agents Against the Screwmen." *Daily Picayune*, May 10, 1903. Advance Local Media.

Chamberlain, Charles D. *Victory at Home: Manpower and Race in the American South During World War II*. Athens: University of Georgia Press, 2003.

Chambers, Henry E. *A History of Louisiana*. Chicago: American Historical Society, 1925.

Chateauvert, Melinda. *Marching Together: Women and the Brotherhood of Sleeping Car Porters*. Champaign: University of Illinois Press, 1997.

"China Aid Group Sets Boycott on Japanese Goods," *Times-Picayune*, April 4, 1938. Advance Local Media.

Choi, Myungshik. "The Impact of Community Land Trusts on Gentrification." PhD diss., Texas A&M University, 2015.

"The City." *The Crusader* 2, no. 23, July 19, 1890.

"City Federation of Women's Clubs." *New Orleans Times-Democrat*, November 28, 1912. Chronicling America.

"City Federation of Women's Clubs." *Daily Picayune*, February 19, 1913. Advance Local Media.

"City Federation of Women's Clubs Forms." *Daily Picayune*, November 27, 1912. Advance Local Media.

"Civic Worker is Taken by Death." *Times-Picayune*, May 29, 1970. Advance Local Media.

Clark, John. Interview with author, June 28, 2012. Cooperative Oral History Project.

Clarke, Grace Julian. "Activities of Woman's Clubs." *Indianapolis Star*, July 13, 1913.

"Clubs Are Oiling Machinery for Year's Program." *Times-Picayune*, October 9, 1921. Advance Local Media.

Clyde Johnson Papers, 1930–1990. Louis Round Wilson Special Collections Library. University of North Carolina at Chapel Hill.

Coady, Moses. *Masters of Their Own Destiny: The Story of the Antigonish Movement of Adult Education Through Economic Cooperation*. New York: Harper and Brothers Publishers, 1939.

Cobb, William H. *Radical Education in the Rural South: Commonwealth College, 1922–1940*. Detroit: Wayne State University Press, 2000.

Cohen, Lizabeth. *Making a New Deal: Industrial Workers in Chicago, 1919–1939*. Cambridge: Cambridge University Press, 1990.

Cohen, Lizabeth. *A Consumers' Republic: The Politics of Mass Consumption in Postwar America*. New York: Vintage Books, 2003.

Colby, Frank Moore, ed. "Cooperation." In *The New International Year Book: A Compendium of the World's Progress for the Year 1916*, 163–65. New York: Dodd, Mead, and Co., 1917.

Coleman, Stanley R. "Dashiki Project Theatre: Black Identity and Beyond." PhD diss., Louisiana State University, 2003.

"Colored Democrats." *Daily Picayune*, May 16, 1897. Advance Local Media.

"Colored Meeting." *Times-Democrat*, June 8, 1898.

"The Committee on City Sewerage." *Daily Picayune*, August 6, 1897. Advance Local Media.

"Committee to Set Store Opening Date." *Times-Picayune*, March 3, 1920. Advance Local Media.

"Committees Named to Serve at Tombs Confederate Memorial Day, Wednesday." *Daily Picayune*, June 1, 1914. Advance Local Media.

Communist Party, District 24. "An Open Letter!" New Orleans: Trades Council Allied Printing, n.d. University of Michigan Special Collections Library. http://quod.lib.umich .edu/s/sclradic.

"Confederate Daughters." *Daily Picayune*, October 22, 1913. Advance Local Media.

"The Conference on Wages." *Daily Picayune*, July 23, 1897. Advance Local Media.

"Consumer Credit Session Today." *Times-Picayune*, October 16, 1966. Advance Local Media.

"Consumer Group Elects Officers." *Times-Picayune*, December 13, 1945. Advance Local Media.

"Consumers' Co-operative Ice Cream Parlor." *Polks' New Orleans City Directory*. New Orleans: R. L. Polk and Co., 1949. Ancestry.com.

"Consumers' Group Plans Celebration." *Times-Picayune*, January 5, 1945. Advance Local Media.

"Consumers' League." *Daily Picayune*, February 19, 1913. Advance Local Media.

"Consumers' League." *Daily Picayune*, March 27, 1914. Advance Local Media.

"Consumers' League Opposes Opening Stores at Night." *Times-Picayune*, December 1, 1917. Advance Local Media.

"Consumers' Union to Install Staff." *Times-Picayune*, January 5, 1947. Advance Local Media.

"Cooks Must Toe Line Under Rule of Women's Body." *Times-Picayune*, July 17, 1918. Advance Local Media.

"Cooks' Union Slogan Brings Protests from Housewives." *Times-Picayune*, May 19, 1918. Advance Local Media.

"Co-op Store Has Big Future, Mrs. Egleston Says." *New Orleans Item*, April 4, 1920. Advance Local Media.

"Co-op Store is Being Formed." *Times-Picayune*, November 14, 1974. Advance Local Media.

"Co-op Store Plan Begins to Sweep Southern States." *Times-Picayune*, March 11, 1920. Advance Local Media.

CoopEcon. "History of the Federation of Southern Cooperatives." 2012. Accessed on July 18, 2014. http://ce2012.sgeproject.org/about-coopecon-2012/history-of-the-federation-of -southern-cooperatives/.

"Co-operative Commonwealth." *Daily Picayune*, February 13, 1897. Advance Local Media.

"Co-operative Laundry and Linen Service, Inc." Louisiana Companies. Accessed on August 21, 2014. http://labusiness.us/co-operati.list-of-louisiana-companies.az.

"Co-operative Plan Enthusiasts Not Afraid of Jobbers." *Times-Picayune*, February 24, 1920. Advance Local Media.

"Co-operative Plan Shown in Detail." *Times-Picayune*, April 16, 1920. Advance Local Media.

"Cooperative Project Began with Eviction." *Washington Post*, January 18, 1953.

"Co-operative Store Rouses Interest in Big Territory." *Times-Picayune*, February 19, 1920. Advance Local Media.

"Cooperative Stores." *Daily Picayune*, August 27, 1879. Advance Local Media.

"Co-operative Stores Become Vital Issue in City's H.C.L. Fight." *Times-Picayune*, February 22, 1920. Advance Local Media.

"Cooperative Support for New Post-Katrina Fishing Co-op in Louisiana." Federation of Southern Cooperatives. Last modified on February 27, 2007. http://www.federation southerncoop.com/press/feb27o7.htm.

"Cost of Living to Be Attacked by Housewives." *Times-Picayune*, March 12, 1920. Advance Local Media.

Coston, William Hilary. *The Spanish-American War Volunteer*. Freeport: Books for Libraries Press, 1899.

Courtbouillon 14, no. 1 (1949). https://archive.org/stream/CourtbouillonVo114No1/court bouillon_vo114_no1009_djvu.txt

Coxey, Jacob S. *The Coxey Plan*. Massillon: Jacob S. Coxey, 1914.

"Coxey's Army: To Have an Imitation in a Parade and Meeting Here." *Daily Picayune*, June 3, 1897. Advance Local Media.

"Coxey Talks to the Co-operative Commonwealth and its Guests." *Daily Picayune*, February 27, 1897. Advance Local Media.

Craig, Tim. "It Wasn't Even a Hurricane, But Heavy Rains Flooded New Orleans as Pumps Falter." *Washington Post*, August 9, 2017. https://www.washingtonpost.com/national/ it-wasnt-even-a-hurricane-but-heavy-rains-flooded-new-orleans-as-pumps-falter ed/2017/08/09/b3b7506a-7d37-11e7-9d08-b79f191668ed_story.html?utm_term=.2fa 42cf20d3e.

"Credit Union Heads to Meet." *Times-Picayune*, March 3, 1966. Advance Local Media.

"Credit Union League Meets." *Times-Picayune*, May 29, 1966. Advance Local Media.

Credit Union National Association. US Credit Union Profit Profile, 2017. file:///Users/ annegessler/Downloads/NationalProfile-M17-Final.pdf.

"Credit Unions in Poverty War." *Times-Picayune*, May 23, 1965. Advance Local Media.

"Credit Unions to Have Program." *Times-Picayune*, January 6, 1967. Advance Local Media.

"Credit Unions Will Celebrate." *Times-Picayune*, October 15, 1951. Advance Local Media.

"Credo." New Orleans Healing Center. Accessed on July 23, 2014. http://www.neworleans healingcenter.org/#!credo/c1fok.

Crow, Scott. *Black Flags and Windmills*. Oakland: PM Press, 2011.

Crow, Scott. Interview with author, January 29, 2012. Cooperative Oral History Project.

Crutcher, Michael E. *Tremé: Race and Place in a New Orleans Neighborhood*. Athens: University of Georgia Press, 2010.

Cullom. "Description and History of the Athenaeum or the Young Men's Hebrew Association in New Orleans, Louisiana." New Orleans: Works Progress Association, n.d. Louisiana Works Progress Administration Digital Collection. State Library of Louisiana. http://louisianadigitallibrary.org/islandora/object/state-lwp:6768.

"Curb Market Is So Successful." *Times-Picayune*, January 6, 1916. Advance Local Media.

Curl, John. *For All the People: Uncovering the Hidden History of Cooperation, Cooperative Movements, and Communalism in America*. Oakland: PM Press, 2009.

"Custom House Notes." *Daily Picayune*, October 27, 1892. Advance Local Media.

Daar, Judith. *The New Eugenics: Selective Breeding in an Era of Reproductive Technologies*. New Haven: Yale University Press, 2017.

Daniel, Evan Matthew. "Cubans." In *Encyclopedia of U.S. Labor and Working-Class History*, ed. Eric Arnesen, 332–334. New York: Routledge, 2007.

Davis, Donald W. "Historical Perspective on Crevasses, Levees, and the Mississippi." In *Transforming New Orleans and Its Environs: Centuries of Change*, ed. Craig E. Colten, 84–106. Pittsburgh: University of Pittsburgh Press, 2000.

"Day Dedicated to Credit Union." *Times-Picayune*, October 16, 1957. Advance Local Media.

"Deaths." *Times-Picayune*, February 12, 1950. Advance Local Media.

"Deaths: Henry W. Hermes." *Times-Picayune*, June 1, 1987. Advance Local Media.

"Deaths: Sylvester Peete." *Times-Picayune*, July 15, 1959. Advance Local Media.

De Certeau, Michel. *The Practice of Everyday Life*, trans. Steven Randall. Berkeley, University of California Press, 1984.

"Decrease Shown in Tuberculosis, Auxiliary Told." *Times-Picayune*, April 2, 1931. Advance Local Media.

"Defense Council Hears Dr. Scherer on Work to Do." *Times-Picayune*, July 22, 1917. Advance Local Media.

De Jong, Greta. *Invisible Enemy: The African American Freedom Struggle After 1965*. West Sussex: John Wiley & Sons, 2010.

De Jong, Greta. "'With the Aid of God and the F.S.A.' The Louisiana Farmers' Union and the African American Freedom Struggle in the New Deal Era." *Journal of Social History* 34, no. 1 (Autumn 2000): 105–139.

De Jong, Greta. *You Can't Eat Freedom: Southerners and Social Justice After the Civil Rights Movement*. Chapel Hill: University of North Carolina Press, 2016.

Dejoie, F. J. "The Origin, Development and Achievements of the N.O. Federation of Civic Leagues." 1929. In Folder 46, Box 77. A. P. Tureaud Papers, 1798–1977. Amistad Research Center, Tulane University.

"Dejoie Funeral Rites Planned." *Times-Picayune*, April 3, 1967. Advance Local Media.

"Delta and Providence Cooperative Farms Papers, 1925–1963 (bulk 1936–1943) Finding Aid." The Southern Historical Collection at the Louis Round Wilson Special Collections Library. Accessed on January 16, 2018. http://finding-aids.lib.unc.edu/03474/.

Democracy Now. "Dr. Robert Bullard: Houston's 'Unrestrained Capitalism' Made Harvey 'Catastrophe Waiting to Happen.'" Radio interview, August 29, 2017. https://www.democracynow.org/2017/8/29/dr_robert_bullard_houston_s_unrestrained.

Denning, Michael. *The Cultural Front: The Laboring of American Culture in the Twentieth Century*. London: Verso, 1996.

Dent, A. W. "The Need for Public Understanding and Support." *Public Health Reports* 67, no. 4 (April 1952): 326–29.

Dent, Tom. "Black Theater in the South: Report and Reflections." In *The Theatre of Black Americans: A Collection of Critical Essays*, ed. Errol Hill, 267. New York: Applause Theatre and Cinema Books, 1987.

Dent, Tom. "New Orleans Versus Atlanta." *Southern Exposure* 7, no. 1 (Spring 1979): 64–68.

Dent, Tom. "Ritual Murder." In *New Orleans Noir: The Classics*, ed. Julie Smith, 159–76. New York: Akashic Books, 2016.

Dent, Tom. *Southern Journey: A Return to the Civil Rights Movement*. New York: William Morrow and Company, 1997.

Dent, Tom, and Gilbert Moses, ed. *Free Southern Theater by the Free Southern Theater: A Documentary of the South's Radical Black Theater with Journals, Letters, Poetry, and Essays, and a Play Written by Those Who Built It*. New York: Bobbs-Merrill, 1969.

Department of Program Development. *Profile of Poverty in New Orleans*. New Orleans: Department of Program Development, 1973.

Deutsch, Tracey. *Building a Housewife's Paradise: Gender, Politics, and American Grocery Stores in the Twentieth Century*. Chapel Hill: University of North Carolina Press, 2010.

DeVore, Donald D. *Defying Jim Crow: African American Community Development and the Struggle for Racial Equality in New Orleans, 1900–1960*. Baton Rouge: Louisiana State University Press, 2015.

Dietrich, John H. "The Cooperative Movement." *The Humanist Pulpit Series* 16. Minneapolis: The First Unitarian Society, 1933.

"Differences Between Worker Cooperatives and Collectives." Cultivate.coop. Last modified on February 24, 2016. http://cultivate.coop/wiki/Differences_Between_Worker_Cooper atives_and_Collectives.

Dinerstein, Joel Interview with author, July 1, 2012.

Dinerstein, Joel. "Second Lining Post-Katrina." *American Quarterly* 61, no. 3 (September 2009): 615–637.

Donaldson, Gary Alan. "A History of Louisiana's Rural Electric Cooperatives, 1937–1983." PhD diss., Louisiana State University and Agricultural and Mechanical College, 1983.

Donohue, Kathleen. "From Cooperative Commonwealth to Cooperative Democracy: The American Cooperative Ideal, 1880–1940." In *Consumers Against Capitalism?: Consumer Cooperation in Europe, North America, and Japan, 1840–1990*, eds. Ellen Furlough and Carl Strikwerda, 115–34. Lanham: Rowman and Littlefield, 1999.

Doyle, Michael William. "Staging the Revolution: Guerrilla Theater as a Countercultural Practice, 1965–1968." In *Imagine Nation: The American Counterculture of the 1960s and '70s*, eds. Michael William Doyle and Peter Braunstein, 71–98. New York: Routledge, 2002.

"Dr. Shaw Comes to Organize War Work for Women." *Times-Picayune*, April 1, 1918. Advance Local Media.

Drake, J. G. St. Clair. "Why Not 'Co-operate'?" *Opportunity: Journal of Negro Life* 14, no. 8 (August 1936): 231, 234, 251.

"Drainage Board Nearing the Work of Building the First Section of the System." *Daily Picayune*, July 30, 1897. Advance Local Media.

Draper, David Elliot. *Mardi Gras Indians: The Ethnomusicology of Black Association in New Orleans*. PhD diss., Tulane University, 1973.

"Drop in Japanese Divorces Cited by Christian Leader." *Times-Picayune*, March 17, 1936. Advance Local Media.

Dubb, Steven. "C-W Interview." Community Wealth. June 2010. Accessed on November 26, 2018. http://community-wealth.org/content/melissa-hoover.

Dubroca, Isabelle. *Good Neighbor: Eleanor McMain of Kingsley House*. New Orleans: Pelican Publishing Co., 1955.

Ducatel, Amadee. "Bacarisse, Lise Augustin Cohen," Notarial Act Index 3 (June–December 1867): 2. http://www.notarialarchives.org/aducatelindexes/ducatel_amedee_vol_90.pdf.

Dunnaway, Nicolle. "Flowers in Their Beauty: The Phyllis Wheatley Club of New Orleans." MA thesis, Southeastern Louisiana University, 2011.

Eakin, Sue, and Manie Culbertson. *Louisiana: The Land and Its People*. Gretna: Pelican Company, 1998.

Easton, Charles L. "A Backward Look at a Utopian Plan: Equality Colony Near Bow, 1896–1906." *Seattle Times*, November 25, 1962. http://www.skagitriverjournal.com/WestCounty/NW/Colony/EastonCL3-Equality1962.html.

"The Ebony Brother as a Statesman." *Daily Picayune*, August 16, 1896.

Eggler, Bruce. "Xavier University Rezoning Request OK'd By New Orleans City Council." *Times-Picayune*, April 20, 2013. http://www.nola.com/politics/index.ssf/2013/04/xavier_ university_rezoning_req_1.html.

Egleston, Edna. "The Co-operative Movement in New Orleans and the South." In *Proceedings of the National Conference of Social Work, at the Forty-Seventh Annual Session Held in New Orleans, Louisiana, April 14–21, 1920.* Chicago: University of Chicago Press, 1920.

Emanuel, Rachel Lorraine, and Alexander P. Tureaud. *A More Noble Cause: A. P. Tureaud and the Struggle for Civil Rights in Louisiana.* Baton Rouge: Louisiana State University Press, 2011.

Emmer, Rod E., Jim Wiggins, Wendell Verret, and Thomas Hymel. 2007. "Louisiana Sea Grant Assists Delcambre, LA, During Hurricane Recovery." Sea Grant Louisiana. http:// www.laseagrant.org/wp-content/uploads/A-Town-Too-Smart-Delcambre.pdf.

"Engineering Society." *Daily Picayune*, November 6, 1898. Advance Local Media.

"Era Club." *Daily Picayune*, December 13, 1908. Advance Local Media.

Esser, George Jr. Papers. Louis Round Wilson Special Collections Library. University of North Carolina.

"Eugene Bacarisse." *Soards' New Orleans City Directory.* New Orleans: Soards' Directory Co. Ancestry.com, 1893.

"Eugene Bacarisse." *Soards' New Orleans City Directory.* New Orleans: Soards' Directory Co. Ancestry.com, 1894.

"Eugene Bacarisse." *Soards' New Orleans City Directory.* New Orleans: Soards' Directory Co. Ancestry.com, 1898.

Evans, Freddi Williams. *Congo Square: African Roots in New Orleans.* Lafayette: University of Louisiana at Lafayette Press, 2011.

Evans, Sara M. *Born for Liberty: A History of Women in America.* New York: Free Press Paperbacks, 1989.

"Eve Up-to-Date." *Times-Picayune*, August 28, 1920. Advance Local Media.

"Ex-Service Men Beneficiaries of Army Sales, Legion Shows." *Times-Picayune*, February 22, 1920. Advance Local Media.

Fairclough, Adam. *Race and Democracy: The Civil Rights Struggle in Louisiana, 1915–1972.* Athens: University of Georgia Press, 1999.

"False Arrest Suit Filed." *Middlesboro Daily News*, July 13, 1938.

"Farm-to-Table Garden Marketing Looms After Price Exposed." *New Orleans Item*, May 5, 1921.

"Farmers Flock to Curb Market of Housewives." *Times-Picayune*, January 20, 1916. Advance Local Media.

"Farmers Get Assistance with Pigford Claims." Southern University Agricultural Research and Extension Center. Last modified on April 5, 2010. https://suagcenter.blogspot.com/ 2010/04/.

"Farmers Program of Mississippi and Louisiana." *Louisiana Association of Cooperatives* e-newsletter, no. 162 (February 2018): 13.

"The Farmers' Union and the City." *Times-Picayune*, July 13, 1915. Advance Local Media.

"FASOLEAF." Propeller. Accessed on January 1, 2019. http://gopropeller.org/ventures/ fasoleaf/

Federation of Southern Cooperatives. "The Ben Burkett Story: The Unlikely Journey of a Small Farmer." Filmed on April 4, 2013. Video: 29:26. https://www.youtube.com/ watch?v=JM7zHWey3DQ#t=168.

Feldman, Nina. "How Anti-Communist Vietnamese Refugees Signed Up for a Cooperative Farm." PRI. Last modified on May 20, 2015. https://www.pri.org/stories/2015–05–20/how-anti-communist-vietnamese-refugees-signed-cooperative-farm.

Ferris, Robert M. *Flood of Conflict: The New Orleans Free School Story*. Roslyn Heights: Alternative Education Resource Organization, 2012.

Fetter, Frank A. *Economics in Two Volumes*. New York: Century Co., 1922.

Fickle, James E. *The New South and the "New Competition": Trade Association Development in the Southern Pine Industry*. Urbana: University of Illinois Press, 1980.

Field, Tony, and Beverly Bell. "The Consumer's Got to Change the System." Other Worlds. Last modified on March 15, 2013. http://www.otherworldsarepossible.org/consumers-got-change-system-farmer-ben-burkett-racism-and-corporate-control-agriculture.

"Finding Common Ground in NOLA Through Food Justice." NOLA Food and Farm Network News. Last modified on April 3, 2012. http://noffn.tumblr.com/post/20426706499/finding-common-ground-in-nola-through-food-justice.

"Flag Present by VFW Auxiliary." *Times-Picayune*, September 20, 1959.

Flucker, Turry and Phoenix Savage. *African Americans of New Orleans*. Charleston: Arcadia Publishing, 2010.

Flynt, Wayne. *Southern Religion and Christian Diversity in the Twentieth Century*. Tuscaloosa: University of Alabama Press, 2016.

"Foes of Fascism Fined $5 Each for Picketing Theater." *Times-Picayune*, March 19, 1935. Advance Local Media.

Foley, Ellen. "New Orleans Federation Will Mark Silver Anniversary." *Times-Picayune*, November 21, 1937. Advance Local Media.

"Food Policy Advocacy." New Orleans Food and Farm Network News. Accessed on August 11, 2014. http://www.noffn.org/category/food-policy-advocacy/.

"Food Production." New Orleans Food Policy Advisory Committee. Accessed on March 15, 2018. http://www.nolafoodpolicy.org/index.php?page=food-production.

Ford, Kristina. *The Trouble with City Planning: What New Orleans Can Teach Us*. New Haven: Yale University Press, 2010.

"The Former Customers of the Housewives' Co-operative Stores, Inc." Advertisement. *Times-Picayune*, November 12, 1921. Advance Local Media.

"Four Areas to Get Credit Unions." *Times-Picayune*, February 26, 1966. Advance Local Media.

"Freret Carnival Club Picks LaMont." *Times-Picayune*, April 30, 1952. Advance Local Media.

"Freret Credit Union Re-elects Barreca." *Times-Picayune*, January 16, 1952. Advance Local Media.

"Freret Street Has Switched to Trolley Coaches Because Trolley Coaches Are Modern." *Times-Picayune*, September 3, 1947. Advance Local Media.

"Freret Street is Wearing a New Look." *Times-Picayune*, November 7, 1981. Advance Local Media.

Fry, Macon. Interview with author, June 10, 2012. Cooperative Oral History Project.

Frystak, Shannon Lee. *Our Minds on Freedom: Women and the Struggle for Black Equality in Louisiana*. Baton Rouge: Louisiana State University Press, 2009.

Fugitive Waves. "King's Candy: A New Orleans Kitchen Vision." Aired on August 25, 2015. Podcast, 22:01. http://www.kitchensisters.org/2015/08/25/fugitive-waves-kings-candy-a-new-orleans-kitchen-vision/.

Fullilove, Mindy Thompson. *Root Shock: How Tearing Up City Neighborhoods Hurts America, and What We Can Do About It*. New York: Ballantine Books, 2004.

"Funding for Cooperatives." USDA. Accessed on July 19, 2014. http://www.rurdev.usda.gov/ BCP_FundingForCoops.html.

"Funeral Today for Mrs. Myers, Woman Leader." *Times-Picayune*, November 3, 1923. Advance Local Media.

Gabaccia, Donna. *We Are What We Eat: Ethnic Food and the Making of Americans.* Cambridge: Harvard University Press, 1998.

Gambit Weekly. "TBC Brass Band Protest." Filmed on June 16, 2010. Video: 3:01. https://www .youtube.com/watch?v=sn2gESJMGuc.

Garlock, Jonathan. *Guide to the Local Assemblies of the Knights of Labor.* Westport: Greenwood Press, 1982.

"Garment Workers Hear Labor Chiefs." *Times-Picayune*, July 30, 1933. Advance Local Media.

"German-American Republicans." *Daily Picayune*, September 30, 1896. Advance Local Media.

Germany, Kent. *New Orleans After the Promises.* Athens: University of Georgia Press, 2007.

"Getting Work: The Unemployed Meeting Success Now." *Daily Picayune*, November 29, 1897. Advance Local Media.

Giese, Paula. "How the Old Co-ops Went Wrong." In *Workplace Democracy and Social Change*, eds. Frank Lindenfeld and Joyce Rothschild-Whitt, 315–34. Boston: Porter Sargent Publishers, 1982.

Gillette, Michael L. *Launching the War on Poverty: An Oral History.* Oxford: Oxford University Press, 2010.

Gilman, Charlotte Perkins. *Women and Economics: A Study of the Economic Relation Between Men and Women as a Factor in Social Evolution.* Boston: Small, Maynard & Company, 1898.

Gilmore, Glenda Elizabeth. *Defying Dixie: The Radical Roots of Civil Rights, 1919–1950.* New York: W. W. Norton and Company, 2008.

Gilmore, Glenda Elizabeth. *Gender and Jim Crow: Women and the Politics of White Supremacy in North Carolina, 1896–1920.* Chapel Hill: University of North Carolina Press, 1996.

"Give First Exhibit of Cooking Today." *Times-Picayune*, April 10, 1918. Advance Local Media.

Godfrey-Smith, Helen. "Oral History Tour Stop 3: Helen Godfrey Smith and Martha Morris of Shreveport FCU." Credit Union History. Last modified on March 10, 2014. http:// cuhistory.blogspot.com/2014/03/oral-history-tour-stop-3-helen-godfrey.html.

Godson, Susan H. *Serving Proudly: A History of Women in the U.S. Navy.* Annapolis: Naval Institute Press, 2001.

Golub, Sally. Interview with author, July 11, 2012. Cooperative Oral History Project.

"Good Business and Elections in Homesteads." *Times-Picayune*, January 16, 1916. Advance Local Media.

Gotham, Kevin Fox. *Authentic New Orleans: Tourism, Culture, and Race in the Big Easy.* New York: New York University Press, 2007.

Gottdiener, Mark and Leslie Budd. *Key Concepts in Urban Studies.* London: Sage Publications, 2005.

Gould, R. B. W. *Official Journal of the Proceedings of the Senate of the State of Louisiana at the Regular Session.* Baton Rouge: General Assembly, 1888.

"Gould, R. W. B." *Soards' New Orleans City Directory.* New Orleans: Soards' Directory Co. Ancestry.com, 1901.

"The Governor Asked to Appeal for a Modification of Quarantine Rigors." *Daily Picayune*, September 25, 1897. Advance Local Media.

G. R. "Floods and Political Crisis are Back in New Orleans." *The Economist*, August 16, 2017. https://www.economist.com/blogs/democracyinamerica/2017/08/left-out-rain.

"Graf Acts Coxey Just for One Day." *Daily Picayune*, June 4, 1897. Advance Local Media.

"Graf, August." *Soards' New Orleans City Directory*. New Orleans: Soards Directory Co., 1894. Ancestry.com.

"Graf Gets a Hall and an Audience." *Daily Picayune*, July 18, 1897. Advance Local Media.

"Grand Opening." *Times-Picayune*, January 7, 1949. Advance Local Media.

"Great American Ports: New Orleans—Second Largest Port in the United States." *Railway and Marine News* 15, no. 8 (August 1917): 19–22.

Green, Elna C. "The Rest of the Story: Kate Gordon and the Opposition to the Nineteenth Amendment in the South." *Louisiana History* 33, no. 2 (Spring 1992): 171–89.

Green, Elna C. *Southern Strategies: Southern Women and the Woman Suffrage Question*. Chapel Hill: University of North Carolina Press, 1997.

Green, James R. *Grass-Roots Socialism: Radical Movements in the Southwest, 1895–1943*. Baton Rouge: Louisiana State University Press, 1978.

Greenwald, Maurine Weiner. *Women, War, and Work: The Impact of World War I on Women Workers in the United States*. Westport: Greenwood Press, 1980.

Greg, Mrs. "The Servant Problem." *Times-Picayune*, July 21, 1918. Advance Local Media.

Gregory, Raymond F. *Norman Thomas: The Great Dissenter*. United States: Algora Publishing, 2008.

"Grocers Blamed for Point Losses." *Times-Picayune*, July 29, 1945. Advance Local Media.

Haas, Edward F. "New Orleans on the Half-Shell: The Maestri Era, 1936–1946." *Louisiana History* 13, no. 3 (Summer 1972): 283–310.

Hair, William Ivy. *Bourbonism and Agrarian Protest: Louisiana Politics, 1877–1900*. Baton Rouge: Louisiana State University Press, 1969.

Hale Boggs, and Lindy Boggs Papers, 1914–1998. Louisiana Research Collection. Tulane University.

Hall, Covington. *Labor Struggles in the Deep South and Other Writings*, edited and introduced by David R. Roediger. Chicago: Charles H. Kerr Publishing Company, 1999.

Hansen, Jonathan M. *The Lost Promise of Patriotism: Debating American Identity, 1890–1920*. Chicago: University of Chicago Press, 2003.

Hardie, Daniel. *Exploring Early Jazz: The Origins and Evolution of the New Orleans Style*. Lincoln: Writers Club Press, 2002.

Harding, James M., and Cindy Rosenthal, eds. *Restaging the Sixties*. Ann Arbor: University of Michigan Press, 2005.

Harold Newton Lee Papers, 1917–1970. Louisiana Research Collection. Tulane University.

Harold R. Battiste Papers, 1928–2010. Amistad Research Center. Tulane University.

Harper, Frederick John. "The Anti–Chain Store Movement in the United States, 1927–1940." PhD diss., University of Warwick, 1981.

Harris, Clarissa Myrick. "Mirror of the Movement: The History of the Free Southern Theater as a Microcosm of the Civil Rights and Black Power Movements, 1963–1978." PhD diss., Emory University, 1988.

Harvey, Daina Cheyenne. "'Gimme a Pigfoot and a Bottle of Beer': Food as Cultural Performance in the Aftermath of Hurricane Katrina." *Symbolic Interaction* 40, no. 4 (July 2017): 498–522.

Harvey, David. *Spaces of Hope*. Berkeley: University of California Press, 2000.

Hayden, Dolores. *The Grand Domestic Revolution: A History of Feminist Designs for American Homes, Neighborhoods, and Cities*. Cambridge: MIT Press, 1981.

Haynes, Elizabeth Ross. "Negroes in Domestic Service in the United States." *Journal of Negro History* 8, no. 4 (October 1923): 384–442.

"Headline News." Louisiana Credit Union League. Accessed on August 20, 2014. http://www .lcul.com/Headline_News_102.html?article_id=2667.

"Healing Center Attacked for Role in Gentrification." NOLA Anarcha. September 11, 2011. http://nolaanarcha.blogspot.com/2011/09/healing-center-attacked-for-role-in.html.

Hearn, Lafcadio. "Jewish Emigrants for Louisiana." In *Inventing New Orleans: Writings of Lafcadio Hearn*, ed. S. Frederick Starr, 162–64. Jackson: University Press of Mississippi, 2001.

Heath, Julian. "Work of the Housewives League." *Annals of the American Academy of Political and Social Science* 48, no. 1 (July 1913): 121–26.

Heinberg, Richard. "Localism in the Age of Trump." Post Carbon Institute. Last modified on December 9, 2016. http://www.postcarbon.org/localism-in-the-age-of-trump/.

Hennick, Louis C., and E. Harper Charlton. *The Streetcars of New Orleans*. Gretna: Jackson Square Press, 2005.

Herman Lazard Midlo Collection. Earl K. Long Library. University of New Orleans, New Orleans, Louisiana.

"Hermes Announces Senate Candidacy." *Times-Picayune*, October 30, 1943. Advance Local Media.

"Hermes Renamed by District Group." *Times-Picayune*, March 17, 1955. Advance Local Media.

Hersch, Charles B. *Subversive Sounds: Race and the Birth of Jazz*. Chicago: University of Chicago Press, 2008.

Hild, Matthew. *Greenbackers, Knights of Labor, and Populists: Farmer-Labor Insurgency in the Late-Nineteenth-Century South*. Athens: University of Georgia Press, 2007.

Hilderbrand, Sue, Scott Crow, and Lisa Fithian. "Common Ground Relief." In *What Lies Beneath: Katrina, Race, and the State of the Nation*, ed. South End Press Collective, 80–99. Cambridge: South End Press Collective, 2007.

"History." North Carolina Association of Community Development Corporations. Accessed on October 15, 2013. http://ncacdc.org/history.cfm.

"History of the Church." Trinity Episcopal Church. Accessed on November 20, 2018. http:// www.trinitynola.com/page.aspx? pid=797.

"The History of the Nation of Islam in New Orleans." NOI New Orleans. Accessed on October 1, 2014. http://noineworleans.org/news/back_issues/history.html.

"History of SSA During the Johnson Administration 1963–1968." Social Security Administration. Accessed on August 20, 2014. http://www.socialsecurity.gov/history/ssa/ lbjoper7.html.

"History of State to Be Theme at Luncheon Friday." *Times-Picayune*, April 28, 1933. Advance Local Media.

Hoffman, Aya. "Seeds of Renewal." Ithaca College. Last modified on April 24, 2012. https://www.ithaca.edu/parkscholars/blogs/park_scholars_in_service/seeds_of_renewal: _community_gardens_in_new_orleans/.

Holley, Donald. *Uncle Sam's Farmers: The New Deal Communities in Lower Mississippi Valley*. Urbana: University of Illinois Press, 1975.

Holly, Derrill. "Louisiana Co-op Helps Entergy with Harvey Recovery." America's Electric Cooperatives. Last modified on September 7, 2017. https://www.electric.coop/ washington-st-tammany-electric-entergy-substation/.

"Home Happenings." *Daily Record*, August 16, 1902. Chronicling America.

"Home Labor's Plea." *Daily Picayune*, July 19, 1897. Advance Local Media.

"Homemakers' Meeting." *Times-Picayune*, July 22, 1918. Advance Local Media.

"Home-Makers Organized at Suffrage House Tuesday." *Times-Picayune*, July 21, 1918. Advance Local Media.

"Homestead News of Interest Here." *Daily Picayune*, October 15, 1911. Advance Local Media.

"Hope Haven Day Feb. 9." *Times-Picayune*, January 20, 1918, 9A. Advance Local Media.

"Hope Haven Farm Wins General Approval." *Times-Picayune*, January 25, 1918. Advance Local Media.

Hoque, Anwarul, and Leroy Davis. *Survey of Cooperatives in Louisiana*. Baton Rouge: Southern University and A&M College, 1980.

"Hospital Insurance." *Negro Star*, December 9, 1932.

Hou, Jeffrey. "Making and Supporting Community Gardens as Informal Urban Landscapes." In *The Informal American City: Beyond Taco Trucks and Day Laborers*, eds. Vinit Mukhija and Anastasia Loukaitou-Sideris. Cambridge: MIT Press, 2014.

"Household Labor Finds New Orleans Homemakers Calm." *Times-Picayune*, July 23, 1918. Advance Labor Media.

"Housewives Await Letter from Dupre." *Times-Picayune*, February 23, 1920. Advance Local Media.

"Housewives' Body Enters Politics at June Meeting." *Times-Picayune*, June 12, 1921. Advance Local Media.

"Housewives Call Meet to Discuss Dearth of Labor." *Times-Picayune*, July 16, 1918. Advance Local Media.

"Housewives' Co-operative Stores, Inc." Advertisement. *Times-Picayune*, May 21, 1921. Advance Local Media.

"Housewives Co-operative Stores, Inc." Advertisement. *Times-Picayune*, September 17, 1921. Advance Local Media.

"Housewives' Co-operative Stores, Inc." Advertisement. *Times-Picayune*, October 8, 1921. Advance Local Media.

"Housewives Find Co-operative Plan Not Money Maker." *Times-Picayune*, October 28, 1921. Advance Local Media.

"Housewives Gain Low Prices from Dealers." *Times-Picayune*, February 27, 1916. Advance Local Media.

"Housewives' Grocery in Operation." *New Orleans Item*, April 17, 1921. Advance Local Media.

"Housewives, Here Are Ways to Utilize All That Bacon." *Times-Picayune*, August 7, 1919. Advance Local Media.

"Housewives' League Branch Organized." *Times-Picayune*, June 12, 1915. Advance Local Media.

"Housewives' League Outlines Plan for Co-operative Stores." *Times-Picayune*, February 22, 1920. Advance Local Media.

"Housewives' League Plan to Establish Co-operative Store." *Times-Picayune*, June 29, 1919. Advance Local Media.

"Housewives Lose One Site, Obtain Another at Once." *Times-Picayune*, January 21, 1916. Advance Local Media.

"Housewives Open Subscription List for Joint Store." *Times-Picayune*, March 6, 1920. Advance Local Media.

"Housewives Report Big Trade at Co-operative Store." *Times-Picayune*, May 3, 1921. Advance Local Media.

"Housewives Seek to Sever League from Federation." *Times-Picayune*, June 5, 1915. Advance Local Media.

"Housewives Sell Products Despite Great Handicaps." *Times-Picayune*, December 23, 1915. Advance Local Media.

"Housewives Still Successful with New Curb Market." *Times-Picayune*, January 16, 1916. Advance Local Media.

"Housewives' Store Assets Inventoried at $1540.35." *Times-Picayune*, January 11, 1922. Advance Local Media.

"Housewives' Store Boosted by Unions." *Times-Picayune*, May 23, 1920. Advance Local Media.

"Housewives' Store Hits $5000 Mark." *Times-Picayune*, March 20, 1920. Advance Local Media.

"Housewives' Store Is Reality." *Times-Picayune*, February 26, 1921. Advance Local Media.

"Housewives' Store Program Indorsed." *Times-Picayune*, March 4, 1920. Advance Local Media.

"Housewives' Store Reports Increase in Subscriptions." *Times-Picayune*, March 26, 1920. Advance Local Media.

"Housework Minus Servants, Subject." *Times-Picayune*, April 9, 1919. Advance Local Media.

"How to Manage with a Servant and Without One." *Times-Picayune*, April 20, 1919. Advance Local Media.

"Howard Egleston Dies of Pneumonia." *Times-Picayune*, February 6, 1926. Advance Local Media.

Howells, Mike. "On the Plunder of Post-Isaac Rebuilding." Occupy New Orleans. Last modified on September 6, 2012. http://onola.wordpress.com/2012/09/06/on-the-plunder-of-post-isaac-rebuilding-onola/.

Humphreys, Margaret. *Yellow Fever in the South*. Baltimore: Johns Hopkins University Press, 1999.

Hutson, Ethel. "Housewives' Body Active to Better Living Conditions." *Times-Picayune*, March 13, 1921. Advance Local Media.

"ICIC Summit: Urban Innovation No. 4: New Orleans Cooperative Development Project." Initiative for a Competitive Inner City. Last updated on October 27, 2013. http://www.icic.org/connection/blog-entry/blog-icicsummit-urban-innovation-no.-4-new-orleans-cooperative-development.

Ifateyo, Ajowa Nzinga. "USFWC: Ten Years of Achievement, Part 2 of 2," 2014. Accessed on July 25, 2017. http://www.geo.coop/story/usfwc-ten-years-achievement-2.

"Important Event to Take Place in April." *New Orleans Item*, April 2, 1920.

"Improved Garbage Collection Asked." *Times-Picayune*, April 4, 1945. Advance Local Media.

"Independents Set Rally for Monday." *Times-Picayune*, December 10, 1939. Advance Local Media.

"Institute to Hear Brooklyn Minister." *Times-Picayune*, February 20, 1933. Advance Local Media.

"Instruction in Canning." *Times-Picayune*, August 12, 1917. Advance Local Media.

"Interactive Session II." National Association of Black Journalists. Accessed on March 15, 2018. http://www.nabj.org/?page=InterSessionII.

International Co-operative Alliance. "Cooperative Identity, Values, and Principles." Accessed on July 15, 2014. http://ica.coop/en/whats-co-op/co-operative-identity-values-principles.

"Invest—Co-OWN It!" New Orleans Food Co-op. Accessed on March 4, 2018, http://www
     .nolafood.coop/ownership/become-a-member/.

Isaacson, Walter. "Foreword." *The Inevitable City: The Resurgence of New Orleans and
     the Future of Urban America* by Scott Cowen and Betsy Seifer. New York: Palgrave
     MacMillan, 2014.

Isay, Dave, and Maya Millett, eds. *Callings: The Purpose and Passion of Work.* New York:
     Penguin Press, 2016.

Jackson, Joy J. *New Orleans in the Gilded Age: Politics and Urban Progress.* Baton Rouge:
     Louisiana State University Press, 1969.

Jackson Lewis. "New Civil Rights Era at USDA Continues with Service Contract to Assist
     Program Administration." Last modified on October 9, 2009. http://www.jacksonlewis
     .com/legalupdates/article.cfm?aid=1874.

Jackson Lewis and United States Department of Agriculture. "Independent Assessment
     of the Delivery of Technical and Financial Assistance: 'Civil Rights Assessment' Final
     Report, March 31, 2011." USDA. http://www.usda.gov/documents/Civil_Rights_Assess
     ment-Final_Report.pdf.

Jacobson, Matthew Frye. *Barbarian Virtues: The United States Encounters Foreign Peoples at
     Home and Abroad, 1876–1917.* New York: Hill and Wang, 2000.

Jacobson, Matthew Frye. *Whiteness of a Different Color.* Cambridge: Harvard University
     Press, 1998.

"James E. Hart." *Daily Picayune,* November 19, 1912. Advance Local Media.

Jameson, Frederic. *Archaeologies of the Future: The Desire Called Utopia and Other Fictions.*
     London: Verso, 2007.

Jamila, Shani. "Creative Resistance: A Study of the Free Southern Theater." *Huffington Post.*
     Last updated on September 14, 2014. http://www.huffingtonpost.com/shani-jamila/
     creative-resistance_b_5586443.html.

Jefferson, Nailah. "Vanishing Pearls: Trailer." YouTube. Last modified on March 18, 2014.
     Video: 2:29. https://www.youtube.com/watch?time_continue=56&v=wBLkLOG5MwA.

Jeffries, Hasan Kwame. *Bloody Lowndes: Civil Rights and Black Power in Alabama's Black
     Belt.* New York: New York University, 2009.

Jerome, Andrew. "President Trump's Budget is an Assault on the Farm Safety-Net, NFU
     Says." National Farmers Union. Last updated on May 23, 2017. https://nfu.org/2017/05/23/
     president-trumps-budget-is-an-assault-on-the-farm-safety-net-and-rural-communities
     -nfu-says/.

Jervis, Rick. "Mardi Gras Tribes Still Follow Suit." *USA TODAY,* January 11, 2008.

Johnson, Cedric, ed. *The Neoliberal Deluge: Hurricane Katrina, Late Capitalism, and the
     Remaking of New Orleans.* Minneapolis: University of Minnesota Press, 2011.

Joint Legislative Committee on Un-American Activities, State of Louisiana. *Report No. 3:
     Activities of "The Nation of Islam" or the Muslim Cult of Islam, in Louisiana,* January 9,
     1963.

Joint Legislative Committee on Un-American Activities, State of Louisiana. *Report No. 8:
     Aspects of the Poverty Program in South Louisiana,* April 14, 1967.

Jones, Angela. *African American Civil Rights: Early Activism and the Niagara Movement.*
     Santa Barbara: Praeger, 2011.

Jones, Beverly W. "Mary Church Terrell and the National Association of Colored Women,
     1896–1901." *Journal of Negro History* 67, no. 1 (Spring 1982): 20–33.

Jones, Jim. "The Legacy of Toyohiko Kagawa." Cooperative Development Foundation. Last modified on March 15, 2011. https://www.cdf.coop/wp/wp-content/uploads/2014/09/Kagawa-article.pdf.

Jordan, John Patrick, et. al. *Leadership in Agriculture: Case Studies for a New Generation.* College Station: Texas A&M University Press, 2015.

Josephson, Matthew. *Union House, Union Bar: The History of the Hotel and Restaurant Employees and Bartenders International Union, AFL-CIO.* New York: Random House, 1956.

"Julia Street." *New Orleans Magazine*, December 2008. http://www.myneworleans.com/New-Orleans-Magazine/December-2008/Julia-Street/.

Juvenile Co-operators Fraternals Benevolent Mutual Aid Association Records. Xavier University Archives and Special Collections, Xavier University.

"J. W. Mason Heads Postal Relief Body." *Times-Picayune*, April 10, 1938. Advance Local Media.

Kaplan, Amy, and Donald Pease, eds. *Cultures of U.S. Imperialism.* Durham: Duke University Press, 1993.

Kelley, Robin D. G. *Hammer and Hoe: Alabama Communists during the Great Depression.* Chapel Hill: University of North Carolina Press, 1990.

Kelley, Robin D. G. *Race Rebels: Culture, Politics, and the Black Working Class.* New York: Free Press, 1994.

"Kelley is to Speak to Wives and Consumers." *New Orleans Item*, April 20, 1920.

Kellogg, Scott and Stacy Pettigrew. *Toolbox for Sustainable City Living.* Cambridge: South End Press, 2008.

Kelman, Ari. *A River and Its City: The Nature of Landscape of New Orleans.* Berkeley: University of California Press, 2003.

Kendall, John. *History of New Orleans.* Chicago: Lewis Publishing Company, 1922. http://penelope.uchicago.edu/Thayer/E/Gazetteer/Places/America/United_States/Louisiana/New_Orleans/_Texts/KENHNO/33*.html.

Kent, Joan. "Closing of Freret Street Canal Villere Upsets Revitalization Boosters," *Times-Picayune*, August 14, 1984. Advance Local Media.

Kitts, Andrew W., and Steven F. Edwards. "Cooperatives in US Fisheries: Realizing the Potential of the Fishermen's Collective Marketing Act." *Marine Policy*, April 4, 2003. http://www.uwcc.wisc.edu/info/fishery/kitts.pdf.

Kmen, Henry A. "Remember the Virginius: New Orleans and Cuba in 1873." *Louisiana History* 11, no. 4 (Fall 1970): 313–31.

Knapp, Joseph G. *The Rise of American Cooperative Enterprise: 1620–1920.* Danville: Interstate, 1969.

Knopp, Lawrence. "Some Theoretical Implications of Gay Involvement in an Urban Land Market." *Political Geography Quarterly* 9, no. 4 (October 1990): 337–52.

Knupfer, Anne Meis. *Food Co-ops in America: Communities, Consumption, and Economic Democracy.* Ithaca: Cornell University Press, 2013.

Kolb, Carolyn. "At the Confluence of Science and Power: Water Struggles of New Orleans in the Nineteenth Century." PhD diss., University of New Orleans, 2006.

Kumar, Krishan. "The Ends of Utopia." *New Literary History* 41, no. 3 (Summer 2010): 549–69.

Kuzmack, Linda Gordon. *Woman's Cause: The Jewish Woman's Movement in England and the United States, 1881–1933.* Columbus: Ohio State University Press, 1990.

"Labor Considering Co-operative Plan." *Times-Picayune*, February 22, 1920. Advance Local Media.

"Labor Indorses Co-op Stores." *New Orleans Item*, May 7, 1921.

"Laboring Men: Approve the Mayor-Mullen-McGary Plan of Relief." *Daily Picayune*, October 31, 1897. Advance Local Media.

"Laboring Men Call a Conference to Urge Quarantine Modification." *Daily Picayune*, October 1, 1897. Advance Local Media.

"Laboring Men: Draw up a Memorial with Reference to City Emergency Employ." *Daily Picayune*, October 25, 1897. Advance Local Media.

"Labor's Indorsement." *Daily Picayune*, November 5, 1897. Advance Local Media.

Land, John E. *Pen Illustrations of New Orleans, 1881–1882*. New Orleans: John E. Land, 1882. http://nutrias.org/exhibits/gateway/mercur.htm.

Larocco, Christina. "Participatory Drama": The New Left, the Vietnam War, and the Emergence of Performance Studies." Conference talk at the American Studies Association Annual Meeting, November 6, 2014.

"The Late Post-Office Robbery Case." *New Orleans Daily Crescent*, September 27, 1861.

"The Latino Farmers Cooperative of Louisiana." National Immigrant Farming Initiative. Accessed on October 31, 2014. http://www.immigrantfarming.org/project-profiles/the-latino-farmers-cooperative-of-louisiana.

"The Latino Farmers Cooperative of Louisiana." Urban Ministry. Accessed on March 3, 2018. www.urbanministry.org/org/latino-farmers-cooperative-louisiana.

"Laundry Prices and Food Costs Held Excessive." *Times-Picayune*, June 11, 1921. Advance Local Media.

"LCFC Board." LA Council of Farmer Co-ops. Accessed on July 19, 2014. http://www.lafarmercoops.org/lcfc_board_5.html.

"Leaders in State Student Conference." *Times-Picayune*, November 9, 1934. Advance Local Media.

League for Industrial Democracy. Vertical File: Political Organizations. Louisiana Research Collection. Tulane University.

Leathem, Karen Trahan. "Ida Weis Friend, 1868–1963." Jewish Women: A Comprehensive Historical Encyclopedia, Jewish Women's Archive. Accessed on January 1, 2015. http://jwa.org/encyclopedia/article/friend-ida-weis.

Lefebvre, Henri. *The Production of Space*, trans. Donald Nicholson-Smith. Oxford: Blackwell, 1991.

"Legal Notices." *Times-Picayune*, October 3, 1965.

"Legion Oaks Will Get First Church." *Times-Picayune*, July 6, 1952. Advance Local Media.

Leonard, Margaret. "Kingsley House: A Great Dynamic Community Force." *Social Service Review* 5, no. 6 (July 1917): 14–15.

"Let Women Make Survey of Duties Daily, is Urged." *Times-Picayune*, November 24, 1918. Advance Local Media.

"Levee Labor." *Daily Picayune*, August 17, 1896. Advance Local Media.

"Levee Labor." *Daily Picayune*, September 1, 1896. Advance Local Media.

"Levee Riot Case a Record Breaker." *Daily Picayune*, June 21, 1895.

Levenstein, Harvey A. *Revolution at the Table: The Transformation of the American Diet*. Berkeley: University of California Press, 2003.

Levy, Diane K., Jennifer Comey, and Sandra Padilla. *Keeping the Neighborhood Affordable: A Handbook of Housing Strategies for Gentrifying Areas*. Washington, DC: Urban Institute, 2006.

Levy, Murray. "Free Southern Theater Plans Afro-American Emphasis." *New Orleans Freedom Press* 1, no. 1 (May 1966): 7.

LeWarne, Charles Pierce. *Utopias on Puget Sound, 1885–1915*. Seattle: University of Washington Press, 1995.

Lewis, George. George Lewis and the Nameless Sound/Shepherd School Ensemble perform George Lewis' Creative Construction Set. October 18, 2018. Rice University, Houston, Texas.

Lichtman, Liz. Interview with author, July 2, 2012. Cooperative Oral History Project.

Lindig, Carmen Meriwether. "The Woman's Movement in Louisiana: 1897–1920." PhD diss., North Texas State University, 1982.

Lipsitz, George. *The Possessive Investment in Whiteness: How White People Profit from Identity Politics*. Philadelphia: Temple University Press, 2006.

"Liquidators' Sale of People's Co-operative Laundry, Inc." Advertisement. *Times-Picayune*, October 30, 1924. Advance Local Media.

Liu, Amy, and Bruce Katz. "Katrina is Everywhere: Lessons from the Gulf Coast." In *Breakthrough Communities: Sustainability and Justice in the Next American Metropolis*, eds. Carl Anthony and M. Paloma Pavel, 81–94. Boston: Massachusetts Institute of Technology, 2009.

Livingston, Jane. "Miracle on the Bayou." *Rural Cooperatives* 74, no. 2 (March–April 2007). http://www.rurdev.usda.gov/rbs/pub/mar07/miracle.htm.

"Local Populists." *Daily Picayune*, October 3, 1897. Advance Local Media.

"Local's Credit Union to Meet." *Times-Picayune*, January 23, 1963. Advance Local Media.

"Locations." Urban Strategies. Accessed on July 9, 2014. http://urbanstrategiesinc.org/by-location/.

Logsdon, Joseph, and Caryn Cossé Bell. "The Americanization of Black New Orleans." In *Creole New Orleans: Race and Americanization*, eds. Arnold R. Hirsch and Joseph Logsdon, 201–261. Baton Rouge: Louisiana State University Press, 1992.

London, Todd, ed. *An Ideal Theater: Founding a New American Art*. New York: Theatre Communications Group, 2013.

"Long Chief Issue in City Election." *Times-Picayune*, January 9, 1934. Advance Local Media.

"Lotto Party Announced." *Times-Picayune*, April 14, 1932. Advance Local Media.

"Louisiana." African Scientific Research Institute. Accessed on February 26, 2018. https://asrip.org/events-and-activities/haiti-america-cultural-economic-connection/louisianna-natives/?v=dc91aeca51b5.

Louisiana Association of Cooperatives, e-newsletter, no. 163 (March 1932). PDF.

Louisiana Department of Agriculture and Forestry. "Who You Gonna Call?" Facebook post, March 1, 2018. https://www.facebook.com/LouisianaDepartmentofAgricultureand Forestry/videos/10155372379518181/?q=kentwood%20co-op.

Louisiana Disaster Recovery Foundation. "Initiating Change for a Sustainable Louisiana." *Initiate Change: 2009 Annual Report*, 2009. http://www.foundationforlouisiana.org/docs/news_reports/ldr_09ar_final.pdf.

Louisiana Grocers' Cooperative. *Annual Report*, 1983. Vertical File: Businesses. Louisiana Grocers Co-op Inc. New Orleans Public Library.

Louisiana League for the Preservation of Constitutional Rights. Political Organizations. Vertical File: Louisiana Research Collection. Tulane University.

Louisiana Recovery Authority Board of Directors. Meeting Minutes, March 14, 2006. Accessed on July 19, 2014. http://lra.louisiana.gov/assets/other/by_month/march07/LRAMinutes031407.pdf.

Louisiana Recovery Authority Board of Directors. Meeting Minutes, January 12, 2007. Accessed on July 19, 2014. http://www.lra.louisiana.gov/assets/other/by_month/jan07/LRAMinutes011207.pdf.

Louisiana Shrimp Harvester Advisory Panel. Meeting Minutes, Baton Rouge, LA, September 21, 2009. Accessed on March 15, 2018. http://www.wlf.louisiana.gov/sites/default/files/pdf/shrimp_task_force/6591-Shrimp%20Harvester%20Advisory%20Board%20Meeting%20-%20MONDAY,%20SEPTEMBER%2021,%202009/Draft_Minutes_Shrimp_Harvestors_Advisory_Panel_9-21-09.pdf.

"Lower Ninth Ward 18." Sustain the Nine. Accessed on August 11, 2014. http://www.sustainthenine.org/sites/default/files/uploaded-documents/L9W%20CSED%20Food%20Action%20Plan%20FINAL_sm_0.pdf.

MacCash, Doug. "Gentrification of Bywater and St. Claude Avenue Was Sped Up by Flood and 2008 Economic Slump." *Times-Picayune*, January 25, 2013. http://www.nola.com/arts/index.ssf/2013/01/the_long_term_gentrification_0.html.

MacCash, Doug. "St. Claude Avenue May Roll Into the 21st Century Aboard a Streetcar." *Times-Picayune*, January 13, 2013. http://www.nola.com/arts/index.ssf/2013/01/st_claude_avenue_neighborhoods_1.html.

MacDonell, Mrs. R. W. "Home Mission Work, Woman's Department." *Missionary Voice* 1 (July 1911): 52–55.

"Magnolia Room in Frank's Steak House Caters to All Organizations." *Times-Picayune*, November 10, 1955. Advance Local Media.

Maloney, Stephen. "Heritage Club Reception Honors Members on October 20." Preservation Resource Center of New Orleans. Last updated on October 9, 2015. http://www.prcno.org/news-and-media/1144.

"Many Food Buyers Back Housewives' Co-operative Plan." *Times-Picayune*, February 29, 1920. Advance Local Media.

Mariscal, George. *Brown Eyed Children of the Sun: Lessons from the Chicano Movement, 1965–1975*. Albuquerque: University of New Mexico Press, 2005.

Market Committee Records. Howard-Tilton Memorial Library. Tulane University.

Martin, Michael S., ed. *Louisiana Beyond Black and White: New Interpretations of Twentieth-Century Race and Race Relations*. Lafayette: University of Louisiana at Lafayette Press, 2011.

Martinet, Louis. *The Violation of a Constitutional Right*. New Orleans: Citizens' Committee, 1893.

Maselli, Joseph and Dominic Candeloro. *Italians in New Orleans*. Charleston: Arcadia Publishing, 2004.

"Mathieu, Louis H." *Soards' New Orleans City Directory*. New Orleans: Soards' Directory Co, 1895. Ancestry.com.

Mathilde Dreyfous (Mrs. Geo. A) Papers, 1937–1989. Louisiana Research Collection. Tulane University.

"Matrons to Decide on Store Monday." *Times-Picayune*, October 30, 1921. Advance Local Media.

"Mayor and Unemployed." *Daily Picayune*, September 18, 1897. Advance Local Media.

McCarthy, Brendan. "About 400 Marches Join 'Occupy New Orleans' Protest." *Times-Picayune*, October 6, 2011. http://www.nola.com/politics/index.ssf/2011/10/about_400_marchers_join_occupy.html.

McConnaughy, Corrine M. *The Woman Suffrage Movement in America: A Reassessment*. New York: Cambridge University Press, 2013.

McCulloch, S. R. "Civic and Social Societies Unite to Combat 'Subversive Activities.'" *St. Louis-Post Dispatch*, November 22, 1936. Vertical File: Communist Party. New Orleans Public Library.

McCutcheon, Priscilla. "Community Food Security 'For Us, By Us': The Nation of Islam and the Pan African Orthodox Christian Church." In *Food and Culture: A Reader*, eds. Carole Counihan and Penny Van Esterik. New York: Routledge, 2013.

McGehee Sr., Dr. E. L. "A Report from the Anti-Tuberculosis League to the State Medical Society." *New Orleans Medical and Surgical Journal* 60, no. 9 (March 1908): 725–29.

McGovern, Charles. *Sold American: Consumption and Citizenship, 1890–1945*. Chapel Hill: University of North Carolina Press, 2006.

McKnight, Albert J. *Whistling in the Wind: The Autobiography of The Reverend A. J. McKnight, C.S.Sp.*, eds. Ronnie Moore. Opelousas: Southern Development Foundation, 1994.

McNulty, Ian. "Community Impact Series: Latino Farmers Cooperative." WWNO. Accessed on March 3, 2018. http://wwno.org/post/community-impact-series-latino-farmers -cooperative.

McWilliams, James E. *Just Food: Where Locavores Get It Wrong and How We Can Truly Eat Responsibly*. New York: Little, Brown and Company, 2009.

Media Relations. "NRECA Statement on President Trump's Paris Decision." America's Electric Cooperatives. Last modified on June 1, 2017. https://www.electric.coop/nreca -statement-on-president-trumps-paris-decision/.

Medley, Keith Weldon. *We as Freemen: Plessy v. Ferguson*. Gretna: Pelican Publishing, 2003.

"Meeting Planned for Credit Union." *Times-Picayune*, January 5, 1957. Advance Local Media.

Meier, August. "Benjamin Quarles and the Historiography of Black America," *Civil War History* 26, no. 2 (June 1980): 101–116.

"Members of the Housewives' League to Try Operating Stalls in the Public Markets." *Times-Picayune*, July 21, 1915. Advance Local Media.

"Memorial Rites Set for Leader." *Times-Picayune*, December 13, 1963. Advance Local Media.

"Merrick School Restraint Asked." *Times-Picayune*, June 21, 1952.

Merrill, Ellen C. *Germans of Louisiana*. Gretna: Pelican Publishing Company, 2005.

"Meyers, Inez." *Soards' New Orleans City Directory for 1914*. New Orleans: Soard's Directory Co., 1914. Ancestry.com.

Michna, Catherine. "Hearing the Hurricane Coming: Storytelling, Second-Line Knowledges, and the Struggle for Democracy in New Orleans." PhD diss., Boston College, 2011.

Mickenberg, Julia. *Learning from the Left: Children's Literature, the Cold War, and Radical Politics in the United States*. New York: Oxford University Press, 2006.

Mickenberg, Julia. "Suffragettes and Soviets: American Feminists and the Specter of Revolutionary Russia." *Journal of American History* 100, no. 4 (March 2014): 1021–51.

"Milk Price Goes Up, Consumption Goes Down, Today." *Times-Picayune*, October 1, 1919. Advance Local Media.

"Mississippi Free Press." Mississippi Civil Rights Project. Accessed on October 21, 2014. http://mscivilrightsproject.org/index.php?option=com_content&view=article&id=499: mississippi-free-press&catid=295:organization&Itemid=33.

Mitchell, Michele. *Righteous Propagation: African Americans and the Politics of Racial Destiny after Reconstruction*. Chapel Hill: University of North Carolina Press, 2004.

Mock, Brentin. "New Orleans' Leading Affordable-Housing Developer Explains its Lack of Affordable Housing." City Lab, September 3, 2015. https://www.citylab.com/equity/2015/ 09/new-orleans-leading-affordable-housing-developer-explains-its-lack-of-affordable -housing/403351/.

Moore, Cecilia A. "Writing Black Catholic Lives: Black Catholic Biographies and Autobiographies." *U.S. Catholic Historian* 29, no. 3 (Summer 2011): 43–58.

Moore, Leonard N. *Black Rage in New Orleans: Police Brutality and African American Activism.* Baton Rouge: Louisiana State University Press, 2010.

"More Hopeful Strike Status in N.O. Is Seen." *New Orleans Item*, April 11, 1920. Advance Local Media.

Morris, Robert. "The Redevelopment of Freret Street." *The Gambit*, August 13, 2013. http://www.bestofneworleans.com/gambit/the-redevelopment-of-freret-street/Content?oid=2238586.

"Moser." *Soards' New Orleans City Directory for 1917.* New Orleans: Soards' Directory Co., 1917. Ancestry.com.

Mottola, Daniel. "Bringing Urban Living in Harmony with Nature." *Austin Chronicle*, January 20, 2006. http://www.austinchronicle.com/news/2006-01-20/325865/.

"Moving Picture Peace." *Daily Picayune*, September 14, 1912. Advance Local Media.

"Mrs. Alvin Porter." *Daily Picayune*, January 27, 1911. Advance Local Media.

"Mrs. Egleston Objects to Fixed Retail Prices." *New Orleans Item*, April 10, 1920.

"Mrs. George Ethel Warren." *Times-Picayune*, October 7, 1971. Advance Local Media.

"Mrs. Gilman's Lecture." *Daily Picayune*, January 21, 1911. Advance Local Media.

"Mrs. Graham Heads City Federation of Women's Clubs." *Times-Picayune*, May 25, 1915. Advance Local Media.

"Mrs. Herbert Moser Complimented." *Times-Picayune*, January 17, 1918. Advance Local Media.

"Mrs. L. B. Elliot." *Times-Picayune*, March 14, 1915. Advance Local Media.

"Mrs. Porter's Memorial." *Daily Picayune*, February 15, 1911. Advance Local Media.

"Mrs. Ruth Braniff Wins Freret Contest." *Times-Picayune*, October 5, 1945. Advance Local Media.

"Mrs. Van Meter Portrait Unveiled." *Times-Picayune*, June 17, 1954. Advance Local Media.

"Mrs. Wilkinson's Last Rites Today." *Times-Picayune*, December 3, 1951. Advance Local Media.

"Municipal Curb Markets Opened in Carrollton." *Times-Picayune*, July 14, 1917. Advance Local Media.

Muniz, Lillian. "Defends Position of Coal Miners." *Times-Picayune*, November 7, 1943. Advance Local Media.

Myers, Mrs. H. B. "Housewives League of Orleans, La." *Housewives Magazine* 11, no. 2 (February 1918): 32.

Myers, Mrs. H. B. "Marketing Problems in New Orleans: Housewives Seek Ways to Bring Producer and Consumer Together." *Housewives League Magazine* 6, no. 5 (October 1915): 46, 48.

Nachmias, Chava, and J. John Palen. "Membership in Voluntary Neighborhood Associations and Urban Revitalization." *Policy Sciences* 14, no. 2 (April 1982): 179–93.

Nau, John Frederick. *The German People of New Orleans, 1650–1900.* Hattiesburg: Mississippi Southern College, 1958.

Navarro, José Cantón. 2000. *History of Cuba: The Challenge of the Yoke and the Star.* Havana: Union Nacional de Juristas.

"NCBA CLUSA Defends Co-ops, Responds to Trump Administration's Budget Blueprint." National Cooperative Business Association CLUSA. Last updated on March 16, 2017. http://ncba.coop/ncba-advocacy/1754-ncba-clusa-defends-co-ops-responds-to-trump-administration-s-budget-blueprint.v.

"NCUA Share Insurance Fund Information, Reports, and Statements." National Credit Union Administration. Accessed on August 22, 2014. http://www.ncua.gov/dataapps/pages/si-ncua.aspx.

"Negro Housing Steps Planned." *Times-Picayune*, April 2, 1953. Advance Local Media.

"Negro School Says City Has Law Keeping H. C. L. at Zenith." *New Orleans Item*, April 25, 1920.

"Negroes Criticize Objections Urged to Cooks' Union." *Times-Picayune*, May 21, 1918. Advance Local Media.

"Neighborhood Activist of Lower 9th Ward Dies." *Times-Picayune*, December 28, 1996. http://files.usgwarchives.net/la/orleans/newspapers/00000161.txt.

Nelli, Humbert S. *The Business of Crime: Italians and Syndicate Crime in the United States.* Chicago: University of Chicago Press, 1981.

Nembhard, Jessica Gordon. *Collective Courage: A History of African American Cooperative Economic Thought and Practice.* University Park: Pennsylvania State University Press, 2014.

Nembhard, Jessica Gordon. "Uplifting and Strengthening Our Community: A Showcase of Cooperatives in New Orleans." Accessed on October 19, 2014, http://www.geo.coop/node/356.

"New Businesses in New Orleans." *Times-Picayune*, February 2, 1975. Advance Local Media.

"New Orleans." Restaurant Opportunities Centers United. Accessed on July 8, 2014. http://rocunited.org/nola/.

New Orleans Black Benevolent Associations Collection. Xavier University Archives and Special Collections. Xavier University.

"New Orleans Building Greater Trade with South American Ports." *New Orleans Item*, May 8, 1920.

New Orleans Coalition. Vertical File: Organizations. Jones Hall Special Collections. Tulane University.

New Orleans Embalmers Association Records, 1952–1996, Collection Number 528. Amistad Research Center, Tulane University.

"New Orleans Gives Thanks for Various Good Reasons." *Times-Picayune*, November 27, 1919. Advance Local Media.

New Orleans Notarial Archives. "Louis A. Martinet Records." Accessed on January 1, 2015. http://www.notarialarchives.org/martinet.htm.

"New Orleans Police Attack Peaceful March at St. Bernard." YouTube video: 3:43. Posted by "bignoisetactical." December 16, 2007. https://www.youtube.com/watch?v=9GPjNhVUzqk.

"New Orleans Society Moves to Gulf Coast for Week-End." *Times-Picayune*, July 4, 1925. Advance Local Media.

New Orleans Young Women's Christian Association Records. Louisiana Research Collection. Tulane University.

"Ninety Cases, Eight Deaths." *Daily Picayune*, October 1, 1897. Advance Local Media.

Nkombo Publications Records, 1968–1974. Amistad Research Center. Tulane University.

"N.O. Moneywise Project Begins." *Times-Picayune*, January 10, 1967. Advance Local Media.

"NOFC History." New Orleans Food Co-op. Accessed on July 24, 2014. http://www.nolafood.coop/about-nofc/beginnings/.

NOLA Locavore. "About Us." The New Orleans 4th Annual Eat Local Challenge. Accessed on July 13, 2014. http://www.nolalocavore.org/nola-locavores/.

Nora, Pierre. "Between Memory and History: Les Lieux de Mémoire." *Representations* 26 (Spring 1989): 7–24.

"Norman Thomas Urges Increases in Civil Liberties." *Times-Picayune*, September 11, 1937. Advance Local Media.

"Norman Thomas Would Organize 'Useful Workers.'" *Times-Picayune*, March 9, 1936. Advance Local Media.

North American Committee to Aid Spanish Democracy, Louisiana Division. Newsletter, April 25, 1937. Vertical File: Organizations. North American Committee to Aid Spanish Democracy. Tulane University.

"Notes About Town." *Weekly Pelican*, November 16, 1889.

Nystrom, Justin A. *New Orleans After the Civil War: Race, Politics, and a New Birth of Freedom*. Baltimore: Johns Hopkins University Press, 2010.

Ochs, Stephen J. *A Black Patriot and a White Priest: André Cailloux and Claude Paschal Maistre in Civil War New Orleans*. Baton Rouge: Louisiana State University Press, 2000.

"Officers Installed at Meeting of Freret Business Men's Group." *Times-Picayune*, June 19, 1958. Advance Local Media.

"Officers Installed by Master Barbers." *Times-Picayune*, January 4, 1934. Advance Local Media.

O'Hagan, Maureen. "Post-Katrina: Will New Orleans Still Be New Orleans?" Institute for Southern Studies, April 10, 2014. http://www.equalvoiceforfamilies.org/post-katrina -will-new-orleans-still-be-new-orleans/.

O'Harrow, Jr., Robert. "A Two-Decade Crusade by Conservative Charities Fueled Trump's Exit from Paris Climate Accord." *Washington Post*, September 5, 2017. https://www .washingtonpost.com/investigations/a-two-decade-crusade-by-conservative-charities -fueled-trumps-exit-from-paris-climate-accord/2017/09/05/fcb8d9fe-6726-11e7-9928 -22d00a47778f_story.html?utm_term=.9e22a2c3a3ac.

Olivera, Otto. "Jose Marti, Cuba y Nueva Orleans." *Guaracabuya*. Accessed on January 1, 2015. http://www.amigospais-guaracabuya.org/oag00002.php.

O'Malley, Keelia, Jeanette Gustat, Janet Rice, and Carolyn C. Johnson. "Feasibility of Increasing Access to Healthy Foods in Neighborhood Corner Stores." *Journal of Community Health* 38, no. 4 (August 2013): 741–49.

O'Neal Papers, 1927–1999. Amistad Research Center. Tulane University.

"Our Farm." Grow Dat Youth Farm. Accessed on July 10, 2014. http://growdatyouthfarm.org/ what-we-do/our-farm/.

"Our Farmers and Producers." New Orleans Food Co-op. Accessed on July 24, 2014. http:// www.nolafood.coop/shopping-at-nofc/meet-our-farmers/.

"Our Mission, Ends, and Goals." New Orleans Food Co-op. Accessed on July 24, 2014. http:// www.nolafood.coop/about-nofc/mission/.

"Organization Chronicles." *Times-Picayune*, July 7, 1918. Advance Local Media.

"Organized Labor Proposes Battle on Living Costs." *Times-Picayune*, May 7, 1921. Advance Local Media.

Orleans Parish Civil District Court. "Amadeé Praderes." *Louisiana, Orleans Parish Will Books* 19, New Orleans: Orleans Parish Civil District Court, 1877–1878. Ancestry.com.

Orleans Parish (La.) Registrar of Voters. "Index to Registration of Foreign Born Persons, Vol 2: 1891–1896." New Orleans Public Library City Archives. Accessed on November 30, 2017. http://nutrias.org/~nopl/inv/vx/vx100g2.htm.

"Over Thirty-Two Thousand Babies Weighed in City." *Times-Picayune*, May 5, 1918. Advance Local Media.

"Over 100 Women Buying Groceries from Own Store." *Times-Picayune*, May 8, 1921. Advance Local Media.

"Parents Condemn Movie Thrillers." *Times-Picayune*, June 26, 1921. Advance Local Media.

Parker, Doug. "Photos: Housing Debate Heats Up." *Times-Picayune*, December 20, 2007. https://www.nola.com/news/index.ssf/2007/12/photo_council_debates_housing.html.

Parker, Florence. *The First 125 Years: A History of Distributive and Service Cooperation in the United States, 1829–1954.* Superior: CLUSA, 1956.

"Parties and Events." *Times-Picayune*, May 16, 1926. Advance Local Media.

Passenger Record, s.v. "Heinrich Hermes." October 27, 1913. The Statue of Liberty-Ellis Island Foundation.

"Patriotic Talks Mark School's End." *Times-Picayune*, July 21, 1918. Advance Local Media.

Payne, Charles M. *I've Got the Light of Freedom: The Organizing Tradition and the Mississippi.* Berkeley: University of California Press, 1995.

Penndorf, Jon. "Hurricane Harvey Reinforces Need for Cities to Plan for Disaster Resiliency." *Washington Post*, August 29, 2017. https://www.washingtonpost.com/news/where-we -live/wp/2017/08/29/hurricane-harvey-reinforces-need-for-cities-to-plan-for-disaster -resiliency/?utm_term=.ef69819a7ac7.

Pente, Graeme. "From Paris to Texas: French Fourierists in Power and in Exile, 1848–1857." Conference talk at Society for Utopian Studies Annual Conference. November 2, 2018. Berkeley, California.

"People's Party." *Daily Picayune*, November 30, 1897. Advance Local Media.

"Personal and General Notes." *Daily Picayune*, March 20, 1892. Advance Local Media.

Phillips, Dave. "Trucks with Aid Roll into FEMA Hub." *New York Times*, August 30, 2017. https://www.nytimes.com/2017/08/30/us/fema-aid-storm-victims-harvey.html?action=cl ick&pgtype=Homepage&clickSource=story-heading&module=span-abc-region&region =span-abc-region&WT.nav=span-abc-region.

"The Picayune's Telephone." *Daily Picayune*, June 2, 1897. Advance Local Media.

"Plan Entertainment of Spring Buyers." *Times-Picayune*, March 5, 1915. Advance Local Media.

Pletcher, David M. *The Diplomacy of Trade and Investment: American Economic Expansion in the Hemisphere, 1865–1900.* Columbia: University of Missouri Press, 1998.

Portney, Kent E. *Taking Sustainable Cities Seriously: Economic Development, the Environment, and Quality of Life in American Cities.* Cambridge: MIT Press, 2003.

Postel, Charles. *The Populist Vision.* Oxford: Oxford University Press, 2009.

Potter, David M. *People of Plenty: Economic Abundance and the American Character.* Chicago: University of Chicago Press, 1954.

Poyo, Gerald E. *With All, and for the Good of All: The Emergence of Popular Nationalism in the Cuban Communities of the United States, 1848–1898.* Durham: Duke University, 1989.

"Practical Domestic Science Taught to Increase Efficiency and Number of Colored Cooks." *Times-Picayune*, January 27, 1918. Advance Local Media.

Prejean, Charles. "Louisiana State Association of Cooperatives: Articles and Bylaws." Lafayette: LSAC, 1967.

"Price 'Outrageous,' Says League Head." *Times-Picayune*, May 10, 1919. Advance Local Media.

"Prof. Wilkinson to Help Organize the Curb Market." *Times-Picayune*, January 3, 1916. Advance Local Media.

"Quarantine's Farewell." *Daily Picayune*, November 5, 1897. Advance Local Media.

"Questions and Answers." *Times-Picayune*, April 30, 1922. Advance Local Media.

Quillen, Kimberly. "The Oil Bust." *Times-Picayune*, January 29, 2012. http://www.nola.com/175years/index.ssf/2012/01/the_oil_bust_the_times-picayun.html.

Rader, Dennis. *Learning Redefined: Changing Images that Guide the Process.* Frankfort: Building Democracy Press, 2010.

Rainey, Richard. "'We Can't Pump Our Way Out': Rethinking New Orleans' Approach to Flood Control." *Times-Picayune*, August 11, 2017.

"Ready to Solve the Great Problem of Finding Work for All the City's Unemployed." *Daily Picayune*, July 16, 1897. Advance Local Media.

"Reception Planned [for] Oldest Clubwoman." *Times-Picayune*, February 28, 1918. Advance Local Media.

Reddix, Jacob L. *A Voice Crying in the Wilderness: The Memoirs of Jacob L. Reddix.* Jackson: University of Mississippi Press, 1974.

Reed, Harvey. Interview with author, June 26, 2012. Cooperative Oral History Project.

Reed, Harvey. "Welcome, Cooperatives in New Orleans and Louisiana: Ted Quant, Harvey Reed." Speech given at the US Federation of Worker Cooperatives Conference. New Orleans, Louisiana, June 21, 2008. Accessed on January 1, 2015. http://www.pdfio.com/k-2694397.html.

Regis, Helen A. "'Keeping Jazz Funerals Alive': Blackness and the Politics of Memory in New Orleans." In *Southern Heritage on Display: Public Ritual and Ethnic Diversity within Southern Regionalism*, ed. Celeste Ray. Tuscaloosa: University of Alabama Press.

Relman, Eliza. "Trump Reversed Regulations to Protect Infrastructure Against Flooding Just Days Before Hurricane Harvey." *Business Insider*, August 28, 2017. http://www.businessinsider.com/trump-reversed-obama-flooding-regulations-before-hurricane-harvey-2017–8.

Reonas, Matthew. "World War I." Know Louisiana: The Digital Encyclopedia of Louisiana History and Culture. Last modified on November 16, 2011. http://www.knowlouisiana.org/entry/world-war-i/.

"The Republican State Convention." *Daily Picayune*, January 30, 1896. Advance Local Media.

Ribó, John D. "Cubans and Cuban Americans, 1870–1940." In *Immigrants in American History: Arrival, Adaptation, and Integration*, ed. Elliott Robert Barkan, 301–308. Santa Barbara: ABC-CIO, 2013.

Rice, Erin. "The USFWC Work Week: Post Conference Event in New Orleans, June 2008." Accessed on September 9, 2017. http://geo.coop/node/355.

Richardson, Joe M. "Albert W. Dent: A Black New Orleans Hospital and University Administrator." *Louisiana History* 37, no. 3 (Summer 1996): 309–323.

Richardson, Maggie H. "A Grocer and a Gentleman." *Greater Baton Rouge Business Report*, April 6, 2009. Accessed on September 21, 2012. http://www.businessreport.com/article/20090406/BUSINESSREPORT01/304069956/0/businessreport0403.

Rightor, Alice. "Housewives' League to Open Co-operative Store This Week." *Times-Picayune*, February 20, 1921. Advance Local Media.

Rivlin, Gary. *Katrina: After the Flood.* New York: Simon & Schuster Paperbacks, 2015.

Rizzo, Mary. "Revolution in a Can: Food, Class, and Radicalism in the Minneapolis Co-op Wars of the 1970s." In *Eating in Eden: Food and American Utopias*, eds. Etta M. Madden and Martha L. Finch, 220–38. Lincoln: University of Nebraska, 2006.

"R.O. Peace Meat Markets." Advertisement. *Times-Picayune*, February 10, 1949. Advance Local Media.

"R.O. Peace Meat Markets." Advertisement. *Times-Picayune*, February 27, 1949. Advance Local Media.

Roahen, Sara, and John T. Edge, eds. *The Southern Foodways Alliance Community Cookbook*. Athens: University of Georgia Press, 2015.

Robinson, Joyce Davis. "Consuming Interests: Food Cooperatives." *Times-Picayune*, July 3, 1977. Advance Local Media.

Robinson, Matt. Interview with author, June 5, 2012. Cooperative Oral History Project.

Rogers, Kim Lacy. *Righteous Lives: Narratives of the New Orleans Civil Rights Movement*. New York: New York University Press, 1993.

Ronnie Moore Papers, 1959–2004. Amistad Research Center. Tulane University.

Rose, Donald J., Nicholas Bodor, Janet C. Rice, Chris M. Swalm, and Paul D. Hutchinson. "The Effects of Hurricane Katrina on Food Access Disparities in New Orleans." *American Journal of Public Health* 101, no. 3 (March 2011): 482–84.

Rosenberg, Daniel. *New Orleans Dockworkers: Race, Labor, and Unionism, 1892–1923*. Albany: State University of New York Press, 1988.

Rossinow, Doug. *The Politics of Authenticity: Liberalism, Christianity, and the New Left in America*. New York: Columbia University Press, 1998.

Rummel, Jack. *African-American Social Leaders and Activists*. New York: Fact on File, 2003.

Russell, Gordon. "New Orleans City Council Meets This Morning; Occupy NOLA Protest Expected at 11." *Times-Picayune*, November 17, 2011. http://www.nola.com/politics/index .ssf/2011/11/city_council_meeting_this_morn.html.

Sainz, Adrian. "Thousands of Black Farmers File Claims in USDA Discrimination Settlement." CNS News. Last modified on March 28, 2012. http://cnsnews.com/news/ article/thousands-black-farmers-file-claims-usda-discrimination-settlement.

Sanchez, George. *Becoming Mexican American: Ethnicity, Culture and Identity in Chicano Los Angeles, 1900–1945*. New York and Oxford: Oxford University Press, 1993.

Sanson, Jerry Purvis. *Louisiana During World War II: Politics and Society, 1939–1945*. Baton Rouge: Louisiana State University Press, 1999.

Sartain, Lee. *Invisible Activists: Women of the Louisiana NAACP and the Struggle for Civil Rights, 1915–1945*. Baton Rouge: Louisiana State University Press, 2007.

Sartain, Lee. "'It's Worth One Dollar to Get Rid of Us': Middle-Class Persistence and the NAACP in Louisiana, 1915–1945." In *Long is the Way and Hard: One Hundred Years of the National Association for the Advancement of Colored People (NAACP)*, eds. Kevern Verney and Lee Sartain, 121–34. Fayetteville: University of Arkansas Press, 2009.

"Says Husbands, 'Ring' Followers, Keep Wives Away." *Times-Picayune*, November 22, 1919. Advance Local Media.

Schiffer, Steven Jay. "'Glocalized' Utopia, Community-Building, and the Limits of Imagination." *Utopian Studies* 29, no. 1 (March 2018): 67–87.

Schneider, Nathan. "Economic Democracy and the Billion-Dollar Co-op." *The Nation*, May 8, 2017. https://www.thenation.com/article/economic-democracy-and-the-billion-dollar -co-op/.

Schoenberger, Podine. "Homemaking Art Taught to Women at Night Classes." *Times-Picayune*, May 31, 1936. Advance Local Media.

"School Location Policy Defended." *Times-Picayune*, April 17, 1951. Advance Local Media.

Scott, Anne Firor. *The Southern Lady: From Pedestal to Politics, 1830–1930*. Charlottesville: University Press of Virginia, 1970.

Scott, Effie Leese. "Activity in Women's Clubs." *Daily Star*, January 11, 1914. Chronicling America.

Scott, James C. *Domination and the Arts of Resistance: Hidden Transcripts*. New Haven: Yale University Press, 1990.

Scott, Rebecca. *Degrees of Freedom: Louisiana and Cuba after Slavery*. Cambridge: President and Fellows of Harvard College, 2005.

Segal, Martin E. "Senior Citizens Trained in Consumer Education." *Times-Picayune*, June 24, 1968. Advance Local Media.

"Sensations in the Levee Riot Trial." *Daily Picayune*, July 26, 1895. Advance Local Media.

"Servant Problem Occupies Meeting of Women's Clubs." *Times-Picayune*, October 29, 1920. Advance Local Media.

Sessums, Cleveland. "Quits Sorting Mail, Turns to Pictures of Postoffices." *Times-Picayune*, April 3, 1938. Advance Local Media.

"Sewerage as the Private Prerequisite." *Daily Picayune*, October 7, 1898. Advance Local Media.

Seymour Alcorn. 74th US Colored Infantry, Compiled Military Service Records of Volunteer Union Soldiers Who Served the United States Colored Troops (USCT): 56th–138th USCT Infantry, 1864–1866, Record Group 94, NAMS M-594, reel 213. Ancestry.com.

Shaffer, Jack. *Historical Dictionary of the Cooperative Movement*. Lanham: Scarecrow Press, 1999.

Shapiro, Laura. *Perfection Salad: Women and Cooking at the Turn of the Century*. Berkeley: University of California Press, 1986.

Shire, Gavin. "President Proposes $1.3 Billion FY 2018 Budget for U.S. Fish and Wildlife Service." US Fish and Wildlife Service. Last updated on May 23, 2017. https://www.fws .gov/news/ShowNews.cfm?ref=president-proposes-$1.3-billion-fy-2018-budget-for —u.s.-fish-and-w&_ID=36050.

"Shober Rites This Morning." *Times-Picayune*, August 27, 1959. Advance Local Media.

Shogren, Elizabeth. "Obama's Climate Legacy will be Harder to Undo Than Trump Thinks." *Mother Jones*, January 7, 2017. http://www.motherjones.com/environment/2017/01/ obama-climate-change-legacy-west/.

Siegmeister, Dr. Walter. "The Downfall of Capitalism and the Birth of the New Cooperative System," *Llano Colonist*, April 1, 1933.

Smith, Eric. *American Relief Aid and the Spanish Civil War*. Columbia: University of Missouri Press, 2013.

Smith, Jazmin. "l'Athénée Louisianais Records, 1834–1987: Collection Overview." Louisiana Research Collection. Accessed on June 23, 2014. http://specialcollections.tulane.edu/ archon/index.php?p=collections/findingaid&id=125&q=Natalie+Scott.

Smith, Neil. *The New Urban Frontier: Gentrification and the Revanchist City*. London and New York: Routledge, 1996.

Smith, Norman R. *Footprints of Black Louisiana*. Bloomington: Xlibris Corporation, 2010.

Smethurst, James. *The Black Arts Movement: Literary Nationalism in the 1960s and 1970s*. Chapel Hill: University of North Carolina Press, 2005.

Social Ecology Newsletter 1, no. 2 (March 1983).

Social Welfare Planning Council. *Community Organization in Low-Income Neighborhoods in New Orleans*. New Orleans: Social Welfare Planning Council, 1968.

"Socialist Leader Will Speak Here." *Times-Picayune*, September 2, 1934. Advance Local Media.

Socialist Party of New Orleans. *Two Packs of Cigarettes a Month*. 1934. Williams Research Collection. Historic New Orleans Collection.

"The Socialists." *Daily Picayune*, September 20, 1903. Advance Local Media.

"Socialists to Hear of New Llano Plan." *Times-Picayune*, December 14, 1934. Advance Local Media.

"Socialists to Meet." *Times-Picayune*, March 9, 1934. Advance Local Media.

"Societies and Institutions." *Catholic Charities Review* 1 (May 1917): 150.

"Society." *Daily Picayune*, December 18, 1887. Advance Local Media.

"Some of Our Patrons." *The Crusader* 2, no. 23, July 19, 1890.

Sommer, Robert, Deborah Schlanger, Robert Hackman, and Steven Smith. "Consumer Cooperatives and Worker Collectives: A Comparison." *Pacific Sociological Association* 27, no. 2 (April 1984): 139–57.

Southeastern Cooperative League Records. Louis Round Wilson Special Collections Library. University of North Carolina.

Souther, J. Mark. *New Orleans on Parade: Tourism and the Transformation of the Crescent City*. Baton Rouge: Louisiana State University Press, 2006.

St. Julien, Mtumishi. *Upon the Shoulders of Elephants We Reach the Sky: A Parent's Farewell to a Collegian*. New Orleans: Runagate Press, 1995.

Stanley, Brian. "The Legacy of George Sherwood Eddy." *International Bulletin of Missionary Research* 24, no. 3 (July 2000): 130–31.

Stanonis, Anthony J. *Creating the Big Easy: New Orleans and the Emergence of Modern Tourism, 1918–1945*. Athens: University of Georgia Press, 2006.

"State Farmers' Union to Hold Annual Meeting." *Times-Picayune*, May 15, 1915. Advance Local Media.

Stein, Judith. *The World of Marcus Garvey: Race and Class in Modern Society*. Baton Rouge: Louisiana State University Press, 1991.

Stevens, Sally. Interview with author, June 27, 2012. Cooperative Oral History Project.

Stevens, Sally. "Urban Innovation No 4: New Orleans Cooperative Development Project," Initiative for a Competitive Inner City. Last modified on October 27, 2013. http://www .icic.org/connection/blog-entry/blog-icicsummit-urban-innovation-no.-4-new-orleans -cooperative-development.

Stone, Ronald H. *Professor Reinhold Niebuhr: A Mentor to the Twentieth Century*. Louisville: Westminister John Knox Press, 1992.

Storrs, Landon. *Civilizing Capitalism: The National Consumers' Leagues, Women's Activism, and Labor Standards in the New Deal Era*. Chapel Hill: University of North Carolina Press, 2000.

Storrs, Landon. "Left-Feminism, The Consumer Movement, and Red Scare Politics in the United States, 1935–1960." *Journal of Women's History* 18, no. 3 (September 2006): 40–67.

"Strike 'Male' From Utilities Bill, Housewives League Asks." *New Orleans Item*, May 16, 1920.

"Strikers Fill Exchange Alley." *Daily Picayune*, July 26, 1901. Advance Local Media.

Student Nonviolent Coordinating Committee. "Position Paper on Black Power," in *Modern Black Nationalism: From Marcus Garvey to Louis Farrakhan, Issue 2*, ed. William L. Van Deburg, 120–26. New York: New York University Press, 1997.

Subramni, Shreya. "New Orleans's Gentilly Resilience District." Princeton H2o. Last updated on October 15, 2016. https://princetonh2o.wordpress.com/pane13/http://www.nola.com/ weather/index.ssf/2017/08/new_orleans_flooding_living_wi.html.

"The Suffrage Committee." *Daily Picayune*, February 25, 1898. Advance Local Media.

"Suffrage House to Give Service Dances." *Times-Picayune*, August 23, 1918. Advance Local Media.

"Suffrage Rally at City Park." *Daily Picayune*, August 31, 1913. Advance Local Media.

"Suffrage to Seek Working Women." *Daily Picayune*, January 18, 1914. Advance Local Media.

Sugrue, Thomas. *Origins of the Urban Crisis: Race and Inequality in Postwar Detroit.* Princeton: Princeton University Press, 1996.

"Supervisors of Election." *Daily Picayune*, October 27, 1888. Advance Local Media.

Sutton, Robert P. *Communal Utopias and the American Experience: Religious Communities, 1732–2000.* Westport: Praeger, 2003.

Svitek, Patrick. "Trump Visits Corpus Christi, Austin to See Harvey Recovery." *Texas Tribune*, August 29, 2017. https://www.texastribune.org/2017/08/29/trump-visit-corpus -christi-austin-see-harvey-recovery/.

Swearingen, Jr., William Scott. *Environmental City: People, Place, Politics, and the Meaning of Modern Austin.* Austin: University of Texas Press, 2010.

"Take the Virtual Tour." Rhizome Collective. Accessed on October 17, 2011. http://www .rhizomecollective.org/node/7.

Tansey, Charles D. "Community Development Credit Unions: An Emerging Player in Low Income Communities." Brookings Institute, 2001. http://www.brookings.edu/research/ articles/2001/09/metropolitanpolicy-tansey.

Tarbell, Ida M. "Mobilizing the Women." *Harper's Monthly Magazine* 135 (November 1917): 841–47. https://harpers.org/archive/1917/11/mobilizing-the-women/.

Tellez, F. J., and E. P. Roy. "Economic and Socio-Economic Relationships Between Farmer Cooperatives and Low-Income Farmers in Louisiana." *Department of Agricultural Economics and Agribusiness Research Report*, no. 359 (December 1966): 34.

"Temporary Site for Store Found." *Times-Picayune*, January 29, 1921. Advance Local Media.

Texas War Records Collection. Dolph Briscoe Center for American History. University of Texas at Austin.

"Thanksgiving in Shorthand." *Daily Picayune*, November 25, 1892. Advance Local Media.

"That Mass Meeting." *Daily Picayune*, June 8, 1897. Advance Local Media.

"The Theosophists." *Daily Picayune*, May 27, 1892. Advance Local Media.

"The Theosophists." *Daily Picayune*, February 28, 1897. Advance Local Media.

"These Dealers Are Featuring Swift's Premium Ham." *Times-Picayune*, April 7, 1950. Advance Local Media.

Thompson, C. H., P. L. Prattis, A. W. Dent, F. C. Horne, and M. W. Johnson. "Discussion of Papers and Closing Remarks." *Journal of Negro Education* 21, no. 3 (Summer 1952): 434–44.

Thompson, Shirley. "Adventures in Black Life Insurance," April 14, 2014. Invited talk at the University of Texas at Austin, Austin, Texas.

Thompson, Shirley. *Exiles at Home: The Struggle to Become American in Creole New Orleans.* Cambridge: Harvard University Press, 2009.

"Thompson States Claim of Grocers." *Times-Picayune*, February 22, 1920. Advance Local Media.

"Three Hundred Negro Servants in Union for More Pay, Less Work." *Times-Picayune*, May 9, 1918. Advance Local Media.

Tiger, Rebecca. "A Bitter Pill Indeed: The War on Poverty and Community Action in New Orleans, 1964–1970." MA thesis, University of New Orleans, 1997.

"To Show Electric Appliances Tuesday." *Times-Picayune*, April 14, 1919. Advance Local Media.

"To Try to Keep Out Italians." *The Sun*, August 20, 1897.

Todd, Anne. "Disasters Spur Co-op Formations: Louisiana Co-op Association Helps Farmers, Fishermen Recover Following Hurricanes and Oil Spill." *Rural Cooperatives*, July 1, 2012. https://www.rd.usda.gov/files/RuralCoop_JulyAug12.pdf.

Tom Dent Papers. Amistad Research Center. Tulane University.

"Tomorrow' Film to be Exhibited." *Times-Picayune*, April 4, 1943. Advance Local Media.

"Tonight—WNOE" Advertisement. *Times-Picayune*, January 10, 1944. Advance Local Media.

Total Community Action. *Quick Facts: TCA Target Areas* (n.d.). Total Community Action, Vertical Files: Organizations. Louisiana Research Collection. Tulane University.

"Training School for Servants May Hold Husbands." *Times-Picayune*, December 31, 1918. Advance Local Media.

Tripp, Ellen Louise. "Free Southern Theater: There is Always a Message." PhD diss., University of North Carolina at Greensboro, 1986.

"Trolley Busses Move on Freret." *Times-Picayune*, September 4, 1947. Advance Local Media.

Trumbull, Gunnar. *Consumer Lending and America: Credit and Welfare*. Cambridge: Cambridge University Press, 2014.

Trump, Donald J. "Presidential Executive Order on Establishing Discipline and Accountability in the Environmental Review and Permitting Process for Infrastructure." Executive Order, Office of the Press Secretary. Last updated on August 15, 2017. https://www.whitehouse.gov/the-press-office/2017/08/15/presidential-executive-order-establishing-discipline-and-accountability.

Tucker, Susan. *New Orleans Cuisine: Fourteen Signature Dishes and Their Histories*. Jackson: University Press of Mississippi, 2009.

Tyler, Pamela. *Silk Stockings and Ballot Boxes: Women & Politics in New Orleans, 1920–1963*. Athens and London: University of Georgia Press, 1996.

"The Unemployed Miss Their Dinners." *Daily Picayune*, August 9, 1897. Advance Local Media.

"The Unemployed Organized Now." *Daily Picayune*, July 26, 1897. Advance Local Media.

"Union Leader Will Address Socialists." *Times-Picayune*, August 19, 1936. Advance Local Media.

"Union Men Open Their Own Shop." *New Orleans Item*, May 10, 1920.

United Daughters of the Confederacy. *Minutes of the Twenty-Third Annual Convention of the United Daughters of the Confederacy*. Raleigh: United Daughters of the Confederacy, 1917.

United States Bureau of Labor Statistics. *History of Wages in the United States from Colonial Times to 1928*. Washington, DC: US Government Printing Office, 1934.

Ureña, Max Henríquez. "Poetas Cubanos de Expresion Francesa," *Inicio* 3, no. 6 (May 1941): 6, http://revista-iberoamericana.pitt.edu/ojs/index.php/Iberoamericana/article/view/1031/1265.

"Urge Home Economics." *Times-Picayune*, May 25, 1919. Advance Local Media.

"Urges Co-operative Grocery Store Plan." *Times-Picayune*, June 21, 1919. Ancestry.com.

US Bureau of Labor Statistics. "The Recession of 2007–2009," February 2012. Accessed on January 1, 2018. https://www.bls.gov/spotlight/2012/recession/pdf/recession_bls_spotlight.pdf.

US Census Bureau. "Louisiana: Race and Hispanic Origin for Selected Cities and Other Places: Earliest Census to 1990." Accessed on August 13, 2014. http://www.census.gov/population/www/documentation/twps0076/twps0076.html.

US Congress. US Public Law 88–452: The Economic Opportunity Act of 1964. Washington, DC: 88th Congress, 1964.

US Department of Housing and Urban Development. "HUD History." Accessed on July 8, 2014. http://portal.hud.gov/hudportal/HUD?src=/about/hud_history.

US Senate Committee on the Judiciary. *Bolshevik Propaganda: Hearings before a Subcommittee of the Committee on the Judiciary, United States Senate, Sixty-Fifth*

Congress, Third Session and Thereafter, Pursuant to S. Res. 439 and 469, February 11, 1919, to March 10, 1919. Washington, DC: US Senate, 1919.

"USDA Names Minority Farmers Advisory Committee." USDA. Last modified on November 6, 2015. https://www.usda.gov/media/press-releases/2015/11/06/usda-names-minority -farmers-advisory-committee.

"USDA Support for Historically Black Colleges and Small Agricultural Producers." North Carolina Agribusiness Council. Last modified on September 20, 2010. https://www.ciclt .net/sn/new/n_detail.aspx?ClientCode=ncagbc&N_ID=23740.

Van Meter, Catherine C. "What Women Are Doing." *Times-Picayune*, September 15, 1918. Advance Local Media.

Vandal, Gilles. "Black Utopia in Early Reconstruction New Orleans: The People's Bakery as a Case-Study." *Louisiana History: The Journal of the Louisiana Historical Association* 38, no. 4 (Autumn 1997): 437–52.

Varela-Lago, Ana Maria. "Conquerors, Immigrants, Exiles: The Spanish Diaspora in the United States (1848–1948)," PhD diss., University of California, San Diego, 2008.

Varney, James. "A Dubious Grant for a Dubious Outfit." *Times-Picayune*, June 16, 2013. http:// www.nola.com/opinions/index.ssf/2013/06/a_dubious_grant_for_a_dubious.html.

"VEGGI Farmers Cooperative." Propeller. Accessed on April 7, 2018. http://gopropeller.org/ ventures/veggi-farmers-cooperative/.

Velasco, Jocine. Interview with author, June 24, 2012. Cooperative Oral History Project.

Vernon, Walter N. *Becoming One People: The History of Louisiana Methodism.* Bossier City: Everett Publishing Company, 1987.

Victor Schiro Papers, 1904–1995. Louisiana Research Collection. Tulane University.

Voinea, Anca. "What Will Donald Trump Do for Co-operatives? Co-op News. Last updated on November 10, 2016. https://www.thenews.coop/110987/sector/banking-and-insur ance/will-donald-trump-co-operatives/.

Voorhis, Jerry. *American Cooperatives: Where They Come From, What They Do, Where They Are Going.* New York: Harper, 1961.

Ward, Brian. *Just My Soul Responding: Rhythm and Blues, Black Consciousness and Race Relations.* London: UCL Press, 1998.

Ward, Jr., Thomas J. *Black Physicians in the Jim Crow South.* Fayetteville: University of Arkansas Press, 2003.

Warner, Coleman. "Freret's Century: Growth, Identity, and Loss in a New Orleans Neighborhood." *Louisiana History* 42, no. 3 (Summer 2001): 323–58.

Warren, Bob. "New Orleans Flooding: What We Know Sunday." *Times-Picayune*, August 6, 2017. http://www.nola.com/weather/index.ssf/2017/08/new_orleans_flooding_what_ we_k.html

"Water." Propeller. Accessed on August 2, 2017. http://gopropeller.org/sectors/water/.

"WCTU Gets New Members." *Times-Picayune*, January 29, 1915. Advance Local Media.

Webster, Richard. "Demolition of Iberville Housing Development Beings." *Times-Picayune*, September 10, 2013. http://www.nola.com/politics/index.ssf/2013/09/demolition_of_ iberville_housin.html.

Webster, Richard. "St. Claude Neighbors Wary of Healing Center Plans." *New Orleans City Business*, June 17, 2011. http://neworleanscitybusiness.com/blog/author/richardweb ster.2013.

Weems, Robert E. *Desegregating the Dollar, African American Consumerism in the Twentieth Century.* New York: New York University Press, 1998.

Wegmann, Earl F. "'Rebel,' 'Invader' Scored in Films." *Times-Picayune*, July 10, 1938. Advance Local Media.

"Weil Social Center Dedication Today." *Times-Picayune*, January 4, 1925. Advance Local Media.

"What America's Society Women of Wealth Are Doing to Correct Wastefulness." *Ogden Standard*, June 30, 1917.

"What We're Working On." Austin Cooperative Think Tank. Accessed on August 14, 2014. http://www.thinktank.coop/what-we-do.

"White Laboring Men." *Daily Picayune*, November 25, 1897. Advance Local Media.

White, Richard. *The Middle Ground: Indians, Empires, and Republics in the Great Lakes Region, 1650–1815*. Cambridge: Cambridge University Press, 1991.

"Who We Are." VEGGI Farmers Cooperative. Accessed on August 14, 2014. http://www.veggifarmcoop.com/.

"Why Jones, Noe Joined Forces in Drive Explained." *Times-Picayune*, January 25, 1940. Advance Local Media.

"Will Open Canning Clubs This Week." *Times-Picayune*, July 21, 1918. Advance Local Media.

Williams, Elizabeth M. *New Orleans: A Food Biography*. Lanham: AltaMira Press, 2012.

Williams, Mrs. George H. "Of Interest to Housekeepers." *Times-Picayune*, April 19, 1914. Advance Local Media.

Williams, Oscar Renal. *George S. Schuyler: Portrait of a Black Conservative*. Knoxville: University of Tennessee Press, 2007.

Williams, Sarah P. "The Servant Problem." *Times-Picayune*, July 28, 1918. Advance Local Media.

Wilson, Matthew. "Republican Spaces: An Intellectual History of Positivist Urban Sociology in Britain, 1855–1920." PhD diss., University of London, 2015.

Wilson, Matthew. "Victorian Sociology, Trade Unionism, and Utopia: A Social Programme for an Ideal Republic: The Positivist Sociology of Frederic Harrison." Paper presented at the Society of Utopian Studies Annual Conference, November 10, 2017. Memphis, Tennessee.

Windel, Aaron. "Co-operatives and the Technocrats, or 'The Fabian Agony' Revisited." In *Brave New World: Imperial and Democratic Nation-Building in Britain Between the Wars*, eds. Laura Beers and Geraint Thomas, 249–68. London: Institute of Historical Research, 2011.

"Winifred Dabney." New Orleans, Passenger Lists, 1813–1963. Records of the Immigration and Naturalization Service, Record Group 85. National Archives and Records Administration, Washington, DC. Ancestry.com.

Winter, Jay. *Dreams of Peace and Freedom: Utopian Moments in the Twentieth Century*. New Haven: Yale University Press, 2006.

Wofford, John. "The Politics of Local Responsibility: Administration of the Community Action Program, 1965–1966." In *On Fighting Poverty*, ed. James L. Sundquist, 70–102. New York: Basic Books, 1969.

Wolff, Tamsen. *Mendel's Theatre: Heredity, Eugenics, and Early Twentieth-Century American Drama*. New York: Palgrave Macmillan, 2009.

"The Woman's Club." *Daily Picayune*, November 7, 1905. Advance Local Media.

"Women Appeal to Men to Subscribe for Balance of Co-operative Stock." *New Orleans Item*, April 2, 1920. Advance Local Media.

"Women Give Assistance to Food Control Department." *Times-Picayune*, July 21, 1918. Advance Local Media.

"Women in Industry: Plans for Improvement of Domestic Service." *Monthly Labor Review* 10, no. 5 (May 1920): 112–16.

Women in Industry Committee, Council of National Defense, New Orleans Division and Louisiana State Division. *Conditions of Women's Labor in Louisiana: New Orleans and Louisiana Industrial Survey.* New Orleans: Tulane University Press, 1919.

"Women of City Show Admiration for Russ[ian] Sisters." *Times-Picayune*, August 7, 1917. Advance Local Media.

"Women's Meetings." *Times-Picayune*, March 19, 1918. Advance Local Media.

"Women Work for Humanity Cause." *Daily Picayune*, September 1, 1913. Advance Local Media.

Wood, Edgar Wallace. "Credit Union Development in Louisiana." PhD diss., Louisiana State University, 1967.

Woods, Clyde. "Katrina's World: Blues, Bourbon, and the Return to the Source." *American Quarterly* 61, no. 3 (September 2009): 427–53.

Woods, Jeff. *Black Struggle, Red Scare: Segregation and Anti-Communism in the South, 1949–1968.* Baton Rouge: Louisiana State University Press, 2004.

The Workers Defense League Collection Papers, 1935–1971. Walter P. Reuther Library. Wayne State University.

"Workers Will Hear Frank McCallister." *Times-Picayune*, March 3, 1938. Advance Local Media.

Works Progress Administration. "Floods and Overflows in New Orleans During the 1890s," 1930. State Library of Louisiana. http://cdm16313.contentdm.oclc.org/cdm/ref/collection/LWP/id/8833.

Wright, Beverly Hendrix. "New Orleans: A City That Care Forgot." In *In Search of the New South: The Black Urban Experience in the 1970s and 1980s*, ed. Robert D. Bullard, 45–74. Tuscaloosa: University of Alabama Press, 1989.

Wright, Beverly Hendrix. "Race, Politics, and Pollution: Environmental Justice in the Mississippi River Chemical Corridor." In *Just Sustainabilities: Development in an Unequal World*, eds. Julian Agyeman, Robert Bullard, and Bob Evans. London: Earthscan Publications, 2003.

Wright Jr., Richard R., and John R. Hawkins, eds. *Centennial Encyclopedia of the African Methodist Episcopal Church.* Philadelphia: AME Church, 1916.

ya Salaam, Kalamu. "Art for Life: My Story, My Song." *Chickenbones.* Accessed on January 1, 2015. http://www.nathanielturner.com/artforlife7.htm.

ya Salaam, Kalamu. "Enriching the Paper Trail: An Interview with Tom Dent," *African American Review* 27, no. 2 (Summer 1993): 327–45.

ya Salaam, Kalamu. "Historical Overviews of the Black Arts Movement." *Chickenbones.* Accessed on October 7, 2013. http://www.nathanielturner.com/kalamuessay.htm.

Young, Cynthia. *Soul Power: Culture, Radicalism, and the Making of a U.S. Third World Left.* Durham: Duke University Press, 2006.

Zarnowitz, Victor. *Business Cycles: Theory, History, Indicators, and Forecasting.* Chicago: University of Chicago Press, 1992.

Zieger, Robert H. *For Jobs and Freedom: Race and Labor in America Since 1865.* Lexington: University Press of Kentucky, 2007.

INDEX

Addams, Jane, 58, 67, 70
Alexander, William W., 119–20
Algiers, 111, 152, 160
American Federation of Labor (AFL),
    74; and Congress of Industrial
    Organizations, 88; female consumer
    allies, 74; founding principles, 38;
    and Laboringmen's Protective
    Association, 41; New Orleans
    affiliates, 94; Samuel Gompers's
    leadership, 38; socialist coalitions,
    33; white supremacist attitudes, 38,
    43
Army Corps of Engineers, 35
Association of Commerce, 52, 54, 58, 62,
    71, 75
Atlanta, Georgia, 118–19, 126, 130

Bacarisse, Eugene: arrest, 23; Cuban
    background, 27–28; French
    political and cultural organizational
    membership, 29; legacy, 85, 91; and
    Panic of 1893, 30; political writings,
    32–33, 36, 46; populist affiliation, 30,
    44; sociality and political action, 28;
    speeches, 32; theosophical influence,
    29–30; and women's equality, 46. *See
    also* Brotherhood of Co-operative
    Commonwealth; Laboringmen's
    Protective Association; White
    Laboringmen's Protective
    Association
Bakara, Amiri (LeRoi Jones), 130, 134, 141
Baker, Ella, 126
Battiste, Harold, 129, 135–36

Behrman, Martin, 54, 56, 75
Bellamy, Edward, 31, 70
benevolent associations, 11–13, 28, 95,
    123–25, 135
Bishop, Julia Truitt, 62, 63
Black Arts Movement, 18, 117, 130, 134, 138,
    143–44
black insurance companies, 119
Black Panther Party, 139, 143, 159
Blanco, Kathleen, 170
Boggs, Hale, 102, 109
Bookchin, Murray, 174
Brittin, Abraham, 36–37, 42, 47
Brotherhood of Co-operative
    Commonwealth, 23–26, 32–37, 91,
    161, 179–80. *See also* Bacarisse,
    Eugene; Graf, August
Burkett, Ben, 155
buying clubs, 58, 70–71, 73, 163, 174
Bywater, 158, 168

Cameron Parish Gulf Coast United
    Fisheries Cooperative, 173
Cassin, René, 101
Central Business District (CBD), 31–32, 45,
    111, 135, 140, 179
Central City, 18, 117, 140–41, 143–44, 161–62,
    186
Charles, Rudolph, 9, 197n76
Chenault, Reese, 162–63, 164
Citizens' Committee to Test the
    Constitutionality of Louisiana's
    Separate Car Act (Separate Car
    Act), 12, 29, 38, 39, 40
Citizens' League, 35, 36, 54

civil rights movement, 112, 121, 131
Clark, John, 20, 163, 188
Cohen, Walter, 29, 40
Colored Domestic Union, 66–69. *See also*
    Peete, Elenora Alcorn
Common Ground Relief Collective, 5,
    159–60, 164–65
Commonwealth College, 91, 102
Communist Party of the United States of
    America (CPUSA), 88, 92, 101
Congress of Racial Equality (CORE), 132,
    139, 145
consumer rights' movements, 17, 51, 60,
    70–71, 93. *See also* Consumers'
    League
Consumers' League, 57, 60–61, 68, 70
Cooperative League of America (CLUSA),
    17, 73, 79, 91, 93, 100–102. *See also*
    Voorhis, Jerry
cooperatives: attitudes toward race,
    69–70; capitalist critique, 70,
    128–29; Catholic models, 5, 98,
    107, 116, 128, 145; definitional
    categories, 13; emergency
    responses, 3, 5, 81, 102, 179, 183, 185;
    and environmental sustainability,
    184, 186–87; expansion and
    contraction of membership, 64,
    73, 79, 91, 183; federal relationships,
    108, 155, 183–84; and female
    reformers, 17, 69–70; gentrification,
    5, 165, 167–68; globally informed
    neighborhood models, 4, 14, 73,
    100, 126, 129; grocery industry,
    93; international cooperative
    movements, 100–101, 116, 129,
    155–56; as political and economic
    development models, 6, 20, 73,
    79, 100; political co-optation of,
    6, 109–10, 184; sociability and
    cooperative formation, 7, 14, 20,
    165; socialist models, 57, 73, 91, 129;
    See also specific cooperatives
Coxey, Jacob, 26, 34, 92
credit union movement, 18, 103–12, 174
Credit Union National Association
    (CUNA), 107–8, 183

Creoles of color: and African Americans,
    12, 39, 121; and Cubans, 26, 28–29,
    38–39; influence on Haitian
    Revolution, 8; interracial social
    mixing, 8; music and performance,
    134–36, 138; mutual aid traditions
    and political equality movements,
    9–12, 38–39, 124–25; and utopian
    socialism, 15; Ward community
    hubs, 10, 28, 121, 151, 179
Cuba, 26–29, 30, 38–39, 41, 44, 55

Dashiki Project Theatre, 144
Deacons for Defense, 132
Dent, Albert W. (A. W.): attitudes
    toward Creoles of color, 116, 125,
    128; background, 118–20; black
    cooperative milieu, 116, 125–26,
    128–29; critique of capitalism,
    116, 128–29; as Dillard University
    president, 18, 95, 115–16, 128–29, 142;
    factors in success, 181; international
    focus, 128–29, 142; legacy of, 116,
    128–29, 131, 132, 145, 161; Mothers'
    Clubs, 116, 119, 123; New Deal
    partnerships, 116, 122, 123; Penny-A-
    Day hospital insurance plan, 18, 95,
    116, 126, 127; and political equality
    movements, 116, 117, 119, 122, 123;
    professionalization of benevolent
    associations, 116, 123, 126, 128; public
    health initiatives, 122; regional
    economic development, 116, 118,
    126; SCEA membership, 115–16, 142.
    See also Dillard University; Flint-
    Goodridge Hospital
Dent, Jessie Covington, 127, 144
Dent, Tom: and African diasporic
    traditions and culture, 142;
    background, 130; and Black Arts
    Movement, 18, 130, 138; critique of
    civil rights movement, 139, 140; and
    Congo Square Writers Association,
    147; father's influence, 116, 118,
    130; leadership in Free Southern
    Theater Collective, 131; and political
    equality, 116, 131; and regional

cooperative development, 116, 130, 147; successes and limitations, 181–82; Total Community Action, 140

Works: *Ritual Murder*, 133–34; *Society of Umbra*, 130; *Southern Journey*, 148; *Uncle Tom's Secondline Funeral*, 138–39. *See also* Free Southern Theater Collective

Desdunes, Rodolphe Lucien, 25, 29, 40

Dillard University, 116, 119, 128, 129–30, 144. *See also* Dent, Albert; Drake, John Gibbs St. Clair

Drake, John Gibbs St. Clair, 128

Duberman, Martin B., 132, 138

Du Bois, W. E. B., 116, 119

Economic Opportunity Act, 108

Eddy, Sherwood, 129

Edwards, Thyra, 90

Egleston, Edna: background, 72; commercial ties, 55, 76; cooperative models, 72–74, 79–80; goals, 79; legacy, 91, 163; political philosophy, 59, 64, 72–74. *See also* Housewives' League; Housewives' League Co-operative Store

Episcopal Church, 58, 76, 131, 146–47

Era Club, 56–57, 59

Ethiopian Theater, 143–44

Fabian Society, 60, 73, 77, 79–80

Farmers' Union Commercial Association of Louisiana (Farmers' Union), 30

Federal Credit Union Act of 1934, 107

Federation of Southern Cooperatives: civil rights movement, 5, 145, 169; government backlash, 145–46; and international cooperative movement, 155; legacy, 5, 148, 151, 169, 174; in Louisiana, 5, 145, 169; work with Free Southern Theater Collective, 147, 169

Flint-Goodridge Hospital, 95, 116, 120–23, 126–27. *See also* Dent, Albert

Flower, Walter, 35, 36, 43, 45–46

Fontaine, Edgar, 108, 109

Foster, Murphy, 31, 35, 36, 37

Free Southern Theater Collective: and Albert Dent, 116, 117, 139, 142; Central City development, 117, 131, 140–41, 143–44; civil rights movement, 117, 131–32; creative and performing arts incubator, 136, 138, 139, 140, 143; contemporary theater collectives, 131; cooperative partnerships, 19, 117, 139, 143–44, 147; factors in success and limitations, 134–35, 136, 140, 145, 181–82; hybrid racial justice model, 117, 131, 138, 139, 142, 143; legacy, 117, 131, 148–49, 161; Lower Ninth Ward development, 117, 131, 134–39; membership, 138, 141; New Orleans collective traditions, 117, 123, 131, 134, 138; organizational structure, 19, 117, 131, 134, 141–42, 143; origins, 18, 131; pan-African black liberationist ideologies, 117, 131, 134, 138, 141–42, 144; place-based production themes, 138; political philosophy, 117, 131, 134, 141–44, 147; Popular Front, 117, 132–33; regional development, 117, 139, 144, 145; religion, 133; resident participation, 133–34, 136, 143; role in Black Arts Movement, 117, 134, 138, 143; SNCC, 132, 141, 144; theatrical aesthetics, 19, 117, 131, 134; War on Poverty organizations, 19, 117, 139, 140–41, 145; work with Federation of Southern Cooperatives, 169. *See also* Dent, Tom; Levy, Murray; Moses, Gilbert; O'Neal, John; ya Salaam, Kalamu

French Quarter, 54, 83, 90–91, 95, 157, 158

Freret Business Men's Association, 86, 99, 105–6, 111–12. *See also* Hermes, Henry

Freret Neighborhood: beginnings, 85; city redevelopment funds, 112; community-led development, 86, 99, 105–6, 111–12; and cooperative development, 17, 84, 86, 111;

demographics, 85–86; and Great
Depression, 17, 83; Hurricane
Katrina and redevelopment, 112; and
integration, 111; racial segregation
and development, 85–86, 106, 111;
World War II, 17
Friend, Ida Weis, 47, 56, 64, 65, 66, 82–83.
See also Consumers' League;
Housewives' League
Fry, Macon, 151–54, 164–66, 168–69,
178, 182. *See also* Gathering Tree
Growers Collective

Garden District, 54, 106, 111, 157, 158
Garvey, Marcus, 116, 121, 128, 129
Gathering Tree Growers Collective,
150–51, 165–69. *See also* Fry, Macon;
Velasco, Jocine
Gaudet, Frances, 65
General Federation of Women's Clubs
(GFWC), 57, 58, 66, 69
German immigration, 45, 55–56, 83
Gershwin, George, 133
Gert Town, 9–10, 159, 165–68, 186
Gilman, Charlotte Perkins, 59
glocalism, 186
Godfrey-Smith, Helen, 104, 110
Gordon, Kate, 46, 51
Gould, Robert Boyer, 40
Graf, August, 23, 32, 35–36, 45. *See also*
Brotherhood of Co-operative
Commonwealth; Laboringmen's
Protective Association; White
Laboringmen's Protective
Association
Grand Marie Vegetable Co-op, 145, 146, 147
Great Depression, 26, 115–16, 120
Great Recession of 2008, 151, 158, 162, 183
Grow Dat Youth Farm, 164, 169

Hermes, Henry: background, 83, 85, 90;
and consumers' movement, 84,
86, 87; cooperative goals, 84–85,
100, 103–5, 107–9; and federal
antipoverty initiatives, 92, 109, 139;
Freret Neighborhood development,
93, 99; global cooperative

movement, 99–101, 128; legacy,
112, 183; political expediency of,
85, 92; political repression of,
83–84, 88; Popular Front political
network, 83, 84, 86, 88, 92, 100; race
and class, 84–86, 100, 105, 108–9;
and Rochdale model, 84, 85, 93,
115, 116; SCEA membership, 99,
104; unionizing, 87–88; wartime
patriotism, 96. *See also* Louisiana
Credit Union League; New Orleans
Consumers' Co-operative Union
Hollygrove Market and Farm, 164, 165, 166,
167, 168–69
Holmes, Albert J., 40, 42–43, 44. *See
also* Laboringmen's Protective
Association
Homemakers' Association, 67–70, 72
Hope, John, 119, 120
Hope Haven Industrial Farm, 64
Housewives' League: coalition
building, 52–53, 60, 61, 62, 71, 74;
commercial ties, 52, 53, 58, 61,
62, 75; comparisons with other
models, 52–53, 83, 84, 91, 94, 101;
consumers' movement activism,
51, 53, 61–64, 70–72; cooperative
philosophy of, 52, 63; formation,
60; goals, 52, 53, 55, 60, 63;
government and business, 62, 63,
72, 75; international cooperative
influence on, 53, 55, 56, 60; legacy
of, 53, 81–82; meeting spaces, 52, 58;
member demographics, 53, 54, 55;
Progressive reform, 52, 58; and race
and class issues, 53, 55, 59, 64–65,
69–70; Rochdale cooperative
projects, 47, 51–52, 61–63, 69, 72,
81; suffrage activism, 52, 56, 63, 77;
World War I organizing, 63. *See also*
Egleston, Edna; Friend, Ida Weis;
Housewives' League Co-operative
Store; Meyers, Inez
Housewives' League Co-operative Store:
alliances, 72–73, 74, 77; backlash,
74–76; business model, 73, 77, 78–79,
180; consumers' movement, 72–73;

factors in success and limitations, 80–81, 180; goals and philosophy, 73, 74; opening, 77–78; services' impact, 78, 81; southern cooperative network, 74, 77, 81; store identity, 76, 80; women's advocacy, 74, 76–78. *See also* Egleston, Edna; Housewives' League

Housing and Community Development Act of 1974, 111, 164

Housing and Urban Development (HUD), 158, 164

Housing Authority of New Orleans (HANO), 120, 137, 158

Hurricane Betsy, 136

Hurricane Harvey, 185

Hurricane Ike, 174

Hurricane Katrina: cooperative emergency response, 143, 150, 179; disruption of cooperative networks, 175; federal deregulation, 157–58; food insecurity, 159; gentrification, 5, 158, 162, 163–65, 167; impact on communities of color, 151, 169; rebuilding plans, 3, 156–57, 159; reduction of public housing, 157, 158; tourist economy and aesthetic racism, 157, 162

Hurricane Rita, 169, 170

industrial unionism, 32, 87, 116

International Cooperative Alliance, 19, 100, 171–72

Irish Channel, 45, 58, 66, 106

Jessen, Louise, 89, 91

Jewish activism, 15, 55–56, 69, 76, 89

Jindal, Bobby, 173

Johnson, Lyndon Baines, 107–8

Julius Rosenwald Fund, 119, 123, 126

Juvenile Co-operators Fraternals Benevolent Mutual Aid Association (Juvenile Co-operators), 39, 123–24

Kabacoff, Pres, 158, 164

Kagawa, Toyohiko, 129

Karenga, Maulana, 134. See also *Nguzo Saba*

Kelley, Florence, 54, 61, 70, 82

Knights of Labor, 10–11, 33, 41

Laboringmen's Protective Association (LMPA): aims, 37, 38; anti-racism, 24, 38, 39, 40, 43; black membership, 24, 37, 38, 39; coalitional organizing, 38, 42–43; formation, 37; infrastructural improvements, 43; integrated meeting spaces, 24, 38; legacy, 44; nativism, 24, 41–42; political expediency, 41; yellow fever outbreak, 42–43. *See also* Bacarisse, Eugene; Graf, August; Holmes, Albert J.; Mathieu, Louis Henry

labor movement: alliances with female activists, 52, 61; cooperatives, 71, 161; interracial unionizing, 25, 40; police harassment, 83; post-World War I strikes, 71. *See also* American Federation of Labor; Knights of Labor

Latin Americans: anti-racism of, 95; New Orleans immigrant community, 85, 90, 158, 160; political activism, 90, 160; racialization, 90; role in Hurricane Katrina rebuilding, 158, 160–61; US relations, 27, 54

Latino Farmers Cooperative of Louisiana, 160–61

League for Industrial Democracy (LID), 82, 83, 91

Legion Oaks, 105

Levy, Murray, 134, 136. *See also* Free Southern Theater

Lichtman, Liz, 150

Local Council of Women, 46–47, 51

local food movement, 151, 164, 168

localism, 183–84

Long, Huey, 83, 86–87, 88, 92

Louisiana: anti-immigrant attitudes, 41–42; cooperative policies, 171; credit union and state economic development, 103, 108; government resistance to suffrage, 75; Regular Democratic Organization (RDO), 11, 54, 75, 83, 86–87; and second

Red Scare, 101–2; white flight
and development, 106; white
supremacist laws and legacy, 11, 24,
43, 44; World War I mobilization, 63
Louisiana Association of Cooperatives
(LAC), 5, 150, 151, 171–78, 182,
186–88. *See also* Reed, Harvey
Louisiana Council of Farmers
Cooperatives, 176–77
Louisiana Credit Union League (LCUL),
85, 104, 106, 107–10. *See also*
Hermes, Henry
Louisiana Division of the North American
Committee to Aid Spanish
Democracy, 90
Louisiana Farmers' Union (LFU), 98, 102,
126. *See also* McIntire, Gordon
Louisiana Fishing Community Recovery
Coalition, 170
Louisiana League for the Protection of
Constitutional Rights (LLPCR), 89
Louisiana Recovery Authority (LRA), 170,
173
Louisiana State Farmers' Educational and
Cooperative Union of America
(LSF), 61
Louisiana State University Agricultural
Leadership Development Program,
154–55

Maestri, Robert, 83, 88–89
Mardi Gras, 10, 12, 59, 125, 138, 157
Marigny, 163
Marshall, Thurgood, 125, 130
Martinet, Louis, 12, 29, 39, 40
material feminism, 59–60, 70, 75, 180
Mathieu, Louis Henry, 38–39, 123–24
McCormack Baron Salizar, 5
McIntire, Gordon, 98, 102
McKnight, Father Albert, 130, 141, 145–48,
155, 172, 174
Meaux, Susan, 170, 171, 173–74
Mendez, Amelia, 85
Meyers, Inez: background, 54; commercial
ties, 55; and consumers' movement,
71–72; and General Federation
of Women's Clubs, 57; illness,

72; legacy, 85; occupation, 55;
Progressive activism, 55; racial
attitudes, 66, 70; socialist beliefs,
52, 58, 59; and women's movement,
55, 56, 59, 77. *See also* Housewives'
League
Mid-City, 80, 158, 160
Moore, Ronnie, 139, 141
Morehouse College, 119, 130
Morial, Ernest "Dutch," 111–12
Moses, Gilbert, 131, 138, 143. *See also* Free
Southern Theater Collective
Muniz, Lillian, 90, 95. *See also* New
Orleans Consumers' Co-operative
Union
mutual aid organizations, 8–11

Nagin, Ray, 156–57
National Association for the Advancement
of Colored People (NAACP):
cooperative development, 95, 110,
124, 126; neighborhood ties, 124;
New Orleans chapter, 121–22, 124;
New Orleans, national organizing
in, 125; political and economic
campaigns, 119, 123, 126; support of
Colored Domestic Union, 66, 67
National Credit Union Administration
(NCUA), 104, 110
National Cooperative Business
Association, 184
National Union of the Brotherhood of
Co-operative Commonwealth
(National Union), 31
Nation of Islam, 129, 134, 135, 144
neighborhoods. *See individual
neighborhoods*
New Deal, 86, 98, 101, 119, 120–21, 127
New Llano, Louisiana, 20, 91
"New Negro," 119, 123
New Orleans, Louisiana: anti-immigrant
violence, 36; city boosterism, 54,
157; Community Action Programs,
108, 110; cooperatives as economic
development model, 174, 179–83,
186–88; credit union movement, 108;
Democratic factionalism, 86–87;

demographic history, 7–8; highway construction and displacement, 135; historical flooding, 34–35, 46, 186; Hurricane Katrina and recovery, 3, 5, 150–51; neighborhood boundaries, 53–54, 105, 120; New South, 53; oil boom and urban reinvestment in, 111; post-World War I economy, 71, 106; public markets, 52; Reconstruction debt, 34; social movements, 56, 83–84; suburbanization, 85, 120, 174; urban disinvestment, 84, 135, 140, 174; utilities and infrastructure management, 99, 135; white flight, 84, 140

New Orleans Consumers' Co-operative Union (CCU), 82, 84, 93–99, 103–5, 180–81. *See also* Hermes, Henry

New Orleans Federation of Civic Leagues, 124–25

New Orleans Food Co-op, 163–64, 166

New Orleans Free School Network, 150

New Orleans Healing Center, 163–64

Nguzo Saba, 134, 135, 148

Ninth Ward: cooperative organizing, 110, 135, 139, 160, 163, 183; demographics, 136; and Free Southern Theater Collective, 18, 117, 134–39; gentrification, 158–59; Hurricane Betsy recovery, 135; Hurricane Katrina rebuilding plans, 156; War on Poverty community economic development, 139

Nixon, Richard, 146

Obama, Barack, 177, 183, 184

Occupy Wall Street, 162, 183

Office of Economic Opportunity (OEO), 108, 110, 139, 141, 144–47

oil industry, 151, 152, 169, 172, 174

O'Neal, John, 131–32, 138, 141–42, 146–48. *See also* Free Southern Theater Collective

Parker, John, 63, 71, 75

Parkway Partners, 152–54

Peete, Elenora Alcorn, 66–69. *See also* Colored Domestic Union

Perkins, Blanche Armwood, 67

Pigford v. Glickman, 155, 177

Pleasant, Ruffin, 64

Plessy v. Ferguson, 12, 25, 38–39, 40, 46, 122

Popular Front, 82, 88–89, 91–94, 98, 121, 133

populism, 30, 31, 41, 44, 61

Positivist sociology, 33

post-Katrina cooperative movement, 151, 159, 161, 162–65

post-World War II United States, 84, 99–101, 104–5

Potter, David, 100

Prejean, Charles, 145, 155

Prior, Angelina Lopez, 94, 96

Progressive Movement, 52, 119

Propeller, 186

public housing: Albert Dent's commitment to, 116, 127; cooperative development, 127, 139, 151, 157–58, 162; Desire Housing Project, 135, 136–37; segregation and public housing development, 120; slum clearance, 120, 127, 135; sociality and political activism, 127

Rabins, Aviva, 150

racial justice cooperatives: anti-poverty initiatives, 110, 118, 141, 145; cadre structure, 142–43; capitalism and white supremacy, 116, 130, 141; economic development, 116, 118, 130, 141, 155, 174; funding sources, 146; government backlash, 145–46; international orientation, 129, 148; as leadership training, 110; legacy, 118, 148; mainstream and radical political cooperation, 5, 106, 118, 129, 141, 144–48; post-Katrina recovery plan, 19, 143, 151, 155; and regional network, 19, 141, 148, 155; Rochdale model, 116, 125–26, 130

Rahim, Malik, 14

Reddix, Jacob, 126

Red Scare: First, 52, 68, 74–75, 180; Second, 84, 101, 146

Reed, Harvey: background, 151, 154–56; cooperative allies, 155–56, 169–70, 176–77; Hurricanes Katrina and Rita, 169–72; and international cooperative movement, 19, 155–56, 169; legacy, 178; local food movement, 164; models, 4, 155, 174; state and national advocacy work, 4, 173, 176–78. *See also* Louisiana Association of Cooperatives

Resettlement Administration, 119

Restaurant Opportunities Center of New Orleans (ROC), 161–63. *See also* Chenault, Reese

Rhythm Conspiracy, 161–62. *See also* Stevens, Sally

Robinson, Matt, 143, 165, 179, 183, 185, 188

Rochdale cooperatives: and African Americans, 18, 128–29, 141; beginnings and expansion of, 16–17, 73; and capitalism, 17, 73, 128; Christian Socialism, 129; consumers' movement, 73, 93; global democratic movements, 17, 73, 128–29; and white supremacy and imperialism, 18, 79, 141–42. *See also* Cooperative League of America; Housewives' League Co-operative Store; New Orleans Consumers' Co-operative Union

Roosevelt, Franklin Delano, 86, 93, 101, 104

R.U.B.A.R.B., 150

rural electricity cooperatives, 92, 184, 186

Schechner, Richard, 138

Schiro, Victor, 137

Schuyler, George, 126

Servicemen's Readjustment Act of 1944 (GI Bill), 104–5

settlement house movement, 58, 64

Sherrod, Fletcher, 95

Sinclair, Upton, 91

socialism, 59, 88, 89, 91–92, 180

Solidarity Economy, 150, 162–63

Southeastern Cooperative Educational Association (SCEA), 97–99, 104, 107, 115–16, 126–28, 145

Southern Conference for Human Welfare, 95, 102

South Plaquemines United Fisheries Cooperative, 170–71, 173

Spanish-American War, 44

Stevens, Sally, 157, 161–63

St. Julien, Mtumishi, 147–48

St. Roch, 162–64

Student Nonviolent Coordinating Committee (SNCC), 131–32, 138, 141, 144

Szilard, Leo, 101

Tarbell, Ida M., 64

Terrell, Mary Church, 123

theosophy, 29–30, 32–33

Third World Left, 117, 141, 144

Thomas, Norman, 89, 91

Total Community Action (TCA), 108, 110, 139, 140

Tremé: Congo Square and Globe Hall, 23, 30, 36–37, 38, 39; cooperative development, 29, 123–25, 135, 154; Creole of color community life, 10, 124; highway construction debates, 135; political equality movements, 36, 124–25; public housing, 154; racial violence, 9

Trevigne, Paul, 10

Truman, Harry, 101

Trump, Donald, 183–84, 185

Tureaud, Alexander Pierre (A. P.), 124–25

United Daughters of the Confederacy, 67

United Federation of Worker Cooperatives (USFWC), 3, 4, 183

United Nations, 101, 102

United States Custom House, 40

United States Department of Agriculture (USDA), 155, 172, 173, 177–78, 187

Uptown, 17, 56, 74, 140, 158, 165

urban gardens, 152–53, 164–65

USSR (Soviet Union), 74, 75, 92

utopian socialism, 14–15

VEGGI Farmers Cooperative, 172

Velasco, Jocine, 166–68. *See also* Gathering Tree Growers Collective

Vivien, Rene, 76, 81
Voorhis, Jerry, 100, 102

Walmsley, T. Semmes, 86–87, 88, 92
War on Poverty, 18, 107–10, 139, 140, 146
Warren, George Ethel, 110
Washington, Booker T., 67, 116
Weber, August, 111, 112
White Laboringmen's Protective
        Association (WLMPA), 24, 44–47.
        See also Bacarisse, Eugene; Graf,
        August
Wilkerson, Robert King, 152
Williams, Sylvanie, 65
Wilson, Woodrow, 51, 70, 71
Woman's Suffrage Party, 57
Woman's Committee of the Council of
        National Defense (WCCND), 63,
        64–65, 66, 67, 68
Women's International League for Peace
        and Freedom, 67, 68
women's movement, 52–53, 57, 63, 67, 75, 77
World War I, 63–66
World War II, 17, 84, 94, 96–97, 116

Xavier University, 159, 165, 166

ya Salaam, Kalamu, 138–39. *See also* Free
        Southern Theater Collective
yellow fever, 42–43, 44
Young Women's Christian Association
        (YWCA), 91, 95

Zippert, John, 145–46, 147

ABOUT THE AUTHOR

Anne Gessler is a clinical assistant professor in the First-Year Seminar Program, History, and Humanities Program at the University of Houston-Clear Lake. She has published in *Utopian Studies, American Studies in Scandinavia, Radio Journal,* and the *Journal of Southern History.* Engaging with women's and gender studies, social movement history, consumer activism, and media studies, her current book project examines women in Cold War amateur radio.

CPSIA information can be obtained
at www.ICGtesting.com
Printed in the USA
LVHW041503260720
661568LV00002B/158